THE WARS OF THE FRENCH REVOLUTION AND NAPOLEON, 1792–1815

In this essential addition to French military history, Owen Connelly examines both the wars of the French Revolution between 1792 and 1799, and those of Napoleon between 1800 and 1815. Arguing that the importance and drama of the Revolutionary Wars have been neglected, and that the unceasing cut-throat politics that continued into the Napoleonic era has been overlooked, this analysis examines the two eras together to provide a broader context for warfare. Connelly demonstrates how the wars of the Revolution shaped Napoleon as a military leader and how the practices of warfare developed and deployed during this period were to influence modes of combat throughout the nineteenth and twentieth centuries, establishing trends discernible in the First and Second World Wars.

Wars of the French Revolution and Napoleon, 1792–1815 examines the causes of the wars of the Revolution and Napoleon and examines key questions, including: what was the impact of the population explosion of the eighteenth century on armies and war? How did the legacy of the *ancien régime* impact upon revolutionary armies? What was the impact of the Revolution on leadership, strategy, organization and weaponry of the armies? Was Napoleon's leadership style unique or could other generals have played his role as well? What contributions were made by governments of the early Revolution, the Terror, the Directory and the Napoleonic regime? What did twenty-three years of successive wars accomplish? Was the era of the Revolutionary and Napoleonic Wars a turning point in the history of warfare and the conduct of combat?

Based on extensive research and including twenty maps, this fascinating study provides a thorough re-examination of this crucial period in the history of France.

Owen Connelly is McKissick Dial Professor of History at the University of South Carolina, as well as being a Director of the Consortium on Revolutionary Europe. He is the author of ten books, including *Napoleon's Satellite Kingdoms* (third edition, 1990), *The French Revolution and the Napoleonic Era* (third edition, 1999), *Blundering on to Glory: Napoleon's Military Campaigns* (second edition, 1999) and *On War and Leadership: The Words of Combat Commanders from Frederick the Great to Norman Schwarzkopf* (2002).

WARFARE AND HISTORY
General Editor, Jeremy Black
Professor of History, University of Exeter

MODERN INSURGENCIES AND COUNTER-INSURGENCIES:
GUERRILLAS AND THEIR OPPONENTS SINCE 1750
Ian F. W. Beckett

MUGHAL WARFARE: IMPERIAL FRONTIERS AND HIGHROADS
TO EMPIRE 1500–1700 *Jos Gommans*

NAVAL WARFARE, 1815–1914 *Lawrence Sondhaus*

OTTOMAN WARFARE, 1500–1700 *Rhoads Murphey*

THE PELOPONNESIAN WAR: A MILITARY STUDY *J. F. Lazenby*

SAMURAI, WARFARE AND THE STATE IN EARLY MEDIEVAL
JAPAN *Karl F. Friday*

SEAPOWER AND NAVAL WARFARE, 1650–1830 *Richard Harding*

THE SOVIET MILITARY EXPERIENCE *Roger R. Reese*

VIETNAM *Spencer C. Tucker*

THE WAR FOR INDEPENDENCE AND THE TRANSFORMATION
OF AMERICAN SOCIETY *Harry M. Ward*

WAR AND THE STATE IN EARLY MODERN EUROPE: SPAIN,
THE DUTCH REPUBLIC AND SWEDEN AS FISCAL-MILITARY
STATES, 1500–1660 *Jan Glete*

WARFARE AND SOCIETY IN EUROPE, 1792–1914 *Geoffrey Wawro*

WARFARE AND SOCIETY IN EUROPE, 1898 TO THE PRESENT
Michael S. Nieberg

WARFARE AT SEA, 1500–1650 *Jan Glete*

WARFARE IN ATLANTIC AFRICA, 1500–1800: MARITIME
CONFLICTS AND THE TRANSFORMATION OF EUROPE
John K. Thornton

WARFARE, STATE AND SOCIETY IN THE BYZANTINE WORLD,
565–1204 *John Haldon*

WAR IN THE EARLY MODERN WORLD, 1450–1815
edited by Jeremy Black

WARS OF IMPERIAL CONQUEST IN AFRICA, 1830–1914
Bruce Vandervort

WESTERN WARFARE IN THE AGE OF THE CRUSADES, 1000–1300
John France

WAR AND SOCIETY IN IMPERIAL ROME, 31 BC–AD 284
Brian Campbell

WARFARE AND SOCIETY IN THE BARBARIAN WEST, 450–900
Guy Halsall

WAR IN THE MODERN WORLD SINCE 1815   *edited by Jeremy Black*

WORLD WAR TWO: A MILITARY HISTORY   *Jeremy Black*

WAR, POLITICS AND SOCIETY IN EARLY MODERN CHINA,
900–1795   *Peter Lorge*

WARFARE IN THE ANCIENT NEAR EAST, TO c. 1600 BC
William J. Hamblin

THE WARS OF THE FRENCH REVOLUTION AND NAPOLEON, 1792–1815

Owen Connelly

Routledge
Taylor & Francis Group

LONDON AND NEW YORK

First published 2006
by Routledge
270 Madison Avenue, New York, NY 10016

Simultaneously published in the UK
by Routledge

2 Park Square, Milton Park, Abingdon, Oxfordshire, OX14 4RN

Routledge is an imprint of the Taylor & Francis Group

© 2006 Owen Connelly
Typeset in Bembo
by Keystroke, Jacaranda Lodge, Wolverhampton
Printed and bound in Great Britain
by Antony Rowe Ltd, Chippenham, Wiltshire

British Library Cataloguing in Publication Data
A catalogue record for this book is available from the British Library

Library of Congress Cataloging in Publication Data
Connelly, Owen, 1929–
The wars of the French Revolution and Napoleon, 1792–1815 /
Owen Connelly.
p. cm. – (Warfare and history)
Includes bibliographical references and index.
1. First Coalition, War of the, 1792–1979. 2. Second Coalition, War of the,
1798–1801. 3. France–History–Revolution, 1789–1799. 4. Napoleonic Wars,
1800–1815. 5. France–History, Military–1789–1815. 6. Europe–History,
Military–1789–1815. I. Title. II. Series.
DC220.C66 2005
940.2′7–dc22
2005009602

ISBN10: 0–415–23984–2 (pbk)
ISBN10: 0–415–23983–4 (hbk)

ISBN13: 9–78–0–415–23984–4 (pbk)
ISBN13: 9–78–0–415–23983–7 (hbk)

CONTENTS

CONTENTS

MAPS

INTRODUCTION

The spectacle of the French Revolutionary/Napoleonic era has captivated ordinary people for over 200 years and still does. Movie and TV producers today see in it the stuff that dominates the daily news – riots, violence, destruction, natural and man-made disasters, espionage, terrorist plots and actions, assaults, murder, executions, suicides, moral crusades, political and personal scandals, romance, intrigue, and of course *WAR*.

For those catering to the popular taste, however, concentration has been on Paris and the crashing blade of the "National Razor" (guillotine) under the Terror (1793–94). After that, the tendency has been to jump to Napoleon – largely his campaigns, and the building of the French Empire. Scholars have followed the same pattern, except for a fixation on the Revolution to the neglect of the Napoleonic era, which has yet no altogether acceptable comprehensive history.

Since 1950, at least, both popularizers and scholars have given short shrift to the Wars of the Revolution (without which there would have been no General Buonaparte/Bonaparte). Military historians have not ignored these wars, but usually have limited themselves to Valmy, Frejus, and a few other battles – or studied the French soldier during the transition from royal to revolutionary army, or as zealot and deserter during the Revolution and Napoleonic era – or the impact of the wars on society. On the other hand, the Napoleonic Wars have had excessive treatment – although not based on detailed monographic research necessary to make the accounts valid. It is hoped that this book will be useful in that it covers both the Wars of the Revolution *and* Napoleon. Curiously enough, one has to go back to the multi-volume histories of the nineteenth century to find a work – such as that of Antoine Jomini – that deals with both.

The importance and drama of the Wars of the Revolution have been neglected, together with the unceasing cut-throat politics that continued into the Napoleonic period. One reason was the insistence of Marxist historians – dominant in France until the 1980s – on glorifying the revolutionary élan of the common soldier to the exclusion of all else military. However, generals with both political and military ambitions make the Wars of the Revolution more interesting. There was elegant Marquis de Lafayette, in 1789 the popular "Hero of Two Worlds"; in 1792 commander of the Army of the North, fleeing for his life from the newborn Republican regime. Among others were the handsome Vicomte Alexandre de Beauharnais – first husband of Josephine, Napoleon's empress – a revolutionary, legislator, and commander of the Army of the Rhine, but guillotined by the Terrorists – Adam-Philippe Custine de Sarreck, "general moustache," a favorite of his troops, but executed anyway – General Charles-François du Perier, called "Dumouriez," confidant of ministers under the *ancien régime*, an opportunist in the Revolution, who cultivated whoever was in power, including the Jacobins of the Terror, and commanded several armies, but deserted to the enemy to save his head. And there was the fiery Louis-Lazare Hoche – handsome, violent, politically savvy, and many times a hero, who died suddenly at 27, on campaign in Germany, of a long-concealed lung infection. He might have been a true competitor of Napoleon.

Ex-Captain of Engineers Lazare Carnot, the "Organizer of Victory" of the Terror, had no high political ambitions himself, but inadvertently promoted men who did, notably Napoleon. Carnot was a revolutionary, despite his unusual status under the *ancien régime* – a member of the Academy of Sciences and a *chevalier de l'ordre de Saint Louis*. From the dozens of might-have-beens, Napoleon Bonaparte finally emerged – a general of genius and canny politician who eventually dominated France and most of Europe.

In the pages that follow we shall lay out evidence on questions to be answered in the Conclusions. Among these are: (1) What was the impact of the eighteenth-century population explosion on armies and *war* (as well as politics, society, culture)? (2) What were the causes of the Wars of the Revolution? of Napoleon? (3) What was the legacy of the revolutionary armies from the *ancien régime*? (4) What was the impact of the Revolution on the leadership, techniques of leadership, organization, strategy, tactics and weapons of the armies? (5) What contributions were made by governments of the early Revolution, of the Terror, of the Directory, and of the Napoleonic regime? (6) Was Napoleon one-of-a-kind or were there other generals who might have played his role as well? (7) What did twenty-three years of successive wars accomplish? (8) Was the period of the Revolutionary and Napoleonic Wars a turning point in the history of warfare (or in the conduct of war)?

One of my goals was to write a military history without using the word "brilliant" even once. I trust I have succeeded.

On the sources

This is a work of synthesis, and owes something to the works of all the authors listed in the Bibliography – and to the memoirs, letters, and histories of con-temporaries. Since a survey of this kind would scarcely benefit from braving the French archives – and archivists – printed primary sources have been used. This has its benefits. For example, it allows comparison of secondary accounts with

Napoleon's (not always creditable) version of events. Regarding the famous incident near Grenoble after his return from Elba, where – by hundreds of accounts, paintings, films, and the like – he walked out in front of his Guard, opened his coat to the soldiers of the 5th [Infantry regiment] and called out: "I am your Emperor. If there is a man among you who would kill his Emperor, here I am!" In exile on St Helena, Napoleon told General Henri Bertrand that he was *on horseback*, rode to within earshot of the troops and shouted: "Soldiers of the 5th, kill your Emperor if you dare."[1] This may not be of crashing importance, but it is interesting – more so because it has gone unnoticed since the publication of Napoleon's *Correspondance* some 150 years ago. This is footnoted, although the footnotes do not reflect all my sources; I have cited only quotations, new material and (what I judged to be) original thinking.

As to other printed primary sources, the reader need only to consult the Bibliography at the end of the book. Essential for the French Revolution are the documents of the Société des Jacobins, the papers of Robespierre, and the *Mémoires* of Lazare Carnot, among others. On the wars of Napoleon, one might begin with the standard *Correspondance* and the newer *L'Oeuvre et l'histoire*, edited by Jean Massin, Jean Tulard, *et al.* (1969), along with the letters and/or memoirs of the marshals, Eugene de Beauharnais, and Jerome and Joseph Bonaparte. (Full French titles are in the Bibliography.)

As to secondary works, there are the exhaustive old multi-volume histories of the Wars of the Revolution – Antoine-Henri Jomini, Arthur Chuquet, Ramsay Weston Phipps, *et al.* Of more contemporary works, the best is Jean-Paul Bertaud, *La Révolution Armée: Les soldats-citoyens et la Révolution française* (1979) (translation by R. R. Palmer, 1988.) On the Napoleonic wars there are excellent older works by David Chandler, John R. Elting, Henry Lachouque, Jean Tulard, *et al.*

It seems proper, however, to highlight here a selection of books from the plethora of works published since 1989, the bicentenary of the French Revolution. Among bibliographical aids is the truly indispensable work of Jean Tulard, *Nouvelle bibliographie critique des mémoires sur l'époque napoléonienne*, 2nd edn. (1991). New primary sources include Jean-Baptiste Kléber, *Mémoires politiques et militaires, Vendée, 1793–1794* (1989), with graphic accounts of the fighting in the Vendée by a Republican general, and a new edition of the *Mémoires pour servir à l'histoire de la guerre de la Vendée* of General Louis-M. Turreau de Garambouville (1992), who sent out the "infernal columns" to destroy offending villages and kill all the inhabitants of offending villages in the Vendée. These reflect the conservative reaction generated by the violent partisan debates in the legislative chambers over *what phase* of the Revolution to commemorate. The extreme Left was for the Year II (1793–94), the year of the Terror; the Right for the early Revolution, with a nod to the aristocrats who supported it. In the end, France barely celebrated it at all. Aristocratic families found their voice, however, and published hundreds of letters from prison, and the like, of which a listing would seem inappropriate here.

More generally useful are Carl von Clausewitz, *Historical and Political Writings*, ed. and trans. by Peter Paret and Daniel Moran (1992), and for the Napoleonic Wars Clausewitz's *Campaign of 1812 in Russia* (1992) with an introduction by George F. Nafziger. On the war and society, R. R. Palmer, among his last publications, edited and translated *From Jacobin to Liberal: Marc-Antoine Jullien, 1775–1848* (1993), the letters of an eighteen-year-old *représentant* under the Terror, who reported with boyish frankness directly to Robespierre from the Vendée and elsewhere, but survived to serve later governments. The old history of Aleksandr Ivanovich Mikhailovskii-Danilevskii (*c.* 1789–1848), *History of the Campaign in France in the year 1814*, was translated from the Russian (1992). Finally, Peter Hofschröer translated Freiherr Friedrich von Müffling's *Aus meinem Leben* as *The Memoirs of Baron von Müffling: A Prussian Officer in the Napoleonic Wars* (1997).

Among secondary works, Jean-Paul Bertaud's *Histoire du Consulat et de l'Empire: chronologie commentée, 1799–1815* (1992) is heavy on military affairs. The most revisionary are Charles Esdaile's *The Peninsular War: A New History* (2003) and *Fighting Napoleon* (2004), which redefine the Spanish guerrilla and explode the myth of a continuous grass-roots war against the French. Along the way, he has also contributed the *The Duke of Wellington and the Command of the Spanish Army* (1990), *The Wars of Napoleon* (1995), and the interpretive *French Wars, 1792–1815* (2001). Jean-Louis Reynaud's *Contre-guérilla en Espagne (1808–1814): Suchet pacifie l'Aragon* (1992), adds weight to Esdaile's thesis that the French might have conquered Iberia but for Napoleon's Russian disaster (1812).

Alan Forrest's *Napoleon's Men: The Soldiers of the Revolution and Empire* (2002) continues his seminal work on the attitudes of French soldiers of the period, begun with *Conscripts and Deserters* (1989) and *Soldiers of the French Revolution* (1990). Both of the latter have been translated into French, a unusual gesture from France's academics.

Peter Hofschröer is runner-up to Esdaile in revisionism. His recent books have caused a storm among historians, roused the interest of the BBC, and incurred the wrath of admirers of Wellington. They are *Waterloo Campaign: Wellington, His German Allies and the Battles of Ligny and Quatre Bras* (1998), *The Waterloo Campaign: A German Victory* (1999), and *Wellington's Smallest Victory: The Duke, the Modelmaker, and the Secret of Waterloo* (2004), the latter on the Duke's alleged suppression of an unflattering model of the Battle of Waterloo by William Siborne, whose *History of the Battle of Waterloo* has been reprinted (1996).

The 900-page work of Paul W. Schroeder, *The Transformation of European Politics, 1763–1848* (1994), sees a change in great-power policy from confrontation to cooperation; he also postulates that the French Revolutionary Wars had their origin in French diplomatic blunders in the eighteenth century. T. C. W. Blanning took much the same line in his *Origins of the French Revolutionary Wars* (1986) emphasizing Louis XVI's failure to intervene in the

Netherlands in 1787, and briefly in *The French Revolutionary Wars, 1787–1802* (1996), which is the best recent book on the subject. It rates above Gregory Fremont-Barnes, *The French Revolutionary Wars* (2001). *L'Histoire militaire de la France*, Sous la direction de André Corvisier, Vol. II (1992) [the official French Army history], is a good reference for both the Wars of the Revolution and Napoleon.

The industrious Philip Haythornthwaite has published *The Napoleonic Source Book* (1990), *Weapons and Equipment of the Napoleonic Wars* (1996), *The Armies of Wellington* (1994), *Die Hard!: Dramatic Actions from the Napoleonic Wars* (1996), and, with others, *Napoleon: The Final Verdict*, Foreword by David G. Chandler (1996). Rory Muir's *Tactics and the Experience of Battle in the Age of Napoleon* (1998) is in competition with Brent Nosworthy's *With Musket, Cannon, and Sword: Battle Tactics of Napoleon and His Enemies* (1995) and Paddy Griffith's *The Art of War of Revolutionary France* (1998), none of which is perfectly accurate. A more specialized volume is that of Kevin F. Kiley, *Artillery of the Napoleonic Wars* (2004), which describes the artillery of all nations from design and manufacture to tactics. David Hopkin, *Soldier and Peasant in French Popular Culture, 1766–1870*, holds that relations between the people and the military improved during the French Revolutionary-Napoleonic period.

On armed forces of Napoleon and his enemies: Ian Fletcher, *Wellington's Regiments: The Men and their Battles from Rolica to Waterloo, 1808–1815* (1994); John G. Gallaher, *Napoleon's Irish Legion* (1993); Roger Lepelley, *Marins de l'Isle de France, 1803–1810: des marins meconnus* (1995); and Frederick C. Schneid, *Soldiers of Napoleon's Kingdom of Italy: Army, State, and Society, 1800–1815* (1995).

On espionage and intelligence gathering there are Steven E. Mafeo's *Most Secret and Confidential: Intelligence in the Age of Nelson* (2000) and Elizabeth Mary Sparrow, *Secret Service: British Agents in France, 1792–1815* (1999). Mark Urban's *The Man Who Broke Napoleon's Codes* (2002) opens up a neglected subject.

On the long-range effects of the *Levée en masse* there is *The People in Arms: Military Myth and National Mobilizaton since the French Revolution*, ed. Daniel Moran and Arthur Waldron (2003), with essays on the Revolutionary period by Owen Connelly and Alan Forrest. Among truly exceptional monographs are Ken Adler's *Engineering the Revolution: Arms and Enlightenment in France, 1763–1815* (1997) and Howard G. Brown's *War, Revolution, and the Bureaucratic State: Politics and Army Administration in France, 1791–1799* (1995). Adler argues convincingly that French engineer and artillery officers promoted meritocracy under the *ancien régime* and Revolution, and finally took control of the war ministry and effected a technocratic revolution. Brown traces the increasing power of the war ministry during the Revolution.

To augment his earlier work on converting the king's army into a revolutionary one, Samuel F. Scott published *From Yorktown to Valmy: The Transformation of the French Army in an Age of Revolution* (1998). The difficulties of the process were downplayed in Bernard Deschard's *L'armée et la Révolution: du service du roi au service de la nation* (1989).

New books on the Vendée, in addition to the primary sources mentioned above, are Gabriel du Pontavice, *La Chouannerie* (1991); Bernard Raymond, *Chronique d'une paroisse vendéenne pendant la Révolution: Saint-Laurent-sur-Sevre, 1789–1799* (1994); Reynald Secher, *La guerre de Vendée: itinéraire de la Vendée militaire* (1989) and *Le Génocide Franco-Français: La Vendée vengé* (1986). The latter is statistical, but both books by Secher reflect the conservative trend evident in 1989, noted above.

Books on Britain in the wars include Desmond Gregory's *Malta, Britain, and the European Powers, 1793–1815* (1996); Rory Muir's *Britain and the Defeat of Napoleon, 1807–1915* (1996), which discusses the greater role of the Royal Navy and British pounds as compared to the army in defeating Napoleon; François Crouzet, *Britain Ascendant: Comparative Studies in Franco-British Economic History* (trans. from French, 1990); Christopher D. Hall, *British Strategy in the Napoleonic War, 1803–15* (1992); Robin Neillands, *Wellington and Napoleon: Clash of Arms, 1807–1815* (1994); and Christopher Hibbert, *Wellington: A Personal History* (1997).

On Napoleon, there are two outstanding books on his youth: Dorothy Carrington, *Napoleon and his Parents* (1990) and Jean Defranceschi, *La Jeunesse de Napoléon: Les dessous de l'Histoire* (2001), augmented, as it were, by Antoine-Marie Graziani's *Pascal Paoli: Père de la patrie Corse* (2003). And there are several new biographies, of which the best is Geoffrey Ellis, *Napoleon* (1997). R. S. Alexander is equivocal in his conclusions; Alam Schom depicts Napoleon as an early-day Hitler – reverting to a game played during the Second World War. Alistair Horne's *Age of Napoleon* (2004) is entertainingly written. On Napoleon's brother Jérôme, King of Westphalia, there is a partial biography: Glenn Lamar, *Jerome Bonaparte: The War Years, 1800–1815* (2000).

On Napoleon's campaigns in Italy and Egypt: Gianni Rocca, *Il piccolo caporale: Napoleone alla conquista dell'Italia, 1796–97 e 1800* (1996). Jacques Derogy, *Bonaparte en Terre sainte* (1992); Tom Pocock, *A Thirst for Glory: The Life of Admiral Sir Sidney Smith* (1996), and Piers Mackesy, *British Victory in Egypt: The End of Napoleon's Conquest* (1995), which argues that the defeat of Napoleon's army (minus one-third or more of its original strength) was important in preventing him from fomenting new disturbances in the Middle East and India.

On the campaigns of 1805–07, we have David G. Chandler, *Austerlitz 1805: Battle of the Three Emperors* (1990); Holger Nowak and Brigitt Hellmann, *Die Schlacht bei Jena und Auerstedt am 14. Oktober 1806* (1994); Wolf-Jorg Schuster, *Man ladt uns ein zum Stelldichein: Napoleon in Thuringen 1806* (1993); Jaroslaw Czubaty, *Wodzowie i politycy: generalicja polska lat 1806–1815* (1993); and Gherardo Casaglia, *Una zattera per l'Europa: Alessandro e Napoleone a Tilsit: 25 giugno 1807*, Prefazione di Jean Tulard (1993).

On the Peninsular War (1808–13), in addition to Esdaile's revisionist books mentioned above, we have Ian Fletcher and Ron Poulter, *Gentlemen's Sons: The Guards in the Peninsula and at Waterloo, 1800–1815* (1992); Ramisa i Verdaguer,

Maties, *Els catalans i el domini napoleonic: Catalunya vista pels oficials de l'exercit de Napoleo* (1995); John L. Tone, *The Fatal Knot: The Guerrilla War in Navarre and the Defeat of Napoleon in Spain* (1994).

On the Austrian Campaign of 1809: Ferdi Irmfried Wober, *1809: Schlacht bei Aspern und Essling* (1992); James R. Arnold, *Crisis on the Danube: Napoleon's Austrian Campaign of 1809* (1990), and the American version, *Napoleon Conquers Austria: The 1809 Campaign for Vienna* (1995); Ian Castle, *Aspern & Wagram, 1809 . . . Clash of Empires* (1994); Robert M. Epstein, *Napoleon's Last Victory and the Emergence of Modern War* (1994); John H. Gill, *With Eagles to Glory: Napoleon and his German Allies in the 1809 Campaign* (1992).

On the Russian Campaign: Paul Britten Austin, *1812*, 3 vols: I. *The March on Moscow*, II. *Napoleon in Moscow*, III. *The Great Retreat* (1990–95); Richard K. Riehn, *1812: Napoleon's Russian Campaign* (1990). On the wars of 1813–14: Peter Hofschröer, *Leipzig 1813: The Battle of the Nations* (1993), based liberally on German sources; Michael Leggiere, *Napoleon and Berlin* (2002); Pierre Miguel, *La campagne de France de Napoléon, ou, Les eclairs du genie* (1991); and George F. Nafziger, *Napoleon at Dresden: The Battles of August 1813* (1995). That of Leggiere is a detailed study of the sort which may eventually support a true history of the Napoleonic wars.

Waterloo has retained its fascination. In addition to Hofschröer's books, noted above, there are David Hamilton-Williams, *Waterloo: New Perspectives: The Great Battle Reappraised* (1993) and *The Fall of Napoleon: The Final Betrayal* (1994); Andrew Uffindell, *The Eagle's Last Triumph: Napoleon's Victory at Ligny, June 1815* (1994), and Uffindell with Michael Corum, *On the Fields of Glory: The Battlefields of the 1815 Campaign* (1996), a historical guided tour; Geoffrey Wootten, *Waterloo 1815: Birth of Modern Europe* (1992); Sir Peter Hayman's *Soult: Napoleon's Maligned Marshal* (1990) presents a new view of a marshal whose performance in Spain and at Waterloo (where he was chief-of-staff) has long been questioned.

Two well-researched books have appeared on generally neglected "sideshow wars," where Napoleon was not personally involved: Milton Finley, *The Most Monstrous of Wars: The Napoleonic Guerrilla War in Southern Italy, 1806–1811* (1994); William H. Flayhart, III, *Counterpoint to Trafalgar: The Anglo-Russian Invasion of Naples, 1805–1806* (1992).

Summing up on Napoleon's impact on Europe are: Alexander Grab, *Napoleon and the Transformation of Europe* (2003); Michael Rowe (ed.) *Collaboration and Resistance in Napoleonic Europe: State Formation in an Age of Upheaval, c. 1800–1815* (2003); Philip G. Dwyer, *Napoleon and Europe* (2002); and Alistair Horne, who, in *How Far from Austerlitz?: Napoleon, 1805–1815* (1996), in his "patented" literary style, traces the decline of Napoleon as a commander, plagued, after Austerlitz, Jena and Friedland, by better-prepared enemies and struggling to direct ever-larger armies.

Owen Connelly
Bitter Root, Montana
15 February 2005

1

THE EIGHTEENTH CENTURY: THE FRENCH MILITARY AND ITS ENEMIES – THE REVOLUTION BEGINS

The Enlightenment and the French military

The eighteenth-century Enlightenment is generally associated with the *philosophes*, of whom Jean-Jacques Rousseau had the most influence during the Revolution. However, the army of the *ancien régime* produced an uncanny number of advocates of military reform and change.

General Charles de Gaulle (president of France, 1959–69) wrote that the Enlightenment "impassioned the army for ideas and for progress." He named Gribeauval, Guibert, Broglie and Saint-Germain (identified below) as principal figures of the military enlightenment.[1] We should add Bourcet, and note that the military intellectuals were also motivated by the disaster (for the French) of the Seven Years War.[2]

The most radical military reformer was General Jacques-Antoine-Hippolyte de Guibert (1743–90), who served as junior officer in the Seven Years War, and later in the War Ministry. In his *Essai général de tactique* (1772), he proposed a national militia, motivated by patriotism (instilled by indoctrination). He proposed that it live off the enemy's land, attack in columns, and rout him by numbers, flexible tactics, and aimed fire. *In his Defense du système de guerre moderne* (1779) he discarded his militia as politically impossible, and concentrated on tactics. However, in his last book, *De la force publique* (1790), published after the Revolution had begun, he proposed a militia comprising all healthy male adults, and discussed conscription.[3] De Gaulle emphasized Guibert's proposal to organize all arms into divisions, integrate arms, and decentralize command for speed and flexibility in maneuver. He praised the Maréchal de Broglie's order that staffs and troops maneuver in various terrains rather than continually parade. Finally, de Gaulle cited Frederick the Great as setting the example for all armies.[4]

Guibert ultimately touted the battalion column for rapid maneuver, with deployment into line for greater firepower, but he felt that field commanders should decide on such matters. His ideas were formalized in the *Drill Regulations*

8

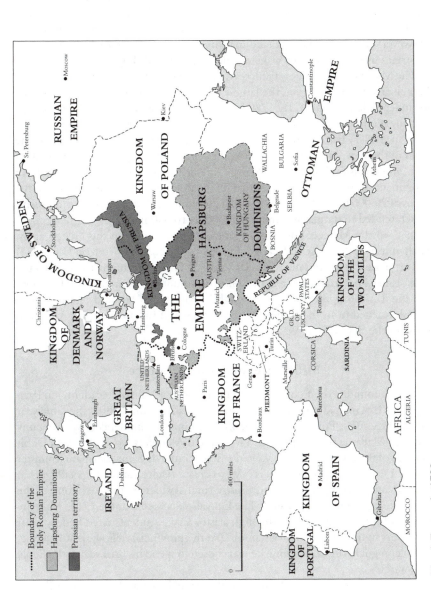

Map 1 Europe in 1789

of 1791, which became the drill manual of the Republican army, but field commanders adopted whatever formations best suited their troops, whether regular or volunteer.[5] The book that influenced Napoleon most was *L'Usage de l'artillerie nouvelle dans la guerre de campagne* (1778), by Chevalier Jean de Beaumont du Teil, which advocated rapid movement and massing of artillery in battle. However, Bonaparte did not take massing guns to heart until 1809 when the Austrians used a great battery against him at Aspern-Essling.

The Marshal Duke Victor-François de Broglie introduced the division into the French army in 1759. It was the largest unit of maneuver (though not intended for independent combat). By 1780 it was standard, but was not of uniform size. Initially it comprised one or two infantry regiments (1,000 to 1,500 men each), with an artillery battery attached, for a maximum of 3,200 men. By the time the Wars of the Revolution began (1792), the regiment had grown to almost 4,000 men, and "division" (sometimes "corps") described formations of any size above a regiment, sometimes up to 20,000 men. Napoleon, as we shall see, created the corps of 20,000 to 30,000 men, of which divisions formed the major component, which tended to standardize them at 8,000 to 10,000 men.

In 1743 the Maréchal de Saxe organized light infantry in the French army. Such units were popularized all over Europe by the *Essay on the Art of War* (1754) of Turpin de Crisse, and many similar studies.[6] The Austrians had learned in the wars against Frederick the Great by calling up volunteers from their border troops (on the Turkish border), who were lightly armed, but fast and effective. The British learned from the Indians in the French and Indian War (the American phase of the Seven Years War).

Military education in France

Louis XV founded the École Militaire royale (Royal Military Academy) in Paris in 1751. (Britain had no comparable military academy until 1802; the same year the USMA, West Point, was founded.) The king was influenced by his brainy mistress, Madame de Pompadour, a friend of d'Alembert, co-editor with Denis Diderot of the philosophes' *Encyclopédie*. The Comte de Saint-Germain (minister of war 1775–77) persuaded Louis XVI to create twelve *écoles royales militaires* in the provinces, so that the poorer, mostly rural aristocrats (the backbone of the officer corps) could be educated. The king also decreed that the École Militaire would admit – in addition to the high aristocracy – students rated best by their professors in the lower military schools. (At the provincial *école royale* at Brienne, Napoleon got his initial training; he was chosen to spend his final year at the École Militaire.)

France also had postgraduate schools for artillery and engineer officers, founded in 1720 and 1748. The Artillery's school (1720) admitted both artillerymen and engineers. The Engineers (*Corps du Génie*) formed their own school in 1748. Perforce, merit counted in these arms; education was essential, especially in mathematics. Thus they were the most democratic. In the artillery corps under the *ancien régime* 14 percent of the officers were commoners; 86 were nobles, but not high nobles. Many were descendants of judicial or financial officers ennobled by the king, including the Comte de Gribeauval.

Weapons of the French and opponents

General Count Jean-Baptiste Vaquette de Gribeauval designed new field cannon for Louis XV, and improved them as Louis XVI's inspector of artillery. Every gun was standard as to caliber, carriages, and limbers, and had packaged shot and powder (a cartridge), which made for more rapid fire. (Interchangeable parts were engineered by Honoré Blanc, but were rejected as too expensive.) With more accurate casting, it was found that the gun barrels could be made lighter and still deliver the same fire.[7] His light, smooth-bore, 12-, 8-, 6-, and 4-pound guns were used by the French armies of the Revolution and Napoleon, and remained the best in Europe until 1825. The Gribeauval guns were lighter by one-third than those of any other country. For example, the Gribeauval 12-pounder's barrel weighed 2,174 pounds (986 kg); the gun with carriage 4,367 pounds (1,981 kg). The British 12's barrel weighed 3,150 pounds; gun and carriage about 6,500 pounds. The firing rate for the French 12-pounder (using a cartridge) was one round per minute; for the 8-, 6-, and 4- two a minute was possible. The French 4-pounder required only three horses and eight men to move with the army.

All the powers used 12-pounders; the Prussians had 12s, 6s, 3s, and some 18s; the Austrians 12s, 6s, and 3s; the British 12s, 9s, 6s, 3s, and 1-pounders, all very heavy.

Followers of Gribeauval – engineers and artillerymen – standardized small arms. Their efforts netted the 1777 Charleroi infantry musket, five feet long, muzzle-loading, 0.69 caliber (17.5 mm). The cavalry, engineers, and others carried the 0.69 musketoon or carbine – the same weapon, but ten inches shorter. The standard sidearm was the 0.69 muzzle-loading pistol. A cartridge was furnished for these weapons, but they had to be primed at the breech and fired with a flintlock. The rifle was known, but not used by the French except for snipers and a few skirmishers.[8] Though more accurate, military rifles were still muzzle-loading; balls were more difficult to ram home, and a few seconds delay could mean death for a soldier.

The infantry and cavalry weapons of the other powers were similar and of about equal range and effectiveness. Russian muskets and carbines were generally 0.74 caliber; Austrian and Prussian muskets were about 0.74 also. Some Russian, Austrian and Prussian infantry units were equipped with British weapons. The British standard was the "Brown Bess," 0.75 caliber (with Baker rifles in the 95th Regiment only).

Before the death of Frederick (1786), the Prussians had one regiment of *Jäger* (light infantry) equipped with rifles – but formed no more. A little later, the British armed a company of the 60th Infantry with rifles, but held up because of the high cost. After they entered the Wars of the French Revolution (1793), however, they formed a regiment, the 95th Rifles, and after Napoleon became their opponent, they issued rifles also to three battalions of the 60th Infantry and some companies of the King's German Legion.

Except for the use of better steel, cavalry sabers changed only in decoration. Typically, light cavalry carried the slightly curved saber with a 33-inch blade; the heavy cavalry saber had a straight, 38-inch blade; specifications varied with the regiment.

The French officer corps

The French army should have had the most professional officer corps in Europe, but to quote Lee Kennett: "French society was . . . far from being militaristic. It was a . . . breach of court etiquette to appear at Versailles in uniform."[9] There was also the obstacle of tradition. The highest-ranking officers – the politically well-connected – often had attended none of the king's schools. Their ingrained belief was that they were *born* to lead, and schooling was superfluous. One of these, at the time of the Revolution, was the Marquis de Lafayette.[10] Appointed a major-general (at age 20) by the American Congress, he commanded troops in the American Revolution (and survived, thanks to the guidance of George Washington). Before he volunteered to fight in America (1776) he had been a junior officer, assigned at age *twelve* to a regiment he seldom visited. Lee Kennett says that most officers in the Royal Army were "amateurs," but that their NCOs were tough veterans of many campaigns and their troops products of six-year enlistments (which encouraged re-enlistment).[11]

In 1781, the old nobility of the sword (*noblesse d'epée*), demanded that access to commissions be limited. The result was the *reglèment Ségur* (22 May 1781) which required four quarterings of nobility to enter the officer corps.[12] The same requirement applied to entry into the military schools. That was no obstacle to country nobles, who usually were more than qualified but had lost their fortunes. They benefited most from king's schools, and were the backbone of the officer corps.

The artillery and engineers welcomed royal school graduates who excelled in mathematics and science (Napoleon was one), but also made officers of qualified commoners (one was Lazare Carnot, the "Organizer of Victory" in the Government of Terror). In September 1792, after Louis XVI was deposed, there was a mass emigration of officers, adding to those who had fled earlier. Only 18 percent of infantry and cavalry officers remained in France, but 42 percent of artillery officers.[13]

The artillery was the key to the first French victories of the Wars of the Revolution. In exile, Napoleon said: "If France, in 1790, promptly set on foot such good armies, it was because [the army] had a good foundation; *the emigration [of noble officers] made it better, not worse.*"[14]

Legacy of the "Sun King"

Louis XIV (1643–1715), the "Sun King," perfected absolute monarchy and presided over the literary and scientific "classical age" in France. However, Louis XIV also gave France a professional army – the largest and best in Europe. The Marquis de Louvois (1641–91), his minister of war for twenty-five years, built a standing army of 200,000, and mustered 400,000 troops in wartime. Further, Louvois created a general staff, the office of chief-of-staff (*maréchal général des logis*), and appointed inspectors for each arm of service.[15] The basic structure was inherited by the armies of the French Revolution and Napoleon.

Louis XIV chose exceptional commanders such as the Vicomte Henri de Turenne and Prince Louis II de Condé.[16] His armies won wars and expanded France. The War of the Spanish Succession (1701–14) gave the throne of Spain to his great-great grandson.[17] However, Britain won Newfoundland, Nova Scotia, and the Hudson's Bay area from France; and from Spain, Gibraltar and trade monopolies in her colonies.

Louis XIV had neglected his navy.

The French staff

Under Louis XV (1715–74), Louvois' general staff became a haven for palace generals, but there were serious members. Pierre de Bourcet proved himself in the wars of 1740–63. During the Seven Years War, generals vied for his services. He originated what came to be called an "estimate of the situation." It offered commanders alternative courses of action, based on the numbers of friendly and enemy forces, their positions, strengths, and weaknesses. Between 1764 and 1781, Bourcet, then a general, was director of a staff college at Grenoble. While there, he wrote *Les principes de la guerre de Montagnes*, which later influenced Napoleon. In 1766 Bourcet organized a new general staff, the Service d'état-major des logis des armées.[18] It had a short life, but was brought back by Philippe de Ségur, minister of war just before the Revolution. Meanwhile, staff officers became common in major commands. Alexandre Berthier, who was on the staff of the Duc de Rochambeau in America, made a reputation during the wars of 1792–95, and became Napoleon's chief-of-staff in Italy (1796), and afterward in every campaign except Waterloo.

The eighteenth century proper:
Louis XV and XVI

Louis XV and XVI continued to favor the army over the navy. France remained (potentially) the first power in Europe, but lacked leadership – royal and military. Louis XV (1715–74), in five wars, gained only the Duchy of Lorraine (and bought Corsica from Genoa). In the Seven Years War (1756–63) in Europe, France had allies – Austrian, German (the Holy Roman Empire), and Russian. Her enemy, Prussia, under Frederick the Great, had only sporadic aid from

Britain. Nonetheless, France lost the major battles, such as Rossbach (5 November 1757), where Frederick, with 20,000 men, routed a French–Imperial army of 64,000 under the Prince de Soubise.[19] Overseas, Louis XV lost Canada, North America east of the Mississippi, and Senegal to Britain, and ceded Louisiana to his ally Spain. In India, France retained only trading stations at Pondicherry and Chandernagor.

When Britain's American colonies revolted in 1775, French pride still suffered from defeats in the Seven Years War. (Voltaire had dismissed the overseas empire as "*quelques arpents de neige*" [some acres of snow], but he lamented its loss in his *Age of Louis XIV* (1751), a sly criticism of Louis XV.[20])

However, Louis XVI lost a chance to wound Britain severely by declining to support the Americans until 1778, and then sending only 7,000 troops. France recovered Senegal (1783), but gained nothing else, not even American trade, and had spent two billion *livres*.[21] By 1788 the debt was four billion livres, and played a role in forcing Louis XVI to call the Estates General (1789),where the French Revolution began.[22]

Military power: France and Britain

France and Great Britain were major antagonists in the wars of the French Revolution and Napoleon. Opposition to French dominance in Europe became constant and unrelenting only after France declared war on Britain in 1793. Except for one year (1802–03), Britain stood against France, alone if necessary; when she found allies, she helped finance their armies.[23]

France's concentration on her army and Europe was partly out of necessity. She had potential enemies on three frontiers and vulnerable coastlines. Louis XV and XVI maintained a peacetime standing army of 200,000, including about 65,000 foreign mercenaries. Britain was protected by the sea. Her army, at best, was one-third the size of the French, and most of it was stationed in her colonies. At home, she used militia.

Britain gave priority to the Royal Navy. In 1715 she had 120 ships-of-the-line (fifty guns or more); France had thirty-nine. In 1789, when the French Revolution began, Britain had 176 ships-of-the-line and about 300 lesser vessels; France had seventy line vessels and perhaps 150 others. By 1810, the French had eighty ships-of-the-line; Britain 243.[24] British officers began training at or before puberty as midshipmen on warships. They learned to sail ships in every detail, and leadership. Their men took pride in serving in the Royal Navy, often even if they had been impressed.

France led in naval technology because of the work of the Académie des Sciences and Académie de Marine. She had bigger ships, with more guns and better navigation instruments. But the British often had French inventions in use before the French themselves.

In the eighteenth century, Britain became the dominant naval power in the world, and the top colonial and commercial power. During the French

Revolutionary–Napoleonic period, she maintained control of the seas, and, with revenues from international trade and home industry, supported allies on the Continent.[25] The French exploited nearby markets – in Europe and the Ottoman Empire – and did well until 1789.[26] In the wars of 1792–1815, however, the Royal Navy drastically limited French commerce to Europe, while British merchants cut into the same markets. The revolutionary governments and Napoleon's worked to ruin British trade with Europe – with scant success.

Eighteenth-century warfare

In the 1700s, warfare in Europe was conducted by nobles of all nations, of which the major ones were Austria, Prussia, Russia, and Great Britain. Austrian generals in their seventies were common. In Prussia, over 40 percent of generals were over 60, almost 10 percent over 70, and 2–3 percent over 80. Russia had many elderly officers as well; her younger generals were mostly foreign. Not all oldsters were inept, but most opposed change.

Britain "sold" commissions to commoners and nobles alike, but the officer corps was dominated by aristocrats. They had to suffer continual prying by ministers and parliamentary committees, however, regarding alleged misconduct, failure, or ineffectiveness, which induced many to resign or retire. So commanders were relatively young, on average. Wellington was the same age as Napoleon; both were 46 at Waterloo.

An advantage of having aristocratic generals was that titled and wealthy men did not scratch and claw for reputations. They tended to avoid unnecessary bloodshed, settling for putting their opponents "in check," and often letting them march away. Armies were small; a "big battle" was one with 60,000 engaged (both sides). However, during the century armies grew in size. In the Seven Years War, the French and Austro-Russians massed 90,000 against Frederick the Great several times, although he seldom had half their numbers. Fighting was serious and bloody when it occurred, but battles were fewer.

Troops were regulars and mercenaries; the latter comprised one-third of the French army and half of the Prussian. All countries hired foreigners to fill the ranks – the Austrians and Prussians largely from the German states. The British had the fewest foreigners – the King's German Legion (Hanoverians), Hessians, and men recruited on campaign. Rulers preferred to have their peasants at home, cultivating the fields and paying taxes. Wars were dynastic, over succession to thrones or territories. Civilians normally were uninvolved (except for being taxed). Of course, armies sometimes went out of control and looted, burned and worse, but not often in the civilized eighteenth century.

National conscription was unknown. All countries had militias, but rarely used them in foreign wars. France, for example, sent militia to man fortresses and perform other garrison duties while regular troops went to war. Armies carried supplies; officers kept looting to a minimum.

Impact of the Revolution on warfare

The French Revolution changed that, and more. Requisitioning in foreign territory – which often amounted to looting – became policy. Under the Terror, Lazare Carnot proclaimed that "the war must feed the war" (troops should live off the land). Napoleon was of like mind.

The Revolution brought organized civilian involvement in wars – physically, through the draft (*levée en masse*) and "home front" labor. Both were glorified by government propaganda in newspapers, flyers, pamphlets, posters, and by speakers (usually old soldiers). Propaganda was geared also to excite emotions – to teach people to hate the enemy and love "La Patrie" (the Nation; literally Fatherland).

The Revolution produced (on the French side) ambitious, cut-throat officers, and mass armies. The gentlemanly customs developed in the seventeenth and eighteenth centuries no longer applied. Generals, noble or commoner, had to win or face charges of treason, and often death. Battles were fought with unexampled ruthlessness.

The revolutionaries' inherited army

French strength on the Continent was grounded in the work of the *ancien régime*. The French revolutionaries introduced national conscription to furnish more troops, and it was continued by Napoleon. However, the French army, though it suffered severe shocks when France became a Republic, was always strong, and retained sufficient numbers of professional officers and NCOs (non-commissioned officers) to train raw troops. From the beginning, French Revolutionary armies could be challenged only by coalitions of powers. The Imperial French armies of Napoleon were defeated, ultimately, only by the combined forces of all of Europe. Even at that, victory owed much to British supremacy on the high seas.

Estates General/Revolution/response of the army

Louis XVI acceded to the throne at age 20 in 1774. He meant well, but lacked willpower and energy, and was bored by the business of government. He dozed during meetings with his advisory councils, and preferred to hunt or indulge in his hobbies, making mechanical gadgets and *eating*. A typical breakfast (1787) consisted of four veal cutlets, one baked chicken, six eggs, a slice of ham, and one and a half bottles of champagne. Louis wanted the best for his people; he cultivated *philosophes* and favored liberal policies. However, he lacked the courage to support reforming ministers, especially those who displeased Marie-Antoinette.

During the period 1774 to 1788, Louis XVI faced economic-fiscal crises that grew steadily worse. The population had grown from 18 to 26 million (44 percent) during the century, creating a land shortage. Landless peasants had migrated to the cities, but since France lacked sufficient industry they faced unemployment and misery. In Paris, with 600,000 people – six times that of any other French city – unemployment was always 10 percent, and 50 percent in the summer of 1789. After 1787 there were bread shortages and skyrocketing prices. Paris had a volatile population of unskilled workers who were easily led. At the same time, the crown (national) debt exceeded four billion *livres*, and was growing by 100 million a year.[27] Loans had become difficult to obtain.

The king tried to reform by royal decree (normal under French absolutism). However, his efforts were blocked by the *parlements* (high courts), whose judges were hereditary nobles, nobles in general and the Church hierarchy. In 1788, the king's attempt to discipline the *parlements* (also his right), resulted in riots in the cities with *parlements*, where people credited the courts with keeping royal taxes low. The king sent army units to restore order, but they were exhausted by marching and countermarching; some units became undependable, and a few mutinous.

Nobles, bishops and abbots (who were also nobles) demanded that the king call the Estates General (the French parliament), which had not met in 175 years (since 1614). Louis XVI, all good will and no backbone, summoned the Estates. A great irony of the Revolution is that the nobles forced the calling of the Estates General, out of which grew the Revolution.

The king decreed the most democratic election ever seen in France. All males over twenty-five could vote for delegates from their estate (clergy, nobles, commoners) – and women property owners and nuns also, through male agents. The Third Estate (commoners) were to have double representation – in response to a campaign led by Lafayette.[28] Louis hoped to get a majority of rural priests and nobles – both traditional and monarchist – in the First and Second Estates. Since by custom, the estates cast one vote each, the first two estates could outvote the third two to one. Thus, the king expected to control the Estates General.

The Estates General

The Estates General met on 4 May 1789 at Versailles. All began well, but the king soon lost control. Neither he nor Jacques Necker, his finance minister, had a plan of action. With nothing to vote on, the Third Estate had time to organize and declare itself the National Assembly. Louis offered to allow the estates, together, to vote by head on most taxes, and abolished some noble privileges. It was too little and too late.

The Third called on the other estates to join the National Assembly. Rural priests (a majority of the clergy) responded, as did liberal bishops and nobles, such as Lafayette. Louis XVI finally ordered all the nobles to join the Third Estate. He seemed to have given in, but had called 30,000 troops to Paris, probably to disperse the National Assembly.

Louis did not realize, however, that in Paris he had grossly inept generals, mostly favorites of Marie-Antoinette.

2

THE REVOLUTION AND WAR: FIRST CAMPAIGNS, 1789–93

Failures of Louis' commanders

By 11 July 1789, some 15,000 of the king's troops were in or near Paris. The Royal German Cavalry and four Swiss regiments were encamped on the *Champ de Mars*, the parade ground of the *École militaire*, south of the Seine. Judging Paris neutralized, Louis XVI dismissed his Swiss-born finance minister, Necker, whom *sans-culottes* (workers)[1] were convinced could assuage their miseries. On 12 July, the people marched in protest, demanding arms to protect Paris. Manufacturers who favored Necker (or were intimidated) gave workers days off and supplied drink for all.

General Baron Pierre-Victor de Besenval, Swiss by birth, was commander of troops in Paris. On 12 July he sent the 300 of his German cavalry to quell the disturbances – but with no clear orders to use force or infantry support. The crowds surrounded them, pulled some from their mounts; and they retreated into side streets. In the black night of 12–13 July, it was "Besenval to the Rescue." He ordered 9,000 Swiss to make a "combat crossing" of the Seine – on confiscated boats and barges – *not* using the intact, unguarded bridges.

They reached the north bank in total disarray. In the early morning light they reorganized, found the cavalry and marched back – *using the bridges*. The maneuvers had been so idiotic that military men muttered of treason.

On 14 July, Besenval did nothing while 80,000 people marched on the Bastille in search of arms.[2] The governor of the Bastille was General Count Bernard-Jordan de Launay (59), a veteran of the royal army, but virtually in retirement. His garrison was small – eighty-two *invalides* (soldiers unfit for field duty) and thirty Swiss. But they were behind stone walls nine feet thick (which no artillery of the day could breach), had cannon and shot, and could have defied an army. However, Launay chose not to fight – from timidity or reluctance to fire on the crowd, full of women and children.

Falsely believing that the mob had a leader, Launay sent him a message offering to surrender the Bastille if his men could withdraw "with honor." He got no answer, but apparently assumed his proposal had been accepted. In late afternoon he ordered the gates opened and the people flooded in. The Bastille was not stormed. Few of the garrison were harmed. Launay was arrested, however; a

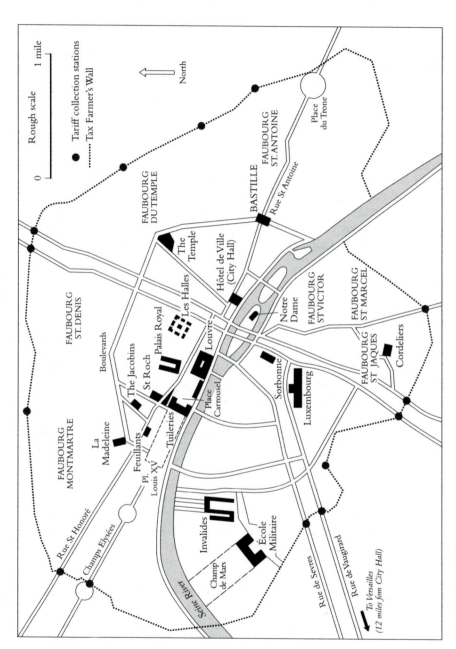

Map 2 Paris in 1789

zealot killed him at the City Hall and the crowd put his head on a pike.

The performance of the king's commanders in July 1789 seems to show that the *ancien régime* perished in part from inner decay. Under Besenval the king's troops were useless; Launay surrendered the Bastille for no reason. One can blame Louis XVI, who was out hunting, but competent generals would have needed no royal orders.

Paris celebrated the "storming" of the Bastille as a victory of the people over tyranny, and began tearing down the fortress – a task finished by commercial companies.[3] Those in the final "assault" formed the honorary "Conquerors of the Bastille" (*Vainqueurs de la Bastille*).

Louis XVI, typically, caved in, restored Necker to office and sent his troops away. He then came to Paris, and to the cheers of the crowd at the City Hall, pinned on the blue and red cockade of the Paris militia. (White, the color of the Bourbon dynasty, soon was added, forming the tricolor of the Revolution.) The Paris militia became the National Guard, commanded by the Marquis de Lafayette, "the Hero of two Worlds." This dapper, vain (and very rich) soldier of thirty-two expected his position to give him political influence.

March of the women

On 5 October 1789, some 6,000 Parisian women (and a few men), spurred by lack of food in Paris, marched on Versailles to ask Louis XVI for help. Weeping, a delegation told the king of their starving children; Louis wept also, and ordered food be sent. The marchers were given places to sleep, food, and wine. All was quiet when Lafayette belatedly arrived with the National Guard. Many nobles thought he had delayed so that if there were an incident he could sweep in and "save the day." He got an incident the next morning.

At dawn on 6 October, men broke into the palace, scared the queen out of her wits, and killed two *Gardes-du-Corps*. National guards expelled them, but they dragged one victim outside and put his head on a pike. Roused by the noise, a crowd formed and (probably prompted) shouted for the king to return to Paris where his subjects could protect him. (At this point, the people believed that the king was above politics, and their advocate.) Lafayette encouraged the king to go, and he did, with his family. In Paris, the royal family moved into the Tuileries palace. The National Assembly was ensconced in a riding school nearby. Lafayette became (nominally) the king's chief adviser. The queen had doubts: "I know Monsieur de La Fayette wants to save us, but who will save us from Monsieur de La Fayette?"

The "March of the Women" or "October Days" was the most important turning point of the Revolution. Moving to Paris was Louis' first step toward the guillotine. The king became a prisoner of Paris, and the National Assembly (and subsequent assemblies) were under direct mob pressure. The people were at first friendly toward the king, but that changed with time.

Flight to Varennes

During the period 1789 to 1791, the National Assembly gradually transferred the king's powers to the Assembly or his ministers. Louis XVI feared for his soul; God had given him the throne; God expected him to rule. Supporters (but not Lafayette) had long advised him to escape from Paris, daily more dangerous. The Marquis de Bouillé,[4] commanding an army at Metz, urged Louis to come to the frontier, where his troops would escort him back to Paris and restore his authority. Leopold II, Austrian Holy Roman Emperor, Marie-Antoinette's brother, promised Austrian troops if Louis could reach the frontier. In June 1791 the king and his family fled in disguise for Montmédy, on the northern border.

Once away from Paris, however, Louis made stops to enjoy his favorite dishes, lost his secret escort, and could not resist hinting who he was. The post-master at Sainte-Menehould recognized the king; he rode ahead to Varennes, where crowds stopped Louis' carriage. A cavalry squadron nearby offered to rescue Louis, but he elected to await more troops under Bouillé. Before the marquis arrived, the Paris national guard appeared and took the royal family back to the capital.

The National Assembly, unwilling to risk proclaiming a Republic, announced that the king had been kidnaped. Parisians were skeptical, and flocked to see a placard posted on the Champ de Mars that called for deposing the king. Violence ensued; Lafayette restored order with National Guardsmen, but there was bloodshed, and his popularity faded. He lost a bid to be mayor of Paris and retired to his estates, but was soon recalled to command an army.

France foments war

During the summer, the National Assembly finished the Constitution of 1791. In September, Louis XVI formally accepted it. A Legislative Assembly was elected, and the members took an oath to King and Constitution, but the largest faction, the Girondins, led by Jacques-Pierre Brissot, favored a Republic. Moreover, their goal was to bring liberty to the peoples of Europe, only possible by war.

In March 1792, the king appointed a Girondin ministry, whose leading figure was Lieutenant-General Charles-François Dumouriez (53).[5] An officer in the royal army, he had secured rapid promotion since 1789 by backing successive revolutionary leaders – the Duc d'Orléans and Mirabeau, then Lafayette, and finally the Girondins.[6] Under the *ancien régime*, he had fought in the Seven Years War and been a secret agent.

Dumouriez was foreign minister, but dominated the War Ministry. He sent General Adam-Philippe de Custine to Berlin to try to break Prussia's alliance with Austria (more about Custine on pp. 56–57). Amazingly, he authorized the general to offer command of the French armies to the Duke of Brunswick, who in September 1792 would lead a Prussian–Austrian invasion of France.

Meanwhile, the rulers of Austria and Prussia met at Pillnitz and called on the monarchs of Europe to destroy the revolution. Most states, and the papacy, were hostile to the Revolution, but were not ready for war – especially Britain, whose participation was essential. Nonetheless, the French Assembly decided that France was surrounded by enemies, and must strike at them to save herself. It pressed the king to make demands – abrasively framed by Dumouriez – on Leopold II, the Holy Roman Emperor (suzerain of Germany). At first, the emperor was compliant, and, for instance, ordered French *émigrés* to leave some Rhineland states. But when asked to nullify all anti-French treaties, Leopold refused in violent terms. He died in March 1792, but his son and successor, Francis II, was more bellicose.

Louis declares war

By April 1792, all the Assembly's factions were for war. Brissot's Girondins felt that if France lost, Louis would be blamed, and they could depose him and found a Republic. Lafayette's constitutional monarchists believed France could win, and strengthen the monarchy. The queen's ultra-royalists believed that if France won the monarchy would be stronger; if not, friendly Austrian and Prussian troops would enter Paris. Marie-Antoinette called the Girondins imbeciles. "They are playing into our hands." (Still a pretty child at age 34, she thought royal persons safe from harm.)

Maximilien Robespierre and a few followers were sole voices against war. The future architect of the Terror warned the Assembly that the Girondins were preaching a "new European crusade" and that "no one loves armed missionaries." Robespierre's fear was that a popular general would take over the government.[7] On 20 April 1792, Louis XVI asked the Assembly to declare war on "the king of Hungary and Bohemia" – the Austrian Holy Roman Emperor. He was trying to limit the war to Austria, but Prussia and lesser German states joined her.

Dumouriez's war plan

Dumouriez believed that Austria could be brought to terms by a quick strike into Belgium (the Austrian Netherlands). At the time, the emperor's primary goal was getting his share of Poland, being partitioned among Austria, Prussia, and Russia.[8] Also, the Belgians had recently revolted against Austria, and Dumouriez thought they might welcome the French.

His position was logical, but he counted without the sorry state of the French army. Something over 50 percent of the officers had fled the country. They could be (and were) replaced by NCOs from the ranks and volunteers from the middle class, but that would take time. Moreover, there was bad blood between the old regulars (the "whites," from their uniform) and the volunteers of 1791–92 (the "blues"). Finally, democratic ideas were in the air, and made soldiers distrust noble officers, and question orders.

The attack into Belgium

France had the armies of the North, Center, and Rhine (Nord, Centre, and Rhin) on her northern frontiers. Marshal de Rochambeau, headed the Nord (on the Belgian border). On his right were the Marquis de Lafayette with the Centre, and Marshal Nicolas Luckner with the Rhin.[9] The Comte de Rochambeau (Jean-Baptiste-Donatien de Vimeur, 67), was tall and elegant in dress, but a gruff professional. Americans had liked him; he was taciturn but affable, blunt, and set on winning.[10]

The king (on Dumouriez's advice) ordered the Nord to invade Belgium. Rochambeau protested that the army was not in condition to fight, but obeyed orders and sent out columns from Lille, Valenciennes and Dunkirk (see Map 3).

On 28 April, the first column marched from Lille toward Tournai – 2,300 men under General Count Théobald Dillon ("Dillon le Beau," another queen's favorite).[11] When it had advanced about 10 miles, just north of Baisieux, Austrian hussars appeared. The French cavalry panicked and rode through the infantry, behind it, disorganizing the whole force. Dillon restored order, but early on 29 April his men fled for Lille. Dillon tried to rally the troops, but was shot, dragged into Lille, and hanged.[12]

Meanwhile, also on 28 April, the second column, under the Duc de Biron,[13] left Valenciennes with 15,000 troops to take Mons.[14] His cavalry chased away Austrian Ulans, but he found the enemy in force on the heights of Jammapes. He bombarded them with cannon fire, and camped for the night without reaching Mons. About 10 p.m. a rumor flew through the camp that Austrian cavalry was upon them. Two regiments of French cavalry – shouting "We are betrayed!" – fled for Valenciennes. Biron and his officers leapt on their horses and brought them back, but the next morning they proved unmanageable. Biron let them return to Valenciennes. His advance had totaled 18 miles.

On 30 April, the Dunkirk column marched to Furnes (15 miles), found no enemy, and returned.[15]

Quiet and reorganization

Rochambeau resigned in disgust and retired to his estates. That decision distanced him from Paris, and spared him the fate of subsequent losing generals – the guillotine.

Dumouriez offered the Nord to Biron, who responded, "I would rather be killed as a soldier than be hung as a general." He then ordered Marshal Luckner from the Rhin to the Nord. Bavarian by birth, Luckner (70) had fought against France in the Seven Years War, but in 1783 had entered the French army as a lieutenant-general. Short, but broad-shouldered and strong, and could still sit a horse from morning until night. His men liked the old veteran with the saber scars on his face. He did not want army command; he felt unqualified, and his French was poor.

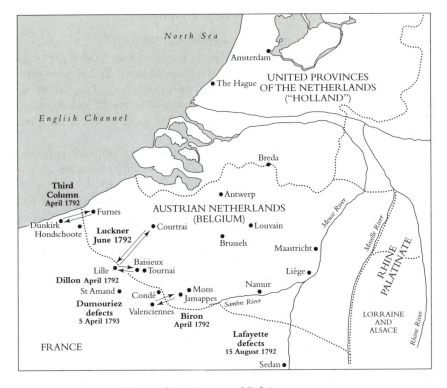

Map 3 First actions, 1792, northern France and Belgium

Second invasion of Belgium

However, Luckner went to Valenciennes, headquarters of the Nord, and induced Rochambeau and Lafayette to advise him. In May 1792, the three planned a second invasion of Belgium, and Rochambeau left for retirement. By the plan, Luckner was to attack the Austrian right, while Lafayette struck at the left. Luckner wanted to stand on the defensive, but the war minister would not have it.

On 9 June 1792, Luckner marched into Belgium with 20,000 men and captured Menin and Courtrai (19 June). However, the Austrians, under Johann Peter Beaulieu, counter-attacked. On 30 June the French retreated to Lille, ending the second strike into Belgium. They had penetrated about 5 miles.

Louis XVI replaced the Girondin ministry with Lafayette's followers. Dumouriez was obsessed with taking Belgium, which he dreamed of ruling, along with Holland (the United Provinces of the Netherlands). He travelled to Lille without orders, but the invasion was over. Luckner was puzzled to see him, but gave him nominal command of the left wing of the Nord, with headquarters at the Camp de Maulde, under Pierre Riel de Beurnonville.[16]

24

The *chassé-croisé*

Parisians blamed the king for the defeats in Belgium. On 20 June a mob invaded the Tuileries, made the king put on a "liberty cap" and toast the Revolution, but did him no harm.[17] Lafayette rushed to Paris and demanded that the Assembly punish those responsible. Radicals wanted to charge him with deserting his army, but the Assembly merely sent him back to the front. Back with his army, Lafayette, bent on saving the king, proposed the *chassé-croisé* to put his army closer to Paris. Lafayette's Centre would change places with Luckner's Nord. Lafayette would then command the Nord, Luckner the Centre and Rhin. The trusting Luckner agreed, and the war minister approved. Lafayette moved most of his troops from the Centre to Sedan, and had the army swear loyalty to the "nation, the law, and the king." Seemingly routine, it was in preparation for saving Louis XVI. On 2 August, the marquis moved his headquarters to Brouelle, and sent Alexandre Lameth (a comrade in America) with two regiments of cavalry to Compiègne. He then offered the king asylum with his army. Louis (whose intuition was nil) declined. He did not feel endangered, and did not trust Lafayette.

The king deposed: "10 August"

Very shortly, however, the people of Paris took control of events. Since the "Flight to Varennes" (June 1791) their distrust of the monarchy had deepened. The military defeats, Lafayette's visit to Paris, and the Assembly's failure to indict him had outraged the people further. Also, Parisians were still suffering from unemployment and hunger.

Finally, there was news that a Prussian army under Karl Ferdinand, Duke of Brunswick (Braunschweig), was marching on Paris.[18] On 11 July, the Legislative Assembly declared the "Nation in Danger" and ordered 100,000 National Guards (*Fédérés*) to Paris. The king vetoed the bill, but the *Fédérés* came anyway. The Guard from Marseilles entered singing "La Marseillaise."[19] On 14 July, the first Bastille Day celebration (*Fête de la Fédération*), with the king participating, was held peacefully.

Meanwhile, at the behest of the Jacobin Club, Jacques Danton framed a petition for the exile of the king, the election of a new *commune* (city government), the arrest of Lafayette and "all public enemies." Too few of the forty-eight sections (wards) of Paris approved it and no action was taken – but soon would be.

On 1 August the "Manifesto" of the Duke of Brunswick arrived and was posted all over Paris. The duke promised that his troops would not harm civilians or loot if the French royal family were kept safe, but: "*If the least violence, the least outrage, be done to their majesties . . . [my troops] will take . . . unforgettable vengeance [on] the city of Paris . . .*" The document, written by French *émigrés* with Brunswick's army, was supposed to intimidate Paris, but instead it confirmed suspicions that Louis XVI was in league with the enemy. Danton's petition was submitted again and forty-seven of the forty-eight sections voted for it.

During the night of 9–10 August, the section leaders expelled the old *commune* (city government) and installed a new one. Early on 10 August the Marquis de Mandat, commander of the Paris National Guard, was dismissed (and killed by a mob). His successor was Antoine Santerre, a self-made millionaire with whom the *sans-culottes* identified. The radicals had most of the Guard. On 10 August, at daybreak, a huge mob, chanting "La Marseillaise," marched on the Tuileries. The palace was protected by 900 Swiss guards and some 300 Chevaliers de St. Louis. However, Louis XVI, his family, and the Chevaliers fled to the Legislative Assembly. The king left the Swiss without orders, they did not deploy to fight, and 600 were massacred. It was Louis' last mistake.

Pressed by the *commune*, threatened by crowds, the Assembly suspended the king and imprisoned him and his family. It then decreed the election of a Convention – by universal manhood suffrage – to write a Republican constitution. In September, the Convention met, and the Legislative Assembly dissolved itself.

Provisional government

Until the Convention met, there was a provisional government under Jacques Danton. He was beloved of Paris, though defiantly ugly – short, overweight, with a pock-marked face and mane of unkempt hair, careless of dress, and often wine-soaked. A poor lawyer in 1789, he mysteriously had become rich. Parisians did not care; he was one of them. He was a "ward politician," who tried to help people one-by-one, and distrusted utopian projects for the masses.

Danton's clout declined in the coming months while Robespierre's rose. Up close, Robespierre could hardly bear the people's smell, but he loved them in the abstract, and had grand welfare schemes for them.

Lafayette flees France

On 15 August Lafayette reviewed his troops at Sedan and asked them to repeat the oath they had taken earlier to "the Nation, the Law, and the King." They refused, so he could not march on Paris. On 19 August Lafayette fled into enemy territory with twenty-two followers. The Austrians arrested him as a "dangerous revolutionary," and imprisoned him at Olmütz, in Moravia, until 1797, when Napoleon got him released.[20] Luckner, called to Paris on suspicion of treason, was returned to command the Centre. The Rhin was placed under the Duc de Biron, and the Nord under Dumouriez.[21]

Brunswick marches on Paris

Paris was in furor, but Brunswick was taking his time. From 19–23 August his army crossed the Rhine at Koblenz. The duke, a tall, soldierly figure, with penetrating blue eyes and a bright smile, was a more regal figure than his king, Fredrick William II, who accompanied him. Brunswick was professional and cautious; the king too aggressive. The army comprised 45,000 Prussians, 5,500 Hessians, 15,000 Austrians under General Clerfayt and 14,000 under the Prince von Hohenlohe-Kirchberg, and some 2,000 French *émigrés*; the Allied army totalled 86,000. Among the *émigrés* were Louis XVI's brothers, the Comte d'Artois and Comte de Provence. Brunswick had sent them to the rear to rid himself of their incessant yammering.[22]

At Fontoy, the small French garrison did not resist. On 20 August the Prussians attacked Longwy, commanded by Lieutenant-Colonel Louis- François Lavergne-Champlorier, recently of the National Guard. Bombardment slowly leveled the town, and local officials forced the garrison (2,600 men) to surrender.

On 29 August Brunswick invested Verdun, a major fortress, but skimpily manned and short of cannon and rifles. Again, the town was shelled, propertied civilians were distraught, and there were negotiations. On 2 September the second-in-command signed a capitulation. The commandant, Nicolas-Joseph Beaurepaire, committed suicide by firing two 0.69 caliber pistols into his ears. In thirty-three years in the royal army, he had risen from private to lieutenant-colonel; the king and his world were gone.[23]

The French prepare for a major battle

General Joseph Servan de Gerbey, the war minister, shifted commanders to better stop Brunswick. He had given Dumouriez the Nord. On 2 September, he gave the Centre to Lieutenant-General François Kellermann,[24] who brought 5,000 men to Metz from the Rhin, bringing his army to 15,000. Luckner was made generalissimo, commanding the Nord, Centre, and Rhin from Châlons – but the generals ignored him.[25]

General Kellermann (57), was an Alsacian, and had served forty-two years in the royal army. He was made *maréchal de camp* (major-general) before the Revolution, and lieutenant-general in 1792. A Jacobin since 1789 (when the club was moderate), he had preferred the constitutional monarchy, but was loyal to France. Kellermann was a fighter, unflappable in combat, which offset his poor education and Germanic French. He went into battle with regulars and "veteran" volunteers of 1791, leaving the green volunteers of 1792 behind; it was a good decision.[26]

Before Verdun was invested, Servan told Dumouriez to march directly to Sainte-Menehould or Châlons and block the road to Paris. Kellermann was ordered to march from Metz and to reinforce him.[27] However, Dumouriez argued that if he invaded Belgium – of which he hoped to be king – the Austrians would abandon Brunswick to protect it. He did not move, which might have meant disaster for the French had Brunswick not been so slow. "On he came, halting till six days' bread was baked and then, when his wagons were full, going on till a fresh baking was required."[28]

On 31 August, Dumouriez could hear Brunswick's guns firing on Verdun, and marched with part of the Nord (19,000 men) for the western side of the Argonne Forest. Swamps, hills, and dense woods made the Argonne practical to cross only in five places. Dumouriez covered them all. On 3 September he was at Grandpré, where he expected to meet the Prussians. He sent Arthur Dillon to Les Islettes, the southern crossing point, and detachments to La Croix-aux-Bois, Le Chesne, and La Chalade.

On 12 September, however, Clerfayt took La Croix-aux-Bois, north of Dumouriez, and outflanked him at Grandpré. However, Brunswick did not attack Grandpré, as Dumouriez had expected, but camped at Landres for three days (15–17 September). Most of his men had dysentery; some could barely get up, much less march. (They had eaten green apples in the Argonne.)

While Brunswick rested, Dumouriez marched without even cavalry pursuit – not for Châlons, where Luckner was receiving reinforcements, but for Sainte-Menehould. On 15 September, a division of his volunteers ran into a Prussian cavalry patrol, panicked and ran, shouting "Treason!" and "*sauve qui peur!*"[29] Dumouriez and his officers, on horses, stopped them at Dommartin, where the exhausted troops collapsed and slept.

On 16 September, Dumouriez regrouped his forces near Sainte-Menehould. Beurnonville reinforced him with troops from the Nord that brought his army – soon renamed the Armée des Ardennes – to 35,000, the majority raw volunteers.

Kellermann had most of the available regulars – including artillery – and "veteran" volunteers of 1791. He feared that Dumouriez's troops might panic (again), flee through his ranks, and disorganize the whole, which could lead to the fall of Châlons and then Paris. He had written to Servan (minister of war) asking that the armies be allowed to withdraw to a position before Châlons, and build fortifications, behind which Dumouriez's men would be less likely to panic. However, Kellermann was ordered to join Dumouriez at Sainte-Menehould.[30]

Kellermann marched, and on 18 September was at Dampierre-le-Château, six miles from Dumouriez. He had only 16,000 men from the Armée du Centre, but they were the most professional. On 19 September he made contact with Dumouriez.

Brunswick had finally left Landres on 18 September and marched south, intending to fight Dumouriez at Sainte-Menehould. However, King Frederick William II, misled by false news that Dumouriez was withdrawing toward Paris, wanted to march for Châlons, cut the French line of retreat, smash the army, and march on Paris. The king was Brunswick's superior, so he marched for the Châlons road. Hohenlohe's force that had crossed the Aisne River had to re-cross to join him. On the night of 19–20 September, in pouring rain, the Prussian army camped by the road from Suippes to Valmy. "The night came, black, profound, without moon and without stars; a raging wind blew."[31]

Valmy

The French were southeast of the Prussians, not barring their way to Châlons. When the armies faced off the next day, the Prussians had their backs to Paris; the French had theirs to Germany – a strange start to a strange battle. Further, the change in the Prussian march route meant that Brunswick would not face Dumouriez's volunteers, but march straight into Kellermann's army, deployed in an arc, with the left on the Châlons road, the center on a hill west of Valmy, and the right on Mount Yron.[32]

On 20 September, marching in cold rain and fog, Brunswick's advance guard approached the hill near Valmy and came under French artillery fire – inaccurate, because of the fog. But a battery on the Châlons road, near the inn of La Lune, stopped the advance cavalry. The artillery then joined Kellermann on the heights. Dillon, at Les Islettes, kept Hohenlohe's troops from reinforcing Brunswick. Beurnonville's forces were behind Kellermann's; Dumouriez's army was southeast of Sainte-Menehould. *Both were spectators on this day. Kellermann fought the battle.*

Brunswick's main army slowly assembled opposite Kellermann's center, and began returning French artillery fire. The Prussians were surprised at the numbers of French troops before them, but by about 1 p.m. Brunswick had his infantry up and in line, and they went forward to the sound of drums and fifes.

Kellermann had concentrated most of his troops in his center – regular artillery, with veteran officers, infantry, and cavalry, the latter to encourage the footsoldiers.[33] He saw the Prussians advancing, and led his infantry forward. Standing up in his stirrups, he held his hat high on the point of his saber, showing its tricolor cockade and red, white and blue feathers, and shouted "Vive la Nation!"[34] The troops shouted back, "Vive La France! Vive Notre Général!" Some accounts say cheering continued, and a band struck up "Ça ira." However, the French infantry advanced only a few hundred feet.

French artillery was hitting the Prussian ranks hard. Brunswick halted his troops after an advance of perhaps 200 yards. They fell back, and the battle became an artillery duel. The French inflicted the most casualties, but the Prussians – probably by chance – blew up three French ammunition wagons.[35] Brunswick sent his infantry forward, hoping the French were in confusion, but Kellermann moved up a new artillery battery and steadied his infantry. The Prussians advanced a few hundred yards, were decimated by the French guns, and fell back. Neither infantry attacked again, but cannonading continued until dark.

Just before night fell, Brunswick, the king, and the staff rode to the promontory of La Lune and held council. Brunswick expressed the consensus with "Hier

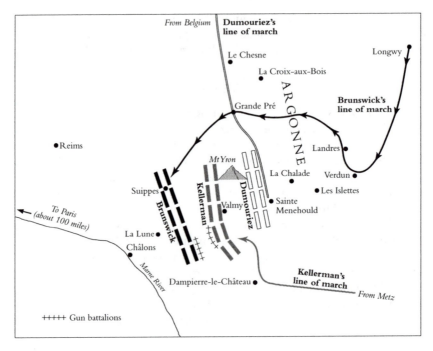

Map 4 Battle of Valmy, 20 September 1792

schlagen wir nicht." (Here we will not fight [or win].) All agreed. The morning drizzle had turned into a heavy downpour, and the officers sought cover – Frederick William and Brunswick at the inn of La Lune.

It had not been much of a battle – French casualties were 300 to 500 and the Prussian 180. But the Prussians knew they had lost. Their mood was grim.

On the morning of 22 September, Kellermann moved south of the Châlons road – surely to give Brunswick an avenue of retreat. Dumouriez, made commander of both armies after Valmy, was negotiating with the Prussians – while reinforcing his armies to 72,000.[36] He was successful; on 30 September Brunswick moved unopposed around the French and made for Germany. Dumouriez ordered Kellermann to follow Brunswick with 16,000 troops from the Rhin and Centre, together with Dillon and 16,000 from the Armée des Ardennes; neither was to engage him. At the frontier, Dillon left to join Dumouriez on the Belgian border.

Dumouriez' first priority was the "liberation" of Belgium.[37] After Brunswick and Kellermann departed he sent his remaining 40,000 troops, under Beurnonville, to rejoin the Nord on the Belgian border.

Turning point in history?

The great German novelist/poet, Wolfgang von Goethe, who was with Brunswick's army, was set upon to analyze the Battle of Valmy by his fellow Germans. From his many remarks, one line is remembered: "*Here and today begins a new epoch in the history of the world.*" He believed French volunteers had defeated the fabled Prussian regulars in open battle.

Doubtless there were many aggressive troops in the French armies. Stories abounded of young men, shabbily clothed and poorly armed, throwing themselves on the Prussians like wild animals. However, since the French infantry hardly closed with the Prussians, most tales are not credible. Observers sent by the Convention told the deputies what they wanted to hear about the volunteers of 1791, 1792, and from the local area.

The patriotic Chuquet says that the Prussians were not defeated by greater numbers, or mistakes, disease, rain, but by the *nation-in-arms*.[38] Elsewhere, he admits that the battle was won by the French artillery – veterans of the royal army.[39] Nonetheless, the myth of victory by citizen-soldiers became truth for most of the French. Some historians and the French military uphold the myth. Charles de Gaulle wrote: "The military is the most complete expression of the spirit of a society . . . *Who thinks of the Revolution without evoking the volunteers?*"[40]

The Battle of Valmy was a turning point. Goethe was right, if for the wrong reasons.

Not surprisingly, the French army did not win constantly after 21 September 1792. However, it began to improve; many volunteers stayed in service rather than "go back to the farm," and became hardened fighters; bourgeois volunteers and ex-sergeants learned how to be officers. By the time Napoleon took command in Italy in 1796 he had "regulars" who won handily by dint of his leadership.

Custine in the Rhineland

In July, Biron took command of the Rhin.[41] Lieutenant-General Adam-Philippe Custine de Sarreck served him as a sort of chief-of-staff, and resented (justly, Biron thought) not having an army command. Biron and the troops admired Custine, called "General Moustache" – big, bluff, loud and hearty – and a disciplinarian who got things done. On 19 September Biron created the Armée des Vosges for Custine, subordinate to him but to operate independently.[42] When the crisis of Valmy had passed, he ordered Custine with 14,300 men from Landau to cut off the supplies of the retreating Prussians and Austrians, and prevent their sending reinforcements to Belgium.

On 29 September the expedition moved toward Speyer, its first objective. Custine's men marched to Heimbach, then divided into three columns. One hit Speyer head-on, another took the fortress from the rear, and a third reinforced the frontal assault. Custine personally directed artillery fire, then led the infantry, who hacked through the gates with axes. The commander at Speyer, a Colonel Winckelmann, had vowed to destroy the "French dogs," but fled, was trapped at the Rhine and capitulated. The capture of Speyer was a triumph, and Custine baldly touted his part in it, writing to the war minister of his twenty-two hours on horseback.[43] However, he had led his volunteers to victory. Custine marched on to take Worms and Philippsbourg without a fight, and went straight for Mainz, which opened its gates to him (21 October). On 31 October he took Frankfurt.

He benefited, of course, from the lack of cooperation between the Austrians and Prussians, resulting from the conflict among Austria, Prussia, and Russia over Poland.[44]

Dumouriez invades Belgium

After Valmy, Dumouriez went to Paris and got authorization for the conquest of Belgium. On 20 October 1792, at Valenciennes, he took command of the new Armée de la Belgique, comprising 40,000 men from the Valmy campaign, 20,000 from the Nord, and some 10,000 volunteers from Châlons. Supporting his right was the Armée des Ardennes (20,000).

On 30 October 1792, Dumouriez marched for Mons, and arrived before the heights of Cuesmes and Jemappes with 40,000 men. There he faced the Duke of Saxe-Teschen with 12,000 Austrians, dug in on the high ground. He decided to attack frontally with 30,000 men, while General d'Harville, with 10,000 volunteers, hit the enemy on the flank. He ended up attacking altogether frontally, but heavily supported by artillery.

Dumouriez's men advanced in columns, to reduce casualties, then charged in line by battalion.[45] Men fell left and right; some units panicked and fled to the rear. However, Dumouriez's officers rallied the men. The Duc de Chartres (later King Louis-Philippe) became the hero of the day by rounding up stragglers to form the bataillon de Mons, which assailed the Austrian center. The enemy retreated the next day. Paris celebrated Jemappes as a major victory.

Dumouriez credited his artillery with the victory, but the Convention and Paris street glorified the volunteers, whom représentants reported had advanced singing "L'Amour sacré de la patrie" and "La Marseillaise." But many regulars had attacked with cheers of royal army units. "En avant, Navarre sans peur!", "Toujours Auvergne sans tache!", and the like.[46]

On 14 November, the tricolor flew over Brussels; by 30 November Dumouriez was at Liège; the Nord, under Francisco de Miranda, the Venezuelan revolutionary, was besieging Antwerp. Dumouriez had all but conquered Belgium, but he had decided to conquer Holland (the United Provinces) as well. He began planning, although his volunteers' one-year enlistments were running out and his army had shrunk from 100,000 to 45,000.

In Paris, the Convention divides

On 21 September, the Convention, ecstatic over the news of Valmy (fought the day before) held its first regular meeting – in the Tuileries palace. It was a largely middle-class body of 749 members, athough there were twenty-three nobles, including the Duc d'Orléans, "reborn" as Philippe Egalité.

At first, there was virtual unanimity. On 21 September 1792 it abolished the monarchy. On 22 September it decreed that all public documents be dated the "First Year of Liberty" or Year I of the Republic.[47] On 25 September the Convention proclaimed France a Republic "one and indivisible," since members feared she might lose her unity (previously assured by allegiance to the king), and fall into internal conflicts.[48]

On 19 November 1792, made smug by French victories, the Convention issued a decree that confirmed the worst suspicions of France's enemies: "The Convention declares . . . that [France] will give fraternity and aid to all peoples who desire to recover their liberty."[49] In short, the Convention adopted the previously Girondin policy of international revolution.

In other matters, however, Girondins (now considered conservatives) increasingly lost power. The Convention split between them and the Montagnards (radicals) or Jacobins, since they took over that club.[50] In the eyes of the Paris street, the Girondins had committed many sins. They had formed a ministry under the king, catered to aristocratic generals, and were conservative on domestic issues. Led (again) by Brissot and followers, they seemed to be obstructionists to those aware of the fragility of the Republic.

The Girondins' strength was in the provinces and the bourgeoisie of provincial cities – too far away to be able to intimidate the Convention.[51] The Paris masses backed the Jacobins, led by Jacques Danton, Maximilien Robespierre, Jean-Paul Marat, Joseph Fouché, Philippe Egalité (the Duc d'Orléans), and the 25-year-old Louis-Antoine Saint-Just, fiery speaker and beloved of the galleries. Their "bible" was Rousseau's *Social Contract*; thus they assumed the right to determine the "general will" (defined by Rousseau as what was best for the people). In fact, it was often the will of Paris.

The struggle over the king's fate highlighted the Girondins' weakness.

The King's Trial

Louis XVI had been deposed on 10 August, but there remained the problem of his fate and how to determine it. The Constitution of 1791 barred trial of the king for treason unless he had led an army, condoned an attack against the nation, or abdicated. The Convention voted to try "Louis Capet" anyway, for *conspiracy* against the nation – not treason but *planning* to commit treason. Even that could not be proved, but it did not matter. Saint-Just, the Jacobins' "golden boy," had said: "To be a king is a crime!" The Convention convicted Louis by an almost unanimous vote (15 January 1793).[52] It sentenced him to death (16–17 January) by a vote of only 387 to 334 (immediate death 361 to 360).[53] The Girondins demanded a plebiscite; the Jacobins blocked it. On 21 January 1793, Louis XVI died at the guillotine.[54]

War, Convention, and Paris

The execution of Louis XVI made the foreign war a matter of victory or death for the Republic. Dumouriez and Custine had won victories in Belgium and the Rhineland, respectively. Generals Pierre de Montesquiou and Jacques Anselme had invaded Savoy and Nice, which were annexed to France "by popular demand." However, there was a question as to how long the French could prevail.

After the king's execution, Britain, Holland, and Spain recalled their ambassadors. In February and March 1793, the Convention declared war on all three.[55] Piedmont-Sardinia and Naples declared war on France; German states sent troops to the Austrian or Prussian armies; the Pope lent moral support and paid subsidies. By April 1793, France was at war with all of Europe save Russia.

The French army numbered only 300,000 men, distributed among armies in the Netherlands, Germany, and on the Swiss, Italian, and Spanish borders. Moreover, it was shrinking as the terms of volunteers expired. In February 1793, the British navy began sinking French merchantmen, interdicting grain shipments from the Baltic and North Africa, making the French army harder to feed.

Dumouriez attacks Holland

On 1 January 1793, Dumouriez was in Paris, fresh from his triumphs in Belgium. Trading on his popularity, he got the war minister (Jean-Nicolas Pache) dismissed and replaced by his friend General Beurnonville. Dumouriez planned to save the king – with the collaboration of the Girondins – but of course failed. After the king's execution, he departed for the front, but was having misgivings about invading Holland, which might bring Britain into the land war.[56]

To his surprise, the Convention ordered him to conquer Holland, and on 16 February Dumouriez marched with the Armée de la Hollande, 23,000 men (including 7,000 raw levies). He left behind the Armée de la Belgique (30,000), under Miranda, besieging Maastricht, the Ardennes (23,500), and d'Harville's corps (12,000) at Namur. The Nord had 18,000 on the coast; there were 15,000 in garrisons. The total number of troops involved thus came to about 122,000.[57] However, the enemy was building up. Some 54,800 Austrians, 11,400 Prussians, 4,200 imperial (German) and 38,000 English, Dutch, and Hanoverian troops under the Duke of York reached Belgium.[58]

Notwithstanding, Dumouriez marched. He took Breda and Gertruydenberg, and at the Holland Deep he rested his men prior to pushing on to Rotterdam, the Hague, and Amsterdam. (Miranda was to join Dumouriez at Utrecht when Maastricht fell.)

On 1 March 1793, however, the French armies in Belgium were surprised and routed by the Prince of Coburg with 40,000 men. They fell back in confusion on Louvain.[59] On 9 March, Miranda arrayed three armies at Louvain to meet Coburg – the Ardennes, Belgique, and Nord, but his armies were at half strength because of the departure of time-expired volunteers.

Dumouriez delayed leaving Holland, but the Convention ordered him to join Miranda. On 11 March he took command at Louvain, but he had arrived with a small escort, without his army, still on the march. Without the Armée de la Hollande or the corps of d'Harville, still at Namur, he decided that the troops could not stand on the defense, and organized them to attack.[60] He had 40,000 infantry and 4,500 cavalry; Valence commanded the right, Chartres the centre, and Miranda the left. Coburg had 30,000 infantry and 9,000 horse.

On 16 March Dumouriez took Tirlemont. Coburg withdrew, but formed up to fight at Neerwinden. Dumouriez followed, and on 18 March attacked. The right and center were bloodied and stalled, but Miranda, on the left, kept reporting advances, and Dumouriez held on. At dusk, however, he found that Miranda had retreated to Tirlemont. The word spread and the army fell apart.

On 21 March, Dumouriez fell back on Louvain, with his volunteers deserting in droves – joyously heading for home, singing patriotic songs. He made a stand at Louvain with such troops as he could gather, but Coburg defeated him again. After the battle, he negotiated with Coburg, who agreed, in return for the evacuation of Belgium and Holland, to let him retreat into France (the Armée de la Hollande marching through enemy lines).

On 24 March 1793, Dumouriez retreated across the French border, directing his troops to the camps of Maulde and Buille, and to Valenciennes, Condé, and Lille.[61]

On 25 March, in further talks with Coburg, Dumouriez revealed a grander plan. He would rally his troops, march on Paris, destroy the Jacobins, dissolve the Convention, and restore the royal government. Presumably the new king would be Louis XVI's son, still imprisoned with his mother in the Temple.[62] He expected the French would support him if he succeeded.

Dumouriez might have rallied the troops if he had acted quickly. Many regulars, tired of uncertainty and the stampedes of the volunteers, probably would have followed him. But before he got organized to march, Miranda, a "professional revolutionary," addressed the Convention.[63] He blamed the defeat at Neerwinden on Dumouriez, and questioned his patriotism.

The Convention sent the minister of war, Buernonville, and four deputies to arrest Dumouriez at his headquarters in Sainte-Amand. When they arrived (1 April), he had them arrested and turned them over to Coburg.[64]

Meanwhile, Dumouriez tried to put the fortresses in the hands of royalist generals, and harangued the troops. But *représentants* from the Convention had got to the troops first, and offered incentives to them and to junior officers to remain loyal. The volunteer battalion of Nicholas Davout (future marshal of Napoleon) actually fired on Dumouriez, who then made the mistake of appearing with an Austrian cavalry escort. The (regular) artillerymen marched stiffly away, followed by the volunteers, then the other regulars.

On 5 April Dumouriez deserted to the enemy, with some of his staff, some cavalry, and a few generals, including the Duc de Chartres.[65] The Austrians occupied Valenciennes and the camps.

Effects on the Girondins in Paris

Dumouriez was identified with the Girondins, and his desertion was a death blow to the party. It was blamed for defeats in the foreign war, and encouraging counter-revolution. It angered the Paris *sans-culottes* by opposing measures for their relief. Finally (2 June), the Girondins were expelled from the Convention. (More on this in Chapter 3.)

The wars continue

General Marquis Auguste Dampierre was given command of the Armée de la Belgique. (In defiance of Dumouriez, he had held Le Quesnoy, and was considered above suspicion (briefly). Belgique and Hollande were abolished, but he got the Nord and Ardennes.)

On 15 April 1793, he recaptured Valenciennes and the Camp de Famars. On 1 May, he attacked Coburg with the Ardennes, but was thrown back and finally beaten when the Duke of York reinforced Coburg with the Coldstream and Grenadier Guards.

The defeat brought a swarm of *représentants* from the Convention to Dampierre's headquarters, certain that they could charge this aristocrat with treason. But Dampierre was mortally wounded in battle (8 May), and avoided the guillotine. Lieutenant-General François-Joseph Drouet took over the Nord; Irish-born General Charles-Édouard-Jennings de Kilmaine was given the Ardennes.[66] They pulled the armies back into Valenciennes and the Camp de Famars.

Beginning on 23 May 1793, Coburg moved toward Valenciennes, overrunning French advance positions at Anzin; the Duke of York took Famars. The Allies then beseiged Valenciennes.

Defeats in the Rhineland

Brunswick retook Frankfurt on 2 December 1792. Custine fell back to Mainz. Brunswick, moving at his usual snail's pace, began crossing the Rhine at Bachrach on 21 March 1793. On 27 March he demolished the French right, and Custine's army was in jeopardy. But Lieutenant-Colonel Henri-Jacques Clarke (later

Napoleon's minister of war) saved it by attacking and convincing the Prussians that they faced a larger force.

Clarke's action enabled Custine's army to retreat across the Nahe to Pfeddersheim. Jean-Nicolas Houchard covered the retreat, and deployed at Ober-Flörsheim, where on 30 March Brunswick attacked him. However, Custine saved him by rejoining the army, which fought well under "General Moustache," whose zest for battle was infectious. Brunswick was stopped.

Nonetheless, Custine had to abandon hope of rescuing the garrison at Mainz (22,000 men, commanded by Lieutenant-Colonel Jean-Baptiste Kléber, soon a general). Custine continued his retreat, burning supplies stocked at Worms and Speyer. On 1 April he was back in Landau, where his offensive had begun. Within a few days, news came of Dumouriez's defection, and Custine, an aristocrat, found himself under suspicion. Some officers refused to serve him, and there were disciplinary problems in the ranks, but he weathered the storm.

On 6 April he was given command of both the Moselle and the Rhin, but he gave Jean-Nicolas Houchard command of the Moselle, reinforced by the Corps des Vosges. He arrayed the Rhineland forces with the Moselle at Saarlouis, the Rhin at Wissembourg, and the Vosges between them.

However, on 13 May Custine left to command of the Nord, which was defending Valenciennes, under crushing siege.

The Committee of Public Safety

In April 1793 the Convention created a national executive (to replace the king) – the Committee of Public Safety (Comité de salut public, hereinafter Comité or great Comité). Jacques Danton emerged as the leader. By June, he had multiple crises on his hands – beginning with defeats by foreign enemies, unrest in Paris, and internal revolts against the government. The Republic had never been more in danger. (Detail in later chapters.)

Gloom on the frontiers

On the foreign battle fronts prospects were grim. At Valenciennes, Custine called for replacements for the Nord from the Rhin, under Alexandre de Beauharnais, and from the Moselle, under Houchard. Neither sent troops. Custine was forced to stand on the defensive, but nevertheless, by mid-July 1793, he had in the Nord 35,013 trained infantry and 4,385 cavalry – armed and ready to fight. Davout praised Custine's "discipline sévère et républicaine."[67] Despite his toughness, the troops liked Custine, thought he could win, and were ready to fight for him. But Custine was called to Paris, and without him his army lost Valenciennes.

Meanwhile, in Custine's former Rhin-Moselle command, Kléber had lost Mainz on 22 July. He had directed punishing sorties against the Prussian besiegers, but the armies could not relieve him. With his garrison reduced to 18,000, and his men starving and short of ammunition, he capitulated.

In the Alps two French armies comprising 50,000 men were in stalemate against a Sardinian army they had earlier scorned. In May, an army of 40,000 Spanish troops had moved across the eastern Pyrenees, defeated a smaller French army, and threatened Perpignan. In the west, the Spanish were besieging Bayonne.[68]

Danton urged "Audacity and more audacity!" on the armies, but secretly tried (and failed) to negotiate peace settlements.

The Vendée

To the country folk in the Vendée and along the Loire in Anjou and Brittany[69] the Revolution was an outrage – especially its acts against the Catholic Church. The revolutionaries had outlawed their priests, abolished monasteries and convents, and put Church properties on sale (not churches, but were they next?). The assemblies had ousted their easy-going lords in favor of money-grubbing *bourgeois*, who had neither grace nor pity (the larger cities and towns favored the Revolution).

Taxes were higher, inflation destroyed their profits, government agents paid pitiful prices for their crops, and the weaving industry in the villages was in ruins. Parisians had *murdered* the king. The last straw was the levy of 300,000 by decree of 24 February 1793 (long before the *levée en masse*). The peasants revolted rather than send more of their sons to defend the Republic, to them a creation of godless madmen.

Exhorted by clergy to save the Church, and led by nobles (some returned *émigrés*) and some commoners, they formed the "Catholic and Royal Army," which controlled the countryside and threatened Republican cities, such as Nantes and Angers. The rebellion began in the Mauges, the trackless hedge country of the northeastern Vendée.[70] (Detail on the war in the next chapter.)

Danton's Comité had not slowed, much less stopped, the rebellion in the Vendée. In March 1793 it had sent General Labourdonnaye, who marched 6,000 men of the national guards of Nantes and Angers into the center of the Vendée. Rebel bands scattered his force. (The Vendéan leaders will be identified in the next chapter.) Republican officials fled from the district capitals; the countryside belonged to the royalists.[71]

In April, the Comité sent General Jean-François Berruyer (56) to stamp out the rebellion. An officer of the old army, he had gained a certain morbid fame for ordering a drum roll to drown out the speech of Louis XVI at his execution. He was promised 60,000 men – including 24,000 veterans from the Armée du Rhin, but the generals defied the weak Comité and sent none. Berruyer got only detachments of gendarmes and volunteers from the "Conquerors of the Bastille" (*Vainqueurs de la Bastille*). However, from his headquarters in Angers, he gathered 12,000 volunteers from adjacent departments, and sent columns toward rebel strongholds.

The Vendéans knew his every move, however, and on 9 April they routed Republican columns at Coron, Aubiers, Beaupreau, and Challans, where the battle was decided by the young Comte de la Rochejaquelein's cavalry. On 9 June, the Vendéans, 40,000 strong, took Republican Saumur.

Heady with success, the Vendéans decided to seize Nantes, a major port city, where they could be supplied and possibly reinforced by the British. In mid-June, a Vendéan army, 30,000 strong, marched down the north bank of the Loire on Nantes. South of the Loire, 10,000 of the Marais army marched in support. The rebels were opposed by General Canclaux, with 6,000 infantry and 300 cavalry, mostly national guards, but behind strong walls.

On 28 June, the Vendéans launched a murderous day of battle. At dusk, leading the seventh attack, the commmander-in-chief was mortally wounded. Deprived of their leader, the army retired helter-skelter on Saumur.

The Vendéans gained nothing by attacking Nantes. It appears that they should have marched on Paris, which was vulnerable. The government was in chaos, the Paris "street" hungry and full of undirected anger. The bulk of the army was on the northern and Rhine frontiers. As it was, the Republic had its first victory over the Vendéans – but too late to save Danton's Comité. Moreover, he had not moved against the "federal cities."

The federal cities

On 2 June 1793 the Girondins were expelled from the Convention by the Jacobins, assisted by 80,000 Paris National Guards. Twenty-nine were arrested, and most guillotined.[72] The majority escaped, however, and fomented the revolts of Lyons, Bordeaux, Marseilles, and Toulon – the "federal cities".[73] The first three were the largest in France, after Paris; the fourth the key naval base on the Mediterranean. Danton's Comité had done nothing to quell these rebellions.

Failures of Danton's Comité

In addition to its failures in war, Danton's Comité had not enforced legislation enacted by the Convention to placate the *sans-culottes* of Paris – the Law of the Maximum, controlling prices, and one authorizing a worker's "revolutionary army" to requisition food in the countryside and arrest "suspects."[74]

For survival, the Republic needed a government with near dictatorial power – one with the will, decision, and imagination to mobilize France's resources and manpower for total war.

3

THE TERROR: POLITICS
AND ARMY REFORM, 1793–94

A new Committee of Public Safety

On 10 July 1793 the Convention removed Danton and his followers from the Committee of Public Safety and manned it with militant Jacobins. On 27 July, Maximilien Robespierre, "the Incorruptible," was added and became the leader. The new Comité numbered twelve – eight lawyers (one a noble), one Huguenot minister, one actor, and two army officers (both engineers). The political tone was set by Robespierre (35), a humorless and prim idealist; Georges Couthon (37), a paralytic cripple, but active and a top legal mind; and Saint-Just (26), the handsome, flamboyant and bloodthirsty favorite of the galleries. Ex-captain Lazare Carnot (40) managed the military.

Carnot: "the organizer of victory"

Lazare Carnot was forty, tall, stooped, square-jawed, with a full head of hair, and usually careless about his appearance.[1] He was an engineer and mathematician with judgment, imagination, and decision. Under the *ancien régime* he had been a member of the Academy of Sciences and a chevalier de l'ordre de Saint Louis (amazing for a commoner). Really a moderate Republican, he had joined the Jacobin government because he believed he could save the French Republic, that must win or perish.

Charles de DeGaulle called Carnot "a professional . . . who had been a *représentant du peuple* and *commissaire aux armées* . . . [and who] brought to the government both natural talent and experience by which he drew victory out of chaos." Further, he became "*le véritable ministre de la guerre*".[2]

The new Comité inherited all the problems of its predecessor, and more. In July, hysteria reigned among the *sans-culottes* after Marat, the "Friend of the People," was murdered by Charlotte Corday d'Armont, a beautiful Norman noblewoman.[3] Parisians saw enemies everywhere.

Government of Terror

Robespierre called for a "Government of Terror." The Convention voted *terror* the "order of the day." The new Comité, assuming dictatorial power, ruled France from July 1793 to July 1794 – the most bloody year of the Revolution. The guillotine stood as a warning to anyone who defied the government, and terror enabled the government to mobilize all France's resources, human and material. To empower the Comité, the Convention passed a new Law of Suspects, mandating the arrest of anyone whose "conduct, relationships, talk, or writings" showed them to be "partisans of tyranny or federalism," and a new Law of the Maximum, with death for major violations.

The Comité was supported by the Paris "street," which was greatly influenced by Jacques Hébert, known as "The Homer of excrement,"[4] editor of the newspaper *Père Duchesne*. He crusaded for guaranteed jobs, cheap food, death to aristocrats and the rich, and the destruction of Christianity.

Structure of the Government of Terror

The Comité was the executive branch of government, and dominated other branches and the Revolutionary Tribunal, which meted out "people's justice." Jacobin clubs, nationwide, supported it. Its *représentants en mission* (representatives-on-mission) had authority over local governments and the armies. They could relieve generals and/or change their plans. Generals and fighting men alike generally resented these civilians, identified by huge tricolor sashes, but obeyed them. Rare *représentants* took command in critical situations.

Représentants committed many atrocities. Jean-Baptiste Carrier ordered *noyades* (drownings) at Nantes, where "traitors" were chained in barges, which were sunk in the estuary of the Loire – killing Girondins and royalists, with their families, along with monks, nuns, and priests. The Comité sent felicitations.[5] Almost every *représentant* took "heads," but some favored histrionics. Laignelot, at Brest, coined a famous epigram: "Peoples will never be truly free until the last king is strangled with the bowels of the last priest!" But he ordered few executions.

Changes in the military

The crowds of Paris (not without prompting) demanded military terror in addition to political–social terror. They demanded a "rising of the masses" to form a people's army, in which the people would not only serve but choose its officers – and control them.

Robespierre's Comité knew that a totally democratic army could not save the nation; discipline was needed, under loyal officers, and the best-trained were nobles or NCOs of the old army. Nonetheless, for good relations with the street, the Comité created a *sans-culotte* "revolutionary army," comprising mostly unemployed workers. Its missions were to scour the countryside for food, firewood, and supplies for Paris, and accuse traitors. Similar armies were put together in other cities.

The *levée en masse*

On 23 August 1793, to avoid the mass rising touted by the Paris street, the Comité had the Convention pass the *levée en masse* – a national draft of young men – the first in history. Initially, Robespierre had opposed the *lévee*, since he felt that competent and loyal *officers* were needed, not soldiers, but soon realized its political benefits. It completed the radicalization of the Revolution by converting military service into a *duty* of all male citizens.

Danton had consistently favored the *levée* – for political reasons – as had the frenetic Hébert and the Paris Commune. Danton professed the wish to eliminate Parisians' "unfair burden" under the volunteer system, about which they groused continually, although 85 percent of "volunteers" were newcomers, chosen by long-time Parisians in the sections (wards). Danton was not under the illusion that the *levée* immediately strengthened; time would be needed to feed, equip and supply the men, and more to train them. The *levée* law mandated that all men between the ages of 18 and 25 register for military service. Unmarried men (only) were called (as needed) – the youngest first – unless physically unfit, insane, or felons. No substitutes were allowed, but after 1797 this democratic rule was abandoned.

The manpower pool was so large that only one-quarter of the 18-year-olds were called, and many of those were rejected because they failed to meet height (5 feet) or fitness requirements.[6] Resistance was heavy. Fifteen percent of those called in 1793 (September to December) deserted, 20 percent during the next year (1794), and more in later years. Evasion was common.[7]

Nevertheless, the "draft" succeeded, helped by propaganda that called the *levée en masse* "Republican," and recruitment monarchial and subversive. Newspapers and placards proclaimed the *levée* was creating an army of loyal citizen-soldiers to replace the king's mercenaries. An army of *représentants* preached that in a republic, every citizen had a *duty* to serve; it was the price of liberty. Citizen-soldiers, they said, would keep democracy alive; citizens not bearing arms must work harder to support the army. Every means was used to make *patriot* and *citizen-soldier* synonymous. Carnot organized the *levée* and gave it the force of law, with penalities for "nonsubmission."

Even with the *levée en masse*, however, Carnot could not assemble a mass army quickly. Until early 1794, battles were fought by armies of regulars, national guards, and volunteers. Afterward conscripts became the majority in the ranks. Within a year (by September 1794), France had an army (on paper) of 1,000,000 men; 800,000 were actually serving.[8]

The *Amalgame*

The *amalgame* was devised by the Comité (before Carnot joined) to integrate the ranks – and make regulars, volunteers, and, later, conscripts "brothers in arms." A law of 13 August 1793 mandated infantry *demi-brigades* of three battalions, with companies of forty volunteers and twenty regulars.[9] The Comité thought the *amalgame* would break up units of the royal army, and reduce the threat of a military coup against the Republic.[10]

Représentants were to name officers in the demi-brigades. All troops were to have the same uniform and the same pay. Under Danton, the king's white coat had been outlawed (21 February 1793), but the law had gone unenforced. Under the *amalgame* the blue "Republican" coat was to be issued to all – when the army had enough coats.

Carnot wisely delayed the *amalgame* so as not to interfere with combat operations, and only ordered it implemented by a law of 8 January 1794, adding one of 28 January for the integration of independent legions and corps into the demi-brigades.

The generals had meanwhile responded by forming "practical" demi-brigades, at the extremes all regular or all volunteer, since they wanted to win, and might be beheaded if they didn't. They were more receptive of a law of 22 November 1793 that required that conscripts be incorporated into battalions. Manpower was needed. The law finally was applied army-wide in 1794. Meanwhile, replacements were largely conscripts, and they were soon the majority in battalions.

Innovations

Carnot gave the army observation balloons – a first – and built the first "telegraph" from Paris to Lille (with stations on hilltops that relayed messages by semaphore). He improved the royal foundries and created new arms works, some in Paris, where workers needed employment, and shops could serve as propaganda. Those in the gardens of the Tuileries and Luxembourg palaces provided the spectacle of people serving *La Patrie*. The latter turned out pikes, long obsolete (if fashionable for carrying severed heads), but others produced muskets, powder, and some cannon.

Reforming the officer corps

Carnot gradually purged the officer corps of the older officers – if incompetent or diehard royalists – but avoided involvement with the execution of noble generals, such as Custine, Biron, and Beauharnais. In mid-September, following a Hébertist uprising, the Comité suspended all officers of noble birth. This allowed Carnot to rehabilitate those he needed to win the wars – talented ex-nobles who were loyal to the Republic.

When Carnot finished, most generals were younger than he (40). The new ones had been promoted because of combat performance; all were tough and ambitious. Among Carnot's new generals were Napoleon Buonaparte (24), J.-B. Jourdan (31), André Masséna (35), Pierre Augereau (36), Dominique de Pérignon (39), Nicolas Davout (23), François Lefebvre (38), Guillaume Brune (30), and Jean-Philibert de Sérurier (50). They were nine of the twenty-six men whom Napoleon made marshals of the Empire.[11]

The new Republican army

The army became a school of patriotism. Regulars, volunteers and conscripts marched together, singing "La Marseillaise," "Ça ira," and the "Carmagnole" with the tricolor and their regimental flag. Their lives were ordered by bugles and drums and the strains of the regimental band. Moreover, promotion was rapid for those who led and fought well. Privates became sergeants, sergeants became officers, and seasoned lieutenants and captains might find themselves generals. Recruits learned the Republican gospel: the army must save the French Republic and spread liberty abroad; the Republic was the salvation of mankind from tyranny. The saying "every private carries a marshal's baton in his knapsack" originated with Carnot (although often attributed to Napoleon). The War Ministry bought 15,000 subscriptions to patriotic Paris newspapers for the armies; it sent thousands of copies of Hébert's radical *Père Duchesne* to the fronts. The troops also got 400,000 copies of the Jacobin Constitution of 1793 (though a dead letter) and the Declaration of Rights. Carnot himself founded and edited a journal for soldiers.[12]

New soldiers got no "basic training," but were simply issued arms and (where available) uniforms, and assigned to units in the armies where they learned by doing. Armies so produced lacked organization and discipline, but made up for it by numbers and the sense of mission that the men absorbed.

Organizer of Victory

Carnot earned the sobriquet "Organizer of Victory" because of the success of French armies against both domestic and foreign enemies. He adopted the general strategy of holding fast on the Rhine (and other borders), and striking with speed and violence into Belgium and Holland. To free the armies to crush foreign enemies, however, it was necessary to repress the internal rebellions in the Vendée and the "federal cities."

Carnot's decision

Carnot judged that the peasant rebellion was most dangerous; the federal cities had lost the backing of surrounding towns and villages, and were isolated. The Vendéans had support in a wide area, and commanded the coast – if not its major ports – where the British might land troops, weapons or supplies.

4

THE TERROR AND WAR, JULY 1793–JULY 1794

The Vendée: rebel leadership

Leadership made the Vendéan rebellion a danger to the Republic. After a stumbling start, it was superb – canny and from the front – but more in the style of the seventeenth century, which meant ultimate failure. Moreover, the men (and ferocious women) of the Armée Catholique et Royale absolutely required personal leadership. They fought as if possessed under their chieftains, but panicked if the leaders fell.[1]

Most beloved of the peasantry was the baby-faced, curly-haired Count Henri de Vergier de La Rochejaquelein (21), who led the cavalry. A graceful rider and swordsman, recognized in battle by his top hat with a tall feather, he could have inspired D'Artagnan of Dumas's *Three Musketeers* – handsome, fearless and late of the King's Guard.[2]

Among other leaders were the bullheaded François de Charette de la Contrie (30), an ex-naval officer; Jean-Nicolas Stofflet, tall and brutal, a former game-keeper (*garde-chasse*); Maurice d'Elbée (40), a Saxon ex-officer of the French cavalry; Charles Artus, Marquis de Bonchamps (33) and Piron de la Varenne, of the King's cavalry; Antoine-Philippe de la Tremoïlle, Prince de Talmond (28); Dommaigné, Comte de Brulon, cavalryman; and Louis-Marie de Salgues, Marquis de Lescure, the most respected.[3]

Many nobles, including Elbée and Bonchamps, were "drafted" by the peasants, who visited their châteaux, flattering them: "You know how to fight, Monsieur, you must come and lead us."[4]

Area of rebellion and armies

The "military Vendée" comprised the department of the Vendée and parts of old Anjou, Poitou, and Brittany (see Map 5). It was bordered on the north by the Loire valley; on the east by the road from Saumur to Niort; in the south by the Sèvre River by Niort; and in the west by the Atlantic Ocean.

The Armée Catholique et Royale comprised three armies – one on the Loire, a second in the northern Vendée and southern Anjou, and a third along the coast

Map 5 The Vendée and the Federal Cities, 1793–94

under Charette.[5] Command rotated in all but the latter. The Vendéan standing (paid) army numbered about 10,000. But by sounding the *tocsin*, the ranks could be swelled quickly to 30,000–60,000. The army had weaknesses other than requiring up-front leaders. There was no overall commander, and the chieftains always planned in council – never good in war.

To oppose the rebels, the French Republic had in the area the Army of Brest (L'Armée des côtes de Brest), under Jean-Baptiste-Camille de Canclaux (53), an officer of the old regime; and the Army of La Rochelle (L'Armée des côtes de la Rochelle), under Jean-Antoine Rossignol, a former soldier in the royal army. The cities loyal to the Republic had national guards – 6,000 in Nantes and 5,000 each in Angers, Saumur, and La Rochelle.

From the start, fighting was vicious. Both sides cut down and killed prisoners and non-combatants, even children. Both sides comprised zealots – devout

46

catholics/royalists versus fanatic Republicans. Each thought the other deserved only death, but the Republicans were less merciful.[6]

Biron in command

In July 1793 Robespierre's Committee called General Biron to command in the Vendée,[7] and ordered up 35,000 troops for him from various armies. In addition, Antoine-Joseph Santerre, commandant of the Paris National Guard, raised 10,000 volunteers. A millionaire gin manufacturer, Jacobin, and hero of the *sansculottes*, he had no military training or service.

Biron received 40,000 inferior troops at Niort (the armies had not sent their best). He discharged half of them, reorganized the rest, and sent them in widely separated columns toward the coast between the Loire and the lower Sèvre.

Vendéan General Elbée divined the Republican strategy, and rallied 25,000 men south of the Loire. On 15 July, the rebels surprised and struck a column under General Labarollière at Martigné-Briand. But the Vendéans' lost the day because Bonchamp, La Rochejacquelein, Stofflet and other chiefs were wounded and evacuated; their troops retreated pell-mell to Vihiers. Labarollière proudly notified Santerre, who was near Saumur. Lusting for glory, Santerre marched through the night, and on the 16th joined the Republicans at Vihiers.

The Vendéans retreated toward Coron. Santerre pursued, but the wounded rebel chiefs returned, rallied the rebels near Cholet, and rang the *tocsin* for reinforcements. On 17 July the Vendéans drove the Republicans in disorder to Vihiers. The *représentant* Pierre Bourbotte rallied some 1,500 men, but Santerre's troops fled past them, and the army dissolved. Santerre and Bourbotte barely escaped.

Santerre was called to Paris, but ruled innocent by his fellow Jacobins. Instead, the *ci-devant* Duc de Biron was blamed for the defeat, convicted of treason, and guillotined.

Erosion of Vendéan power

As July 1793 ended, the Vendéans were victorious, and full of hope. The British tentatively promised support, and the rebels made plans to capture a port to receive a British expedition.

In early August, however, the Vendéans lost Luçon (in the south) to troops from La Rochelle. Charette, Lescure, Elbée, and La Rochejaquelein raised 36,000 men, and tried to retake the city, but Republican artillery thwarted their attempt. In the north, however, Bonchamps outfought the Republicans on 4 September at Erigny, and Lescure won minor victories. On 5 September, Elbée scored a triumph at Chantonnay, scattering the Republican army and capturing its artillery and plans.

The Mainz garrison

Meanwhile, on 23 July, in the Rhineland, the French garrison at Mainz – reduced to 18,000 – surrendered to Allied forces. The officers and men were paroled, pledging not to fight against foreign enemies for a year, but could serve against Frenchmen. So the troops were dispatched to the Vendée under General Jean-Baptiste Kléber (40).[8] Kléber's men loved his zest for fighting. His Rhin veterans were a boon to the Republic's forces, but not at first.

In mid-September Kléber's corps joined Canclaux's Army of Brest and they invaded rebel territory. Kléber drove Charette into Torfou, but the rebel's 10,000-man force grew to 40,000 as other bands arrived, and Kléber retreated. He joined Canclaux against Elbée, but the "brigands" bested them. On 22 September, with losses at 2,000, they took shelter in Nantes.

On the Loire, meanwhile, Santerre arrived again with 15,000 troops, and won a skirmish with the Vendéans. Rossignol joined Santerre with most of the Army of La Rochelle, and unaware of Canclaux's retreat, ordered Santerre to take Cholet. Santerre was bloodied by rebels under Piron, and retreated to Coron.[9] Piron, reinforced with artillery, attacked Coron; the Republicans fled.

Santerre was called to Paris and flung into prison, to live in dread until after Robespierre fell in July 1794.

Carnot focuses on the Vendée

On 22 September Carnot created an Army of the West (Armée de l'Ouest; hereinafter Ouest) to replace the armies of Brest and La Rochelle. (Like the better generals, he believed in single command.) Jean Léchelle, a native of the Mauges and a "good Jacobin," was named commander – but not by Carnot (Kléber would have been his choice).[10] However, the united Republican armies had an advantage over the Vendéans, who did not unite theirs.

Vendéan decline

On 15 October Léchelle attacked Cholet, a major rebel stronghold, with Kléber in the lead. The Vendéans defended staunchly, but after the battle Lescure, their chief, lay dying, and they retreated to Beaupréau. The Republicans occupied Cholet, 36,000 strong. Bonchamps rallied 35,000 Vendéans, placed Breton allies at the Loire bridges, and on 16 October attacked Cholet. "Fury guided the Vendéans" – but fury – although sustained for 10 hours – was not enough.[11] The rebels withdrew, with Bonchamps mortally wounded and Elbée maimed.

Cholet was a crucial Republican victory, but that escaped Léchelle. To pursue the enemy, he sent only François-Joseph Westermann's legion (about 1,200 men, many German deserters) and two uninspired brigades.[12] Nevertheless, Westermann surprised the Vendéans at Beaupréau, routed them, and slaughtered all stragglers, sparing neither women, children, nor old men. His drunken troops sacked the town. Westermann, an Alsacian and ex-sergeant of the royal army, was notorious for his brutality, even in the savage Vendée war; the Comité soon sacked him.[13]

The Vendéans move north

In mid-October, at St Florent, the rebels assembled some 60,000 fighters and 20,000 wives, children, old people and camp followers. A council of leaders decided to cross the Loire into Brittany and try to capture a port to receive British aid. They made La Rochejacquelein commander-in-chief, a good choice, but the Vendéans had no agreement with the British on a port or time schedule, which proved fatal.

The Armée Catholique et Royale had many crippled troops, and was short of food and munitions. It expected 50,000 Breton volunteers, but got 7,000. Finally, the fighters had to protect the crowd of non-combatants, who impeded the march.

Nevertheless, on 23 October the Vendéans took Laval, defended by 6,000 National Guards, with the loss of only 100 men. Léchelle was resting the Republican troops, with the approval of the *représentants*, but after Laval fell they realized Nantes and Angers were vulnerable, and ordered the general to march.

Léchelle attacked Laval in two columns, one on either side of the Mayenne River. One column floundered in difficult terrain, and was smashed. La Rochejacquelein and the cavalry pursued the remnants, forcing survivers to swim the Mayenne River. Stofflet's bands destroyed the second column. The Republicans fled southward to Château-Gonthier, then Ségre and Craon.

Léchelle repaired to Nantes, where he died, apparently of depression. Rossignol, ex-commander of the La Rochelle army, took command of the Ouest.

Cheered by the Laval victory, the Vendéans dismissed thoughts of moving to safety south of the Loire, and the chiefs spent ten days debating the next move. Stofflet lost patience, and marched his army north, flags flying and drums beating. The army followed, and took Fougères, where a message came from Henry Dundas, British minister of war, promising to send aid if the Vendéans took a good port. They made for Granville, on the west side of the Cherbourg peninsula.[14]

The *représentant* Jean-Baptiste le Carpentier commanded Granville's defense. The city was walled and had artillery, and he had moved the regulars of the Cherbourg garrison to Granville, replacing them with 12,000 volunteers from the coastal area.[15]

On 12 November the Vendéans took Avranches. On the night of 13–14 November they attacked Granville, breached the outer defenses, and assailed the main walls all the next day. After thirty-six hours, the rebels had 1,500 casualties. With no British sails in sight, La Rochejacquelein ordered withdrawal.

The Vendéans moved back to Avranches, where the council decided to march for Caen, old capital of Normandy. They were 94 miles from the Loire; at Caen they would be 160 miles away. The peasant soldiers demanded to return home. La Rochejacquelein ordered retreat toward Laval.

Meanwhile, Rossignol, with 40,000 Republicans, marched north. On 21 November, at Dol, La Rochejaquelein's Vendéans met his two columns, under Kléber and Westermann, coming from Avranches and Fougères. La Rochejacquelein's artillery, on heights above the roads, pounded the Republicans. Green volunteers fled toward Antrain, infecting the regulars, who fell back, cursing officers and *représentants* who tried to halt them. Rossignol lost over 5,000 men; the Vendéans had a victory.

The way was open to the Loire, but the rebels didn't take it. The council decided to march on Granville again, but again the peasant-soldiers rebelled. The Vendéans fell back on Angers via Fougères, but had to fight for Angers, and after thirty-six hours withdrew toward Le Mans, pursued by Westermann and Bouin de Marigny's cavalry.[16] The rebels defeated 6,000 Republicans at La Fleche and took Le Mans without a fight.

Meanwhile, the Comité relieved Rossignol, gave the Ouest to François-Séverin Marceau, and added to his forces. Marceau won a victory at Le Mans, killing 10,000 rebel soldiers and civilians, and executing 661 men and women (22–24 December 1793).[17]

On 14 December the Vendéan forces, united at Laval, got word that the British were ready to land 10,000 troops in Normandy. There was a fleet off Cherbourg carrying 8,000 troops and many *émigrés*, but the Vendéans doubted it and marched for the Loire.

On 16 December, La Rochejacquelein crossed the Loire at Ancenis, but a Republican patrol, helped by a gunboat on the river, drove him away from the landing. On the north bank, the army began to disintegrate, as its fighters left for home.

Westermann's legion, reinforced, closed in; some 10,000 Vendéans rallied, but failed to stop him and fled westward. At Blain, with La Rochejacquelein absent, they elected the Chevalier de Fleuriot commander-in-chief. At night, in bitter cold, with snow falling, he led the wasted army to heights near Savenay. There, some 6,000 rebels made their last stand.

On 23 December, Marceau attacked, led by the divisions of Kléber and Beaupuy (12,000 men). The Vendéans fought bravely, but after 2,000 fell and they lost their artillery, they broke and fled in all directions. Tracked for eight days like wild animals, they perished anonymously in "an infinity of small actions."[18] "The carnage was horrible," Kléber wrote. "Everywhere, one saw piles of *cadavres*."[19] The army sent captives to Nantes; where the *représentant*, Jean-Baptiste Carrier, executed 1,971 rebels in twenty-eight days, the last on 25 January 1794.[20]

Vendéan forces were broken. Charette held out briefly, then hid in the Bocage.[21] La Rochejacquelein and Stofflet raised a small army in January 1794, but both were killed within a month. Elbée, badly wounded, took refuge on the island of Noirmoutier, long a Vendéan sanctuary.

In April 1794, General Louis Turreau was given command of the Ouest. He captured Noirmoutier, found Elbée there, still bedridden, interrogated him and had him shot, along with the island's garrison and many inhabitants.[22] Meanwhile, he sent out "infernal columns" to wipe out the rebellion – burning homes and crops, and butchering villagers.[23] Republican generals lived high, hoping the war would last.[24]

The rebel spirit lived on, however, in the guerrillas of southern Brittany, called Chouans (night owls). New leaders appeared, whom we shall meet later, and there were more risings.

The French navy

In midsummer, 1793, Admiral Samuel Hood sailed a British fleet (carrying 12,000 troops) into the harbor of the federal city of Toulon – by request of the rebels. Royalists had joined the Girondins there and taken over leadership. When Hood's fleet appeared, French vessels ran up the king's "lily banner."

While war blazed in the Vendée, French sailors mutinied in the Atlantic fleet and seized control of ships. In September 1793 twenty-one ships-of-the-line (of seventy in commission), and many lesser vessels, lay at anchor at Brest while crews caroused.

In October 1793 the Comité, hoping to save Atlantic ports from the British, sent two members, Prieur of the Marne and Jeanbon Saint-André, to "redeem" the fleet. Saint-André (a former Huguenot minister) preached the glories of the Republic, where every man could be an admiral, ending "services" with all singing "La Marseillaise."[25] Prieur liquidated "enemies of the people." With Republican troops nearby, they saved Brest. Prieur went on to the Vendée, where he addressed the Jacobin clubs, paraphrasing the Roman senator Cato, scourge of Carthage: "London must be destroyed! London must be destroyed!"

Missed British opportunities

The British might have made the Vendée rebellion a success if they had acted early on. However, they were uncertain of its strength, and offended by its presumed representative, the prissy and arrogant Comte d'Artois (brother of Louis XVI), an outspoken absolutist (with debts of two million pounds in England).

The British distrusted Artois. He was obviously not a military man. His military intelligence was suspect, since all his agents in France had been captured. Yet he demanded British money to raise troops (French or mercenary) for an invasion, which he would lead. They doubted he could command troops if he found any. In 1793, the British gave Artois nothing; in 1795 they relented, but later regretted it.

The federal cities

In June 1793, the federal cities – Bordeaux, Marseilles, Lyons, and Toulon – revolted against the Terror government, led by Girondins, as we know. They could have posed a strong challenge to the Terror government and French Republic if they had joined forces with the royalists. But with the exception of Toulon, and marginally Lyons, they did not. If they had, more cities would have been federalist. For example, at Nantes, the Girondins balked at uniting with royalists, and the Jacobins kept control.

The federal cities alarmed the Convention. Not only were they Girondist strongholds but it was known that royalists hoped to gain footholds in the cities and begin the reestablishment of the monarchy. While Artois focused on the Vendée, his brother, the Comte de Provence (regent for the boy-king, Louis XVII, imprisoned in Paris) was planning to enter Toulon.

The Comité sent armies to reduce the cities.

Bordeaux

Bordeaux presented few problems. Out of contact with the other cities, and finding Toulouse – on the route to Marseilles – staunchly Jacobin, the Girondins rejected royalist overtures and made peace with the local Jacobins. Meanwhile, Bordeaux had expelled Jacobin *représentants* but left its National Guard with the Republican army at La Rochelle. It recalled the troops to defend the city, but the city council decided not to fight.

In October 1793 an expedition commanded by Guillaume Brune (of whom much later) moved on Bordeaux.[26] The force comprised 1,800 regulars, *sans-culottes* of Réole, and peasants. *Représentants*, headed by Jean-Lambert Tallien (26), a journalist,[27] expected Brune to attack Bordeaux, but he was welcomed by the city's 12,000-man National Guard. Not to be deprived of a conquest, Tallien stripped the guardsmen of their insignia, and the *représentants* formed a "revolutionary army" from Brune's men and local *sans-culottes*. It stood guard while they massacred Girondins and aristocrats by firing squad, noose, and guillotine (four on one scaffold).

However, Tallien saved the beautiful Thérèsa Cabarrus, recently divorced from a nobleman, and later married her. It was at her salon, in Paris, that Napoleon met Josephine.

Marseilles[28]

In Marseilles the merchant oligarchy wanted to call in the British fleet, but the popular party won out. In August 1793, the Republican army of General Carteaux captured the city without a fight. He imprisoned a few hundred Girondins and royalists and made Marseilles a base for the recapture of Toulon. When the *représentants* arrived in October they were preoccupied with

Toulon, because of the presence of Hood's British fleet. They executed fewer than 200 persons in Marseilles.

Lyons: "liberated city"

Lyons, meanwhile, had suffered a municipal civil war. The Girondins won, and guillotined the Jacobin leaders. At the end of September, Lyons was holding out, and flying the tricolor of the Republic, although the Comte de Precy commanded the defense.

General Kellermann, co-victor at Valmy (1792), was called from his Armée des Alpes to quell the revolt of Lyons. He came with 30,000 troops; the *représentants* added national guardsmen, the riff-raff of "revolutionary armies," volunteers, and local conscripts. He besieged Lyons, reinforced by Auxonne artillery, still largely a "royal army."[29]

Lyons was a prime target; the countryside had supported it; it was rich; there were all too many royalists in the city. The Comité sent a member, Couthon, to reduce Lyons. Beginning on 2 October, moving by carriage and wheelchair, helped by his wife, he directed the assault with little attention to Kellermann or the other five *représentants*. On 9 October the city fell.

The Convention ordered Lyons "destroyed," which meant the homes of the rich; it was to be renamed *Ville Affranchie* (Liberated City). Couthon tagged a few houses, set up a tribunal, and departed, leaving the punishment of rebels to Collot d'Herbois (an actor) and Joseph Fouché (ex-cleric turned atheist, professor, and future minister of police). They executed some 1,700 "traitors" most by firing on them with cannon, some by the guillotine. Added to the thousands killed in battle, it was enough to appease the Comité and Convention.

Kellermann, who had not participated in the executions, was arrested on suspicion of royalism, and imprisoned in Paris, but freed after Robespierre's fall (July 1794).[30]

Toulon

In Toulon, royalists, mostly *émigrés*, were in control – with the consent of the Girondins. Admiral Hood had landed troops – 2,000 British, 7,000 Neapolitan, and 8,000 Spanish – who almost doubled Toulon's forces. (Her population was 35,000 at best.) The city flew the lily banner of the Bourbon dynasty. The royalists' grand scheme was to conquer the south of France, bring in the Comte de Provence (brother of Louis XVI; the future Louis XVIII) via Toulon, and restore the monarchy. Much of the Rhône valley was royalist in sympathy.

In August 1793, General Jean-François Carteaux, an artist turned soldier, arrived from Marseilles with a Republican army of 30,000 and laid siege to Toulon. The defenders were outnumbered, but held the heights which ringed the city, and were supported by the guns of the British fleet. The siege dragged on into winter.

Victory for the Republic was finally won by an obscure young Corsican captain of artillery, Napoleon *Buonaparte* (who changed his name to *Bonaparte* in 1796).

Napoleon

Napoleon was the second child of Carlo (Charles) and Letizia Ramolino Buonaparte, born in Ajaccio, Corsica, on 15 August 1769, and christened *Napoleone*. The ruling class was Italian; the island had belonged to Genoa. Napoleon was born French, however, since in 1768 Louis XV had bought the island, and crushed an independence movement led by Pasquale Paoli. Napoleon's father had been on Paoli's staff, but took the French king's amnesty.

Napoleon had attended the king's military schools (Brienne and L'École militaire, in Paris), where only aristocrats were admitted; his father had become a French count (based on a Florentine title). He had graduated and been commissioned (at age 16) second lieutenant (*sous-lieutenant*) of artillery in 1785.

In 1791 he had been elected a lieutenant colonel in the Corsican National Guard, but his family was exiled (as francophiles) when Corsica declared independence (July 1793). Napoleon returned to the French army as a captain. Robespierre's Government of Terror ruled France, but Buonaparte was a Jacobin.

Napoleon at Toulon

Captain Buonaparte had been posted to L'Armée d'Italie. But in passing Toulon he heard that Carteaux's artillery commander, General Auguste de Dommartin, had been wounded and evacuated. He went directly to the *représentants* at Toulon, headed by Joseph-Christophe Saliceti, a Corsican and friend of the Buonapartes, and asked for the artillery command; he was qualified, and a good Jacobin. Saliceti and the other *représentants*, Paul Barras and Augustin Robespierre (the chief terrorist's brother), gave the position to Buonaparte, with a promotion to temporary major.

In August the Republicans began the grinding reduction of federal strong points. Buonaparte, however, kept pressing General Carteaux for an attack to seize Éguillette, a high promontory overlooking the harbor. From there, he argued, his artillery could fire down on Hood's fleet, and force it to withdraw.[31]

Carteaux (or his willful wife, *de facto* co-commander) ruled Buonaparte's plan too risky; it required concentrating French forces, and the defenders might envelop his army.[32] Further, he expected reinforcements from Lyons, which had fallen on 9 October. Carteaux also knew that generals who lost battles were likely to lose their heads to the "National Razor." To Napoleon, risk was the name of the game; he despised Carteaux.

In November 1793, however, Carteaux was replaced by General Jacques-François Dugommier (65), tall and gray-haired, a Creole from Guadeloupe and a veteran commander.[33] He gave Napoleon a free hand.[34] Carnot, to whom Napoleon had written, approved. There ensued a month-long assault on Fort Mulgrave (guarding Éguillette). Buonaparte attacked with the infantry (11 November 1793) and sustained a bayonet wound in his thigh. On 14 December, the fort fell and Napoleon began to bombard Hood's fleet. The British blew up the arsenal, burned twenty-one French warships, and on 18 December 1793 evacuated the port, taking away their soldiers.[35] On 19 December Toulon fell.

The capture of Toulon marked the end of the federal revolts. Furious that many of the leaders had escaped (with Hood or otherwise), the *représentants* executed – by firing squads, without trial – every rebel, soldier, or sailor they could find (1,000 or more), and then set up a court for suspects. Buonaparte refused any part in the vengeance.

Carnot promoted Captain Buonaparte (24), to brigadier-general.[36] The *représentants*, notably Saliceti and Barras (of whom more later), arranged that he be praised in the Convention. Napoleon was a product of the Terror. It is ironic that in 1792 Maximilien Robespierre had warned against starting a war. It could end, he said, only in the restoration of the monarchy or military dictatorship. He was right, although Napoleon would be much more than a military dictator.

Domestic peace restored, the Comité focused on foreign wars.

Fate of Custine

One of the first victims of Robespierre's Comité had been General Custine, commander of the Nord. Called to Paris, he was not allowed to return to his army, although his men agitated in his favor. *Représentants* sent to malign him were roughed up by the troops, who trampled their pamphlets in the mud.

On 28 July, without Custine, the Nord lost Valenciennes to the Austrians. Further, in Custine's former Rhin-Moselle command, Kléber had surrendered Mainz on 22 July. Custine had been called to Paris for minor offenses, such as scornful remarks: "When I don't like a decree of the Convention I throw it in the fire."[37] His only crime was being an aristocrat. However, the Jacobins charged him with the loss of both Valenciennes and Mainz, and added other accusations. General Moustache – a colorful, popular, and loyal leader – was tried, and on 27 August 1793 sent to the guillotine. The mob jeered when he knelt to pray at the scaffold; he ignored them, then went quietly.[38]

Foreign wars

In August 1793, Jean-Nicolas Houchard (55) was called from the Moselle to command the Nord. "A royalist's nightmare vision of a *sans-culotte*,"[39] he was six feet tall (a giant at that time), with a scarred face and misshapen mouth from saber cuts and bullet wounds. He was crude and uneducated; his French was sprinkled with German words. He was not a noble, but had been a cavalry captain in the old army, and had tried to avoid promotion to general because it was dangerous, and he felt unqualified. The troops liked Houchard, who was jovial, and obviously a fighter.

In the Nord's sector, the Austrians and the British, under the Prince von Coburg and the Duke of York, held Valenciennes and Condé, fortresses only 100 miles from Paris. The Duke of York with 37,000 British, Hanoverians, and Hessians, was marching on Dunkirk; Coburg with 35,000 Austrians, on Le Quesnoy. On 1 September 1793, York besieged Dunkirk with 21,000 men, with 16,000 guarding his flanks and rear.

The Comité urged Houchard to break the siege, but he hesitated. He wrote to Carnot that he needed more troops, food, ammunition, and supplies, and added that his generals were not aggressive because of fear of punishment if they failed. The Comité sent men from the garrisons of Lille and other posts to him, building the Nord to 51,000, and *ordered* him to attack York.

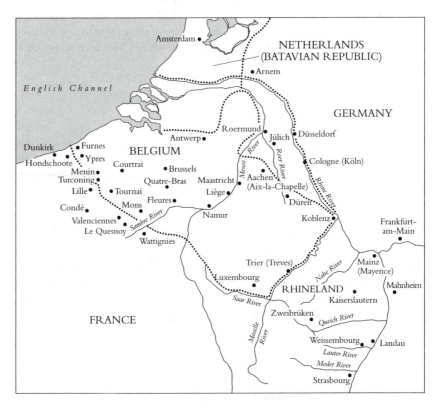

Map 6 The foreign war, 1794–95 (key places only)

Hondschoote

On 6 September 1793, Houchard moved against York's Hanoverian-Hessian covering force.[40] There was heavy fighting, and despite *représentants'* interference, Houchard broke through and took Hondschoote. York had taken 3,000 casualties, and began abandoning the siege of Dunkirk; his Hanoverians retreated to Furnes, in Belgium. The *représentant* Levasseur urged Houchard to follow, but the general, who resented the civilians in tricolored sashes, roared: "You are not an army man!"[41] However, Carnot sent orders for Houchard to take Furnes and block York before he could withdraw his siege lines at Dunkirk.

Houchard still did nothing; perhaps he thought saving Dunkirk for France was enough. The Comité had sent felicitations, and Paris had celebrated victory at Hondschoote. However, Houchard went on to other disasters. He took Menin from the Dutch, and moved to Courtrai. But on 15 September Coburg attacked him with swarms of cavalry, and his troops, heavy on green volunteers, broke and fled back to Menin, only to be hit by a column of the Duke of York. Houchard withdrew to Lille. He was recalled to Paris and tried for "softness toward the enemy." Despite his pleas that he was a simple soldier doing his best to serve, he was convicted and sent to the guillotine (17 November).

Hondschoote was a turning point in the war, all the same. Houchard had saved Dunkirk and shaken the coalition locally.

Wattignies

Carnot gave Jean-Baptiste Jourdan (31) command of the Nord.[42] Promoted to brigadier in May 1793, and (by Carnot) to major-general in September, he had been an outstanding division commander at Hondschoote. The son of a surgeon of Limoges, Jourdan had been a soldier under Rochambeau in America, then had left the army and become a merchant. In 1790, he had reentered the army via the National Guard.

A big man with the manner of a genial bishop, Jourdan easily got his way in everyday matters, and could be a forceful commander, although he lacked zest for battle. Carnot visited him, but went back to Paris to get him supplied; he lacked arms, ammunition, food, clothing, and especially shoes. Conscripts were wearing peasants' wooden clogs. Carnot saw to Jourdan's needs, and returned to guide him on campaign.

On 15 October, with 45,000 men, Jourdan attacked Austrian-held Wattignies to take pressure off the French garrison at Maubeuge, under attack by Coburg. The prince had Condé and Valenciennes, and wanted Maubeuge to clear the way to Paris. Coburg's cavalry stopped Jourdan cold, and he pulled back.

On 16 October, Jourdan attacked again, and on Carnot's advice threw his weight against the Austrian center. Casualties were heavy, but one column of Jourdan's army took Wattignies, emplaced a twelve-gun battery of artillery, and held the place. On 17 October Coburg retreated into Belgium.

The garrison of Maubeuge (17,000 men) had not entered the battle. But Carnot was more angry at the ungrateful people of Maubeuge. He informed the Comité that they should be given a dose of terror to "rebuild the public spirit."[43]

The Comité declared Wattignies a major victory. Excited over Jourdan's prospects, they ordered him to pursue Coburg, surround him, and cut him off from his allies in the Rhineland. Jourdan protested that this was unrealistic, and (thanks to Carnot) was allowed to go into winter quarters.

However, he refused to send reinforcements to the Moselle and Rhin, under heavy attack, or to the Vendée. When the Comité told him he had 140,000 men under his command, he questioned their records, and complained of desertions, disease, and lack of food, clothing and shoes for the troops (who were wrapping their feet in straw). Moreover, he said, his able-bodied men were not ready for combat.

On 12 January 1794, the Comité called Jourdan to Paris. He lived in dread for a week, half-expecting the fate of Houchard, but on 19 January he was simply retired. Jourdan went home and reopened his store, where he displayed his uniform and sword. Jean-Charles Pichegru was given the Nord. (Much on him follows.)

Jourdan was not finished with military service, however.

The war in the Rhineland

The Prussians and Austrians had been advancing – slowly – in the Rhineland, led by the Duke of Brunswick (58), and the Austrian general Count Dagobert Siegmund von Wurmser (69). Neither was very aggressive, and Brunswick had secret orders *not* to cripple the French army, and to give the Austrians minimal aid. The Prussian king felt betrayed by the Austrians regarding Poland.

In 23 May 1793, after Custine departed, command of the Rhin passed to the ex-viscount Alexandre de Beauharnais (33), a blond, handsome officer of the old army, separated from his wife, Josephine, Napoleon's future empress.[44] In the National Assembly, he had presided during Louis XVI's attempted flight and voted with the radicals.

Beauharnais was a good staff officer, but had never held high command. His primary mission – with Jean-Nicolas Houchard, commanding the Moselle – was to relieve the French garrison in Mainz. He held councils of war on 7 and 27 June,[45] and decided to go for Mainz at once.

Since the Rhin had 60,000 troops and the Moselle 40,000, the task seemed easy. En route to Mainz, Houchard went toward Kaiserlautern, and Beauharnais marched on Neustadt. The enemy commanders anticipated their moves, but Beauharnais won his first skirmish with Wurmser, and Houchard drove to the outskirts of Kaiserlautern. But then news came that the Mainz garrison had surrendered on 23 July.

Beauharnais proclaimed to his army, and wrote to the *représentants* and Comité, that an offensive was now impossible. Houchard went into retreat, and at the Saar he was called to command the Nord (which, we know, was a death sentence). He was replaced by Balthazar Schauenburg, an officer for thirty years.

The Prussians merely demonstrated before the Moselle, but the Austrians attacked Beauharnais' Rhin in earnest. In late July 1793, Wurmser and General Mezaros hit the French. Beauharnais retreated, with many casualties, over rough ground and through undergrowth, to the Queich, then behind the Lauter. He was angry with his generals and men (who had given up easily), hurt by the hostility of local Jacobins, confused and depressed. He offered his resignation to the *représentants* and wrote to the minister of war that he could not longer command a Republican army; he was ill, and a noble, "tainted by original sin."[46]

The *représentants* wanted to keep Beauharnais – a model ex-noble officer. But he sent his heavy artillery from Wissembourg toward Strasbourg, and began moving troops. On 23 August 1793 they accepted his resignation.[47]

Charles-Hyacinthe le Clerc de Landremont – under protest – took command of the Rhin. In 1792 a colonel with thirty-five years' service in the royal army, in 1793 a major-general, he felt unqualified, and knew the penalty for failure. Further, the Rhin had only 45,000 men.[48]

Nevertheless, in September 1793, Landremont (Rhin), and Schauenburg (Moselle) launched an offensive, but they ended up separated, with Landremont withdrawing toward Strasbourg. Both were called to Paris, but thanks to Carnot were not executed.

Dismissal of noble officers

During the fall, in the Rhineland, the *représentants* arrested all noble officers they could find (an unguided execution of a directive suspending noble officers). Some were executed, some retired. Top army commands were in flux, and the armies were under strength. (The *levée en masse* was not yet very productive.) France was saved in great part by the Austro-Prussian dispute over Poland. On 30 September, King Frederick-William left the Rhineland for negotiations. The Prussians on the Rhine went on the defensive, leaving the French to the Austrians.

Rotating commands

In late September 1793 the Rhin went to Delmas (besieged at Landau), then to General Munnier, the oldest division commander, who was afraid to issue orders. On 2 October the *représentants* gave the Rhin to Jean-Paschal-Raymond Carlenc (promoted to major-general after twenty days as a brigadier). He had been a captain of the royal army, but an *officier de fortune* (commoner); all the same, he feared being taken as a noble.

Carlenc found the Rhin behind the Lauter, where Landremont had left it. He dawdled. In mid-October the Wurmser's Austrians (with about 2,000 *émigrés*) attacked, and Carlenc retreated to the walls of Strasbourg. He was arrested, sent to Paris, and retired.

Pichegru and Hoche

On 23 October two powerful *représentants* arrived in the Rhineland – Saint-Just, cold-blooded second to Robespierre on the Comité, and Philippe Le Bas, a fanatic *Conventionnel* and friend of the *Incorruptible*. They gave the Rhin to Charles Pichegru (32). In 1789 he had been a royal artillery sergeant, in March 1793 a captain, in August a major-general, and now army commander.

Pichegru was plain of face and short, but muscular and broad-shouldered; and taciturn, active and energetic.[49] Educated for the Minimes, a teaching order, he was unusually literate for a commoner-general. His lifestyle was austere. Seemingly an ardent Jacobin, he later turned royalist.

On 31 October Saint-Just and Le Bas gave Louis-Lazare Hoche (26) the Moselle. Son of a minor royal official, he had entered the army from the National Guard. Carnot had cited him for his defense of Dunkirk against the Duke of York. He found his army of 32,000 dispirited and disorganized, and spent three weeks whipping it into shape. It was assumed he would operate under Pichegru; he had other ideas.

Hoche was big, strong, brash, and loud – but not stupid – and handsome, with a saber cut on his face that merely made him look more soldierly. Off duty, he was a libertine. However, "Hercules" had a weakness – infected lungs – which sometimes made him spit blood and which killed him in 1797.[50]

Mainz or death!

Hoche's personal mission was simple – get to Landau before Pichegru and lift the siege. On 17 November 1793 he started from the Saar with some 36,000 men, styled "*L'Élite de la sans-culotterie.*"[51] He surprised the Prussians and drove them through Blieskastel, Hombourg, and Zweibrüken to Kaiserslautern. There, however, Brunswick was waiting for him. Hoche's amateur subordinates began an infantry charge two miles from the enemy. The *sans-culotterie* was exhausted when it made contact, and the artillery was late. Attacks on 28, 29, and 30 November failed. At the end, Brunswick demolished the French infantry with all his artillery in line. Hoche retreated and on 3 December was back at Zweibrücken. He had lost 2,000 men; Brunswick 829.

Saint-Just and the *représentants*

Meanwhile, Saint-Just (and ten other *représentants*) had set to restoring discipline in the armies. Saint-Just and Le Bas undertook to supervise Pichegru and the Rhin, and became involved in operations, not just discipline. Pichegru responded to their orders with apparent gratitude, and gained their favor.

Saint-Just instructed the troops in republicanism, but carried out a purge of the officers, concentrating on those he believed had been corrupted by Strasbourg's pleasures. He executed two generals – one in front of his troops – and a score of others. He ordered officers to camp with their men, cancelled all leave, and required that men drill when they were not fighting. Saint-Just also improved the supply system by having shady *commissaires* shot, forcing Alsace to supply the Rhin with clothing and shoes, and levying a forced loan of 1,000,000 *livres* (francs) on the richest citizens of Strasbourg.

The *représentants* also descended on Hoche, at Zweibrücken, furious at his retreat. He met them smiling, joking that they could surely *write* his army to victory. They were not amused. They wanted him to cooperate closely with Pichegru, and ruled his attack on Kaiserslautern a disaster.

Pichegru moved up and threatened to outflank Wurmser's left at Buchsweiler. Since Wurmser could not depend on Brunswick, opposite the Moselle, he withdrew behind the Moder. In December 1793 Pichegru attacked, but was repulsed. Hoche appeared with some 18,000 troops for a coordinated effort, but the left of the Rhin was not there. On 22 December he attacked anyway. Artillery felled a tree, which knocked him off his horse; then his horse was killed under him.[52] But he won the day.

Wurmser abandoned the lines of the Moder and fell back. At year's end, 1793, he was crossing to the right bank of the Rhine, and Brunswick was retiring to Mainz where he could cross easily.

On 27 December Hoche entered Wissembourg without a fight. The *représentants* with him (Lacoste and Baudot), jubilantly appointed him commander of both the Rhin and Moselle – without consulting Saint-Just and Le Bas. On 31 December Hoche ordered the armies united as the Armée d'Entre-Rhin-et Moselle. His troops chanted "Landau ou la mort" (Landau or Death).[53]

However, it was Pichegru who took Landau. In December 1793 Pichegru entered Wissembourg, and went down the Rhine, led by his hussars and chasseurs, sabers drawn, to Landau. With him were the *représentants* Saint-Just, Le Bas, Lacoste, and Baudot. They found Landau undefended. Pichegru notified the minister that the siege of Landau was broken. Saint-Just assured Pichegru the credit.

Hoche accused of treason

Hoche's Moselle (February 1794) numbered 76,489 on paper, 50,000 in fact; more than Brunswick – but he had complaints. His army lacked everything. The "patriots" he appointed to command were no good. His troops had been promised rest when Landau was recaptured, but instead were ordered to march on Trier. There were mass desertions, mainly of volunteers. Finally Hoche was thrown by a horse, which put him in bed; "Hercules" cried in frustration. Carnot sent the army into rest camps.

Hoche had been too independent and too outspoken. The Terror government feared his political potential. Moreover, Hoche had supported Danton, destined for execution in March 1794, and had been (a corporal) in the royal army's Gardes Française. He was acccused of treason by the *représentants*. The politicians ordered Hoche to Toulon, as if to take command of the Armée d'Italie. Instead he was arrested, and in mid-March 1794 was imprisoned in Paris. However, Carnot saved him from the guillotine. When the Terror ended in July, he was given command in the Vendée, and showed great maturity and judgment in treating with the rebels. (See the next chapter.)

The Belgian front

The French held at bay the Austrians and Prussians on the Rhine, the Sardinians in Savoy, and the Spanish before Perpignan. The Comité decided to concentrate on Belgium.

Jourdan was recalled and given command of the Moselle. Pichegru was moved to the Nord. Jourdan, in May, marched for Belgium with the left of the Moselle (42,000 men). René Moreaux took over the right of the Moselle (soon combined with the Rhin to form the Rhin et Moselle). He took up holding positions while threatening Trier.[54]

In February 1794, the Allied (enemy) line ran, west to east–Ypres–Denain–Valenciennes–Meuse River–along the Meuse to Namur–then to Trier. The forces comprised English, Dutch, Austrian, and imperial (German) troops. There were no Prussians because of the conflict over Poland.

On 29 and 30 April 1794, 25,000 troops from the Nord took Courtrai and Menin (Battle of Mouscron). But on 30 April the Austrians, under Coburg, took Landrecies. On 10 May the Allies tried to recapture Menin and Courtrai. Austrian cavalry routed several newly formed demi-brigades near Menin, but the next day Pichegru appeared with more troops and beat off the Allies.

On 17 May Coburg then mustered 60,000 men and took and occupied Tourconing. But the next day the French, with equal numbers, took it back. Coburg retreated to Tournai. On 22 May Pichegru thunderously assailed Tournai with all available forces, but amassed 6,500 casualties, and fell back.

Coburg had taken 4,000 casualties, however, and began shifting men from the Sambre–Meuse front – a bad move, since the French were reinforcing their armies (soon under Jourdan) in that area. With Saint-Just directing the attacks, the French crossed the Sambre on 11 May, but on 14 May were forced back across the river in heavy fighting (French losses 4,000; Austrian 2,800). On 20, 26, and 29 May the French again forded the river, only to be hurled back. On 3 June Austrian and Dutch forces thwarted another French attempt to cross the Sambre, and drove them into retreat.

The French pinned their hopes on Pichegru's Nord, in the west (Flanders). Pichegru invested Ypres on 1 June, and took it on 17 June. On 25 May the Allies held a council of war at Tournai; of the generals, only Coburg and York wanted to fight. The Allies went on the defensive. Carnot, meanwhile, had ordered an offensive on the Sambre.

Jourdan takes command

In May, at Thionville, Jourdan had put together 50,000 men – 18,000 from the Rhin and the entire Armée de la Moselle. He was directed to march for Belgium and (after changes) take Charleroi. In June, Carnot added to his command the Armée des Ardennes and the right wing of the Nord. This gave Jourdan an army of 96,000 troops, which was dubbed the Armée de Sambre et Meuse (13 June 1794). Saint-Just appeared to supervise for the Comité, breathing fire and skepticism, but aware that Carnot believed in Jourdan. Jourdan deployed his troops to take Charleroi (see Map 7). Marceau, with the right wing, was to cross the Sambre below Charleroi and anchor its left on Lambusart. To his left, Jourdan, with 32,000 troops, was to cross the river at Le Châtelet and take positions north of Charleroi. François-Joseph Lefebvre, with the advance guard, would drive on Campinaire. On his left, forces under Jean Championnet, with Dubois' cavalry, would cross at Marchienne-au-Pout. The left wing, Kléber, with about 20,000, was to cross the Sambre and little Piéton rivers, and deploy west of Charleroi. Farther up the river, Joseph Schérer's force was to demonstrate to distract the Austrians.

General Jacques Hatry began the siege of Charleroi (Austrian garrison 2,800), using heavy guns moved from various fortresses. But Jourdan got word that the Prince of Orange (of Coburg's army), with 43,000 men, was advancing to relieve Charleroi. On 12 June Jourdan, leaving a token force behind, crossed the Sambre with 58,000 men, bypassed Charleroi to the east, and moved northward. On 16 June he fought the enemy near Quatre-Bras in fog and rain. Jourdan's artillery ammunition ran out, and his left, with the rawest draftees and volunteers, collapsed. He withdrew across the Sambre and lifted the siege of Charleroi.

Meanwhile, Coburg, the Allied comander, transferred troops from Orange to himself in the hope of stopping Pichegru, who was besieging Ypres. Jourdan moved north again. On 18 June, Pichegru took Ypres. Coburg camped at Tournai for several days, trying to decide whether to go against Pichegru or Jourdan. The Prince of Orange, his army weakened, fell back to cover the fortress of Mons, and ordered Beaulieu, at Namur, to cover the Brussels road at Quatre-Bras. Orange then went to Tournai, where he persuaded Coburg that Jourdan could block their escape route to Germany, and was the greater threat.

On 18 June, when Jourdan recrossed the Sambre, Hatry resumed the siege of Charleroi. This time he had his forces dig trenches at Campinaire, Lambusart, Gossilies, and Heppignies. They formed a formidable semi-circle north of Charleroi.

Saint-Just vented his energy on Hatry, appearing with a shiny new sword, sent by Carnot on request, and howling that the siege of Charleroi was going too slowly. Finish! *Tout de suite*! He found that the artillery gunners were young and

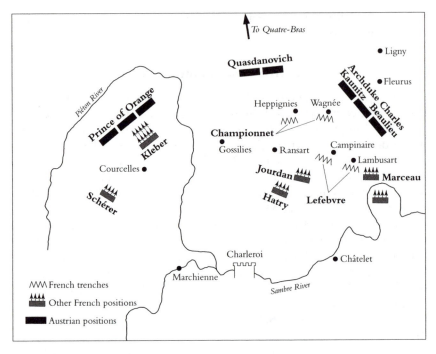

Map 7 Battle of Fleurus, 26 June 1794, at the end of battle (dusk)

untrained, and were holding back the army. He sent the artillery commander and chief engineer to Jourdan, with an order to have them executed immediately. Jourdan refused. Saint-Just settled for the life of one young captain, whose performance he had observed.

Saint-Just next ordered Jourdan to send 30,000 men to Pichegru, whom he felt had the more important mission. Jourdan refused; to win, he needed every man. On 26 June 1794 Charleroi fell, and Jourdan allowed Saint-Just to take the surrender.

Jourdan was busy. The Prince von Coburg had attacked his fortified positions at 3 a.m. The Austrians threw 52,000 men at Jourdan's 75,000 entrenched soldiers, backed by Hatry's division and a cavalry regiment. Coburg's left was commanded by the Archduke Charles (age 25), brother of the Austrian emperor, eventually rated second to Napoleon among generals of the period. Kléber held the left solidly, and at about 2 p.m. ordered an advance. However, on the right, under attack by Beaulieu, Marceau's green troops panicked and fled back across the Sambre. Marceau took insane risks to restore order among his troops, with help from Lefebvre, and with part of them recrossed the Sambre. Lefebvre's right flank had been exposed by Marceau's retreat, however, and he pulled back from Fleurus. Championnet, on his left, withdrew from Saint-Fiacre. Enemy columns moved almost to the Sambre on both sides of Charleroi. They were too close to the fortress, however, and faltered under the cannon fire of the newly arrived French garrison.

In the Campinaire trenches, Lefebvre ordered his men to let the enemy get close, then fire. When the Austrians slowed, he sent cavalry through gaps in his line to charge the enemy (under the Archduke Charles). Meanwhile, Beaulieu, blasting the French with case shot, followed by cavalry who broke through the hedges, took Lambusart. The French set fire to part of the town, and the flames spread to nearby fields of grain.

Lefebvre, always in the front lines, inspired his men to hold, although his headquarters, behind him, was afire. In smoke, fighting from trenches full of dead men, the French center held. On Lefebvre's left, Championnet held Heppignies and Wagnée, and high ground nearby. However, Championnet could hear enemy guns in his rear on both flanks, and retreating troops said Lefebvre's advance guard had been routed.

Jourdan ordered Championnet to withdraw, but before the troops could move a rider came at breakneck speed through the grain fields with the news that Lefebvre had recovered Lambusart (not true, but soon would be). Jourdan ordered the troops to turn about again and attack, and sent his reserve cavalry to lead them. The cavalry recoiled, but Championnet's division surprised the Austrians, who thought they had won, and they retreated in disarray. Lefebvre made headway against the addled enemy, and took Lambusart. His flankers reorganized and attacked on his right; Marceau reinforced them. Jourdan sent part of his force to advance on Lefebvre's left. After fifteen hours of fighting the Austrians retreated.

Coburg had ordered the retreat. The Archduke Charles wanted to continue the fight, but he was not in command. The Austrian army moved north. Jourdan put his army on the right flank of Pichegru's Nord and they drove the Austrians out of Belgium. Jourdan then made for the Rhineland, where the Prussians were fighting listlessly, in view of the continuing dispute over Poland. In 1795 they would make peace with France (see Chapter 5).

The Battle of Fleurus relieved foreign military pressure on France. The sense of danger, which had given the Terror support, dissipated. Robespierre's Comité had conducted the war too well for their own good. The victory of Fleurus removed the *raison d'être* for Robespierre's government.[55]

Robespierre destroys his appeal

Fleurus was a heavy factor in bringing down Robespierre, but during the Terror he had made himself increasingly unpopular. By July 1794 he was a heinous tyrant.

Once firmly in power (fall 1793), Robespierre centralized control of Paris, operating with a cowed Convention and Commune. He silenced the Paris section assemblies by outlawing permanent (day and night) sessions and offering pay to attend (which packed them with the unemployed). Under the Law of Suspects, he jailed active section leaders. The *Incorruptible* also abolished women's clubs, and sent outspoken members to the guillotine.

Robespierre sent Jacques René Hébert, the voice of the street, to the guillotine, aided by Danton and his followers (see p. 41). He then turned on the *Dantonistes*, and rushed them to the National Razor. These executions alienated the *sans-culottes*, and frightened the politicians. Oblivious to public opinion, Robespierre had the effrontery to introduce a new religion, the "Cult of the Supreme Being," designed to please freethinkers and Christians alike. It pleased no one.

The Paris Jacobin Club lost faith in Robespierre; many provincial clubs became hostile. The *Incorruptible* responded with the Law of 22 Prairial (10 June 1794), another Law of Suspects, allowing arrests for "spreading discouragement," and the like. In the next seven weeks there were 1,376 executions, compared to 1,251 in the previous fourteen months. The *Incorruptible* further offended the *sans-culottes* by proposing a ceiling on wages.

The Convention, especially *ex-représentants*, lived in fear that Robespierre would prosecute them for crimes they had committed with Comité approval. Barras, Saliceti, Tallien, and others organized the Convention against Robespierre.

After a six weeks' absence (reasons unknown), Robespierre appeared on 8 Thermidor (26 July 1794) to address the Convention. Fingering what appeared to be a list of "traitors" (which he never read), he lectured, preached his new religion, and hurled threats. When he left, no one present felt safe.

On 9 Thermidor (27 July), Robespierre again tried to address the Convention, but was shouted down. Emotionally drained, he screamed, "I demand that I be sent to death!" The Convention obliged, and also arrested his followers. Sympathizers helped them escape, but they were recaptured. There was the pretense of a trial. Robespierre, who had turned a pistol on himself, lay outside, strapped down, his jaw in a bloody bandage.

On 10 Thermidor (28 July 1794), the *Incorruptible*, his lieutenants, and nineteen followers were guillotined. The next day, seventy-one more were executed.

The Terror was at an end and the Convention again controlled the government. The conservative Thermidorian Reaction, called after the month of the Revolutionary calendar, began. Radical politicians tried to join the majority in the Convention. Barras was eminently successful. Others were not.

Domestic accomplishments

The Terrorists demonstrated for the first time the power of a nation totally mobilized for war, but attempted much more. They planned a system of public education, for which France had to wait a hundred years, and "great schools" that became permanent (thanks to Napoleon) – the École Polytechnique (Polytechnic School) and École Normale Supérieure (High Normal School). They founded the Institut de France. They even attempted to provide minimal social security for aged, ill, and disabled.

They promoted science and technology, notably for war – but such as balloons and the semaphore "telegraph" had wider potential. Their outstanding gift was the metric-decimal system of weights and measures, devised by Joseph-Louis Lagrange. Napoleon pushed the system in France, and sponsored its adoption by other European countries.

5

THE GOVERNMENT OF THERMIDOR AND ESTABLISHMENT OF THE DIRECTORY, JULY 1794–OCTOBER 1795

Thermidor

With the end of the Terror (July 1794), the Convention took control of the government. The Comité de salut public remained the executive – with conservative members and reduced powers. By October, only Lazare Carnot remained of Robespierre's Comité.

The Convention moved cautiously in order to restructure the government without mistakes that would invite royalists or Jacobins to seize control. Only in the last months of 1794 was the Jacobin Club suppressed, and surviving Girondins (73) reinstated in the Convention. Trials ran into 1795 of those accused of committing atrocities under the Terror.

The Thermidorian government still had to fight the foreign wars, suppress a new Vendéan revolt, and deal with incessant hunger and unemployment in Paris. The Convention also preserved the Terrorists' constructive work (mentioned in the previous chapter). Finally, the Convention had to write a Republican constitution – its original purpose.

Society

Release from tyranny prompted licentiousness in society. The *Gilded Youth* (*Muscadins* or *Incroyables* [Incredibles]) – violence-prone sons of the rich – dominated Paris streets. They were known by their long hair, expensive but filthy clothes, and muddy boots. Their women, the *Merveilleux* (Wonderfuls), also wore boots, and hats with stuffed birds or flowers. They flaunted their wealth, insulted *sans-culottes*, and attacked ex-Terrorists.

Paris celebrated the release of political prisoners, and whatever else it could, with balls for the rich and parties in the streets for the people. At "Victims' Balls," those who had lost relatives to the guillotine wore red ribbons around their necks.

Salons of prominent women reappeared, notably that of Theresa Tallien, "Our Lady of Thermidor." Imprisoned as an aristocrat, she was freed by her husband, Jean Tallien, now on the new Comité. He also secured the release of her friend Josephine de Beauharnais. Theresa and Josephine set the styles – for the evening, gowns translucent above the waist.

The misery of workers increased, however, and they came to hate the new government. The Thermidorians repealed the Law of the Maximum, and allowed paper money (*assignats*) to "float," so that by fall 1795 the "money of the people" was worthless. The Convention set the price of bread at 20 *sous* (one franc) per pound, but bread was scarce. In April 1795 the cost of food was eight times what it had been in 1790, and rising.

In April and again in May 1795, after a freezing winter of starvation and death, *sans-culottes* invaded the Convention shouting for bread, and held the deputies captive until driven out by the National Guards. The second time they killed a deputy, and waved his head on a pike. Regular troops, under General Jacques Menou, were stationed in Paris to ensure peace.

The foreign wars

The foreign wars continued under the direction of Carnot. After the Battle of Fleurus (26 June 1794), Jourdan moved to link the Sambre-et-Meuse to Pichegru's Nord. He left Barthelemy Schérer with 30,000 men to besiege the fortresses held by the enemy. The Austrian general, Clerfayt, and the Prince von Coburg opposed Jourdan, while the Prince of Orange and the Duke of York opposed the Nord. On 13 July Pichegru was at Antwerp.

On 27 July, Jourdan took Liège. The Sambre-et-Meuse had its right on the Meuse at Namur, and its left at Tongeren. Between 15 July and 30 August Schérer reduced the fortresses in the rear – Landrecies, Valenciennes, Le Quesnoy, and Condé. He then joined Jourdan's Sambre-et-Meuse, bringing it to 100,000 men. Schérer commanded the right wing; Jourdan the center; Kléber the left.

Opposite Jourdan, on the right bank of the Meuse, the Austrians (now under Clerfayt, *vice* Coburg) had their left opposite Liège, center at Maastricht, and right at Roermond.

Schérer struck the Austrians at the Ourthe River, fighting his way across the racing torrent under cannon fire. The Austrians retreated eastward, through Aix-la-Chapelle (Aachen), and turned to fight behind the Roer, west of Cologne (Köln).

Clerfayt had his right at Roermond on the Meuse, with his line running south along the Roer to Nideggen. On 22 September Jourdan sent two divisions across the Meuse at Liège and seized Aix-la-Chapelle. Kléber (left wing) surounded Maastricht, but per Jourdan's order left a 15,000-man blockade and went for the Rhine.

On 2 October heavy fighting began along the Roer. On the French right, one division of Schérer's wing took Düren, but the rest were unable to cross the

Roer. Kléber attempted to cross opposite Ratheim, but had to bombard Ratheim while bridges were built. Meanwhile Jourdan (the center) – 26,000, plus 4,000 cavalry – took Aldenhoven, and followed the Austrians to the walls of Jülich. However, except for Schérer's one division, none of the French had crossed the Roer.

Nonetheless, Clerfayt withdrew from the Roer line and on 6 October 1794 retreated acoss the Rhine at Mulheim, near Cologne. Jourdan followed him to the right bank. Kléber's wing of the Sambre-et-Meuse took Roermond, and the Austrian commander, Kerpen, crossed the Rhine to Düsseldorf (4 October 1794). Kléber brought up his main body and bombarded Düsseldorf, which surrendered on 7 October 1794. Jourdan sent Kléber back to besiege Maastricht.

The bulk of the Sambre-et-Meuse, on the Rhine between Cologne and Düsseldorf, made contact with adjacent armies. The Moselle and the Sambre-et-Meuse took Coblenz (Koblenz), headquarters of the French *émigrés*, and celebrated.

At the end of October 1794, four French armies were in line between the North Sea and Switzerland. The Nord, under Jean Pichegru, was invading Holland (the United Provinces of the Netherlands). Jourdan's Sambre-et-Meuse was resting while Kléber took Maastricht. René Moreaux's Moselle lay between Coblenz and Mainz; Pierre-Antoine Michaud's Rhin between Mainz and Basel.

On 4 November 1794, Maestricht surrendered to Kléber (given the honor by Jourdan, who was present). Jourdan then sent Kléber to command the blockade of Mainz.

Conquest of "Holland"

In January 1795, Pichegru sent his right (Macdonald's and Moreau's divisions) over the Rhine to Gröningen. Jourdan put two divisions on the Nord's right; they crossed the mouths of the Rhine and took Arnhem and towns farther north.

Meanwhile, Pichegru's cavalry performed an unprecedented feat at Amsterdam, galloping across the frozen harbor to capture the Dutch fleet and the city. This created a sensation in Paris, where the Convention heaped praise on Pichegru (whose advance was made possible by Jourdan's victory at Fleurus).

By the end of March 1795 the French occupied the whole of the Netherlands. Cooperating with Dutch revolutionaries, the French converted Holland into the Batavian Republic, the first of many "sister Republics" of France. The Stadthouder went into exile in England, to which he ceded control of Dutch colonies.

On the Rhine

Meanwhile, divisions of the Moselle and Rhin combined to take Mainz, Mannheim and Luxembourg. In April 1795, the two armies were combined as the Rhin-et-Moselle. But since none of the generals wanted command, Pichegru was called from the Nord, which went to Jean-Victor Moreau.

On 16 April, Pichegru assumed command of the Rhin-et-Moselle at Mainz. He was more morose and secretive than in 1793, when he had commanded the Rhin. During the summer of 1795 he seldom visited his army, even the divisions blockading Mainz. Some began to suspect (rightly) that he was a secret royalist.

Breakup of the First Coalition

The year 1795 proved a good one for the French. The Prussians, jaded over their (perceived) disproportionate burden in the war (and over the question of Poland), made peace with France (Treaty of Basel, 5 April 1795). Prussia ceded the left bank of the Rhine to France, although the Austrians still defended Mainz. On 6 July the French defeated the Spanish at Irurzun and drove them toward Bilbao. On 22 July, Spain made peace with France, also by a Treaty of Basel (and in 1796 allied with France). The Armée des Alpes and the Armée d'Italie were holding their own, although Italie had problems.

Thermidorian foreign policy

The Thermidorians reversed the foreign policy of Robespierre, who, in 1793 and 1794, had declined aid to Dutch, Swiss, Italian, and Polish revolution-aries – even to General Tadeusz Kosciuszko. That hero of the American Revolution had raised a rebellion (1794–95) in a futile effort to preserve Poland as a nation. (Afterward, he fled to France and formed a Polish legion, which served the Republic and Napoleon.)

The Thermidorians had annexed Belgium (the Austrian Netherlands) and turned Holland into the Batavian Republic. They had resumed the policy of international revolution espoused by the Girondins in 1791 and 1792.

Carnot thought the Thermidorians' policy was an obstacle to permanent peace, and in August 1795 he resigned from the Comité in protest (but resumed power in the Directory in October). He felt European monarchs could not tolerate for long the promotion of subversion by France, and if France continued to expand her sphere of influence the powers would fight back.

In 1795, however, the Thermidorians' policy was offensive largely to Austria; only Austria and her minor allies in Germany and Italy held out on the Continent. Britain fought at sea.

Again the Vendée

In 1794, the royalist–Catholic movement had revived in the military Vendée, with all the bitterness of 1793. The slaughter sponsored by the Terror government had driven peasants into guerrilla bands (*Chouans*), notably in Brittany. New leaders had arrived from England, notably Count Joseph de Puisaye, Louis-Auguste-Victor de Bourmont, and Georges Cadoudal. They brought British funds and the promise of more. After Thermidor, the Vendéan forces increased, taking vengeance on Jacobins and putting the French army on the defensive.

In September 1794, the Convention gave command in the Vendée to General Louis Hoche. He was the hero of the defense of Dunkirk, but then overstretched his army on the Rhine; Carnot had saved him from execution. Given an army equal to the Nord, he won every battle with the Vendéans, but became convinced, after talking with many prisoners, that what the rebels wanted most was the restoration of their church (not necessarily the king), and amnesty if they laid down their arms.

The government authorized Hoche to parley on that basis. In February 1795, veteran Vendéan leader François de Charette signed an agreement with Hoche, and in April and May so did other leaders, including the dashing Jean Cottereau, chief of the Chouans. Puisaye fled to England. Priests, even ex-*émigrés*, were allowed to reopen the churches. Rebels got amnesty, the promise of compensation for lost or damaged property, and exemption from service in the Republican armies.

Hoche did not disarm the rebels, however, which was a mistake. All too many Vendéans hoped still that Louis XVII (the imprisoned boy-king), would be restored to the throne. There was peace, but not for long.

Quiberon

In June 1795, Louis XVII (age 10) died in his prison, the Temple. His uncle, the Comte de Provence, was proclaimed Louis XVIII by the *émigré* court in Verona. Louis accused the "Jacobin" government of murder, and promised to return to France and wreak vengeance on revolutionaries. Almost simultaneously, the British government (under William Pitt the Younger) finally granted aid to the Comte d'Artois and agreed to land an *émigré* army on the Atlantic coast of France. Georges Cadoudal, a Chouan hero of 1793, was sent to rally the guerrillas in Brittany.

Between 27 June and 15 July the British landed 4,500 presumed *émigrés* near Quiberon (see Map 5, p. 46), (some 3,500 of whom were actually impressed French prisoners of war); Cadoudal brought 15,000 Chouan reinforcements, and Charette rallied the Vendéans. A British fleet blockaded French warships at Brest. However, Quiberon, on the tip of a narrow peninsula, was a foolish choice of beachhead. Warned in advance, Hoche mustered his forces, allowed rebel forces to assemble, then drove them down the peninsula and trapped them "like rats" (as he reported to the Convention). Puisaye, a few other émigrés, and Cadoudal escaped to England, but Hoche's men killed hundreds of royalists and captured 8,000.

Tallien was sent by the Convention to try the prisoners. He gave the death sentence to 748 genuine émigrés (by his judgment), and freed the impressed French prisoners and Chouans. Charette was hunted by police and finally captured and shot in 1796.[1]

The Comte d'Artois had planned the Quiberon landing as part of a scheme to restore the monarchy in France. A small British army was to follow up the émigré landing, and in the Rhineland Condé's émigré army was to invade France (helped along by General Jean Pichegru). But after the disaster the British declined to land their troops, and there was no invasion from Germany.

Nevertheless, the Comte d'Artois refused to give up. The British invasion force allowed Artois, who was aboard ship, to land on the island of Yeu, off the Vendéan coast. From there, until October 1795, he attempted to organize royalists in France to support another invasion. Then, however, the British, weary of his fantasies of mass support in France, loaded him and his few troops into ships and returned them to England. Artois had meanwhile divided émigré leadership by insisting that absolute (rather than constitutional) monarchy must be restored, which also damped the ardor of the British.

Guerrillas continued to fight in the Military Vendée, but too few to alarm Paris until 1798. Napoleon finished them off in 1800.

The Convention in danger

In October 1795 the National Convention, sitting in the Tuileries palace, feared an attack by Paris mobs. It had written a new constitution, creating the Directory, a moderate Republican government. The nation at large had approved the constitution, but not Paris. The people were still miserable, and felt the new government to be no different from the Thermidorian. They still suffered unemployment (35 percent), shortages of bread and fuel, and frequent deaths from starvation and exposure. Thousands were ready to march, under the leadership of royalists (who downplayed restoring the monarchy, emphasizing "taking care" of the people). The Convention appointed Paul Barras (40) to defend the Tuileries. Although once an officer in the royal army, his most recent conquests had been political or of the boudoir (Josephine de Beauharnais was his mistress). On 4 October, Barras offered Napoleon Buonaparte the actual command, and he unhesitatingly accepted it. Years later, in exile on St Helena, he would say: "Fortune is a woman; if you lose her today, do not expect to find her tomorrow."[2]

Napoleon was available in Paris because, in early 1795, Barras and Saliceti had gotten him a place on the Topographic Bureau (general staff).[3] (He had refused a command in the Vendée, and been dropped from the army list, but the former *représentants* at Toulon saved his career.) He had been making plans for the Armée d'Italie. Life was dull; his future grim.

Barras knew Buonaparte would do whatever was required to stop the mobs. Also, he considered Buonaparte expendable; he was a "foreigner," and resented for his early promotion in the officer corps. If his actions offended the powerful, he could be sent to a remote post.

To Napoleon, Barras's offer of command was a godsend.

The "whiff of grapeshot"[4]

The Convention had called in 5,000 regular troops, some volunteers (the "Patriots of '89"), and a few artillerymen, but without cannon. Buonaparte needed guns. Infantry alone could not stand against 80,000 people – an average mob when Paris was aroused. To bring him artillery, Napoleon picked a tall Gascon cavalry major, Joachim Murat – a man of obvious force and a devil-may-care attitude. As dark fell, Murat led a cavalry squadron on in a wild ride through Paris to the National Guard's artillery park at Sablons. Once there, he galloped through the gate, giving the guards no time to react, and his troopers followed. He returned with forty cannon early on 5 October.

Buonaparte placed the guns to cover all approaches to the Tuileries – mainly the Rue de la Convention, which ran south from the Rue St-Honoré – where the mobs always gathered – directly to the palace gardens (see Map 2, p. 19). He had the guns loaded with canister, plus nails, links of chain, and scrap metal.

On 5 October thousands of people gradually gathered on the Rue St Honoré, hidden by buildings from the defenders of the Tuileries, who, however, could judge the crowd's size by the noise, which got louder all the time. Napoleon sent a warning to the leaders, unnamed, that he would use all his weapons, but it was ignored. Meanwhile, the people bolstered their courage with beer and wine (gifts from middle-class backers).

At 4 p.m. the mob could be seen forming up at the head of the Rue de la Convention. At about 5 p.m. the people came on, shouting the "Marseillaise," a sea of pikes and red liberty caps. Napoleon's gunners stood, torches lit, awaiting his command. The mob moved to within 100 yards, 50 yards; Buonaparte sat on his horse behind the gunners, impassive.

Finally, at point-blank range, Buonaparte shouted, FIRE! The cannon did their bloody work, and the people fled, leaving dead, wounded, and pools of blood on the cobblestones. In a few minutes, it was all over. Some diehards held out in the church of St-Roch, but not for long. Napoleon disarmed the city.

Conservative hero

The Convention was saved. By grace of Napoleon, the Directory, called after its five-man executive, became the government of the Republic. Four years later, Bonaparte would replace it with a government of his own. In 1795, however, he sought promotion from Barras, the *de facto* head of state. (And the only director who would serve for the life of the Directory.)

Napoleon reported that "General Barras" had made victory possible, even to ordering the cannon brought from Sablons. He called all the attackers "royalists," and gave no casualty figure, but said that among the dead were *émigré* nobles, reactionary priests, and Vendéan rebels.[5]

Possibly, he wanted Barras on his side if he were accused of excessive brutality. But on 11 October, he wrote his brother Joseph: "We were victorious, and all is forgotten."[6] Paris was quiet; the Republican establishment was jubilant.

Napoleon was promoted to major-general and given command of the Army of the Interior.

Josephine

Napoleon, who had never had much of a social life, found himself deluged with invitations from the most celebrated hostesses in Paris. At the salon of the outrageous and beautiful Madame Theresa Tallien, he met Josephine de Beauharnais (called "Rose" by her friends), the widow of the Vicomte Alexandre de Beauharnais, a victim of the Terror. Rose was 32, six years older than Napoleon, and had two children, Eugene (14) and Hortense (12). Nonetheless, Rose was lovely, chic and charming – and of the old aristocracy – which secretly impressed Napoleon.

Before they were well acquainted, Napoleon proposed marriage to Josephine. She had survived by becoming the mistress of powerful men, most recently Paul Barras. She decided the little general might be useful (Barras was losing interest in her); she became his mistress, but refused to marry him. However, when Buonaparte was made commander of the Armée d'Italie, she agreed. On 9 March 1796 they were wed in a civil ceremony.

The foreign war continues

In September 1795, on orders from the Thermidorian government, the armies on the Rhine had begun an offensive into Germany to defeat Austria, the last major member of the coalition still at war with France. On 6 September, Jourdan, with the Sambre-et-Meuse (91,000), crossed the Rhine, and took Düsseldorf. On 20 September, Pichegru, with the Rhin-et-Moselle, crossed and took Mannheim. Meanwhile, Jourdan had invested Mainz and struck south to the Lahn River. The Austrian commander, Clerfayt, attacked and drove Jourdan back across the Rhine. On the night of 28–29 October, Austrian troops from Mainz suddenly attacked the French besiegers, who retreated in disarray. They joined Pichegru, who retreated, abandoning his garrison at Mannheim, which soon surrendered. Clerfayt then turned on Jourdan, who signed an armistice on 21 December. Pichegru, who had not supported Jourdan, was blamed for the defeat, and replaced by Jean-Victor Moreau.[7]

However, the troops of both armies were without pay, and short of supplies and munitions. Moreover, the French army was shrinking. The *levée* of 1793 went unenforced and many troops just went home. By the end of 1795 it was down to 450,000; by the winter of 1796 to 346,000.

General Barthelemy Schérer, commanding the Armée d'Italie, had better luck, if temporarily. On 23 November he attacked Loano, while André Masséna took a division through the mountains to flank the enemy. The Austrians retreated to Genoa, but soon counter-attacked and forced the French to retreat almost to Nice.

Bonaparte to command in Italy

In March 1796 Bonaparte was made general-in-chief of the Armée d'Italie, where his victories made him world-famous. He left for Nice to take command two days after his marriage to Josephine de Beauharnais, who declined to accompany him.

6

WAR IN ITALY AND GERMANY, 1796–97

In the spring of 1796 Austria was the only major continental power waging land war with France; Britain was fighting at sea. On the Rhine, Jourdan, with the Armée de Sambre-et-Meuse (78,000), and Moreau, with the Rhin-et-Moselle (80,000), were preparing to strike at the Austrians in Germany.

In late March, Bonaparte assumed command of the Armée d'Italie (38,000 effectives) at Nice. He was to engage the Austrians and their minor allies in northern Italy, and create a diversion while the war was being won in Germany. However, he needed no engraved invitation to try to win the war with his little army, while Jourdan and Moreau created a mammoth diversion in Germany.

Buonaparte/Bonaparte

In 1796 Bonaparte was merely one of Carnot's new generals. However, with the Armée d'Italie, he began to shape his image as a man-of-destiny, a man with a "star," a commander who read his enemies' minds. (On his early life, see pp: 54–55.)

Bonaparte was not a nice man; few great commanders have been. He inspired respect, awe, fear, and loyalty in officers and civil officials whose fortunes were tied to his, but rarely affection. His popularity was greater among the rank-and-file, with whom he cultivated camaraderie.

He was a handsome man, if short for an officer (among his men, he was average at 5'2").[1] The sculptor Canova thought his body ideally proportioned. He had perfect teeth and a winning smile, but used it sparingly. He was a consummate actor, at his best before troops. In private, he could invariably charm men (and most women) into doing his bidding.[2]

Bonaparte was acutely sensitive; he could "read" people by their expressions, attitudes and gestures. On the battlefield he had what Frederick the Great called *coup d'oeil* – the ability to assess the situation at a glance. Although icy calm under fire, and usually elsewhere, he had occasional fits of rage, during which he cursed offenders – in Italian and/or French – and might beat them with his riding crop. He once kicked a cabinet minister in the stomach. He dismissed Talleyrand in 1809, calling him "*merde* in a silk stocking." Of course, some scenes were staged.

Napoleon was a loner who worked incessantly to get and hold power. "I love power, I do," he admitted to Pierre Roederer (1809), "I love it like a musician loves his violin". Madame de Staël said: "With him, everything was means to ends."

Napoleon attributed his success to his work habits, a gift from his mother, that, he said, made him "All that I am, all that I have been." He fostered the idea that he was a military genius, but in exile (1816), he told Las Casas: "I was born and made for work. I knew the limits of my legs . . . but never of my ability to work." If not in action, he said: "I have the habit of thinking about what I ought to do four or five months in advance". At war, he drove his army ahead, vigilant and ready to modify all plans "to the infinite."[3]

He hardly slept, or let his officers rest. While he befriended his soldiers, he harassed his generals like a drill-sergeant, damning them for every mistake (and some of his own) – over and over, until they obeyed by reflex.[4] Any rewards came after campaigns. Handling civil affairs in Paris, he roused ministers at ungodly hours, dictated to relays of secretaries, and ate meals in twenty minutes, often standing. Even his dalliances with women were scheduled.[5]

Bonaparte's sense of humor was almost nil; embarrassed high officials amused him. At the theater, he wanted tragedy; opera was a social occasion with noise. He abhorred the high notes of stringed instruments. He once commissioned the composer Méhul to write an opera with no notes higher than a viola could play.

We know of his exploits at Toulon (1793), and in Paris (1795) which netted him promotion to major-general (the highest grade at the time) and command of the Armée d'Italie.[6]

As he departed Paris, an ugly rumor followed him – that Barras had given him command of Italie for taking Josephine off his hands. She was hardly pining for him, but was back in society and had a (presumed) lover, Lieutenant Hippolyte Charles. Bonaparte was hopelessly in love with her, as his naive letters show: "My soul is sad; my heart is enslaved". This did not dispel the rumor. Victories, however, soon would.

General Bonaparte

In March 1796, en route to Nice, headquarters of the Armée d'Italie, Buonaparte began signing his name *Bonaparte* – decidedly more French. He was to command major-generals who outranked him (by date of promotion), and were veterans of many campaigns. He had fought against foreign enemies only at Toulon. Nevertheless, he did not doubt that the generals would accept him, since he was backed by Barras, the "King of the Directory," and Carnot, in 1796 one of the five Directors and controlling the military. Further, Bonaparte knew the Armée d'Italie from service with it in 1794 and 1795, and his work in the topographic bureau.

All this aside, Bonaparte had spent his life preparing to command, and ached to go to war, positive that he would succeed. He had yet to proclaim himself a military genius, but soon would. He had advantages that he took for granted: he was 26 years old, rather than 50 (as army chiefs were under the *ancien régime*). He had robust good health, vigor, good eyesight, good reflexes and phenomenal stamina – which combined to promote optimism and self-confidence.

The Army of Italy/generals

On 27 March 1796, Napoleon took command of the Armée d'Italie at Nice. His army had 96,000 men, but 22,000 were in garrisons and 36,000 in hospital, on leave, prisoners-of-war, or unaccounted for. That left 38,000 effectives.[7]

His key line generals were André Masséna (38), Pierre Augereau (39), and Jean Sérurier (54). Masséna and Augereau were ex-sergeants-major in the royal army; the latter had also served in the Russian and Prussian armies. Sérurier was a handsome aristocrat with over thirty-five years' service in the royal army; Carnot had saved his career because of his skill and loyalty. The chief-of-staff, Alexandre Berthier (42), another aristocrat, came with Napoleon – detached from Kellermann's Armée des Alpes by Carnot. He had been on Rochambeau's staff in America, and in great demand by commanders during the campaigns of 1792 to 1795. Berthier, small and swarthy, would be Napoleon's chief-of-staff on every campaign (except Waterloo, when he was ill).

In the coming campaign, Napoleon would depend heavily on Masséna and Augereau. Masséna – broad-shouldered and strong, with the face of a boxer – had been with Italie for six years, and had been responsible for earlier advances under generals Dumerbion and Schérer. He knew Bonaparte from his time on Italie's staff and at Toulon. Augereau – "whose great height gave him a martial enough air"[8] – had never served with Bonaparte. But Bonaparte knew his reputation as a swordsman (many brawls and duels) and as a tough, smart commander.

Bonaparte takes over

Bonaparte met his generals exuding the intensity of a human bomb that might explode. Masséna said afterward that as he approached he looked like a farm boy on his father's plowhorse, but when he dismounted – nine feet tall. Augereau said, "I don't know why, but the little bastard scares me."

Napoleon immediately demanded the exact position and strength of their divisions, why deserters ran free, why there were malingerers in the hospitals (he knew there were). He was *un homme terrible* with the officers, he said later. With the men, he was familiar, visiting their campfires and asking about their needs. They were skeptical that this small, skeletal, unkempt general could help them, but he did. Carnot had sent provisions for three infantry divisions, and assured the *commissaire*, Saliceti, a 3,500,000 franc loan in Genoa, where he bought food, warm clothing, and shoes. (Genoa was neutral and traded with everyone; British woolens were among items purchased.) It helped that Joseph

Bonaparte was French consul in Genoa.[9] Carnot also sent two regiments of cavalry from Kellermann's Armée des Alpes. Napoleon told both officers and men, however, that if they fought well they would be rewarded in Italy (where, in fact, he banned looting). The proclamation "Soldiers, you are naked, you are starving . . . Rich provinces, great cities will be in your power; you will find there honor, glory, and riches" dates from St Helena. But Napoleon surely told the troops something similar. Significantly, he did not dwell on the revolutionary mission of "liberation of oppressed peoples," but appealed to the baser cravings of the men – like an Italian *condottiere* of old.[10]

On 28 March Napoleon wrote Carnot: "I have been well received by the army, which has displayed great confidence in me". That was a lie, but Napoleon made it true.

Plans and enemy forces

The Directory's plan (which Bonaparte had helped formulate), was for him to separate the forces of Piedmont-Sardinia and Austria, and defeat each in turn.

Austrian general Baron Michel von Colli headed a Piedmontese army of 70,000, with some 50,000 effectives, deployed in the Maritime Alps. General Baron Johann Beaulieu (71) commanded an Austrian field army of 30,000, deployed behind the Ligurian Alps, and 50,000 troops in garrisons and forts in northern Italy.

To get between the enemy armies, Bonaparte had to move his army east toward Genoa – along the coast – then north across the low-lying Italian Alps. The easiest paths over the mountains were the Cadibona pass, above Savona (1,425 feet), and the Bochetta, north of Genoa (1,500 feet).

Into the breach (see Map 8)

On 6 April 1796 Bonaparte sent his army of 38,000 eastward, led by Masséna's "corps" (17,000), with Augereau (11,000) on his left, and Sérurier (10,000) in reserve.[11] On 9 April he sent Masséna toward Genoa with only his cavalry and some light infantry, moving noisily. Beaulieu, who had his 30,000 men at the top of the Cadibona, reacted (as Napoleon expected) by sending 15,000 to the Bochetta, above Genoa.

Meanwhile, Masséna secretly withdrew to Savona, and on the night of 11–12 April led his men over the Cadibona as fast as they could go. On the morning of 12 April he emerged from the fog at Montenotte, hit the Austrians, who were attacking a French redoubt, in the rear, and routed them. Napoleon reported to the Directory that he had troops on the Austrian flank, but praised Masséna for defeating Beaulieu "in person."[12]

Beaulieu's mistake had been dividing his forces – a fault Napoleon found endemic among Austrian commanders, and one which he exploited. Augereau

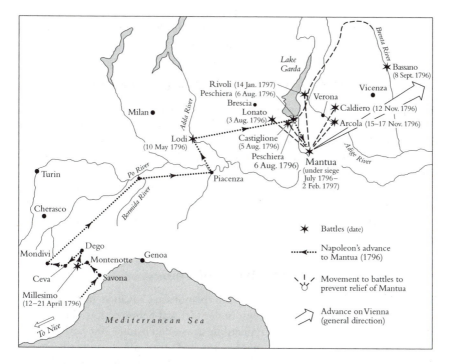

Map 8 Napoleon's first Italian campaign, 1796–97

joined Masséna the same day (12 April), and on 13 April at Millesimo, 10 miles away, they attacked Colli with only 20,000 troops, and drove him toward Ceva. Masséna then turned eastward and on 14 April routed the Austrians at Dego. Beaulieu withdrew all his field forces toward Alessandria.

On 18 April, Augereau and Masséna combined again and defeated Colli at Ceva. He retreated westward, widening the gap between the Piedmontese and Austrian armies. Napoleon then brought his corps together – Masséna, Augereau, and Sérurier – and followed Colli. On 21 April, at Mondovi, he punished the Piedmontese, who retreated, fighting at intervals, toward Turin. Napoleon's corps followed, cutting into the enemy's rear elements. Colli, depressed by his troops' lack of spirit, went to Turin and convinced King Victor Amadeus to ask for a ceasefire.

On 26 April, at Cherasco, the king signed an armistice with Bonaparte – really a surrender; Piedmont left the war. Napoleon got an indemnity in gold and silver. With the first installments, he paid his officers and men, emphasizing his gratitude to them. Most men got the first "hard money" they had seen in years, since they had been paid in script – *assignats* or *mandats* – issued by revolutionary governments, which was next to worthless.

Part of Napoleon's leadership consisted of always seeing to pay, promotions, and "trinkets of glory" (medals) for the troops. He also sent heavy contributions to the Directory, increasing his political influence.

The march through Parma (see Map 8)

Bonaparte allowed the word to spread that he would march directly on Milan, which meant crossing the Po River at Valenza. Beaulieu waited for him there, behind the Po. However, Napoleon marched south into Parma, a neutral state, and crossed the Po at Piacenza (9 May) – south and in the rear of Beaulieu. Bonaparte put winning above international law (or custom).

Beaulieu withdrew eastward toward the Quadrilateral, four fortresses – Peschiera, Verona, Legnago, and Mantua – that guarded the Alpine passes to Austria. Napoleon went into a forced march northeastward, hoping to strike Beaulieu before he got away.

The Battle of Lodi

On 10 May, in the late morning, at Lodi, Napoleon's advance guard overtook the Austrian rear guard – 9,000 men under General Sebottendorf. The enemy was behind the deep Adda River, guarding a wooden bridge 200 yards long.

Napoleon called for artillery – and by dusk had thirty guns blasting the enemy. While other generals – even Berthier – tried leading charges over the bridge, Napoleon worked the guns. Dirt and powder flying, his face black and sweaty, his uniform covered with stains, he aimed the guns (a corporal's job). The troops decided this was *their* general. After Lodi, they called him the "Little Corporal," and he loved it.

Napoleon ignored the failed charges over the bridge. He was waiting for Colonel Jean Beaumont's cavalry, which he had sent upstream to ford the Adda, and return to hit the Austrian flank. The cavalry arrived as dark descended, allowing Masséna to lead a successful charge across the bridge. The enemy went into retreat.

Lodi was not a major battle, or even a necessary one. Sebottendorf was protecting the rear of an army in flight, and by the next morning probably would have been gone. However, it was a memorable little battle, the more so because Bonaparte used it to bolster his reputation. His "bulletin" told the Directory that he had defeated an Austrian force of 18,000 men – double the number actually there – and estimated enemy casualties at 3,000. Such things led to the expression "Lie like a Bulletin," but *Napoleon thought exaggeration was legitimate and useful in war.* More importantly, Lodi solidified Napoleon's self-confidence. Already, he had been disdainful of enemy commanders, and certain that he was better than most French generals. After Lodi he thought he was the best general ever. He told his aide, Colonel (later marshal) Louis de Marmont: "In our time, no one has the slightest conception of what is great. It is up to me to give them an example."[13] His mood was darkened only by Josephine, still in Paris, who was letting her daughter, Hortense (age 13) write her letters to him.

The Cisalpine Republic

After Lodi, Bonaparte made for Milan, where he and Italian Republicans, such as Francesco Melzi d'Eril, organized the Cisalpine Republic, another "sister Republic" of France. He bought two newspapers to advertise his exploits, the *Courrier de l'Armée d'Italie* and *La France vue de l'Armée d'Italie*. The news they printed over the next year was based on real victories, but exaggerated the feats of Napoleon and his army. Without these papers Napoleon would not have become famous so quickly.[14]

Bonaparte knew the value of propaganda early on.

One general better than two (see Map 8)

Napoleon was shocked, however, to receive orders from the Directory to take his army south and secure central Italy and Naples. General François Kellermann of the Armée des Alpes was to finish the war in northern Italy.

He wrote Carnot that he was ready to resign, but praised Kellermann, a hero of Valmy (1792), as was mandatory. However, he said, "One bad general . . . is worth more than two good ones."[15] He demanded unity of command under *one* general. Such candor could have ruined him, but Napoleon believed that the Directors would not recall the only general winning victories. He also "sweetened the pot" by sending along money, art treasures (paintings by such masters as Corregio and Michelangelo), and 100 fine horses to pull the Directors' carrriages. Bonaparte kept his command, and Carnot gave him 10,000 troops from Kellermann's army.[16]

Napoleon rejoined his army, which by early June had taken all the Quadrilateral fortresses except Mantua. Beaulieu left a garrison of 14,000 men in Mantua and retreated into the Tyrol. Napoleon blockaded Mantua in June; by 15 July Sérurier's corps had it invested, and settled down to starve out the defenders. Direct attack or digging siege lines was next to impossible; it lay in the Mincio River, surrounded by rivulets and marshes.

For the next seven months the Austrians attempted to relieve Mantua, under successive commanders, and Napoleon responded. Between phases of the war, while the Austrian army was being reorganized, Bonaparte sent out forces to neutralize the Italian states he had not overrun. Augereau arranged peace with the Pope and the King of Naples. The Holy See ceded Bologna and Ferrara to France (added to the Cisalpine Republic), paid 34,000,000 francs, and "donated" art works. Naples contributed 50,000,000 francs. The Directory was impressed.

Germany: the French meet the Archduke

In April 1796, when Napoleon marched into Italy, the Archduke Charles (92,000) was preparing to invade French Lorraine. He was set also to oppose Jourdan's Sambre-et-Meuse (78,000), when it moved. Field Marshal Count Dagobert von Wurmser (83,000) faced Moreau's Rhin-et-Moselle (80,000), to the south.

The Archduke Charles (Karl), although the brother of the emperor, and young (26, Napoleon's age), had won his field marshal's baton against the French in Belgium and the Rhineland. Dark-haired and handsome, with a strong, classic face, he looked every inch the prince he was. He would prove again in 1796 and 1797 that he was a superior commander (later rated second only to Napoleon by Wellington, among others).[17]

In July 1796 Charles took command of all Austrian forces when Wurmser was ordered to Italy with 25,000 men. He lost other troops to garrisons at Koblenz and elsewhere, and some allied German troops went home. Thus the Archduke's forces were outnumbered by the French (if the two armies united).

The French planned for their armies to come together in Germany – eventually – but meanwhile Jourdan was to move east along the Main River, and Moreau (to the south) along the Danube (see Map 9).

In early June 1796, Jourdan crossed the Rhine at Düsseldorf and drove south. The Archduke crossed the Rhine and defeated Jourdan at Wetzlar, chasing him back to the left bank. But on 26 June, Moreau crossed the Rhine at Strasbourg, and Charles hurried south to defend the Danube route to Vienna.

Jourdan re-crossed the Rhine and marched east, pushing an Austrian force under General von Wartensleben before him. On 12 July Jourdan captured Frankfurt, and on 18 August was at Amberg, 30 miles from the Bohemian border.

Meanwhile, Moreau moved southeast toward the Danube. On 9 July, at Rastadt, the Archduke attacked him before his army was concentrated, but Moreau's advance guard won the first skirmishes. Charles retreated down the Danube, since his major goal was to keep the two armies apart. His cavalry kept him informed on both. On 8 August, Moreau took Ulm. Charles attacked him on 11 August near Neresheim, bloodied the French with cavalry, then artillery, and broke off.

The Archduke had decided to lose Moreau, who moved at a glacial pace, and take on Jourdan. He crossed to the south bank of the Danube, and Moreau followed. Charles eluded him, re-crossed the Danube, and went north to strike at the Sambre-et-Meuse.

Wurmser advances (see Map 8)

In the Tyrol, meanwhile, Field Marshal von Wurmser (72), replaced Beaulieu in command of the Austrian army, which was reinforced to 50,000.

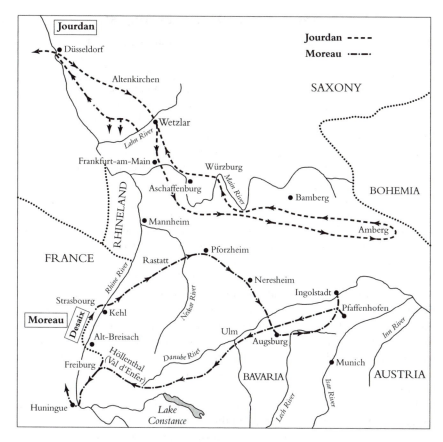

Map 9 Jourdan and Moreau in Germany, 1796

In July 1796 Wurmser marched with his forces divided. He came south, with 35,000 men, along the eastern shore of Lake Garda, while General Quasdanovich, with 20,000 men, moved down the western shore. Wurmser then divided his 35,000 further, sending 5,000 men to besiege Peschiera, and 5,000, under Meszaros, to approach Mantua via Verona, leaving him with 25,000. The Austrians marched slowly, giving Napoleon time to prepare; they had heavy trains with food supplies, cooks, and bakers.

Bonaparte ordered Masséna and Augereau, whose corps were on the Adige River, to meet the enemy, with Masséna, nearest Lake Garda, leading and Augereau following. He ordered Sérurier to move away from Mantua and concentrate at Marcaria, 25 miles to the west. This gave Napoleon a reserve, but was a gamble. It could have allowed Mantua's garrison to emerge and hit his rear.

Lonato and Castiglione (see Map 8)

Masséna moved toward the foot of Lake Garda, but heard of clashes between small French units and Austrians (Quasdanovich) west of Lake Garda, and moved that way. Quasdanovich repulsed his advance guard. But then Masséna hit Quasdanovich with his main force, and overwhelmed him at Lonato (3 August). Quasdanovich retreated rapidly back to the Tyrol, leaving Wurmser with 20,000 fewer men. Masséna then turned south and reinforced Augereau, and they kept Wurmser's main force at bay near Castiglione.

On 4 August, Bonaparte reinforced his two champions with two divisions (Kilmaine and Despinoy), artillery under Marmont, Beaumont's cavalry, and part of Sérurier's corps (on the march). He thus outnumbered his enemy – 30,000 to 25,000.

On 5 August, Napoleon won the Battle of Castiglione, not by superior numbers but by dangerous maneuvers. He ordered Masséna and Augereau to attack, then feign retreat, then, on his order, to again attack. When they went into retreat, Wurmser rushed to take advantage of it. He shifted the weight of his army to his right (north) flank, and attacked. When he was fully committed, Napoleon ordered Masséna and Augereau to turn their corps around and attack. They did. The Austrians fell back in confusion. As the French attack accelerated, Beaumont's cavalry, with an infantry division from Sérurier's corps, hit the Austrian left (south) flank. To his credit, Wurmser kept his force intact – leading cavalry charges despite his 72 years. When 5,000 men from the siege of Peschiera arrived, he was able to break contact and retreat rapidly up the Adige to the Trentino.

Bonaparte had another major victory – thanks mainly to Masséna and Augereau, who had unusual control of their corps. Men in retreat are vulnerable – their backs are to the enemy – and momentum is to the rear; they resist reversing their path. All of Napoleon's commanders performed well, arriving on time, where ordered, including Sérurier, who marched in from the south.

Wurmser was not finished. He knew from intercepted messages that the Directory had ordered Bonaparte to Germany (but not that he refused to go). He left 20,000 men, under Davidovich, to defend the approaches to the Tyrol, not difficult in the rugged Alpine terrain. On 1 September he marched east and then south along the Brenta River, hoping to relieve Mantua without much resistance. Again, he divided his forces. He had 20,000, Meszaros had 10,000 in the advance guard, and Sebottendorf and Quasdanovich 5,000 each on his flanks, marching 15 to 20 miles apart. His route was Bassano to Vicenza, then southwest across the Adige.

Meanwhile, Bonaparte restored the forces investing Mantua under General Sahuguet (Sérurier was ill). He sent General Charles de Kilmaine, with 3,000 men, mostly cavalry, to patrol the northern Adige. On 1 September, Napoleon ordered three corps to come together before Trent – Masséna arrived from Rivoli, Augereau was marching from Verona, General Charles-Henri Vaubois with an improvised division was at the north end of Lake Garda.

On 3–4 September, unaware of Wurmser's march, he sent Masséna and Vaubois to break through the mountains to Trent. On 5 September they took Trent, and found that Wurmser had marched away. Bonaparte put Vaubois in a blocking position north of Trent, and ordered Masséna to pursue Wurmser, then Augereau. They ended up on opposite sides of the Brenta, a deep and swift stream – each with 10,000 men, racing ahead, hell bent for glory. On 8 September, Masséna and Augereau caught half of Wurmser's army (Sebottendorf and Quasdanovich) at Bassano. The town bridge had not been blown, so they joined and routed the Austrians. Quasdanovich fled toward Trieste with 3,000 men; Wurmser marched to Vicenza, where he was joined by Sebottendorf, and on 9 September united the remaining Austrian forces at Villanuova. He was reduced to fewer than 14,000, but still confident he could take Mantua, and marched for Legnago.

Napoleon ordered Masséna to pursue Wurmser and Augereau to seize Padua, to the east, since he thought Wurmser might retreat toward Trieste. This divided Napoleon's forces and gave Wurmser an even chance of relieving Mantua.

On 9 September, Bonaparte realized that Wurmser was going for Mantua. He ordered Masséna to cross the Adige at Ronco, go south along the river, and block Wurmser at Legnago; Augereau was to march west from Padua to Legnago and strike the Austrian rear. Since, however, Bonaparte's two major corps would be on opposite sides of the Adige, Masséna's corps might be destroyed before Augereau could reach him. It was possible that Sahuguet and/or Kilmaine could reinforce Masséna, but Wurmser might get reinforcements from Mantua if Sahuguet marched; perhaps 8,000 of the 15,000-man garrison were in condition to fight.

At first, things went Wurmser's way. On 10 September, he reached Legnago, installed a 2,000-man garrison, and crossed the Adige. On 11 September he marched for Mantua. On the same day Masséna crossed the the Adige and Augereau reached Legnago. On 12 September, since Sahuguet had left the bridges intact, Wurmser entered Mantua with 10,000 men. With the garrison he now had 25,000 men (20,000 effectives). On 13 and 14 September he carried out successful sorties against the French, but on 15 September Napoleon met him with his corps united, and drove him back into the fortress, where he remained until forced to surrender (February 1797).

Germany: Jourdan's retreat

On 20 August, Jourdan was nearing Bohemia, when his flank guard collided with Charles's advance guard. Jourdan got the news at 2 a.m. on 21 August. He delayed acting, however, because he expected help from Moreau, who had written (10 August) that if the Archduke re-crossed the Danube, he would follow.

On 24 August, Jourdan finally went into retrograde toward Amberg, and was attacked from the south by the Archduke, who had joined with Wartensleben, giving him a numerical advantage. Jourdan fought at Amberg, and held, but there was no word from Moreau, so he withdrew toward Bamberg. Charles moved to cut his route of retreat, but ended with Jourdan between his advance guard and main army. Jourdan marched for Würzburg, north of the Main, expecting to brush aside Charles's advance guard and link up with a garrison he had left there. He found the garrison besieged in the citadel, and the Archduke was approaching. On 3 September, in dense fog, Charles crossed the Main and attacked, led by a mass of cavalry; Wartenslaben alone sent forward three squadrons of *cuirassiers*. The French cavalry fought back, but had to take cover behind its infantry. Jourdan's line became too extended and broke; he again retreated westward.

On 10 September he arrayed his forces on the Lahn, and his Sambre-et-Meuse fought well. However, Jourdan knew that he was up against the wily Archduke and most of the Austrian forces in Germany – *and that Moreau would not help him*. On 16 September the Austrians attacked across the Lahn, and Jourdan retreated, fighting, northwest via Hachenburg for Altenkirchen. On 20 September he was across the Rhine.

During his retreat, the Directory had kept urging Jourdan to make a stand. He had tried at every likely spot, but, without help from Moreau, could not stop the Archduke short of the Rhine.

Moreau advances into Bavaria

Moreau, meanwhile, had invaded Bavaria, he said to create a diversion to help the Sambre-et-Meuse. His engineers repaired bridges cut by the Austrians, and on 18 August 1796 he was across the Danube – but Archduke Charles had gone after Jourdan. Moreau could have put the Rhin-et-Moselle in pursuit of Charles – either to attack him in support of Jourdan or to crush him between his army and the Sambre-et-Meuse. Instead, he re-crossed the Danube to the south bank and marched for Augsburg. At the same time, he wrote Jourdan that he would press the Archduke hotly so that he could not move north. In contradiction, he wrote the Directory that Charles was moving north and would soon unite with Wartensleben (whom Jourdan had followed across Germany).

To face Moreau, the Archduke Charles had left behind 36,000 men under the Comte de La Tour (or Latour), a French-Austrian general anxious to destroy the French "Jacobins." Moreau had 70,000 troops in three "corps," commanded by Laurent Gouvion-Saint-Cyr, Louis-Charles-Antoine Desaix, and Brigadier Ferino.[18]

On 22 August, Saint-Cyr was before Augsburg, whose mayor, at his suggestion, closed the gates of the city to *both sides*. Latour's Austrians retreated, marched around Augsburg, and crossed the Lech. The stiffest resistance was by French *émigrés* (fewer than 6,000) under the Prince de Condé.

By nightfall, on 22 August, Latour's force was behind the Lech. Moreau deployed to face it, ignoring the news that the Archduke was about to strike Jourdan's Sambre-et-Meuse. On 24 August Moreau attacked across the rising water of the Lech. The colonel leading Saint-Cyr's advance party drowned, and Ferino's advance guard was washed down the river, but 60,000 French got across. The Austrians stood briefly, then took to open country and crossed the Isar, near Munich, but with heavy losses.

On the Isar, during an informal truce, there were strange scenes. Republicans and *émigrés* talked and joked with each other across the river. The Duc d'Enghien (Condé's grandson) appeared; Moreau's Republican troops doffed their caps.

Moreau had Latour outnumbered two to one, but advanced slowly. On 30 August, Saint-Cyr was at Pfaffenhofen. The plan was for Desaix to take Ingolstadt on 31 August. However, Latour, aware of Moreau's penchant for sluggish movement, moved across the French front to Ingolstadt and joined with General von Nauendorf, who had 6,000 reinforcements from the Archduke. On 1 September, the Austrians attacked Desaix, who fought a furious battle alone. Moreau, at Pfaffendorf with most of the army, did not even try to aid Desaix. If he had, they might have destroyed Latour's army. Moreau was not a quick thinker.

In early September, Moreau advanced farther east, fighting minor actions. Latour marched for Landshut, and Nauendorf for Abensberg to cover what had become the Archduke's rear, and protect a major crossing-point on the Danube, Regensberg (Ratisbon). Moreau sent Desaix with a small force to find Jourdan, whose help he now needed, but Jourdan was nearing the Rhine. On 19 September, Moreau began retreating toward the Rhine.

Italy: Alvinczy commands the Austrians
(see Map 8)

Baron General Jozsef Alvinczy von Borberek (61), a Hungarian officer, succeeded Wurmser in command of the Austrian forces. He had fought in the Seven Years War, and against the French from 1792 to 1794 in Belgium and the Rhineland, and then served in the *Hofkriegsrat* (War Council). His army numbered about 50,000.

Napoleon had only 30,000 effectives, including 9,000 investing Mantua, and they were widely separated, in terms of time required to unite, considering the rugged terrain, bad roads, cold, and incessant rain. In October, Vaubois's division (10,500) was guarding the passes from the Tyrol. Masséna (5,200) was at Bassano, and Augereau (13,000) on the Adige. A division (6,500) under General François Macquard was northwest of Mantua.

Alvinczy, however, divided his army, and Bonaparte took advantage of it – eventually. In October, Alvinczy marched west from Trieste with 30,000 men, while Davidovich came south from the Tyrol with over 18,000. As it turned out, Vaubois was able to block Davidovich in the mountains so that he did not figure in the coming campaign. Bonaparte met only the 30,000 directly under Alvinczy, which he further divided.

Caldiero and Arcola (see Maps 8 and 10)

Alvinczy encountered Masséna's forces near Bassano, but the French withdrew neatly to Verona, where Masséna was reinforced to 7,000, and Augereau joined him with 4,700 infantry and 2,000 cavalry. Macquard, with 2,600 men, moved by forced march to Verona and garrisoned the fortress.

Bonaparte took command of the corps of Masséna and Augereau at Verona (fewer than 14,000 men) and marched east to meet Alvinczy. On 12 November 1796 Napoleon attacked Alvinczy's advance guard (8,000) at Caldiero, but his opponent surprised him by fielding 18,000 troops. Moreover, the attacks of his two corps were poorly coordinated. French troops were tired from days of marching, and they fought in pouring rain, which soaked powder and damped their fire. Masséna was thrown back, then Augereau.

Alvinczy might have destroyed the French if he had fought with all his 30,000 men. However, he had 3,000 far out on his north flank, another 3,000 to the south, and 6,000 lagging behind. Nevertheless, Alvinczy won at Caldiero.

Bonaparte retreated on Verona, his mind working furiously. He decided to hold Verona with Macquard's 2,600, whom he ordered to try to make it seem that the whole army was making a stand. He planned to lead his main force – raised to 19,000 by troops from Vaubois and the lines at Mantua – down the south bank of the Adige to Ronco, cross partly flooded areas, and take Alvinczy in the rear at Villanuova and/or San Bonifacio.

On the night of 14 November the strike force, led by Masséna and Augereau's corps, with Guieu's brigade (from Vaubois), marched the 10 miles to Ronco. Alvinczy, meanwhile, was massing before Verona, after detaching forces to the south to guard his flank. He judged the rice-growing "swamps" north of the Adige to be impassable to a major attack force. Napoleon had chosen the area because of its potential for surprise.

On 15 November Augereau and Masséna crossed the Adige from Ronco in the rain, their men moving along dykes about 35 feet wide and a few feet above the marshes. Augereau made for the bridge at Arcola, from which he could strike for Villanuova, where the Austrian supply trains had stopped. Masséna headed for Belfiore, where Austrian troops (Provera) had been reported.

Augereau attacked the Arcola bridge repeatedly, but failed to take it. Napoleon came up to lead a charge, but ended up in the swamp when his horse shied and threw him. Masséna meanwhile drove the Austrians out of Belfiore, but the day was spent. Guieu crossed the Adige at Albaredo, and marched on Arcola, but had to turn back because Augereau could not support him – the Alpone River was between them. At nightfall they were all back at Ronco. Something had been gained, however, since Alvinczy was backing away from Verona toward Villanuova. His first priority seems to have been to protect his communications

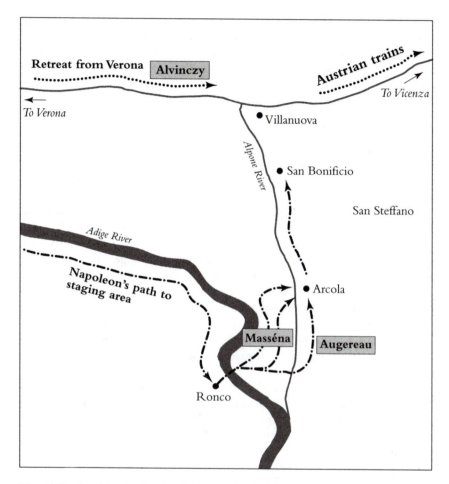

Map 10 Battle of Arcola, last day, 17 November 1796

and trains. To Bonaparte's advantage, his opponent was thinking in terms of escaping, not attacking. Perhaps he did not see that Napoleon was more vulnerable than he was.

Stubbornly, Bonaparte ordered the same advances on 16 November, but with Guieu's brigade in reserve. He could have thrown a bridge across the Alpone, less wide and deep than the Adige, and put Guieu across – or a division, or his whole force. If his whole force, it could have moved east – only a mile or two, onto solid ground – and then attacked north toward the Verona–Trieste highway, bypassing the Austrians at Arcola.

As it was, the forces were again back at Ronco by sundown.

Alvinczy might have bypassed Verona and gone for Mantua – his objective, after all. Instead, he ordered most of his army toward Villanuova, and his supply trains toward Vicenza. He also reinforced his units at Arcola and on the Alpone, but only so they could better protect his rear when he retreated.

On the night of 16–17 November, Napoleon finally ordered a bridge thrown across the Alpone. Augereau was to cross on the morning of the 17th and drive for Arcola; Masséna would cross the Adige at Ronco and attack the bridge at Arcola, detaching a regiment to block Provera if he approached.

On 17 November, Augereau's maneuver went perfectly. Masséna's was delayed by a blown bridge, but not by much. Masséna reached the Arcola bridge, feigned being repulsed, drawing an Austrian attack, and then counter-attacked across the bridge. There was some confusion, during which Napoleon, according to Marmont, went forward with Masséna's troops but stumbled, fell into a canal, and had to be dragged out.[19]

Masséna and Augereau went into pursuit, pushing the Austrians before them. Within a few days Alvinczy was in full retreat toward Trieste.

The Battle of Arcola was touted as a triumph by Napoleon's propaganda machine, with him leading the last attack on the key bridge. David's painting, *Bonaparte at the Bridge of Arcola*, was part of this effort.

It was a triumph, no doubt. However, the victory at Arcola must be chalked up to the incompetence of Alvinczy and the stubborness of Bonaparte.

Alvinczy determined to make a second try for Mantua (see Map 8, p. 81). He reorganized his army near Trent, and again was reinforced to 50,000. In January 1797, when he again marched against Bonaparte, he divided his forces.

With the main body of 28,000, Alvinczy went down the Mincio toward Rivoli, leaving some 6,500 to guard his rear. Bajalich, with 6,000 men, marched via Bassano on Verona, and Provera, with 9,000, on Legnago. As in his first attempt, he did not attack with his whole army; if he had he might have crushed Bonaparte.

Napoleon had arranged his forces to guard the approaches to Mantua from north and east. General B.-C. Joubert (*vice* Vaubois) with 10,000 men, was north of Rivoli; Masséna (10,000) at Verona; Augereau (10,000) on the Adige between Ronco and Badia. Sérurier (8,500), was again on the lines at Mantua. Baron G.-V. Rey (*vice* Macquard) had 4,000 garrisoned at the south end of Lake Garda.

When word that the Austrians were moving reached Bonaparte (10 January), he was in Bologna negotiating with the Pope's representatives. The next day, however, he was at Roverbella, in a better position to command, and had reports of Austrian forces between Legnago and Badia. He decided that Alvinczy's attack again would be from the east, and ordered (12 January) Masséna and Augereau to prepare accordingly, and Rey to reinforce them, plus cavalry.

On 13 January, however, Joubert reported that heavy enemy forces had forced him to withdraw to near Rivoli (see Map 8, p. 81). Alvinczy was approaching from the north. Bonaparte ordered Masséna to Rivoli, and went on horseback to join Joubert. Arriving at 2 a.m., 14 January, he ordered Joubert to occupy the

Trombalora, the highest hill in the area, just north of Rivoli. There, at dawn, Joubert deployed his 10,000 men.

At dawn Bonaparte attacked Alvinczy with Joubert's troops, to keep the enemy off balance until Masséna arrived. It was a risky ploy, but Alvinczy played into Bonaparte's hands by further dividing his army and ordering almost impossible maneuvers. He had sent Lusignon, with 4,500 men, to the west, to negotiate rugged mountains and take the French in the rear. Quasdanovich (8,000) had been ordered to march past the Trombalora and (also) attack the French in the rear. Vukassovich (3,000) was to support Quasdanovich, but was on the opposite (east) bank of the Mincio. Alvinczy faced Napoleon with only 12,000 men.

Bonaparte attacked the three divisions in front of him (Liptay, 5,000; Knoblos, 4,000; Ocskay, 3,000), exploiting the gaps between them. He was close to victory at 10 a.m., when Masséna arrived with some 6,000 men. His new infantry reinforced Joubert's right, while the madcap General Antoine Lasalle's cavalry galloped through the gaps in the enemy line and into his rear. Meanwhile, the forces sent to attack the French rear were defeated. Luisignon was captured by Masséna's rearguard.

The Austrians retreated in disarray. Colonel (later Marshal) Murat with 600 cavalry, had crossed Lake Garda in gunboats, and pursued the enemy, killing, wounding, and taking prisoners. The next day he continued the pursuit, along with Vaux and Joubert, grousing that the infantry got in his way. Meanwhile, Provera tried to take Mantua, but was surrounded by Augereau's corps.

Rivoli, however, like many of Bonaparte's victories, was due in part to his subordinates' skill and his enemy's ineptitude.

Germany: Moreau's retreat

Moreau retreated (19 September) with 64,000 troops, and initially with only Latour (17,000) in his path, with Nauendorf (6,000) following him. But other troops joined Latour from posts on the Iller and Neckar (17,000), bringing the army to 40,000.

Latour divided his forces. He followed Moreau, south of the Danube, with about 26,000, flanked at a distance, north and south, by detachments of 4,000 each. Nauendorf, with about 6,000, went via Tübingen, on the Neckar, toward Kehl.

Moreau passed Ulm and retreated southwest. On 29 September his army stretched from Lake Constance to the Danube. He sent 2,000 men ahead to reinforce Kehl, opposite Strasbourg, where he intended to cross the Rhine.

On 2 October Latour, with 26,000 men, attacked Moreau at Biberach on the Riss River, where steep banks and swamps favored the French. Moreau massed his northern wing – most of Saint-Cyr's and Desaix's corps, 39,000 troops, drove the Austrians back and scattered them, taking 5,000 prisoners.

Typically, Moreau did not pursue Latour, but camped while agonizing over the best route to the Rhine. He preferred the Kinzig River route – to Kehl – but he feared that the Archduke would meet him with his and Latour's armies united. So he chose a more southerly route, the Höllenthal (Val d'Enfer) – to Freiburg, then Alt-Breisach, a crossing point on the Rhine. On 10 October Saint-Cyr forced the Höllenthal, and on 12 October took Freiburg and Waldkirch. Moreau dawdled for three days, the began edging north along the Elz River toward Kehl and Strasbourg.

On 19 October the Archduke Charles crossed the Elz and attacked Moreau, who had 38,000 men; Charles had a maximum of 24,000. Moreau thought he faced superior forces, and called up 10,000 more, but still was beaten. Charles took Waldkirch and barred the route to Strasbourg.

Moreau consolidated his army, but the Archduke struck again on 20 October, and Moreau gave up hope of advancing directly to Kehl/Strasbourg. On the same day, he sent Desaix across the Rhine at Alt-Breisach, and marched down the left (French) bank to Strasbourg and began repairing the defences at Kehl.

Moreau took the rest of the army up the Rhine, toward the Swiss border. On 24 October, Charles, with only 32,000 men, attacked Moreau at Schliengen and drove him into retreat again. Moreau pulled out under cover of darkness, and on 25–26 October his troops crossed the Rhine at Huningue – almost in Switzerland.[20]

The aftermath of the German campaign

The Archduke had beaten both French armies, and offered to send reinforcements to Italy for use against Bonaparte. To his astonishment, the *Hofkriegsrat* rejected his proposal, and ordered him to retake Kehl and Huningue. Moreau proposed a truce (his Rhin-et-Moselle only), but Charles declined and followed orders.

Jourdan had resigned and retired, which pleased Carnot since he thought Jourdan had abandoned Moreau, instead of the reverse, and thus held Jourdan responsible for the debacle in Germany. In September 1797, Pierre Riel de Beurnonville took command of the Sambre-et-Meuse, but under duress. He begged to be replaced by Kléber, Shérer, or Hoche, and refused to help Moreau at Kehl and Huningue. On 9 December 1796 he signed a truce with Charles, for his army only, giving the Archduke more troops.

On 25 December 1796 a frustrated Directory gave Moreau command of both the Rhin-et-Moselle and Sambre-et-Meuse. In January 1797 he made a truce with the Archduke by giving up Kehl and Huningue. There was peace on the Rhine until spring.

Meanwhile, Charles was ordered to Italy to face Napoleon.

Italy: the Archduke Charles

In mid-February, the Archduke replaced Alvinczy in command of the Austrian army in Italy. He was promised 90,000 troops, but got 44,000, counting

Alvinczy's survivors, and his army was scattered and demoralized. Moreover, Wurmser had surrendered Mantua (2 February 1797).[21] It freed Napoleon to move against Charles, not feasible while the Mantua garrison posed a threat to his rear. And in February, Bonaparte had been reinforced by about 19,000 troops from the Rhin-et-Moselle and Sambre-et-Meuse.[22]

In early March 1797, Napoleon marched in force over the Carnic Alps, covering 400 miles in thirty days. At Klagenfurt, in Carinthia, Charles made a fight with only 10,000 men, and emerged bloodied but intact, but judged the situation hopeless. On 7 April 1797, Charles asked for an armistice, and Bonaparte agreed. On 18 April 1797, preliminaries of peace were signed at Leoben, in Styria. Although Austria did not sign a peace treaty until October, the war was over.[23]

Confusion on the Rhine

The French generals on the Rhine – Louis-Lazare Hoche (Sambre-et-Meuse) and Moreau (Rhin-et-Moselle) – had attacked the Austrians (under Latour), and they knew of the talks at Leoben. On 22 April, they heard of the armistice – in which, presumptuously, they had been included by Bonaparte. They stopped fighting, but the reaction of General François Lefebvre, commanding the advance guard of Hoche's army, was typical. When Bonaparte's young aide handed him the news, he rasped "*Putain!* You could at least have stopped for a bottle of wine!"

The shuffling of generals, that had gone on since 1792, continued. In September 1797, Hoche died of a lung infection, and Moreau was called to Paris, charged with withholding evidence against Pichegru. Augereau was given command of the two armies on the Rhine, combined as the Armée d'Allemagne. (Sent to Paris by Bonaparte, he had just to managed a *coup d'état* to favor the Directory.)

Napoleon's accomplishments

Napoleon was a national hero in France, and suddenly famous worldwide. In one year he had defeated five armies, four of them larger than his own, and captured 160,000 prisoners. He had kept the Directory solvent with millions of francs in precious metals and works of art. He sent Augereau (September 1797) to Paris to support a *coup d'état* (mentioned above) which improved his political clout.[24] *His blunders show that Bonaparte was not a psychic who could divine the enemy's plans and move accordingly. He was a "scrambler" – an improvisor – who overcame his mistakes and won repeatedly.* His subordinates, especially Masséna and Augereau, played a large part in his success. He called Masséna "*L'Enfant cheri de la victoire,*" and deservedly. Also, the ineptitude of Bonaparte's enemies worked in his favor. The Austrian commanders (save Archduke Charles, who had no chance) were eighteenth-century soldiers. They lacked Bonaparte's sense of urgency as an upwardly mobile, soldier-of-the-Revolution. Finally the Austrian soldier lacked motivation, while Napoleon's men did not. True, the French soldier's zeal for "spreading liberty" had long-since worn thin, but in compensation they had rapid promotions, increased pay, and the glory of serving Bonaparte, a constant winner.

Peacemaking and return to Paris

At Mombello palace, Milan, Napoleon, observed by his family (including even Josephine), dictated peace with royal flair to representatives of the minor powers, and greatly influenced the negotiations with Austria (October 1797) at Campo Formio.[25]

In December 1797, Napoleon returned to Paris, and was received as a hero, amid parades and celebrations. To his great pleasure, he was elected to the *Institut*, populated by France's elite intellectuals, and made a speech perfect for the occasion: "The greatest conquests are against ignorance". He did not conceal from the Directors that he had political ambitions, but posed no immediate threat. Nevertheless, he made them nervous. They offered him command of an army to invade England, which he refused. Instead, he asked to lead an invasion of Egypt, and the Directory approved, probably to get him away from France, since all deny it in their memoirs.

7

EGYPT AND THE COUP D'ÉTAT DE BRUMAIRE, 1798–99

Bonaparte's campaign in Egypt was a disaster. It was a waste of lives, money and material. It made no difference in the international balance of power, or in the position of the French navy in the Mediterranean. There was little glory in besting enemies with a medieval concept of warfare and weapons to match. It was seen in retrospect that the intellectuals he took along had established the science of Egyptology – that was all. Yet fate and Bonaparte's talent in propaganda and (a surprise) politics miraculously turned it to his favor.

The rationale for the Egyptian venture, presented by Bonaparte and the Directory's foreign minister, Talleyrand (Charles-Maurice de Talleyrand-Périgord), was that it was the best way to strike at the British – the only power still at war with France. From Egypt, the French navy could challenge British control of the Mediterranean and wreak havoc with her trade with the Levant, Persia, and even India.

Egypt was still nominally part of the Ottoman Empire, but the pasha, Abu Bakr, was a ceremonial head of state. Mamelukes, once the guard of the pasha, had ruled Egypt for 300 years. (They had been imported as European boy-slaves, usually bought in Levantine slave markets, and reared as Moslems and warriors.) Talleyrand promised to visit Constantinople (but never did) and convince the sultan that the French would restore his power in Egypt. If the *Porte* cooperated, Bonaparte was confident he could march to India, or to the Indian Ocean, where the French navy could carry his army to India.

The Directors approved the plan. They were willing to risk a small army in what amounted to peacetime. Defeat would hardly ruin France, and the venture would keep Bonaparte busy and away.

Bonaparte's force

Beginning in March 1798, the expedition was organized at Toulon. Bonaparte was pleased with his 35,000 troops, many veterans. He chose mostly younger generals (for ambition and vitality). Among these, Lannes and Murat had served him in Italy. Louis Desaix[1] volunteered, and brought along Louis-Nicolas

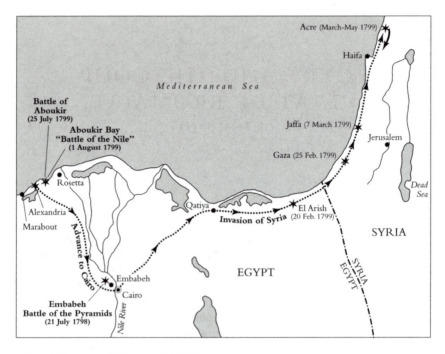

Map 11 Campaign of Egypt, 1798–99

Davout, later an outstanding marshal. Alexandre Berthier came as chief-of-staff; Masséna and Augereau did not come; they were army commanders themselves. The army was well supplied and equipped, but had only 1,350 horses. The cavalry required 700, which left 650 for the artillery, trains, and other uses.

As befitted a soldier-intellectual (and to assure the recording of his performance as both), Napoleon persuaded Gaspard Monge and Claude Berthollet, a mathematician and a chemist, to recruit scientists, cartographers, writers, and artists for the expedition. The London *Times* (which had agents in France) reported that the army at Toulon was "immense" and equipped with artillery and mortars. Further, "ammunition and men of letters have been put on board."

A lucky voyage

On 19 May 1798, the expedition sailed – troops and supplies in four hundred transports, escorted by thirteen ships-of-the-line (50 guns or more) and four frigates, commanded by Admiral François-Paul Brueys d'Aigailliers; his flagship, *L'Orient*, with 120 guns, was the premier warship in the world.

The British had spies "under every rock" in and near Toulon. Henry Dundas, secretary of state for war, knew that Bonaparte was bound for Egypt, but he could not convince the other ministers. Admiral Earl Saint Vincent, commanding the

British Mediterranean Fleet, had to protect against possible invasion of Naples, Spain, Portugal, or Egypt. Saint Vincent sent Rear-Admiral Sir Horatio Nelson, with fourteen ships-of-the-line and seven frigates to find and destroy Bonaparte's expedition at sea.

Nelson opted to patrol off the Egyptian coast. He was there when the French should have arrived – in mid-June. But Bonaparte had stopped to capture Malta, ruled by the Knights of Saint John of Jerusalem (Knights of Malta).[2] The purpose was to secure communication with France, for French naval bases, and to protect French commerce. However, it probably saved his expedition from destruction.[3]

Meanwhile, Nelson was forced to sail to Sicily for supplies, and was far away when the French landed.

Cairo (see Map 11)

On 1 July 1798, the French landed at Marabout, near Alexandria. There was no opposition, and the only casualties were from seasickness. Napoleon sent 5,000 men to take Alexandria (where there was fighting, and generals Kléber and Menou were wounded). That done, Bonaparte marched for Rahmaniya across the desert with 20,000 troops. General Louis Desaix (whom we met in Germany, serving under Moreau), brought the rest of the troops (10,000) up the Nile, covered by gunboats, with Murat's cavalry in the lead. Napoleon's march was harder than he had expected. The troops were in winter clothing, without canteens, and marched in deep sand under a blazing sun. Men who discarded clothing froze at night. Soon, many men were thinking of mutiny, and some deserted; even generals complained loudly, and one, after Bonaparte called him names, committed suicide. Napoleon lost 1,000 men, but reached Rahmaniya in ten days. Desaix was there to meet him.

In 1798, Murad Bey and Ibrahim Bey were the joint chiefs of the Mamelukes. (Bey was a title; a notch below pasha.) They were in no hurry to engage the French, but were confident. Murad boasted that he would split French heads like watermelons.[4]

On 13 July, at Shubra Kitt, north of Rahmaniya, Napoleon battled Murad with 6,000 Mamelukes and 10,000 (relatively useless) Egyptian infantry. Napoleon had his army in division squares – for maximum impact of his fire-power on primitive cavalry. The squares had cannon on the corners, moving outside, firing and retreating into the squares as opportunity offered. The infantry was five or six ranks deep, with the front rank kneeling, firing, then successively replaced by the others.[5]

Great riders, the Mamelukes charged fiercely, but were armed mostly with medieval weapons – the scimitar (curved saber), ball and chain, spiked mace, and dagger. They had some obsolete firearms, but disliked using them, since to them honorable combat meant closing with the enemy and seeing his blood spill. Perhaps to exaggerate his victories, Napoleon wrote the Directory that the Mamelukes were "magnificent," with modern English weapons, and riding horses perhaps better than any in Europe. In fact the short Arabian horses were the best for the terrain – tough, hard of hoof, and fast.[6]

Some Mamelukes broke into Napoleon's squares, and the French knew that if their horses were killed (infantry always took the larger target), they came up fighting, and seemingly had to be killed two or three times before they died.[7] In the end, however, French firepower won the battle. After a few charges, the Mamelukes suddenly withdrew; they would fight another day.

There was harder fighting in the Nile between French and Egyptian gunboats, but that ended quickly too. Napoleon brought up field artillery to support his gunboats, and blew up an enemy munitions ship to boot. French casualties were negligible; the French marched on toward Cairo.

On 21 July, at Embabeh, Napoleon faced 60,000 enemy in the "Battle of the Pyramids," which were out-of-sight but gave the battle's name some glamour. On the west side of the Nile, facing Bonaparte's army, were 6,000 Mamelukes under Murad Bey, 20,000 entrenched Egyptian infantry, and a few Turks. In their rear were 14,000 Arab horsemen. Across the Nile, Ibrahim Bey had 6,000 Mamelukes and 14,000 Egyptian infantry. But apparently, Ibrahim had decided to put himself under Turkish protection in Syria – and perhaps return as sole ruler. Murad did the fighting.

Again, Napoleon put his army in five division squares, and planned to have them maneuver, but they largely stood on the defensive. Only Desaix executed orders fully, moving his square onto the enemy flank. French regimental bands constantly blared the "Marseillaise" and other marches throughout the battle – a bloodier one than Shubra Kitt. Murad's Mamelukes took the most casualties, charging repeatedly until they were bled white; some 2,000 were killed. The Egyptian infantry fought in their trenches, but still lost about 4,000 men. The Arabs, *bedouin* nomads, organized by tribe, made sporadic attacks, hoping for loot, and found none. At day's end, the French were again the victors, with only 300 casualties.

The French, especially Napoleon, were impressed by the valor of the Mamelukes. Their dress appealed to Bonaparte's theatrical bent – turbans, colorful silk shirts, embroidered vests, trousers and slippers with upturned toes. He recruited some Mamelukes for his bodyguard (later the Imperial Guard). There were never more than 100, however, since they proved savage off duty and on; most were eventually replaced by Frenchmen dressed as Mamelukes.

Napoleon also recruited a Mameluke bodyguard, Roustan, a giant, sinister figure, who, for the next fifteen years, was always with his master, on foot or on horseback.

Murad Bey retreated up the Nile, and Bonaparte sent Desaix in pursuit. He defeated Murad at Sadiman, and scattered his army beyond Aswan. Ibrahim Bey went into Syria, where he was protected by the Turkish governor. Napoleon occupied Cairo.

Battle of the Nile

On 1 August, Admiral Nelson, with fourteen ships-of-the-line, sailed into Aboukir Bay (the mouth of the Nile) and attacked Admiral Brueys' fleet – thirteen line vessels, but with overall greater firepower. Brueys anchored his fleet in the shallows, thinking that the British could not get behind him, and would have to sail along his line, where he had enough guns (on one side) to sink them. His flagship, *L'Orient*, had 120 guns, 60 on each side. Sixty was more than the total on most of the British ships. His logic was flawless, but doomed him.

Nelson, whose motto was "Damn tactics; go straight at 'em," did just that. He came at the northwest end of Brueys' line, and his ships sailed both in front of and behind the French, blasting them from both sides. The British sank and/or burned *eleven* French ships-of-the-line; only two escaped, with two frigates, and fled to Malta. Admiral Brueys was killed. Nelson lost not a single ship. French seapower in the Mediterranean and worldwide was reduced drastically, since France had only about seventy ships-of-the-line in commission; Nelson had sunk one-sixth of them.

Bonaparte was marooned in Egypt, and his communication lines with Paris were all but destroyed. For the next year, he had little contact with the Directory.

Nelson's victory and a *jihad* (holy war) declared by the Ottoman sultan against the French sparked a revolt in Cairo. It was a surprise, since the Egyptians had seemed submissive, but bloody. They killed Frenchmen in the streets, soldiers away from their units, and set French hospitals on fire.

Napoleon reinforced his army with Mamelukes who had attached themselves to him. They quickly killed or captured any Egyptians fighting in the open. Informers (for pay, of course) appeared as if by magic. With their help, the French ran down anyone with arms, entering buildings and homes, searching out weapons, and shooting rebels on the spot. In a few weeks, the French had become as merciless as their enemies.

Cairo was soon quiet, and Napoleon, with no orders from Paris, decided to execute the original plan and march into Syria, perhaps on to India. However, he delayed the march until he wiped out all resistance in Egypt, most importantly from Murad Bey's army. Desaix finally sent a messenger from upper Egypt that Murad's army was no more. Napoleon had also developed a hatred for the Arabs in particular: "We are continually harassed by . . . Arabs, who are the greatest thieves and most evil bastards in the world, who assassinate both Turks and French".[8]

Syria

In preparation for the march, Bonaparte sent an ultimatum, aimed at intimidating the military governor of Syria, Ahmed Pasha Jezzar, "the Butcher." He also sent a message to the only Indian prince who was fighting successfully against the British, Tippu Sahib of Mysore, in which he said that he, General Bonaparte, would soon arrive to support Tippu with an "invincible army."[9]

On 10 February 1799, Bonaparte marched into Syria with 13,000 men and 52 field guns. He took El Arish and put most of the Turkish garrison on parole – after they pledged not to fight the French again. (The population of Syria was predominantly Arab, but the fortresses were manned by Turks.) On 3 March, he took Jaffa after three days of fighting, capturing 2,000 to 2,500 Turks, about half of whom he had paroled at El Arish. At this point Napoleon had fewer than 13,000 men. There had been battle losses, and some of his troops had contracted "plague." A few died daily. He could not spare troops to guard prisoners or escort them back to Egypt. If he let the Turks go, they would surely fight him at some place ahead – or strike at his column as it marched. Considering the size of his force, 2,500 enemies was not negligible. He had to choose between killing the prisoners or calling off the expedition. Bonaparte had the prisoners shot, without qualms of conscience, since the Turks regularly tortured French prisoners to death. He was adopting the morality of his enemy, and was never guilty of such behavior during his campaigns in Europe.

Napoleon visited the hospitals, exposing himself to the plague, while confidently stating that it would not strike anyone who did not fear it. Since he did not become infected, his posturing reduced his men's fear of the plague – and of the desert, and of going forward. Leaving a detachment to guard the sick, but too small to stand, in fact, he marched on.

Siege of Acre; retreat to Egypt

On 17 March 1799, 300 miles into Syria, Bonaparte laid siege to Acre. He lacked siege artillery (44-, 24-, and 16-pounders and heavy mortars), which he had sent by sea, where it had been captured by the British naval vessels commanded by Sir Sidney Smith. And although Acre was an ancient fortress, antedating the Crusades but strengthened by European crusaders, its walls were impervious to field artillery, and it was defended by 250 guns.

The defense was well commanded for the Turkish pasha by Colonel Antoine Le Picard de Phélypeaux, a French émigré who had been a schoolmate of Napoleon at the École militaire. With only field artillery, and short of ammunition, Bonaparte could send only infantry against the walls, and it failed. Moreover, he was attacked by the Turkish Army of Damascus, which he defeated in the Battle of Mount Tabor, but with losses of several hundred men and much time. Throughout, Sir Sidney Smith's gunboats harassed the French along the coast. Meanwhile, his men began dropping from plague.

In mid-May, Bonaparte heard that Sir Sidney Smith was ferrying a Turkish army to Egypt, and broke off the siege. He marched on 20 May, after giving orders (which were disobeyed) to administer lethal doses of drugs to plague victims to save them from torture by the Turks. Of his original 13,000 men,

2,500 were dead and another 2,500 were sick or wounded; half of the latter did not reach Egypt.

Battle of Aboukir

Back in Egypt in July, Bonaparte assembled 7,700 men and seventeen guns and marched to meet 20,000 Turks, under Mustafa Pasha, who had landed on 10 July near Aboukir. The Turks might have taken Cairo before Napoleon arrived, and perhaps picked up local support, but they had dug in for a defensive battle. They occupied the fortress of Aboukir, at the tip of a narrow peninsula, and had formed two defensive lines, one behind the other. The first line, was about a mile and a half in front of Aboukir, was anchored by fortified hills on both shores, but had an undefended gap in its center. The second line, about 600 yards from the fort, was a solid line about 1,000 yards long, spanning the peninsula. Some 5,000 men were in Fort Aboukir, the rest divided between the fortified lines. They were supported by thirty guns and gunboats along both shores of the peninsula.

On 25 July, at dawn, Napoleon attacked, sending Lannes' division against the fort on the French right, Destaing's against the fort on the left. Murat, with the cavalry, waited for the infantry attacks to succeed, then swept through the gap between the forts, undermining the defenders in first one fort and then the other. The Turks fled; many were cut down or driven into the sea as they retreated, but most reached the second line. The French infantry advanced, but the heavily manned second line held. Napoleon sent up his artillery, and its pounding forced the Turks to flee from a 200-yard stretch at the western end of the line.

Murat swept through the gap, turned the Turkish position, and drove the enemy into the sea, cutting and slashing until the blood washed up on the beach. Fort Aboukir held out until 2 August, but the Turks were really beaten in one day. They lost 2,000 killed in action, 11,000 drowned, 5,000 captured, and 2,000 more missing and unaccounted for.

Sir Sidney Smith negotiated for the withdrawal of the prisoners, who included Mustafa Pasha. During the talks, as a matter of courtesy, Smith passed to Napoleon copies of the London *Times*. Bonaparte learned from them that France was being hit hard by a new coalition (Britain, Austria, Russia, Turkey, and lesser powers). All of Italy had been lost to the Austrians; the French held only Genoa. An Anglo-Russian force had invaded the Netherlands (Holland); Russian forces were in Switzerland.

Napoleon to France

Bonaparte felt he must return to France and "save the Nation," and surely thought of entering politics. He had no orders, but he was willing to risk court martial. (The Directory had sent orders, which he had not received, to return *with his army* – a near impossibility.) Probably, he believed he could do more for his army in France than in Egypt.[10]

On 24 August Bonaparte sailed; his two brigs carried Berthier, Desaix, Lannes, Murat, some intellectuals, and others, for France. He left sealed orders for General J.-B. Kléber to take command of the army. The journey was harrowing. His ships were becalmed off Egypt for almost two weeks, easy prey for the British navy. But they finally made sail, stopped briefly at Corsica, and on 9 October landed at Fréjus, near Cannes.

Bonaparte brought with him the news of the Battle of Aboukir, which was presented as a triumph. Crowds cheered him in every village and town as he travelled north; on 15 October he was in Paris. The Directory had discussed his "desertion," but had lost the will to discipline him – or even mention his willfulness. Whatever else the Egyptian campaign was, it was an unexampled romantic adventure to the public. It put Paris agog over Egypt and things Egyptian. It produced reports of victories – over exotic and mysterious enemies. Bonaparte made good use of that.

Bonaparte "saves the Republic"

On his arrival in Paris Napoleon was immediately contacted by the "Revisionists," who publicly advocated revising the constitution to strengthen the executive. Actually they meant to replace the government of the Directory – by legislative action if possible, by *coup d'état*, using military force, if necessary. A Director, the wily ex-Abbé Emmanuel Sieyès, a force in every government since 1789, was the chief revisionist. The plotters included another Director, Roger Ducos; the foreign minister, Talleyrand; the minister of police, Joseph Fouché; and Napoleon's brothers Joseph and Lucien. Sieyès picked Napoleon to be his "sword" (command the military), and Bonaparte was to be "Grand Elector" in the new government – a surrogate king with ceremonial duties. Civilian "consuls" – Sieyès and others – were to rule.

Napoleon and the "Revisionists" had the support of most of the Council of Elders (upper house of the legislature) and at least half of the Council of 500 (lower house). The intelligentsia (Madame de Staël, Benjamin Constant, René de Chateaubriand, and others) had been won over by Joseph Bonaparte, who was one of them. (However, Napoleon and the *idéologues* soon clashed.) The propertied classes (bourgeois and noble) were generally supportive, since law and order had broken down. The officer corps and the army were convinced the war was being mismanaged. Most of the French were merely weary after ten years of revolution, one government after another, disorder, bloodshed, and war. When a strong leader appeared, they followed him; when he established a stable government, they gave him support.

The Revisionists' plot resulted, of course, in the *coup d'état* of 18–19 Brumaire (9–10 November 1799). On the first day, under threat of a fictitious Jacobin plot, the Elders gave Napoleon command of troops in Paris and called a meeting of both councils for the next day. He promised the Elders: "You want a republic founded on true liberty . . . on national representation . . . You shall have it . . . I swear it. I swear it in my name and that of my comrades in arms!"[11]

On the second day, the councils met in the palace of Saint-Cloud. Napoleon insisted on addressing both houses, asking that the Revisionists be given power to write a new constitution. The "500" were angry, however, and members pushed forward toward the rostrum. Bonaparte was surrounded, and either fainted or was knocked out by the pressure of bodies. He was carried out by grenadiers and recovered quickly.

Meanwhile, Lucien Bonaparte became the hero of the day. He left the "500," over which he was presiding, when the ruckus started and ran into the courtyard, where lines of soldiers stood. Jumping on a horse, he rode before them, shouting that they must drive out the assassins and Jacobins in the palace. Waving a sword, he promised to plunge it into Napoleon's heart if he betrayed the Republic. The troops entered the palace and put the legislators to flight.

This was more violent than most of the plotters had wanted. To give the *coup* some semblance of legality, they recalled such legislators as were willing to come to an evening session. This "rump" of the councils voted the power to write a new constitution to "provisional consuls" Sieyès, Roger Ducos, and Bonaparte.

Bonaparte then outwitted Sieyès. He insisted that committees of the Councils approve the constitution, and then the Councils themselves before it was submitted to the people. This put the old legislators on his side. He then worked with Roger Ducos and Sieyès on a draft constitution, while encouraging the Councils' committees to frame their own version. They did, led by the liberal Pierre-Claude Danou, heavily influenced by Napoleon. When the consuls and committees met together, they approved Danou's constitution – for practical purposes Napoleon's. The French people shortly approved it in plebiscite.

The Constitution of the Year VIII (promulgated in December 1799) made Napoleon Bonaparte (by name) First Consul of France, the chief executive. Pierre Lebrun and J.-J. Régis de Cambacérès, Second Consul and Third Consul, were merely his advisers. Sieyès and Roger Ducos were relegated to the senate, which was appointive, but were allowed to help Bonaparte choose the first thirty members. There was universal manhood suffrage, but only for electors, who, moreover, only supplied lists from which the senate picked legislators (members of the Tribunate and legislature, Corps Legislatif).

Bonaparte was the government. Why did France accept him? They were tired of the chaos of revolution, of course, with its succession of governments. General Charles de Gaulle put it another way. The army, he wrote, represented "force, order, honor" and was indignant at the "feebleness, license [and] vices" of the Revolution.[12]

At any rate, for the next fifteen years, as consul, then emperor, Napoleon ruled with his appointive senate. He named advisers to his council-of-state, which proposed the laws. The laws were passed by legislative bodies chosen by the senate (which he appointed). He chose ministers, prefects of departments, and administrators down to mayors of cities, officials of police, and commissioned officers of the army and navy. He had, in short, more power than the Bourbon kings. He was too canny a governor, however, not to have his major acts approved in national plebiscite, or to fail to cultivate his senators and legislators with praise and rewards. One thing he had in common with the terrorists of 1793–94 was adherence to Rousseauist principles. He did not believe in government by the people, or their representatives; he believed in government *for* the people, by himself. To do so, however, he thought it necessary to *listen* to people, or their chosen deputies. He thought any ruler a fool who did not listen.

Moreover, he worked steadily at building support among civilian as well as military leaders in and outside the government at every level – men eventually called *notables*. Early on, he allowed political exiles to return – Jacobins and aristocrats alike – except for the former royal family (the Bourbons) and their most fanatic suporters. He then worked to form an amalgam of leadership among nobles of the *ancien régime*, new nobles (whom he created, as emperor) and coming members of the middle class (whether in business or the administration). In this he was very successful. Toward the end of his empire, the business and banking community was behind him, together with the great landholders and the sons of old nobles, new nobles, and bourgeois notables. But for his military reverses, beginning in 1812, his dynasty might have survived – which, however, is not a proposition which this book will attempt to prove.

8

MARENGO AND THE
GRANDE ARMÉE, 1800–05

In the period 1797 to 1799, France's aggressive foreign policy had provoked the European powers. France created four more "sister Republics" in 1798–99 – the Helvetic (Switzerland), Ligurian (Genoa), Roman (papal states) and Parthenopean (Naples), making six with the existing Batavian and Cisalpine Republics. Thus Austria and Russia, plus minor powers, joined Britain and Turkey, already at war, in the Second Coalition. War began in Europe in March 1799.

In August 1799, when Napoleon left Egypt, France was losing the war. By October 1799, however, when he arrived to "save" France, his military leadership was not greatly needed.

The improvement of France's situation was facilitated by the new Jourdan–Delbrel conscription law (September 1798), which furnished the manpower needed by the armies. (The *levée en masse* had lapsed.) The first year, men 18 to 25, and thereafter men turning 18, had to register for military service – subject to call at age 20 – those turning 20 were the "class" of a given year. (The law stayed in effect under Napoleon, who had it amended to allow the buying of substitutes.)

It had taken eight months for French armies to improve their situation. Barely had hostilities begun (March 1799) when the hero of Fleurus (1794), Jourdan, commanding in Germany, was driven across the Rhine by the Archduke Charles. He was relieved and his army given to Masséna, already commanding the Armée d'Helvétie (Switzerland), deployed from the Rhine to the Grisons.

In Italy, Field Marshal Aleksandr Vasilievitch, Count Suvorov (69),[1] commanded Allied forces (Russians plus Austrians under generals Paul Kray and Michael Melas). As a general, he was later compared to Wellington; but he was a "character." The British ambassador at Vienna described him as quite mad, "a little old shrivelled creature in a pair of red breeches and his shirt [and nothing else]."[2] He declined a bed and slept on straw because Christ had been born in a manger. But Suvorov won battles. He advocated relentless mass attack, preferably with the bayonet, and sometimes demonstrated its use in battle. His men worshiped him.

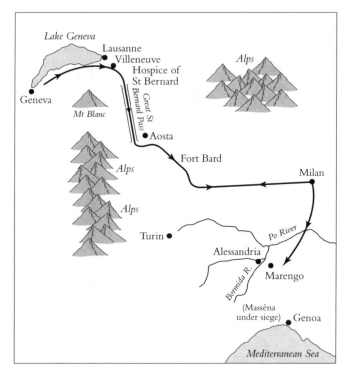

a) Napoleon over the Alps and to the vicinity of Marengo

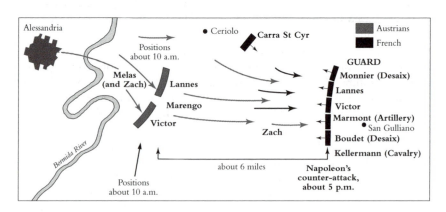

b) Battle of Marengo, 14 June 1800

Map 12 The Marengo Campaign, May–June 1800

Beginning in April 1799, Suvorov (86,000 Austrians, 24,000 Russians) battled successive French generals commanding the under-strength Armée d'Italie. Barthélemy Schérer (30,000 French) lost hope and resigned from the army. Jean-Victor Moreau took over and retreated to Milan, then Turin (18 May), and finally, his army reduced to 21,000, to Genoa. Jacques-E.-J.-A. Macdonald, with the 37,000-man Army of Naples (the Republic had collapsed) tried to reinforce Moreau, to no avail. He then fought Suvorov, against two-to-one odds. On 19 June both Moreau and Macdonald were in Genoa. In August, Barthélemy Joubert – Sieyès' first choice for the role played by Bonaparte on 18 Brumaire – was given the Armée d'Italie to win some glory. He attacked Suvorov, but was killed in the battle of Novi. Jean-Etienne Championnet took command of Italie and Armée des Alps, totalling 41,000, but was ordered to stand on the defensive.

In April, Masséna's army became the Armée du Danube (63,000 men). In June, he faced the Archduke Charles (70,000 Austrian troops) who had marched from the Rhine, and in July also by General Rimski Korsakov with 27,000 Russian troops. The Austrian court soon returned the Archduke to the Rhine, however. Austria, (First Minister Thugut) giddy from Allied victories in Italy, had decided to take total control of Italian territory and also recover Belgium (recently the Austrian Netherlands).

On 18 September, the Archduke took Mannheim, moved on Mainz, and prepared to drive on into Belgium. He was too far north to guard the flank of Allied forces in Switzerland. Suvorov, with 30,000 Russian troops, was marching from Italy to Switzerland, where he was also to command the forces of Korsakov (27,000) and the Prince of Condé (about 3,000 French *émigrés*).

By September, Masséna's army was reinforced to 89,000 men, and an Armée du Rhin created (eventually under Moreau), so that he could concentrate on Switzerland. He promptly attacked Korsakov and then the Prince of Condé's *émigrés* in Constance; both fled into Germany. Masséna then turned on Suvorov and, in battles that took 5,000 Russian casualties, drove him east through the Grisons into Germany.

In October 1799, General Brune, defending the Netherlands, was encouraged by Masséna's victories, and reinforced. He routed the Russians, captured their general, and blundered into a battle at Bergen (or Kastrikum) and won a minor victory over the British. With winter coming on, many troops ill, and disgusted with his Austrian allies, the Duke of York agreed to talk terms. Per an agreement of 15 October, he re-embarked his Anglo-Russian expedition for England.

On 22 October, Czar Paul I withdrew Russia from the coalition, bitterly damning the Austrians for their betrayal of the Allies, and the defeat (by Masséna) of Suvorov, his most celebrated commander. The Czar had an unconcealed admiration for Bonaparte, which the First Consul enhanced by accelerating the repatriation of Russian prisoners. Paul was soon murdered by his courtiers, which brought his son Alexander I to the throne. Meanwhile, Bonaparte benefited by not having Russia against him. Austria was the only major power still fighting in Europe.

After Brumaire, Bonaparte sent Masséna to defend Genoa. As a reward for supporting him on 18 Brumaire, he let Moreau keep the Armée du Rhin (given him in July), but reluctantly, since he knew Moreau's plodding ways.

The Second Italian Campaign

With the Consulate established (December 1799, without elections until spring 1800), Napoleon turned his attention to the war. He elected to take personal command in Italy, still a secondary theater, where he felt, as French head of state, he would not be expected. Further, he had advertised that the constitution prohibited the First Consul from leading troops, which was not true. However, the Austrians did not expect him in Italy until he actually marched. Austrian intelligence believed that France had all the troops she could muster in the field. Most were on the Rhine in Germany; ergo, France would launch her major attack in Germany, as she had in 1796 and 1797.

The Austrian misconception suited Napoleon. He ordered Alexandre Berthier, his perennial chief-of-staff, to organize a reserve army of 60,000 in Burgundy, near the Swiss border. He meant to take it over the Alps – Hannibal style – in the spring of 1800, and descend on the rear of the Austrian army besieging Genoa. As noted above, Masséna, "l'Enfant cheri de la victoire" in the First Italian Campaign, was holding Genoa, the anvil for his hammer. When he arrived in Italy, he expected Masséna to emerge from Genoa and strike the Austrians from the west, while he hit them from the east.

Berthier not only found the troops, but equipped them to cross the Alps with special clothing, shoes, and snow shoes. The army was ready to march in April 1800, when Bonaparte arrived. On 15 May, after the snows began to thaw in the passes of the Alps, Napoleon put the army in motion. The main body crossed the Great Saint Bernard Pass, with Bonaparte on a mule (Americans would say "donkey") – sure of foot and hardy – not the fiery grey stallion of the David painting.

The army reached the crest of the Pass with relative ease, and enjoyed wine and cheese donated by the Hospice of St Bernard. Beyond, however, Austrian garrisons had to be dislodged, and at Bard, they were held up by fire from a fort on high ground which dominated the road. While most of the army painfully bypassed the fort, much artillery and some cavalry was left behind, and could not follow for two weeks, after Bard was reduced.

The First Consul emerged onto the plain of Lombardy on 30 May. On 2 June he was in Milan, where he restored the Cisalpine Republic (restyled the Italian Republic) and received the cheers of the population (who hated the Austrians more than the French). He also applied himself to finding more cannon, and put available forces on the march toward the Po and Lodi, on the Adda, where he had fought a battle (made famous by his propaganda) in 1796. He felt that the

Austrian army before Genoa – if threatened by his and Masséna's actions – would make for the Quadrilateral fortresses, as Beaulieu had done in 1796, and he did not want the Austrians there – especially in Mantua.

A change of plans

Masséna, with a 10,000-man garrison, had held Genoa against the Austrian field army under Field Marshal Michael Friedrich Melas until Bonaparte crossed the Alps. The rest of the Armée d'Italie (17,500) was in the vicinity of Nice. Melas had 51,000 men – 21,000 surrounding Genoa and 30,000 between Nice and Genoa (not counting garrisons, totalling 77,000). On news of Napoleon's approach, he pulled some of his troops back from Nice, but kept pressure on Masséna's garrison.

The French in Genoa were in a bad way, weak from a diet of a few ounces of horsemeat, bread laced with straw, and occasional toasted rats. Only 6,500 of Masséna's original 10,000 men were alive. In early June, he got word that Bonaparte was in Milan; he felt he had accomplished his mission. Melas agreed to let the garrison march out "honorably" – under arms. On 4 June, rather than wait, see more men die, and then probably capitulate unconditionally, he surrendered Genoa.

For his part, Melas was willing to grant terms because he wanted to garrison Genoa himself. He had word that Masséna's troops from Nice (14,000) were marching to join him. Thus Masséna might have over 20,000, and attack him from the west, while Bonaparte came at him from the east (exactly what Napoleon had in mind). With an Austrian garrison in Genoa, Melas felt he could block or impede any force Masséna gathered, and concentrate on beating Bonaparte. In fact, Masséna's army was only a psychological threat; his debilitated garrison troops could barely march, much less fight. They were straggling into Nice, rather than being reinforced.

On 8 June, Napoleon got word that Masséna had lost Genoa, and at first refused to believe it. His old comrade had carried out his orders, but Bonaparte had not fully appreciated his situation, and remembering the "miracles" of 1796–97, expected him to hold longer. However, Napoleon was not one to fret over a setback. He accelerated plans to move toward Genoa, so as not to allow Melas to escape (envisioning that Melas would retreat east, as had Beaulieu in 1796). *His priority was to destroy the enemy army – as it always was, throughout his career.*

Bonaparte had underestimated his opponent, who was 71 but not in his dotage. Melas was concentrating his forces to meet Napoleon. He had left a 10,000-man garrison in Genoa and ordered the rest of his field army to concentrate at Alessandria, about halfway between Genoa and Milan. By 10 June he had 34,000 men there, heavy on cavalry and artillery, and was ready to fight.

Napoleon had only 28,000 of his troops of the 60,000 in northern Italy, but he marched anyway. He wanted a quick and spectacular victory to strengthen his new government and assure his control of France. He was on familiar ground, had been reassured by the plaudits of the Milanese, and was not as wary as he might have been.

Bonaparte, with his small army, swept to the south and west, in the general direction of Genoa. Late on 13 June he arrived east of Alessandria, on the far side of the Bormida River. He had been warned by cavalry scouts and French divisions north of him and in the Alps (who had Austrian prisoners) that Melas was concentrating troops at Alessandria, but did not believe he would give battle there. Nevertheless, he sent out scouts to see if the bridges over the Bormida were up. The report was that all bridges had been destroyed or removed. That meant Melas could not attack unless his men swam the river.

Napoleon did not reconnoiter the area himself (as he habitually did if expecting battle), or send a second patrol – probably because the report confirmed what he already thought: Melas would not fight. Having observed the slow and cautious ways of the Austrian army in 1796 and 1797, he did not believe the force in Alessandria could possibly be ready to fight. He expected Melas either to make for the Quadrilateral or for Genoa. With that in mind, he dispatched two sizeable forces to block the routes – a reduced division (about 3,500) to Piacenza, the probable crossing point on the Po River, and Desaix's corps (two divisions) to block the roads to Genoa. One division (Monnier) went toward Garofoli; Desaix led his second division toward Novi. These detachments deprived Napoleon of 12,000 men.

On 14 June, Napoleon was bivouacked south of the Bormida with only 15,000 men – two reduced corps (Victor on the Bormida, Lannes three miles to the east), some reserve cavalry under François Etienne Kellermann (son of the hero of Valmy), and the Consular Guard (1,100) – in villages on the roads east of the Bormida, one company eight miles from the battlefield.

Marengo (see Map 12)

At dawn on 14 June, Melas hit Napoleon with 34,000 Austrian troops. He first attacked Victor's corps, on the Bormida, and drove it slowly east, while other French units joined the fight (and the retreat). For over four hours, however, Napoleon refused to believe that the Austrians meant to give battle. Meanwhile, Lannes' corps became fully engaged, and, off and on, the reserve cavalry and Consular Guard.

At about 10 a.m., Napoleon began sending out urgent messages for his detached divisions to return. That to Desaix said in part: "Return, in the name of God, if you still can."[3] Neither commander received the messages; they were sent too late, and some copies were taken by Austrian cavalry, who greatly outnumbered the French. Desaix, however, marched to the sound of the guns, and saved the day for Bonaparte.

Throughout the day, the French were forced steadily eastward toward San Giuliano. The strongpoint of San Ceriolo, on the French right, fell at about noon; Napoleon shortened his lines and continued the retrograde action. At 5 p.m. the French battle line was centered on the village of San Giuliano – some five miles from where the battle had begun. Napoleon had been reinforced along the way by about 4,000 men, including his Guard infantry and Monnier's division, but had not been able stop the Austrians. Melas, who had a minor wound, had judged the battle won, placed General Zach in command, and returned to Alessandria.

As French resistance weakened, Zach allowed the Austrian forces to fall into a lazy formation which placed only a few battalions in contact with the French; the remainder were strung out in loose-march formation along the road to San Giuliano.

As the French aligned on San Giuliano, Desaix arrived, ahead of his troops, and said to Napoleon: "This battle is lost, but there is time to win another one." He moved his division, as the regiments appeared, into line; the relatively fresh men steadied the corps of Lannes and Victor. Napoleon had Kellermann consolidate the scattered cavalry and Marmont form an artillery battery, and ordered the attack.

The French infantry drove straight into the overconfident Austrians, supported by Marmont's artillery. But hardly had the battle begun when the handsome Desaix, recognized by his long, jet-black hair, was shot dead and tumbled from his horse. The Austrian account says that the French infantry was "transported with rage," and penetrated the Austrian advance guard, and the enemy began falling back.[4]

Kellermann disorganized the Austrians further by charging through gaps in the French line and into the Austrian rear – repeating the charge as quickly as he could re-form his mixture of heavy and light cavalry. In the process, he captured General Zach, thirty-seven officers, and 1,527 soldiers. The Austrians retreated, crashing into the oncoming ranks behind them, and the retreat became a rout.

The French troops pursued, but they were tired, night came on, and most of the enemy escaped across the Bormida. Overall, Austrian casualties were about 9,500, but only 963 killed; the French had 1,100 killed, and 4,500 wounded or captured – not high figures for a major battle. Afterward, however, the French were exhilarated and confident, the Austrians demoralized.

Melas judged his army unfit for more fighting, and the next morning (15 June) he asked for an armistice, which Napoleon granted. On 18 June Bonaparte turned his army over to Masséna and left for Paris. The war was over in Italy – but not in Germany.

Napoleon's *Bulletin* on Marengo told the story fairly truthfully. He gave credit to Desaix – but without saying that Desaix had saved him from disaster – and expressed grief for his fallen comrade: "Why is it not permitted to me to cry?" He praised Kellermann and Marmont. However, he maintained that his army was never out of control (which was true).[5] Nevertheless, Marengo preyed on his mind. Desaix had saved the day – and on his own initiative.

It is hardly to Napoleon's credit, but over the next few years he had the history of Marengo rewritten until he got a version demonstrating that he had planned it all, including the arrival of Desaix at San Giuliano.[6]

Problems with Moreau

In Germany, Moreau, commanding the Army of the Rhine (120,000) had used five months to prepare his campaign against the Austrians (commanded by General Paul Kray).[7] Once Moreau started, he made steady progress, but agonizingly slow to Bonaparte. Moreau bypassed Kray's entrenched camp at Ulm but took Munich, and the Austrians (15 July 1800) agreed to an armistice. However, the British had given Austria a hefty subsidy, and the emperor avoided making terms, while he rebuilt his forces. Napoleon tended to blame Moreau for all delays, however; he had a reputation for excessive caution.[8]

In mid-November 1800, Bonaparte ordered Moreau to resume fighting. But by that time Austria had fielded an army of 136,000 under the Archduke John (age 18), that struck first, surprising the French east of Munich. Nevertheless, Moreau scattered the Austrian army at Hohenlinden on 3 December 1800. His victory ended the war with Austria.

Moreau was the new hero of Paris. The French had celebrated the victory of Marengo, but the war had not ended. Moreau had brought peace. Paris gave him interminable fêtes, which inflated his ego, and his young wife's more so (they were newlyweds).[9] He foolishly became an overt rival to Napoleon, which angered the First Consul (soon emperor). In 1804 he had Moreau imprisoned and exiled on charges of treason.[10]

Napoleon made peace with the remaining coalition powers and the papacy: Austria, by the Treaty of Lunéville (9 February 1801);[11] Great Britain, by the peace of Amiens (March 1802);[12] Pope Pius VII, by the Concordat of 1801 (June 1801; promulgated 1802).[13] Peace with Britain lasted only a year. Militarily, the Concordat was most important. It ended the peasant revolt in the Vendée (active or festering since 1793). The rebels proved more interested in having their churches back than the restoration of the king.

All Europe was at peace for the first time in ten years, and Bonaparte had time to consolidate his government, and prepare his army for greater triumphs.

Bonaparte in peacetime

With peace in Europe, Napoleon set in motion a colonial scheme. Louisiana (secured from his ally Spain) was to provide food for the "sugar islands" of the French West Indies. It was ruined by the resistance of blacks in Haiti and fevers that killed virtually the entire French army sent to subdue them. Napoleon gave up his colonial schemes (1803) and sold Louisiana to the United States: "Damn coffee, damn sugar, damn colonies!"

Meanwhile, Bonaparte took the opportunity to annex Piedmont, Elba, and part of Switzerland to France; he had himself elected president of the Italian (formerly Cisalpine) Republic. He barred British trade with France and all areas he could control or influence, including Holland and Naples. While damaging British commerce and violating the Treat of Amiens, he demanded that Britain surrender Malta (recaptured from the French in September 1800), per the same treaty. The British declined.

In April 1803 Great Britain withdrew her ambassador from Paris and, without a declaration of war, began attacking French ships at sea. Napoleon retaliated by occupying Hanover, the possession of King George III of England. At the same time, he assembled at Boulogne and camps along the channel coast an Armée d'Angleterre (Army of England), threatening invasion.

The Grande Armée

At Boulogne (and the channel posts, which extended into the Netherlands), Napoleon reorganized the strike force of the French Army – 200,000 men who became the Grande Armée of 1805, his field army. The French standing army numbered about 600,000 men.

Napoleon restored to the army all the glamor of that of the *ancien régime,* and added more. Regiments, notably the cavalry, were given distinctive uniforms in blazing colors, at least two, parade and field, the one as splendid as the other. The new flags had eagles atop the flagstaff ("The Eagle" of the Regiment). Every regiment had a band. He restored the identity of foreign regiments – Poles, Swiss, Hanovarians, and others – for healthy competition. With numbers rather than names, some provincial regiments were re-formed as well.

No new weapons were introduced, however, or tactics. As noted earlier, the weapons were inherited from the monarchy – the 0.69 caliber Charleville musket, the 0.69 carbine, the 0.69 pistol, and the Gribeauval artillery – 12-, 8-, 6-, and 4-pound field guns and heavier siege pieces. The tactics were inherited from the *ancien régime* – attack in battalion column, line, or in *ordre mixte,* or column moving into line for increased firepower. Despite assumptions to the contrary, Napoleon did not expand the artillery. Throughout his wars he maintained an average of three cannon per 1,000 men – about the same ratio as his enemies, and often less.

His emphasis was on improving morale, training, organization, discipline, hardening, and better use of weapons, although the infantry continued to use "area fire," throwing up a hail of bullets in the general direction of the enemy. The effectiveness of his work was fully demonstrated in the 1805 campaign.

Napoleon restored the grade of marshal (1804) to the army and made marshals of generals he considered outstanding (and for political reasons, a few heroes of the Republic) – sixteen in 1804; ultimately twenty-six.[14] He made the corps the standard unit of all arms, replacing the division, which was subordinated to the corps. It numbered 20,000 to 30,000 men, was usually commanded by a marshal or lieutenant-general (a temporary grade), and was capable of giving battle unsupported. It comprised two or more infantry divisions of 8,000 to 12,000 men, a brigade of light cavalry (2,000 to 3,000 men), six to eight companies of artillery, engineers, medics, trains, and headquarters.

The infantry division was divided (ideally) into two brigades of one or more regiments. The regiment (after some experimentation) had a standard complement of four battalions of six companies of 140 men each, or 3,360 line troops, plus headquarters, and a band. The total corps artillery support was forty-eight to sixty-four guns (six cannon and two howitzers per company of 110 men), of which two or more companies were under corps control, and the rest attached to divisions or brigades. Corps guns were mostly 12-pounders; those at lower level 8-, 6-, and 4-pounders, with the 6-s disappearing by 1812.

The infantry battalion had one company of *voltigeurs* or *tirailleurs* (skirmishers), one company of *grenadiers*, and four companies of *fusiliers*, or ordinary infantry-men. The skirmishers were smaller and more agile men; they led the attack, advancing like Indians to disorganize the enemy. (Casualties were high; after 1809 artillery preparations more often did the skirmishers' job.) The grenadiers were the taller men, and were used as shock troops (but did not carry grenades, which had proved too dangerous). The cavalry was of two types, light and heavy. The light cavalry were called *hussars, chasseurs à cheval, dragoons,* and (after 1809) lancers; the heavy cavalry were the *cuirassiers* and *carabiniers à cheval*. They differed in that the heavy cavalry had bigger men who wore body armor (the cuirass) front and back, steel helmets (with roach and plume), and rode heavier horses. The two sorts of heavy cavalry differed only in regimental colors; the light cavalry by headdress (helmet for dragoons, bearskin shako for hussars, etc.) and regimental colors. All were armed with sabers, carbines (0.69 calibre) and pistols (0.69). The sabers of the heavy cavalry were longer, however, and straight, designed to be used like a lance, whereas the light cavalry had curved blades for cutting and slashing.

Army headquarters (Napoleon) controlled 150 or more guns in the field (which did not change the average of three guns per 1,000 men). Army headquarters also controlled the cavalry reserve of 20,000 (1805) to 60,000 (1812), early on commanded by "the First Horseman of Europe," Marshal Murat, later other marshals. Marshal Berthier was the chief-of-staff on every campaign save Waterloo.

Finally, there was the Imperial Guard, Napoleon's trump card. The Guard was much more than a bodyguard; it was a small, elite army, with its own infantry, cavalry, artillery, engineers, trains, and headquarters. It grew from 8,000 in 1805 to 80,000 in 1812. It was commanded in battle by the emperor, though headed by a marshal (latterly a marshal commanded the infantry and a general the cavalry, or vice versa). The Old Guard, of regiments formed 1800–06, was composed of combat veterans of three or more campaigns. The Middle Guard, formed 1806–09, had the same requirements. The Young Guard, formed after

1809, was filled with veterans, but then, as attrition thinned the ranks, with merely promising (usually tall, imposing) soldiers.

The Guard had did not need to "prove itself" in battle. Says Elting, an encyclopedia of army expressions: "They were men who had heard the owl and seen the elephant." Napoleon held it back as his ultimate reserve. He delighted in using the artillery, but seldom committed the infantry, the *grognards* (grumblers), who stood in intimidating mass on high ground behind the lines, usually in full dress uniform. When he committed his infantry, it never failed him – until Waterloo. The Guard was privileged in every way. Privates ranked with sergeants of the line; sergeants-major with lieutenants; colonels were generals or marshals of the line. Said a wag, "Don't you know that the Guard's donkeys have the rank of mules?"[15]

Napoleon's uniform was that of a colonel of Guard Cavalry (1st Chasseurs à Cheval); the field uniform had a green coat with red facings. The Emperor made a fetish of always appearing before the troops in the same faded green coat, by which they knew him; it was part of his style. Charles de Gaulle praised Napoleon's Guard as a factor in motivating his army: the creation of "elites, given privileges which the others burned to share . . ."[16] However, he also emphasized Bonaparte's debt to the Revolution, which had shaped the army, and the Directory, which had given him conscription.[17]

Napoleon's "regular army"

Napoleon fought with a "regular army" for most of his career, contrary to the usual view which is that of an army of draftees. True, many had entered as conscripts, or by volunteering or through the National Guard. However, they had elected to remain in the army. The officers and NCOs were career men, and until 1813, after the Russian disaster, even the rank and file were "regular."

Manpower was available by conscription, but Napoleon used it modestly. Between 1800 and 1810, he called an average of only 73,000 men a year. Only in the crisis years of 1812 to 1814 did he use it heavily, calling 1.5 million men.

The presence of foreign troops in Napoleon's army helped to keep down draft quotas in France. The Grand Armée of 1805 was mostly French, but about one-quarter of it, or 50,000 troops, were foreign – Polish, German, Italian, Irish, and others – and this counts only men in French uniform. There were also Allied troops, in 1805 almost all from the German states; and of course the Italian army – half Italian, half French – which fought in Italy in 1805. The numbers of foreign troops increased yearly.

The Grande Armée formed at Boulogne was decidedly professional, with a greater percentage of Frenchmen than any army Napoleon would ever command.[18]

9

SUBDUING THE EUROPEAN POWERS: AUSTERLITZ–JENA–AUERSTÄDT–FRIEDLAND, 1805–07

Provoking conflict

There is abundant evidence that in 1805 (at least until July) Napoleon intended to invade England. The best proof is that he planned to challenge the Royal Navy in the English Channel. On that subject, Admiral John Jervis, Earl of St Vincent, had said: "*Buonaparte may cross the channel, but it will not be by sea.*" But Bonaparte had appointed Admiral Pierre-Charles de Villeneuve to execute (in 1805) a grand naval strategy (see p. 123 and p. 124) to clear the channel for his invasion.[1] Napoleon's Armée d'Angleterre, soon to be the Grande Armée, had other uses. But he had spent money and blood (in drownings and accidents) practicing with thousands of boats and barges acquired to carry the invasion force.

On the other hand, the major continental powers stood against him. Between 1803 and 1805, Bonaparte had affronted the rulers repeatedly. In 1803, he occupied Hanover, a possession of the king of England, which put French troops on the Elbe River, deep in Germany. That disturbed Francis II of Austria, Holy Roman (German) Emperor, and Frederick William III of Prussia. Napoleon also pushed through the implementation of the Imperial Recess (1803)[2] which attenuated the power of Francis II by eliminating small German states, the most loyal to the emperor since they needed his protection.

In 1804, Napoleon's (Fouché's) secret police arrested royalists plotters in Paris. Georges Cadoudal, a former leader of the *Chouans* in the military Vendée, was executed. Under brutal interrogation, he had implicated generals Pichegru and Moreau, who were imprisoned (Pichegru committed suicide in his cell – or was assassinated; Moreau was exiled).[3] He also said that the royalists were to be aided by an *émigré* army, led by a prince of the blood.

In the last piece of information, Napoleon saw an opportunity, by ruthlessly displaying his power, to condition the *émigré* Bourbons and other hereditary monarchs to accept his elevation to emperor. He sent 300 cavalry across the Rhine into Baden; they captured the Bourbon Duc d'Enghien (grandson of the

Prince de Condé), and on 20 March delivered him to Vincennes.[4] He was tried by a military court during the night, and executed at dawn on 21 March 1804. This act of terror had the desired effect – if temporary – on European monarchs. Only the czar of Russia ordered official mourning.

In 1804 Bonaparte arranged for the senate to proclaim him emperor of the French, and the people voted approval. On 2 December 1804, in Notre Dame cathedral, Napoleon crowned himself "in the name of the French people and the *Army*," using the crown of Charlemagne.[5] Bonaparte thus proclaimed himself the successor of the great Frankish ruler, not of Bourbon kings, disdaining the Holy Roman Emperor, Francis II, Charlemagne's traditional successor.[6]

In May 1805, Napoleon further offended Francis by making himself king of Italy (26 May 1805). (He named Eugene de Beauharnais, 23, Josephine's son, his viceroy.) In the Duomo of Milan, Bonaparte again crowned himself, figuratively, with the "Iron Crown" of the Lombards – solid gold and too heavy for graceful lifting.[7] The commemorative medal bore Napoleon's profile and the Lombard formula *"Rex Totius Italiae"* (King of All Italy), alarming the Pope, ruler of central Italy, and the Bourbons of Naples–Sicily.

In mid-1805, Russia allied with Austria and Great Britain, forming a Third Coalition against France. Czar Alexander I opposed the "illegtimate" Bonaparte dynasty, and wanted Russia to play a greater role in Europe. Further, his interests in the Mediterranean and Balkans were challenged by France.[8]

Napoleon at Boulogne

Napoleon could not ignore the new coalition against France. However, on 2 August 1805, two weeks after returning to France from Italy, he made for Boulogne, where he ostentatiously continued preparations for the invasion of England. He had to know, all the same, that even if he got his army across the channel, the Royal Navy might (nay, probably would) maroon him in England, while European armies invaded France.

In fact, Napoleon was prepared for war in Europe. During 1804 and 1805 he had sent officers to reconnoiter in Germany and had orders drafted for the army.[9] Before departing the Kingdom of Italy, he inspected the Quadrilateral fortresses, which defended against attack across the Alps.[10] En route to Paris, he ordered Marshal Masséna to Italy to command young Viceroy Eugene's army. He neutralized Prussia by promising Hanover to Frederic William III (who kept negotiating to join his enemies).

When he spoke of invasion, it was always "imminent," and he gave conspicuous attention to the movements of the French fleet under Admiral Villeneuve, slated to dominate the channel for his invasion. This both kept British eyes riveted on activities at Boulogne and emboldened Austria and Russia to strike in Germany. Clearly, however, Bonaparte could not strike simultaneously at Britain and his continental enemies.

Naval strategy

In March 1805, Admiral Villeneuve's French fleet sailed from Toulon. His orders were to lead Lord Nelson's Mediterranean fleet to the West Indies, lose him, absorb French fleets from Brest and Rochefort at sea, race to the channel, and cover the invasion. Napoleon surely knew that Villeneuve was a careerist who valued saving his ships over winning – not the sort of commander he preferred. *Possibly he appointed him to fail.*

Nevertheless, Villeneuve began well; he reached the West Indies in mid-May, with Nelson arriving on 4 June. On 9 June, Villeneuve sailed for Europe. Nelson followed on 12 July, but with favorable winds reached Gibraltar in seven days. He sent a frigate to warn the Admiralty of Villeneuve's approach, which sighted the French fleet and reported its position.

Villeneuve, meanwhile, got no reinforcement from the other French fleets; the British sealed up Brest; the Rochefort fleet broke out, but failed to find Villeneuve and returned to port. Then, on 22 July, Villeneuve (forty ships; twenty-six Spanish, fourteen French) blundered into Admiral Sir Robert Calder's fleet (fifteen ships) off northern Spain, and fought a battle, though becalmed until dusk. Villeneuve lost two ships, Calder none.[11] The French admiral, despairing of reaching the channel, put in at Ferrol (northern Spain), then sailed south; on 20 August he was at Cadiz.

On 25 August, Napoleon heard Villeneuve was hiding at Cadiz. In a flood of letters, most sent through the minister of marine, Admiral Denis Decrès, Bonaparte called Villeneuve pusillanimous, *sans courage*, incomparably inept, deserving of ignominious dismissal, and kept adding insults for weeks.[12] Villeneuve, he said, had ruined his invasion plan.

In October, to redeem his honor, the admiral sailed from Cadiz to engage Nelson, and met disaster (see pp. 123–124).

The Grande Armée marches east

Throughout August 1805, however, Napoleon had been sending army units toward the Rhine. On 23–24 August he ordered the entire army to march for Germany. On 25 August, he wrote Talleyrand that he would "*pirouette* my 200,000 men," which he was already doing. On the 27th, he dictated orders to his "seven torrents" (corps). On the 29th, the army became the Grande Armée.[13] The Archduke Charles, with 90,000 men, was prepared to meet him in Italy, where he had made his main effort twice before. Napoleon, of course, meant to attack the Austrians (and the Russians, if present) in Germany before they attacked his German allies.

He was faced by 72,000 Austrian troops under General Karl Mack von Leiberich (53), who had serious command problems. The Archduke Ferdinand (24) was nominally his superior – sent because the Russians insisted on dealing with a Habsburg prince. In the field, however, Ferdinand demanded a voice in decisions, confusing the staff and endangering the army. Mack's nearest support was the Archduke John's army (25,000) in the Tyrol. However, 35,000 Russians, under Field Marshal Mikhail Kutuzov, were to join Mack by 20 October; 60,000 more by 30 October.

Bonaparte's Grande Armée of 200,000 comprised seven corps under his recently created marshals; 40,000 reserve cavalry under Marshal Murat; and an 8,000-man Imperial Guard.[14] France's allies, Württemberg, Baden, Bavaria and Hesse-Darmstadt, supplied 50,000 more troops.[15]

Mack had invaded Bavaria on 13 September 1805. The Bavarian army moved north, waiting for Napoleon. Mack went up the Danube to Ulm, on the border of Württemberg (the Bavarian got out of his way, and waited). Mack did not expect French forces east of the Rhine before mid-October, and by then should have Russian reinforcements. However the *Hofkriegsrat* had underestimated the date the Russians would reach Mack by two weeks, and judged Napoleon's army would reach the Rhine three weeks later than it did.[16]

Napoleon marches by Mack

By 30 September six corps of Napoleon's army (one was in reserve) and Murat's cavalry had crossed the Rhine and were moving east and south toward the Danube River. The leading corps crossed the Danube from 7–8 October at Donauworth, Münster, Neuburg and Ingolstadt; the rest from 9–11 October between Elchingen and Münster. All crossed *east* of Ulm. Early historians of the war, plotting the routes of the French corps, and with the advantage of hindsight, thought they saw a master plan in execution – the envelopment of Mack's army at Ulm. Not so.

Napoleon expected Mack to detect his huge army's approach, and do what any sensible general would do – drop south of the Danube and retreat to a defensible river line – the Lech, Ammer, Isar, or Inn.[17] Napoleon had issued orders on 4 October for his army to move toward the Lech River line, then shortly toward the Ammer, with Bernadotte heading for Munich, on the Isar. Until 11 October, he hustled his corps in that direction, and thus overshot his enemy – at Ulm.

In doing so, he left Mack in a position to drive through his rear – along the north bank of the Danube – tearing up his supply and communications lines. Mack owed his advantage also to the fact that his cavalry had scouted the Black Forest, but missed the French, who went north of it. But Mack had an advantage, and he knew it. On 7 October, he wrote: "It would be easy to make [Napoleon] pay dear . . . for one would only have to descend along the left [north] bank . . ."[18]

On 9 October, Mack ordered exactly that: a march through Günsburg along the north bank of the Danube. However, the Archduke Ferdinand paralyzed the headquarters, and Mack ordered a concentration on Ulm. On 12 October, after all French corps had crossed the Danube, Mack again ordered a march through the French rear – this time to Regensberg – but again Ferdinand opposed him, and Mack lost his chance to cripple the French army.

Meanwhile Napoleon persisted in the belief that the Austrians were to his southeast. On 8 October, leaving his headquarters at Donauworth, he pressed on, with the Guard, toward Augsburg. On 9 October he angrily ordered Ney to get his corps across the Danube *tout de suite*, leaving one division to capture stray Austrian troops at Ulm. On 10 October, Napoleon dismissed reports from Ney and Davout of Austrian units south of Ulm, certain that if it were so they were headed for the Lech River line. On 11 October Ney crossed the Danube, the last corps across, leaving Pierre Dupont's division north of the river.

Dupont, with 4,000 men, mostly cavalry, marched for Ulm and collided with 25,000 Austrians, under Mack himself, on the Michelsberg hill. Dupont took heavy casualties, but managed to fight until nightfall, then escaped eastward. His report went to Ney, then Napoleon, who got the news late on 12 October.

Back to Ulm

About midnight on 12–13 October the French emperor finally realized his errors; the thought of Mack's opportunities chilled his blood. In addition to cutting his supply lines, Mack might, in one fell swoop, capture the army treasury, siege guns, and ammunition trains; they were all near Ellwangen, 40 miles north of Ulm. There were few French combat troops north of the Danube to protect them.

Before dawn on 13 October, Napoleon and his Guard were rushing west toward Günzburg, cold and miserable, with freezing rain pummeling the troops and rattling off his carriage. He sent orders to Murat, Ney and Lannes to recross the Danube and engage the Austrians at Ulm, and damned the marshals for missing the Austrians and crossing the Danube. Napoleon blamed everyone but himself – and his abuse, to which they were accustomed, spurred them on. To support them, he ordered Soult through Memmingen on Ulm and Marmont westward on a more northerly route.

On the 14th, the Archduke Ferdinand fled Ulm with 6,000 troops, making for Prague (to deprive Napoleon of the pleasure of capturing a Habsburg, he said). Napoleon dispatched Murat and the cavalry in pursuit, and the Gascon cut down half of Ferdinand's men before dropping south to lead the Grande Armée toward Vienna. Three of Mack's "corps" had encountered the French south of the Danube and fled for Austria or the Tyrol. Of 70,000 troops in his army, Mack was left at Ulm with 27,000.

Late on 14 October, Ney re-took the wrecked Elchingen bridge. On the 15th he drove the Austrians from their positions on the Michelsberg and he and Lannes sealed them into Ulm. Early on the 16th, Soult and Marmont blockaded Ulm south of the Danube. On 16 October Napoleon began bombarding Ulm with all the guns he could muster. Mack refused to surrender or negotiate, but his generals defied him; on 20 October he surrendered. Mack's force of 27,000 marched out and laid down their arms.[19]

Napoleon reports

Napoleon was quick to get his version of the events on the record. On 17 October he wrote Talleyrand: "My plan has been executed just as I conceived it. I totally deceived the enemy, and of his army of 100,000 men; more than half have been captured, killed, wounded, or deserted."[20] On 19 October, he wrote Josephine: "I have accomplished my design; I have destroyed the Austrian army by simple marches."[21]

Bonaparte's letter to the foreign minister was intended to "inform" government circles, and that to the empress the salons of Paris. As usual, he exaggerated the number of Austrians captured, and attributed his victory to the exact execution of his plan. Actually, his victory was more amazing as accomplished, but he did not want to reveal that he had bypassed Mack, which would soil his image. The blame he placed on the marshals on 12–13 October was part of his "case." So was the reaction of his men, who joked, with a certain gratitude, that he had won with their legs, not their blood.

Mack surely would have done better if the Archduke Ferdinand had not challenged his decisions. He tried twice – on 9 and 12 October – to send his army into Napoleon's rear. If he had succeeded, Napoleon might have suffered a defeat, or, at the very least, victory would have been tougher to win.

Napoleon owed the victory at Ulm to Austrian bungling and his ability to scramble. Despite initial mistakes, he won. Much credit must go, however, to his marshals, particularly Ney, Lannes, and Murat – and his troops, who carried out his orders with alacrity. Another factor – one that Napoleon had never enjoyed before – was superior numbers, an advantage he would have until after the Russian campaign of 1812. *Ulm was a triumph of strategy, but also of improvisation.*

Trafalgar

On 21 October 1805, the day after Mack's surrender, Admiral Lord Horatio Nelson destroyed the core of the French and Spanish fleets off Cape Trafalgar. The Battle of Trafalgar spelled *finis* to Bonaparte's naval strategy.

On 15 September, after continually maligning Villeneuve, Napoleon told the minister of marine to order the admiral to France to explain himself.[22] Villeneuve, however, was bent on redeeming himself. On 21 October, he sailed from Cadiz and met Nelson off Cape Trafalgar. The Battle of Trafalgar was a disaster for Villeneuve, who lost twenty-two of thirty-three vessels, including his flagship. Nelson, with twenty-seven ships, lost not one. Villeneuve, who probably wanted to win or die in battle, survived, while Nelson was killed. Villeneuve was repatriated in 1806, and committed suicide. Lord Nelson's body was reverently preserved in a keg of wine and taken to London, where he was entombed in St Paul's Cathedral with honors of state.

Trafalgar, of course, established British control of the seas. Napoleon had caused this climactic encounter, ignoring that Villeneuve had long since served his purpose (surely for 1805).

Pursuing the Russians

Field Marshal Prince Mikhail Kutuzov, with 38,000 Russians, arrived on the Inn River (the Austro-Bavarian border) in October, heard of Mack's surrender, and did not cross. He was joined by some Austrian units which had eluded capture at Ulm, but the Emperor Francis refused to place them under his command. The next contingent of Russians (40,000 under Field Marshal Friedrich Buxhöwden) had just entered Moravia. Kutuzov decided to retreat into Moravia where he could unite the whole Russian army (80,000), and be reinforced by larger Austrian forces, perhaps those of the Archduke Charles, from Italy.

Kutuzov withdrew east along the Danube, leaving the Inn bridges burning, crossed to the north bank at Krems, 30 miles short of Vienna, and marched for Moravia.

On 26 October Napoleon sent Murat and the cavalry in pursuit the Russians. Murat and Lannes, whose corps was with Murat, chose to interpret the orders to mean *toward Vienna*, whereas Napoleon meant *follow the Russians*. Five corps followed Murat toward Vienna; only Mortier's corps marched down the north bank of the Danube. (Ney's corps was in the Tyrol, guarding the army's south flank.) Napoleon and Murat had neglected Mortier, but he escaped destruction because Kutuzov, who outnumbered him two to one, was focused on retreating north.

Murat, clashing off and on with the Russian rearguard, captured prisoners, who told him where Kutuzov was headed. On 6 November, he sent an officer to notify Napoleon who sent orders for Murat to pursue the Russians "sword in the backs" (*l'epée sur les reins*). Murat (who later said he didn't get the order), pressed on to Vienna, signalling Napoleon: "I see nothing that would delay Your Majesty's march on Vienna . . ." Napoleon was infuriated, but had to follow.[23]

Meanwhile, Murat and Lannes had entered Vienna (12 November), which had been declared an open city, parading with thousands of spectacular cavalry. Napoleon ordered Murat to seize the bridges north of Vienna. He got them by announcing that a truce was in effect. Murat and Lannes, two swaggering Gascons, personally intimidated the Austrian prince commanding the main bridge, and waved their men across.[24]

However, Murat then signed a real armistice offered by the wily Russian General Piotr Bagration. When Napoleon heard, he negated the truce and sent Murat to find the enemy.

Meanwhile in Italy

In September 1805 the Archduke Charles marched into the Kingdom of Italy from the east. His 50,000 troops (reduced from 90,000 by detachments in his rear) pushed back the Franco-Italian army (37,000) under Marshal Masséna. (Napoleon considered Eugene too young to command quite yet.) At the end of October, however, Charles heard of Mack's debacle at Ulm, and began withdrawing toward Vienna.

On 29–30 October, Masséna attacked his rear at Caldiero, but Charles counterattacked and they fought fiercely to a draw. Charles resumed his withdrawal, and on 26 November joined forces with the Archduke John at Marburg in Styria. After detachments, casualties, and desertions, they had 80,000 men, but were no immediate threat to Napoleon since they were 255 miles from Brünn. If battle were delayed, however, they would be.

Czar Alexander commands the Allies

Kutuzov united Russian forces (71,000 men) at Olmütz, and was reinforced with 15,000 Austrians, bringing Allied strength to 86,000. Czar Alexander I (28) then took comand. A tall, athletic figure, he fancied himself a general, and looked the part.

Meanwhile, Napoleon moved north to Brünn, 40 miles west of Olmütz, with the Guard, under Bessières; the corps of Lannes, Bernadotte and Soult were nearby. Murat's cavalry patrolled between Brünn and the Russians. The emperor's direct command comprised about 67,000 troops. Davout and Mortier were near Vienna, in position either to reinforce Napoleon or back up Marmont, who was south of Vienna to block the Archduke Charles if he arrived from Italy. Ney was moving through the Tyrol to Carinthia, with the same mission.

Kutuzov recommended that Czar Alexander wait to be reinforced by the Archduke Charles, and/or Ferdinand, who had 18,000 men in Prague. With both, they would have 184,000 men. Napoleon probably would have to fight with 70,000 or fewer. The Russians, however, were short on food and supplies. Kutuzov recommended that unless Charles arrived soon, Alexander should withdraw the Russians into Poland, resupply, and then link up with the Austrian armies again. He was certain that if they won battles, even in the spring of 1806, Frederick William III would bring Prussia into the alliance. Alexander would not listen. He had Napoleon outnumbered, 86,000 to 70,000 or fewer. His younger advisers, notably Prince Piotr Dolgorukov, told him he could win, and he was determined to try.[25]

On 27 November, Alexander advanced on Brünn. Both sides had pretended to negotiate for peace, which allowed them to send observers through enemy lines. Napoleon had encouraged the Russian movement by showing few troops. On 28 November he withdrew Marshal Soult's corps from the Pratzen plateau, between the armies. Alexander took it as further proof that the French were weak, and accelerated his advance.

Battle of Austerlitz (see Map 13)

On 1 December, Alexander carefully observed Napoleon's army, arrayed behind the Goldbach (brook). The French right (south) flank, was weakly held by part of Soult's corps. He decided to drive through and cut the Vienna road – the French supply line. He could then envelop the French army and destroy it, or at least turn the south flank and drive the French toward Prague – toward the army of the Archduke Ferdinand, while he pursued.

On 1 December, Napoleon had fewer than 67,000 troops, many not visible to Alexander. By the next morning, however, the French emperor was stronger. He had ordered part of Davout's corps (6,000 men) from Vienna, and Bernadotte, with 10,000 of his corps, south from the Prague highway (leaving Wrede's Bavarians to block Ferdinand).

At dawn on 2 December, Alexander attacked. In the next few hours, he sent 40,000 of his 86,000 men against the French south flank. He had 16,000 on the Pratzen, some 14,000 to the north advancing along the road from Olmütz, and his Guard and reserve cavalry (10,500 and 5,500) were between the two.

Davout (6,000), had arrived in the dark of morning after marching 70 miles from Vienna. Between dawn and 10.30 a.m. his men took the place of Soult's men on the Goldbach, covering the southern front of the army – 3 of its 7 miles. At the same time, 10,000 of Bernadotte's corps were behind Lannes (in the north); French strength was 73,000.

Davout drove back the Russians who had crossed the Goldbach, and met more as they arrived. The enemy outnumbered him four to one, but his men were the best trained in the army, and the terrain favored him. They were on dry ground, and the masses of Russian infantry marched into frozen marshes on the enemy side of the Goldbach, and soon found themselves knee-deep in mud and freezing water. Davout's infantry and artillery cut them down as they came. The czar, however, kept throwing more troops into the bloody killing ground, keeping doggedly to his plan.

Davout's corps became the anvil on which Napoleon hammered the Russian army. At about 10 a.m. the emperor ordered Soult to retake the Pratzen – "In fifteen minutes, Sire." But Russian Imperial Guards counter-attacked, and broke one of Soult's divisions. Napoleon committed Bessières, with the Imperial Guard cavalry, who drove them off. Soult, with Bessières and reinforcements from other corps, took the Pratzen.

At about 11 a.m., on Napoleon's order, Soult attacked southward from the Pratzen, driving the Russians in front of Davout toward the frozen rivulets, ponds, and marshes to the south. About 1 p.m., Davout's corps attacked across the Goldbach. The Russians were driven south and finally broke and fled across the marshes and ponds. The ice gave way and hundreds were drowned; the

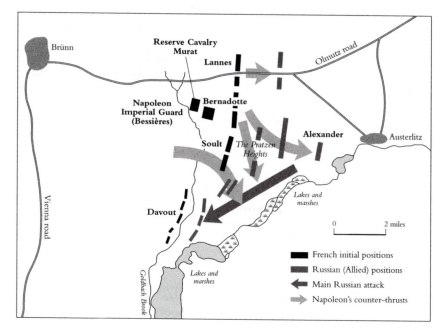

Map 13 Battle of Austerlitz, 2 December 1805

firm ground between the larger ponds was enfiladed by the French artillery, taking a hideous toll.

Meanwhile, Lannes' corps attacked east along the Olmütz highway; Bernadotte's and Murat's cavalry drove toward Austerlitz. By 4 p.m. the "sun of Austerlitz" (Napoleon's words) was setting and snow was falling, and the Russian army was in chaotic retreat. The czar had lost 25,000 men (10,000 killed); the rest took so many directions that Murat's cavalry could not find a major track to follow. Alexander barely escaped with his guard. Napoleon had an overwhelming victory.

Alexander refused to make terms, but merely marched away. The Austrian emperor, on the other hand, anxiously sued for peace, for which he paid dearly. (See below.)

Napoleon's tactical art

"On s'engage, et alors on voit," said Napoleon (Engage, and then wait and see). Austerlitz was *the* prime example of this system. Napoleon engaged the Allies, but kept a large reserve (the Guard, Murat's cavalry, and Bernadotte's corps). When Alexander's gross mistakes were evident, he committed his reserve and rolled to victory

127

A master tactician, he nevertheless could not have won without skilled subordinates, in this case Davout and Soult especially, and superbly trained and motivated troops, who executed his orders without question.

Austerlitz was a classic Napoleonic tactical triumph, but, like all Napoleon's victories, involved improvisation. None of Napoleon's battles was alike, but, unless conditions dictated something different (as at Waterloo), there was always the big reserve, the wait, the enemy mistake – the alteration of plans (improvisation) as necessary – and the attack.

At both Ulm and Austerlitz he accomplished what was always his purpose – to destroy the enemy army. Ulm was an improvised strategic victory; Austerlitz an improvised tactical victory. They marked Napoleon as one of the all-time masters of the art of military command.[26]

The profits of victory

Probably anticipating another war, Napoleon left most of the Grande Armée in Germany.

In the diplomatic settlements, Austria ceded Venice, most of Istria, and the Dalmatian Islands to France;[27] the Tyrol and Trentino to Bavaria, and her Swabian territories to Württemberg. She recognized Württemberg and Bavaria as kingdoms. France ceded Hanover to Prussia, but Napoleon knew that Prussia had been ready to join the Allies before Austerlitz.

In early 1806 – expanding his empire – Napoleon sent Masséna, with the Army of Italy, south to conquer Naples,[28] and made Joseph, his elder brother, king. Simultaneously, he sent Talleyrand to the Batavian (Dutch) Republic; he threated annexation to France, and the Dutch requested a Bonaparte king. Napoleon named his brother, Louis, king of Holland.[29]

In July 1806, Napoleon established the Confederation of the Rhine (*Rheinbund*), comprising most of the German states (and soon all but Prussia). As "protector," he took the place of the Holy Roman Emperor in Germany. Francis II abdicated the ancient title and restyled himself Francis I of Austria. The Holy Roman Empire disappeared – permanently, as it turned out.

Austria was too weak to resist in 1806, but Francis vowed ultimate revenge on Napoleon. He made the Archduke Charles head of the *Hofkriegsrat* and commander-in-chief of the army, which he was to reform and expand.

Prussia goes to war

Prussia had occupied Hanover, but in February 1806 Napoleon demanded that the treaty of December 1805 be renegotiated. Though outraged, Frederick William complied. He retained Hanover, but gave up Cleves and Auspech, in Germany, and Neuchâtel, in Switzerland. In June 1806, however, he heard that Napoleon was offering Hanover to Britain in return for peace. His military staff told him he had the army of Frederick the Great (which, unfortunately for him, he did, not an improved one). His nobles were already angry over

Napoleon's high-handed actions in Germany, particularly the creation of the Confederation of the Rhine, and ready for war.

In July 1806, Frederick William allied with Alexander I of Russia, with the warm approval of beautiful Queen Louise, more bellicose than he. (Napoleon, dazzled and impressed by her grit, said she was "the only man in Prussia.") In August, Prussia mobilized her forces – 250,000 men – with three field armies totalling 145,000. The Russians promised two armies of 60,000 each. Saxony, Brunswick, Hesse-Kassel, and other small states added a few thousand more.

Frederick William (or his commanders and staff) decided to strike at the French in Germany without waiting for the Russians. He planned to take his armies through the Thuringian forest to the Main River and destroy the Grande Armée before it got organized. The armies marched in September, and on 4 October were at Jena and Erfurt near the border of the *Rheinbund*.

Napoleon had left Paris on 21 September to take command of his army in Germany. (On 26 September, Frederick William had sent Napoleon an ultimatum – "evacuate" Germany or face war – but by that date it was irrelevant.) His ambassadors, still at the Prussian and Russian courts, had told him that the Prussians were on the march and that the Russians were not ready to join them.

Marshal Berthier had the Grande Armée ready and deployed in the vicinity of Bamberg, on the Main River. Napoleon played his usual pre-combat games, making misleading announcements about his marching schedule and exaggerating his numbers. On 6 October, he took command at Bamberg. He had 180,000 French, reinforced ultimately by 100,000 troops of his German allies.

Napoleon (37), was at the height of his powers; Marshal Davout (36), the cool, professional "Bald Eagle" was destined to be "co-victor" in this campaign. The six French corps were commanded by marshals whose records promised more glory – Lannes, Ney, Augereau, Mortier, Bernadotte, and of course Davout. Murat headed 20,000 reserve cavalry. The rough old Marshal Lefebvre commanded the Guard infantry (6,000) and the Gascon Marshal Bessières the Guard cavalry (2,500).

Except for the king (nominally in command), the Prussian generals were much older. The Duke of Brunswick (71), a more regal figure than the king, was in actual command of three armies, the largest (75,000) under himself, one of 40,000 under the Prince von Hohenlohe (60), and another of 30,000 under General Ernst Rüchel (52). Decision-making and coordination of the armies' actions were difficult; the king's opinions had to be honored; the staff was too large, and Brunswick and Hohenlohe were not on good terms.

To add to Prussian problems, Napoleon was upon them before they expected. He had struck northeastward without knowing the exact location of the enemy, but threatened to cut them off from Berlin. On 8 October, Brunswick was near Gotha; Hohenlohe east of him, along the Saale, and Rüchel to his west, near Eisenach. Brunswick ordered withdrawal toward Berlin. He planned to join the armies behind the upper Saale or the Elbe.

Napoleon, still not sure of the enemy's location, was advancing northward east of the Saale, with the army forming a rough square, ready for attack from any direction. He expected to draw his corps together when a major battle loomed, and routinely kept them within a day's march of each other.[30] Napoleon was moving toward Leipzig, with the idea of forcing Saxony out of the war, and denying the Prussian army the use of the fortress of Magdeburg, on the Elbe. The army "square" had the corps of Lannes and Augereau on the left, advancing along the Saale; the corps of Soult and Ney, and a Bavarian division under Jerome Bonaparte on the right, about 35 miles to the east, moving toward the Elster River line; between and ahead of these forces were the cavalry of Murat, followed by the corps of Davout and Bernadotte. On 10 October, at Saalfeld, Lannes met Prince Louis Ferdinand, commanding Hohenlohe's rearguard. He attacked with 25,000 men, and pinned the Prince, with only 9,000, against the Saale River. Louis was killed while charging the French with his cavalry. Napoleon wrote Lannes praising him and labeling Louis "the instigator of the war," justly punished by God.[31]

Napoleon decided, incorrectly, that that the Prussians were retreating north along the Elster River and would probably stand at Gera. Lannes' quick victory over only a small advance guard reinforced his fixation on Gera. He ordered Murat and Bernadotte to Auma, Soult and Ney to Gera, and Lannes and Augereau to continue north along the Saale.

On 11 October, the madcap Lasalle's cavalry galloped into Gera. Napoleon got there about noon with the Guard and more cavalry, followed by Bernadotte's corps, but found only Prussian supply units there. However, Lannes, on the Saale opposite Jena, seconded by Augereau and Davout, reported that there were large Prussian armies between Jena and Weimar. Spies, prisoners, and local residents confirmed it.

On 13 October, Napoleon confidently wrote Murat that the Prussian army was at Jena.[32] He ordered Augereau, Ney, Soult, and Murat to march for Jena, and he moved toward Jena with the Guard. He ordered Davout from Naumburg to Apolda, "in the enemy rear," along with Bernadotte, if he was nearby. The order was imprecise, and allowed Bernadotte to go instead to Dornburg; he did, and missed the battles of the 14th completely.

Meanwhile, on the 13th, Lannes crossed the Saale, took Jena and the Landgrafenberg, a key hill to the west. Napoleon joined him at about 4 p.m., confirmed his misconception that the Prussian Army (100,000 or more) was west of Jena, and started preparing for battle. In fact, the largest Prussian army – Brunswick with 64,000 men – was not facing the emperor, but was marching north toward Auerstädt, en route to the Elbe. In its path was the single corps of Marshal Davout, whom Napoleon pictured as in the enemy rear.

In the vicinity of Jena were 38,000 men under the Prince von Hohenlohe, supported by 15,000 under Rüchel at Weimar. They constituted the rear of Brunswick's army. Hohenlohe's right (22,000) was at Capellendorf, 5 miles from the French center, shortly near the Landgrafenberg; his left also 5 miles away at Dornburg. Directly in front of the French was one division (8,000 men) under General Boleslas Frederich Emmanuel Tauenzien.

Napoleon radiated confidence, but wanted insurance against attack by superior forces before all his units arrived – that is, before the morning of 14 October. The danger period was the night of 13–14 October. For the 14th he planned a massive attack on the Prussian center with double the enemy's forces.[33]

During the night of 13–14 October, Napoleon packed Lannes' corps (22,000) and the Guard (8,500), onto the Landgrafenberg. He had a road built to get his artillery to the highest point of the hill. There he put his command post, surrounded by the Guard, with Lannes corps behind him. Troops stood shoulder to shoulder on the hilltop.

Did this reflect Napoleon's apprehension at facing the "Army of Frederick the Great" and the fabled robot-like advance of its infantry? The Prussian Warrior king (d. 1786) was the only modern general he truly respected.[34] Considering that he had only one enemy division facing him, and that his artillery could barely reach the front ranks of the enemy, his preparations seem comic. He did not know, admittedly, that only one division faced him or that the Prussian army was a "paper tiger."

Battles of Jena and Auerstädt

At 6.30 a.m. on 14 October, Napoleon sent Lannes forward. He remained on the Landgrafenberg, with the Guard. The marshal was expected to attack through Clowitz, but in the half-light and fog his divisions got separated. One division took the village, but the rest of the corps moved south toward Vierzehnheiligen. About 9 a.m., Tauenzien's division attacked Lannes' flank, marching robotically (perhaps as in Napoleon's nightmares), in drillfield lines. They split the French, but were overwhelmed by French numbers. Augereau came up on Lannes' left and Ney, with his advance guard, appeared between the two and was badly shot up, but held and advanced. By 10 the French held Vierzehnheiligen. About 11 a.m., Hohenlohe counterattacked, but was stopped dead at Vierzehnheiligen by superior forces. He expected Rüchel's 13,000 men to arrive soon from Weimar, but Rüchel took four hours to cover the 6 miles from Weimar, and was too late to help.[35] Opposite Hohenlohe, Soult's corps and Murat's cavalry arrived, swelling Napoleon's army to 96,000. Just after noon, the French attacked in full force, and broke Hohenlohe's army, which fled in disarray. At 2.30 p.m., Rüchel appeared, and tried to attack through the fleeing troops of Hohenlohe's army. His infantry moved with frightening precision – to a point – but was put to flight by Hohenlohe's retreating horde.

Napoleon with 96,000 men (40,000 engaged) had defeated Hohenlohe (38,000; 33,000 engaged) and Rüchel (13,000). He had 5,000 casualties; the Prussians 11,000, plus 15,000 captured.

Ten miles to the north, near Auerstädt, Marshal Davout had won a more amazing victory. With a single corps of 26,000 men he had met the main Prussian army (64,000 men) under the Duke of Brunswick. Marching from Naumburg to Apolda, via the Kosen bridge (over the Saale), at about 6.30 a.m., Davout's advance guard collided with that of the Prussians at Hassenhausen. The marshal brought up his lead division and formed it into battallion squares. It threw back attacks by a Prussian division and twelve squadrons of cavalry under General Gebhard von Blücher (64), a hard-drinking, aggressive soldier and Francophobe, who had ridden all night to get there.[36]

At about 9 a.m., Davout brought up a second division and a brigade of cavalry. The Prussians attacked with four divisions and pushed the French back. However, about 9.30, the Duke of Brunswick was mortally wounded; King Frederick William assumed command, but luck was with Davout. At 11 a.m., when they seemed about to turn the French left flank, Davout's last division arrived, threw the Prussians back, and turned the enemy flank. By 1 p.m. the Prussian army was broken.[37]

Davout had won an astonishing victory, but not without cost. He had 8,000 casualties – almost one-third of his corps of 26,000. The Prussians lost 12,000, with 3,000 captured, and were scattered, so that later most units were unable to stand against the French. About 2 a.m. on the 15th, Napoleon got a detailed report on Davout's victory. "Your marshal . . . saw double today," he told the messenger. On the 16th, he wrote Davout a letter of congratulation, to be shared by his corps, which he gave the honor of leading the French into Berlin. No more. Napoleon's Bulletin called Jena–Auerstädt one battle – Jena – in which he commanded. "Jena" was emblazoned on the flags of regiments that were in either battle.[38] In 1808, two years later, when the twin battles were dim in the minds of the French, he gave Davout the title Duc d'Auerstädt.

Davout displayed no resentment, but rather wrote Napoleon praising his officers, especially the division commanders, and men. He reported honestly on the battle, and asked only for ammunition before he marched again. However, he also noted the death of Brunswick, and that the Prussian king, his two brothers, and an uncle had been at Auerstädt – proof that he had fought the main Prussian army.[39]

There is no doubt that Davout won the day; Napoleon had misjudged the Prussian positions and fought a lesser action. If Davout had not sent the major Prussian army flying in all directions, consequences would have been grave. The army might have escaped to join the Russians, which would have made final victory over the Allies more difficult, and maybe impossible.

Both victories were due in part to the ineptitude of the Prussians. Their premature offensive and late withdrawal made them vulnerable, and they made lesser blunders. Davout wrote he had an advantage at Auerstädt because he had reconnoitered the Kosen Heights and Saale bridge, and the Prussians had not.[40]

Jena–Auerstädt preyed on Napoleon's mind. On St Helena, he described the twin battles, emphasizing that Jena was crucial. Davout, he said, had merely blocked the enemy's escape across the upper Saale; if he had lost at Auerstädt, he could have held at Kosen with as few as 6,000 men. Bernadotte was at Dornburg, but his absence allowed Davout "to cover himself with immortal glory . . ." But "the victory was assured at Jena."[41]

In 1806, Napoleon felt he could not give major credit to Davout for destroying the Prussian army, since the fate of the empire depended on his military reputation. But on St Helena, he was stirring historical facts into a favorable stew.

Berlin and the Continental System
(*blocus continental*)

On 24 October 1806, Davout's III corps entered Berlin. Napoleon arrived on 27 October, after visiting the tomb of Frederick the Great in Potsdam. Meanwhile, French columns, often aided by Murat's cavalry, pursued the few organized units of the Prussian army. There were almost none left, when, on 7 November, Blücher gave up after a valiant attempt to hold Lübeck. The fortresses soon surrendered except on the Baltic, where Danzig and Königsberg (where the king and queen of Prussia took refuge) held out until the spring of 1807. However, only General Anton W. Lestocq, with 15,000 men (by February only 9,000), joined the Russians and fought on.[42]

On 21 November 1806, Napoleon issued the Berlin Decree, which initiated the Continental System, blockading Europe – or as much of it as Napoleon controlled – against British goods. He hoped to bankrupt Britain by ruining her trade with Europe. It announced a blockade of the British Isles – which he could not enforce, but hoped to – and closed European ports to British vessels, ships carrying British goods, or ships that had taken on cargoes at British or British colonial ports. In 1807, the Berlin Decree was strengthened by the Milan Decree, which mandated confiscation of all ships that touched a British port or submitted to search by the Royal Navy.

The decrees defended Freedom of the Seas, which appealed to the United States. However, Napoleon's words and actions did not jibe. French privateers plundered American merchantmen and French customs officials seized and impounded US vessels until mid-1811. Nevertheless, Napoleon managed to picture France as a better friend to the United States than Britain. In 1811, his bogus promises to stop French interference with American trade helped push the United States into the War of 1812 against Britain. In world perspective, the United States was "allied" with France in 1812 when Napoleon invaded Russia.

The Duchy of Warsaw

At the end of 1806, Napoleon's army of French and allied troops invaded Prussian Poland. After partial partitions, that of 1795 had divided the Kingdom of Poland among Prussia, Austria, and Russia. France, under Napoleon, had demonstrated the power to defeat all three. The Poles thus saw Napoleon as either their savior or only hope. Prince Josef Poniatowski, a Polish cavalier out of legend, led thousands of Poles into the war on the side of France. He recruited and led Polish troops in later campaigns. After that in Russia, Napoleon made Poniatowski a marshal (the only foreigner to be so honored). The Elector Frederick Augustus of Saxony also deserted Prussia; Napoleon made him a king.

Invasion of Poland

On 10 December Davout's corps and Murat's cavalry entered Warsaw, to cheering crowds. Poniatowski greeted them, and the Polish aristocracy entertained them lavishly. On 1 January, Napoleon arrived, and set up temporary headquarters.

Early on, Napoleon met the Countess Marie Walewska, a dazzling blonde of eighteen married to a nobleman in his sixties. Polish nobles – and reputedly even her husband – urged her to please the emperor for the sake of Poland; she became Napoleon's mistress. When he moved his headquarters for the winter campaign, she went with him, and later he brought her to Paris.[43]

The bitter winter campaign

In December 1806, the Russians initiated hostilities, and the Prussian king, prompted by spirited Queen Louise, refused to talk terms. Napoleon had little choice but to fight a war, sure to last through the winter of 1806–07, or longer. He did not want to prolong his absence from Paris. Already, he suspected, plots were being hatched, and the business community was nervous.

Worse, morale was flagging among Napoleon's troops. They had expected peace after the sweeping victories over the Prussians; instead they found themselves in the frozen wastes of Poland. Some cut off fingers, or mutilated their hands in order to be sent home. (Men were sent back if they couldn't use weapons.) Food was short; living off the land was impossible. The troops got hard tack and dried beef only before major battles. French officers had lost some of their enthusiasm. Napoleon still drew cries of "*Vive l'Empereur!*" but not with the spirit of earlier years. Even the Guards – the *grognards* – grumbled more than ever. Eventually, Napoleon solved the problem by bringing in replacements and supplies of food and drink. However, before he did, he had won major battles – a tribute to his leadership.

In December 1806, before Napoleon arrived, Marshal Count Alexander Kamenski (75) had marched on Warsaw with 70,000 Russians and 15,000 Prussians. Lannes' corps was beaten at Pultusk by General Theophil von Bennigsen's Russian corps, but Davout, Augereau, and Murat saved the day. The Russians went north to Königsberg. Czar Alexander shortly gave command of the Russo-Prussian army to Bennigsen (62), a Hanoverian with thirty-odd years' service in the Russian army.

In January 1807 Bennigsen ordered an offensive to the south, since Napoleon had spread his corps for wintering.[44] Bernadotte, backing the sieges of Danzig and Königsberg, and Ney, south of him, retired southward.

Napoleon, on 27 January, ordered a counter-offensive. Bennigsen fell back on his first encounter with the French – Murat's cavalry and Soult's corps – and retreated into East Prussia. On 3 February, at Ionkovo, Bennigsen made a stand, but Napoleon could not assemble enough men to win before sunset, and the Russians withdrew. Napoleon angrily ordered pursuit.

Eylau (see Map 14)

On 7 February 1807, Murat and Soult reached Eylau, in East Prussia. They were joined by Augereau, and then Napoleon, with the Guard. In dark and bitter cold, the marshals fought a bloody battle to take Eylau and gain shelter for the troops.

At dawn on 8 February, Bennigsen's army was arrayed on a long ridge east of Eylau. Napoleon was happy to see the Russians make a stand, confident that he could beat them and end the war. He was outnumbered, but had 45,000 men and 200 guns, and Davout (15,000 and 48 guns) was marching from Bartenstein, 15 miles southeast. He sent orders calling in Bernadotte and Ney. Bernadotte was too far away to reach Eylau before the battle, however, and Ney was chasing Lestocq's Prussians and arrived very late. Only Davout effectively reinforced Napoleon.

The Russians began the battle at 8 a.m. by bombarding Eylau with artillery. At 8.30 Napoleon sent Soult's corps, spread north and south of Eylau, against the Russian right. He hoped the Russians would commit themselves on their right, against Soult; if so, he would throw the rest of his force against the Russian left and win the battle. But he needed Davout, who had not arrived.

Soult's divisions attacked over frozen ground, with falling snow in their faces, were bloodied and disorganized by Russian artillery, and thrown back on Eylau by infantry. Napoleon ordered Augereau to attack with his corps. The marshal was ill, and led the troops forward with his head wrapped in a huge scarf, topped by his hat. His corps was in disarray from the start, because the emperor's order came so early, and suddenly there was heavy snowfall, which hid the enemy. Augereau's men marched headlong into a Russian battery of seventy guns, which fired at point-blank range and cut them down by hundreds, then the Russian infantry came on, and the corps broke apart. By 10.30 a.m. Augereau's corps was destroyed as a fighting unit. Soult was back in his original position at Eylau and too weak to attack. Napoleon seemed on the way to defeat.

There was still the cavalry, however. Napoleon decided to use it to knock the Russians off balance. He ordered Murat to attack with every horseman he had – 11,000 reserve cavalry, the Guard cavalry (Bessières), and surviving corps

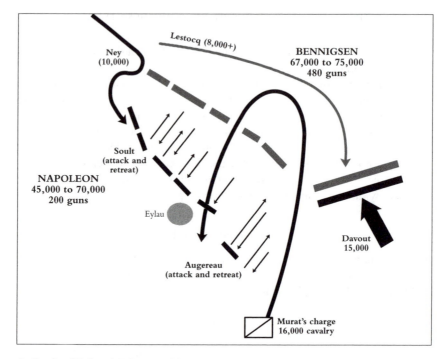

a) Battle of Eylau, 8 February 1807

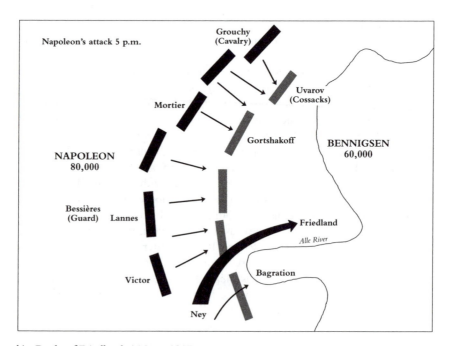

b) Battle of Friedland, 14 June 1807

Map 14 Battles of Eylau and Friedland, 1807

cavalry – a total of over 16,000 horse. The Gascon rode at the Russians with his usual bravado, waving his gold cane instead of drawing his sword.

The maneuver worked. Bennigsen was taken totally by surprise, and apparently went into shock. Instead of attacking with his stolid masses of infantry against the French center, which had very little infantry left, he held fast.

Just before Murat's attack, Russian infantry had overrun Napoleon's command post in the Eylau cemetery. Bonaparte was saved by his escort of the day, 100 Guards, but then took command of a Guard battalion and forced the Russians back.

About 1 p.m., Davout arrived. He attacked Bennigsen's left, and turned the Russian flank; by about 3.30 the French seemed to be winning. However, at this moment, Lestocq's 9,000 Prussians, who had arrived from the north, attacked Davout and forced his tired and hungry men to give ground. At nightfall, Napoleon's lines were at the same place in the center, and forward on his right by about half a mile.

Ney, who had been following the Prussians, had received orders to reinforce Napoleon at about 2 p.m.; he arrived at 7 p.m. He made a pass at the Russian north flank, but did no good in the dark, and fell in on the north end French line.

Neither side had won, but two of Napoleon's four corps had been so badly shot up as to be ineffective. The late-coming corps were understrength; Ney had 10,000; Davout had arrived with 15,000, but had lost men. The cavalry was decimated, although more men had survived than horses, which had been the preferred targets of the Russian infantry, and many had fallen and broken legs on the frozen ground. Only the Guard was reasonably intact. Discounting casualties, Napoleon had never had over 60,000 men and 248 guns. Bennigsen had 67,000 men and 460 guns, and 75,000 men (minus casualties) and perhaps 500 guns after Lestocq arrived at about 3.30 in the afternoon.[45]

Bennigsen had taken heavy casualties, perhaps 15,000, but was left with at least 60,000 organized effectives, and a two-to-one advantage in artillery. However, he was uncertain of French strength – two corps had noisily come up at day's end; were more on the march? He knew Napoleon's reputation, and he was old, cold, and exhausted. In the black of a freezing night he had too many doubts to believe he could win if he fought the next day. The odds were in his favor, but he could not see it. He withdrew during the night.

Napoleon was left with the field, and could count Eylau a victory. "*War*," he said later, "*is three-quarters an affair of morale . . . other factors count only for another quarter.*"[46]

Napoleon admitted 7,600 casualties, but probably had twice that. The Russians lost 15,000. At dawn on 9 February, the French saw a battlefield littered with corpses – men and horses frozen in contorted positions among the wreckage of wagons and caissons. The sight shocked even Napoleon, who wrote Josephine, "The victory is mine, but I have lost many men; I am not consoled that the losses of the enemy were greater."[47]

The battle settled nothing, so the campaign went on.

The French and Russian armies went into winter quarters. The major action was at Danzig, under siege by Lefebvre's corps.

Napoleon spent the cold months in the castle of Finkenstein. He managed to run the French government and perform an astounding miscellany of tasks, including organizing a school for young women at Ecouen, allocating spaces to the daughters of men killed in action.[48] Madame Walewska was there to comfort him.

Napoleon's priority, of course, was the restoration of army strength and morale. He dispatched Augereau – a very sick man – to France and called Masséna to replace him. He also sent home the wounded and deranged, called up 100,000 French conscripts, and demanded more men from allied states. The Grande Armée in Poland reached 200,000 men, with 100,000 in reserve in Germany. He had horses purchased for the cavalry in Germany – Prussian Trakehners and warmbloods from Bavaria, Hesse, and Württemberg. The veterans were allowed to rest and got better rations. The army gained new spirit.

Bennigsen also had rebuilt the Allied army, and had 90,000 men under his (and Lestocq's) command – 30,000 in the Tilsit area and 20,000 opposite Masséna's corps near Warsaw.

The Friedland campaign (see Map 14)

Napoleon's plan for the spring was to destroy the enemy army – his aim in every war. Lefebvre's corps took Danzig on 27 May 1807, which removed a threat to his rear (Allied troops and supplies came through its port). Napoleon felt free to mount a full-scale offensive, but his corps were still widely separated.

Bennigsen knew the French positions from reports of his Cossacks. He planned to planned to destroy the French piecemeal by attacking the nearest corps (Bernadotte), and then the others. For that purpose he assembled 90,000 men north of the Passarge River, but the plan failed because Lestocq attacked prematurely. Because their subordinates knew neither German nor French well, they communicated poorly, but another problem was that Lestocq was an impetuous commander and a poor subordinate.[49] Bennigsen sent Lestocq to defend Königsberg, the Allies' remaining major port on the Baltic, and he took on the French.

Napoleon marched five corps, the reserve cavalry, and the Guard on Heilsberg. His plan was to drive a wedge between Bennigsen and Lestocq, and then overwhelm Lestocq at Königsberg. On 10 June, the French took Heilsberg in an all-day battle. Nevertheless Bennigsen, keeping the Alle River betwen him and the French, continued to move northeast.

Napoleon ignored Bennigsen's actual path, since he was convinced he was headed for Königsberg. He sent the corps of Soult and Davout, and most of the Murat's cavalry – over 60,000 troops – toward Königsberg. He ordered the corps of Victor, Ney, Mortier, and Lannes to follow, but about 40 miles behind, with the left and right 40 miles apart. Lannes was on the right of the army – alone and exposed on the Alle River.

Bennigsen, meanwhile, reinforced Lestocq at Königsberg to 25,000 troops, which left him with 60,000. Bonaparte, contrary to his own rules, had again spread his corps, and was vulnerable to an attack from the east by Bennigsen.

On 13 June 1807, Bennigsen was moving north along the east bank of the Alle River when his Cossacks reported that there was a small French unit just across the river, west of Friedland. They guessed that it was a French division with some cavalry and artillery. In fact, it was Lannes' corps (18,000+), but that probably would have made no difference to the Russian commander.

Bennigsen ordered his army (60,000) across the river to crush the isolated French unit. There were only three narrow bridges, so the crossing took all night.

Lannes notified Napoleon, at Eylau, 15 miles west, who got the message at about 9 p.m. The emperor immediately ordered Mortier (15 miles from Friedland) to reinforce Lannes, and at 10 Ney, who had 25 miles to march.

Napoleon then returned to remote-controlling the attack on Königsberg, dictating instructions for Murat, who was in command there. He believed that Bennigsen would fight a major battle only to protect Königsberg. However, by 2 a.m. (14 June), reading Lannes' urgent reports of a Russian build up, Napoleon decided that a major battle might develop at Friedland. At 4 a.m. he marched with the Guard, Victor's corps, and three cavalry divisions.

Meanwhile, Lannes held the Russians at bay. He had his infantry in high wheat, which hid their numbers, with most of his cavalry on his left flank, under Emmanuel Grouchy, matching Platoff's Cossacks. He held the Russians back all night, giving little ground. About 7 a.m. part of Mortier's corps joined him, raising his numbers to 26,000, and at about 9 a.m. the rest came, bringing French strength to 32,000.

At noon on 14 June, Napoleon arrived with almost 50,000 men. He had been listening to the thunder of Russian artillery as he rode, and the enemy masses persuaded him that Bennigsen was there with his whole army – 80,000 or more. (He did not know about the reinforcements sent to Lestocq.)

Napoleon sent orders to Murat to take Königsberg at all speed – without theatrical charges – and march, with the cavalry and Davout's corps, for Friedland. He said he might hold the enemy back with artillery fire until the next day, but Murat and Davout must arrive by 1 p.m. That would give him numerical superiority. He already had that, but did not know it.[50]

Napoleon reconnoitered the enemy positions, using binoculars from the high ground at Posthenen, well behind Lannes' line, then closer up. He sent his aides to look at enemy positions and report.[51] As he learned about the Russian positions he became more and more optimistic, and finally concluded that Bennigsen had trapped himself. His back was to the river, and he could not withdraw quickly over three bridges. Moreover, Napoleon realized that he outnumbered Bennigsen, and more troops were coming.

By 5 p.m., all his troops had come up, and the emperor was jubilant, shouting to the troops that it was the anniversary of Marengo. They shouted back *Vive l'Empereur!* Napoleon was certain that he could roll over the enemy, and had decided to attack frontally and drive the Russians into the Alle River.

Napoleon ordered Ney to make the main attack on the Russian left (south) flank, break it, and drive the enemy into and through Friedland. His corps had all but missed the Battle of Eylau, and was fresh. The corps of Lannes and Mortier and Grouchy's cavalry were to hold fast. Victor's corps and the Guard were in reserve.

By 5.30, Ney's infantrymen and Latour-Maubourg's cavalry were storming through the Sortlack Forest. By 6 p.m. all the enemy in the south was jammed into Friedland; the village and the bridges were afire. The Russians to the north were bravely attempting a counter-attack, but to no avail. A half-hour later Lannes and Mortier moved forward; Grouchy, on the high ground, watched the Cossacks opposite him retreat up the Alle River. At 10.30 p.m. the battle was over, with Russian survivors still trying to swim the Alle River. Russian losses were about 30,000, half of them killed, burned alive, or drowned. French casualties were heavy – 10,000 – but a climactic battle had been won.

The remnants of Bennigsen's army were demoralized and scattered. On 15 June, the day after Friedland, Lestocq abandoned Königsberg and marched to link up with Bennigsen, but further fighting was impossible. Murat's cavalry moved swiftly east from Königsberg, with the corps of Davout behind him and the corps from Friedland following. The campaign was over.

Lannes, of course, deserves much credit for the victory. The most handsome of the marshals held the field with 18,000 men (against 60,000) through the night of 13–14 June and almost until midday on the 14th. He gave Napoleon time to bring in 80,000 men, a mass that could crush Bennigsen's army. General Emmanuel Grouchy, commanding Lannes' cavalry, fought off the Cossacks and denied them an accurate idea of Napoleon's strength.

Napoleon mustered his force in relative concealment, and thus achieved some surprise. *It is disappointing, however, to see the master of maneuver using greater numbers for victory. He would come to depend too much on mass in succeeding years, which led to carelessness on his part.*

Tilsit

Bennigsen advised the czar, through his brother, the Grand Duke Constantine, to make peace. "It is not combat any more, but a veritable butchery." On 19 June Alexander asked for a truce. Napoleon assented. On 25 June 1807, at Tilsit, the emperor and the czar met in a theatrical setting, on a raft in the center of the Niemen River – the border between Russia and Europe. Napoleon undertook to charm the czar, and Alexander responded in kind. Afterward, there were parties for the monarchs and their military and civil officers. The grenadiers of the French Guard entertained the czar's grenadier guards, and so it went.

Alexander and Napoleon inspected each other's armies, with the French emperor most fascinated by the czar's exotic troops – Cossacks, Kalmouks, and Baskirs.

Napoleon proposed a division of power between Russia and France in Europe – and a future division of the Ottoman Empire between them, to which the czar readily agreed. Talleyrand, not high on loyalty, told the czar that Napoleon could not be trusted, but Alexander would not listen. Bonaparte found it convenient to blame the war on Prussia. Russia was to lose no territory; the czar was to join the Continental System, but was allowed to delay his decision until he attempted to mediate peace between France and England (which of course failed).

Napoleon was much taken with Louise, the Queen of Prussia, who was beautiful, spirited, and outspoken. However, he was not so enthralled as to be soft on Prussia.

In what had been the Prussian part of Poland, Napoleon created the Duchy of Warsaw,[52] giving Poles hope for the resurrection of the Kingdom of Poland. Prussian lands west of the Elbe, and those of her allies – Brunswick, Hesse-Kassel, and lesser states, plus part of Hanover, became the Kingdom of Westphalia, to be ruled by Napoleon's brother Jerome. Murat's Duchy of Berg, enlarged, became a Grand Duchy. Prussia had to join the Continental System, pay an indemnity of 140 million francs, and support French troops in her fortresses until it was paid. Prussia, like Russia, allied with France, but reluctantly.

Napoleon's power was at an all-time high, but he was not satisfied. Spain and Portugal were not yet part of his empire.

10

"THAT MISERABLE SPANISH AFFAIR": THE PENINSULAR WAR, 1808–13

"That miserable Spanish affair [the Peninsular War] is what doomed me," Napoleon told Las Cases in exile (1816) on St Helena.[1] He blamed his "disasters" on the war in Spain and Portugal, and said it "opened a school for English [British] soldiers."[2] Indeed. Britain's army in Portugal and Spain got experience under Arthur Wellesley, one of Napoleon's few peers as a commander, who left Iberia as Duke of Wellington. He trained Portuguese troops also, and eventually commanded all troops in Spain and Portugal.

In Iberia, French armies sustained 300,000 casualties (some 260,000 French or foreigners in French service; 40,000 in the armies of Naples, Westphalia, and other allied states). Spanish resistance, especially guerrilla attacks, and the action of Wellington's forces, surely put a strain on Napoleon's troops. However, they were not demoralized; they fought well to the end if well commanded. Conscripts, however, were prone to desertion if assigned to Spain.[3] The French Empire poured 3,000 million francs in gold into the Peninsula, and many times that in arms, materiel, horses, etc. It weakened the Empire long before the Russian disaster (1812). The people's resistance (or the *perception* of it) encouraged Napoleon's enemies elsewhere.

Napoleon never fought Wellington in Iberia. (He was there only two and a half months, 4 November 1808 to 16 January 1809). He delegated command of French forces, but of course sent the commanders orders from Paris, with scant effect. The failure of Napoleon's subordinates raises questions about how the whole marshalate were chosen, whether they were ever intended for independent command, and how new generals, some of whom appeared in 1813 and 1814, were or would be produced.

Napoleon himself never attempted to answer these questions, but said on St Helena: "My presence was indispensable anywhere I wanted to win a victory. It was a flaw in my armor: None of my generals had the force for a large independent command."[4]

Napoleon's decision not to command in person in Iberia raises questions about his judgment. However, *the Peninsular War is of little use in analyzing his ability as a commander*. This chapter will be brief.[5]

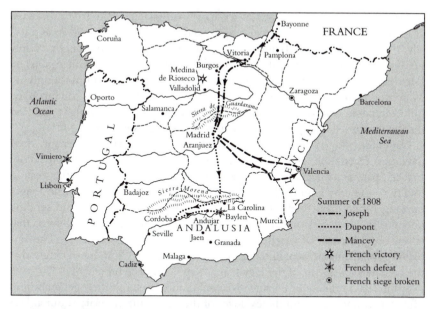

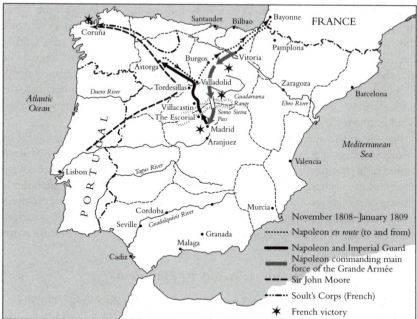

Map 15 Napoleon in Spain and Portugal, 1808–09

Spain and Portugal: Napoleon's views

In 1807, Napoleon's empire was larger than Charlemagne's had been a thousand years before, but he wanted to add Spain and Portugal. He saw Spain as a bad ally;[6] Portugal as a *de facto* British ally. Iberia was dangerous, he thought, mainly because the British navy could land troops in either country at will. Spain and Portugal were trading with the British – Portugal openly, Spain under guises. Moreover, Napoleon considered that the Spanish king, Charles IV, had furnished him unreliable troops, antiquated warships (many sunk at Trafalgar), and no money (promised 1803), to remain neutral; he was at war anyway (1804).

Napoleon judged the governments of Spain and Portugal corrupt, their dynasties degenerate, and their people under feudal and Church oppression. In fact, Spain was still almost medieval. The people's "nationalism" was a zealous loyalty to the crown and the Church. The Inquisition was active, if no longer burning infidels, but banning books (particularly French ones) and sending liberal officials to jail or exile. (The people were taught, and believed, that it was the protector of Christian Spain against Moslems and Jews.) The vast majority of Spaniards were illiterate peasants, whom the Church had taught that the French were agents of the Devil, and Napoleon his representative.

Spain was dominated by Prince Manuel Godoy, first minister, generalissimo of the army and navy, and the ex-lover of the aging queen, Maria Louisa. Her husband, Charles IV, was subject to spells of illness and not very bright; when healthy he was absorbed with hunting, and his horses and dogs. Ferdinand, the crown prince, intrigued constantly to seize the crown and to ruin Godoy. Ferdinand (24) was dumpy and ugly, but prince charming to his subjects; he was their only hope for better times. Many Spanish nobles and some liberals backed his plots, but if caught, he betrayed them to save himself. In Portugal, the prince regent, John (the queen was insane), though officially neutral, worked hand in glove with the British.

Napoleon was sure that the people (surely in Spain) would be grateful if he changed things – a gross misconception. Irrational as it seemed, the Spanish would fight, nominally for king and Church – at least in 1808, though afterward their enthusiasm flagged.[7] Loyalty to Ferdinand is subject to doubt; a catchphrase among guerrillas was "Viva Fernando y vamos robando!" ("Long live Fernando; let's go robbing!")[8] At any rate, some sort of resistance persisted, and Wellington, with his British and Portuguese army, stood ready to help as opportunity arose.

Godoy sells out to Napoleon

Napoleon saw that Godoy would be finished (probably killed) when Charles IV died or was overthrown. Thus, secretly, he promised Godoy a kingdom in southern Portugal, Lusitania, the Roman name for the area. Napoleon, by the Treaty of Fontainebleau (27 October 1807), was authorized to send an army across Spain to invade Portugal and station a 40,000-man "reserve" at Bayonne (on the French–Spanish border). The reserve's real mission was the conquest of Spain.

In November 1807, General Andoche Junot, with 28,000 men, marched to Lisbon, substantially without opposition, and assumed governance of Portugal. The Portuguese royal family and thousands of followers were ferried to Brazil on British battleships.

Napoleon had moved to Bayonne, with his court and military staff; French troops were moving into Spain. In March 1808 he gave command of the Armée d'Espagne (100,000 men) to Marshal Murat. Bessières (22,000) guarded the Bayonne–Madrid route; Duhesme (12,000) was in Catalonia, but blockaded in Barcelona; Verdier (16,000) in Aragon; and Murat (42,000) was approaching Madrid, with two corps (Dupont and Moncey), and a detachment of Imperial Guards. Some 8,000 were crossing the border at Bayonne. The French "allies" marched with flags flying and bands playing.

Since Godoy had not alerted the Spanish army, fortress commanders decided whether to welcome or fight them. In Catalonia, Duhesme had entered Barcelona in February 1808 with 12,000 men, but was then besieged by the Catalans, and was not rescued until January 1809. Catalans were jealous of their freedom; they had "shown the knife" even to Charlemagne; Catalonia was never truly subdued. In the west, on the *camino real* to Madrid, resistance was scant. Murat paraded to Madrid.

Murat in Madrid

Initially, Madrid was friendly. On 23 March, amid cheers and applause, Murat entered on a prancing black stallion, wearing a green velvet uniform, red boots, a black shako with white plumes and diamonds, and a black cloak, lined in red. His army entered, led by Imperial Guardsmen, each regiment with its flags (Eagles), trumpeters and drummers, followed by cavalry, artillery and infantry, and a detachment of turbaned Mamelukes.

The populace assumed that Murat supported Ferdinand VII, the former crown prince, who, on 19 March, had overthrown his father at the summer palace in Aranjuez. On 27 March, Ferdinand, lightly escorted, rode into Madrid and called on Murat. Through the marshal, he appealed to Napoleon recognize him, and asked (as he had before) for a Bonaparte bride. He offered Godoy, his captive, to Napoleon. (The prince had hidden in an attic, rolled in a rug, for two days, but had been forced out by thirst.) Charles IV and Maria Luisa also sent fawning messages of respect, asking for aid in recovering their throne, and the queen begged for Godoy's life. Napoleon was delighted. Both kings and the queen were at his mercy. He believed the worst of all three, and ordered Murat to send all the Bourbons to Bayonne – the kings, the queen – and anyone with a claim to the throne. The old monarchs and Godoy went happily. Ferdinand hesitated, since Spanish supporters and agents in British pay were pressing him to flee and lead an armed resistance, but he lacked the courage, and went to

Bayonne. On 5 May Napoleon forced both monarchs to abdicate, and sent them, their relatives, and Godoy into exile in France.

Napoleon had summoned Joseph Bonaparte from Naples to be king of Spain, and he arrived belatedly on 7 June. Naples went to Marshal Murat and his wife, Caroline Bonaparte, as joint rulers. Napoleon knew that Joseph was no soldier, but did not think he needed to be.

Dos de Mayo

On 2 May (*Dos de Mayo*), a riot began outside the royal palace when French cavalry brought up a carriage to take away Don Francisco, the last of the royal children. People assailed the cavalry, who cut their way out, so they tore the carriage to pieces. Word spread and all Madrid rose against the French.

Napoleon had expected little trouble in Spain – except in Madrid. Thus he had instructed Murat, in detail, how to give the *Madrileños* a "whiff of grape-shot," even to placement of cannon. Murat had his troops poised on the outskirts of Madrid, ready to move down streets, which, like spokes of a wheel, ran to the Puerta del Sol in the center of the capital. Infantry, bayonets fixed, and cavalry drove the rioters toward the central plaza. They bypassed strongpoints held by Spanish regulars (and took them later). Plazas en route, and finally the Puerta del Sol, were swept by cannon fire and then overrun by troops. The Spanish had no firearms, but fought valiantly with kitchen knives, tools, sticks, and stones. They rained chamber pots, cook pots, furniture and roof tiles on the French from windows and housetops, but all in vain. By mid-afternoon Madrid was quiet. Next morning firing squads executed alleged leaders and men caught with weapons. Madrid did not rise again against the French, but Spain was not cowed as Napoleon had expected. He had a war on his hands.

French atrocities of the *Dos de Mayo*, notably of the Mamelukes (eighty-six men of the 40,000) fuelled the anger of Spaniards. The Mamelukes, showered with refuse and missiles from above, had entered buildings, beheaded men, women, and children, and rolled their heads down stairs. The stories became grist for rebel propaganda. Napoleon, the rebels wrote over and over, had brought in Moslems – Moors! – to persecute Christians.

Spain rebels

So quietly that Napoleon ignored it, a grass roots rebellion blazed up throughout Spain. It was inspired in good part by Spanish clergy, notably monks and friars, who considered Napoleon a servant of the Devil. Some took up arms and raised bands of guerrillas.[9] Provincial juntas formed; country nobles, threatened by peasants, and fearful that Napoleon would abolish their privileges, joined in; some led troops. Liberal nobles were sometimes killed, but most joined the rebels. Liberals soon dominated the rebel government – in Madrid in 1808, but in 1810 barricaded in Cadiz and protected by the Royal Navy. Liberal *afrancesados* (francophiles), served King Joseph.

During 1808 and early 1809, volunteers swelled the ranks of the old Bourbon army, but after the first year the people evidently decided the war was won; at least they did not care to participate. The rebel government mandated conscription, but could never enforce it; Spain suffered more from evasion and desertion than France.[10] The armies were often large, but dissolved after a hard battle. Although there were able generals, such as the Marquis de La Romana, Don José Palafox, and Don Francisco Castaños, their officers were undependable, and their armies fragile.[11] The guerrilla bands probably did more damage to the French, although many were at least part-time thieves and pillagers; as time went on, patriot guerrillas became part of the Spanish army.

Junta of Bayonne

In May 1808, Napoleon assembled a Spanish National Junta at Bayonne and was grandly pleased – and misled – by it. Eminent men, largely nobles and churchmen, attended – the Prince de Castelfranco, the Dukes del Parque and d'Infantado – liberals such as Francisco Cabarrus, Gonzalo O'Farrill, Pedro Cevallos, and Don Manuel Romero – two archbishops and the heads of the Franciscan and Dominican orders. The Cardinal de Bourbon, cousin of Charles IV, and Spain's most famous writer, Gaspar Jovellanos, wrote to wish Joseph well.

Joseph Bonaparte seemed to make a crashing impression. In fact, the Comte de Toreño wrote later that if he had not represented Napoleon, the Spanish would have accepted him. An enlightened monarch in Naples, he was socially adroit, handsome, taller than Napoleon, intelligent, a liberal and gentle soul, and something of a *philosophe*.

The junta approved a liberal constitution. On 7 July, Joseph was crowned by the Archbishop of Burgos. On 9 July, he and his ministers (all Spanish) left for Madrid, escorted by Imperial and Royal (mostly French) Guards.

King José Napoléon

En route to Madrid, Joseph wrote to Napoleon expressing increasing anxiety. The Spanish in most villages, he said, stared at him sullenly or there were none in sight. There were places where all doors and windows were boarded up. The emperor tried to reassure him: Remember the grandees at Bayonne; the better people are on your side. Joseph finally said he would go to Madrid, but if the Spanish didn't want him, he did not care to rule. "I would not live long enough to atone for all that evil."

Nevertheless, Joseph asked to command French troops in Spain. General René Savary (who replaced Murat in Madrid), he wrote, was not even keeping him informed. The emperor made Joseph commander, which both would shortly regret.

On 20 July 1808, Joseph entered Madrid – silent and with rags hung from windows and balconies. Almost at once, some of his Spanish followers began deserting him. Men such as Don Pedro de Cevallos, minister of foreign affairs, had polite excuses. Minor officials and servants simply disappeared. It was a week before the king knew why.

Unexpected French defeats

On 20 July 1808, at Bailen, in Andalusia, General Pierre Dupont's corps of 20,000 had been captured by Francisco Castaños's Spanish army of 33,000, partly untrained volunteers.

Displaying the confidence inspired by Napoleon, Dupont had marched to conquer Andalusia with one infantry division (of three in his corps) and some cavalry. On 16 June, after looting Cordoba, he heard of Spanish armies nearby, and withdrew to Andujar, north of the Gaudalquivir, where his men vegetated for a month. Madrid sent his other infantry divisions, but he failed to concentrate his corps, and they were of no help.

On 18 July, Dupont retreated from Andujar toward Bailen and La Carolina, but his men were weak from idleness, and soon lacked water (in the blazing July sun). Theador Reding, a Swiss general, blocked him at Bailen, and Castaños closed in behind. On 20 July, Dupont signed an armistice, and shortly surrendered his corps (17,635; over 2,800 were dead, wounded, or missing).

Just after Joseph got news of Bailen, Marshal Jeannot de Moncey reached Madrid from Valencia. He, like Dupont, had left to conquer Valencia with one division and a few cavalry. On 27 June he had stormed the city of Valencia and lost 1,000 of his 8,000 men, and, under threat from other rebel armies, retreated.[12]

Joseph had asked to command: now he had to make decisions. He had 35,000 troops in Madrid and 20,000 on the highway to Bayonne. Rebel strength was unknown (but was actually fewer than the king's). But Joseph opted to take no chances (his generals agreed). On 31 July the king evacuated Madrid and retreated northward. By early August his army was north of the Ebro. Napoleon accused him of retreating into France.

The emperor soon had more bad news. On 21 August 17,000 British, under Sir Arthur Wellesley (Wellington), had defeated Junot at Vimeiro, north of Lisbon. Junot, overconfident, had attacked with only 13,000 men. Wellesley was in defensive positions on hills, with many of his men hidden on the reverse slopes (still his method at Waterloo). Junot attacked repeatedly, with dash and valor, but was shot to pieces. His infantry met steady aimed fire, and when close, a final volley and a bayonet charge that broke them.[13] Junot agreed to evacuate Portugal; the Royal Navy transported his army to France.

Napoleon reacts

Napoleon was blue with anger for days, sometimes manhandling generals bound for Spain, shouting that they must punish the Spanish. Actually, he had decided to go to Spain and set matters straight. He persuaded Czar Alexander to keep the peace in the north, and marched most of the Grande Armée to Spain, where it expanded the Armée d'Espagne (but for clarity, we shall call it the Grande Armée or the French Army.) By 1 November, Napoleon had 300,000 troops on the Ebro.

Napoleon meant to annihilate the Spanish armies, and force the people to accept Joseph. In Madrid, a rebel junta governed in the name of Ferdinand VII. The defeat at Bailen had encouraged his enemies all over Europe. Rebel propaganda spoke of the "visit" of Joseph (Pepe Botellas; Joe Bottle) to Madrid.

The emperor!

At midnight, 5 November 1808, Napoleon secretly arrived at Vitoria. The next morning, a sixty-gun salute announced his presence; French troops cheered. The emperor would command then, not Don José (Joseph).

Napoleon froze Joseph out of his own headquarters, and undertook to intimidate the Spanish. Their soldiers were no match for the victors of Austerlitz and Eylau, he proclaimed. To an order of friars suspected of encouraging guerrillas, he shouted that if they persisted he would cut off their ears.

The Spanish had fewer than 90,000 troops opposite his 300,000. Moreover, most of the soldiers were green, and very provincial. The Catalans would fight only in Catalonia. There were six other armies on the line (Galicia, Castile, León, Aragon, Andalusia, and Estremadura), all understrength and with gaps between them. There was no central command.

Napoleon marches

On 9 November, the French army marched. Marshal Victor's corps, on the right wing, scattered the army of Don Joaquin Blake. On the French left, Lannes, Moncey, and Ney forced Castaños into retreat and drove Don José Palafox behind the walls of Zaragoza. In Catalonia, Gouvion Saint-Cyr battled toward Barcelona against the only staunch resistance.

Napoleon drove for Madrid with the corps of Soult, Junot, Mortier, Lefebvre, and Victor, plus the Imperial Guard and 50,000 reserve cavalry (half as many horsemen as the Spanish had soldiers). On 10 November his force rolled over Burgos, which was savaged and plundered, to the distress of King Joseph, who had appointed pairs of clerics and laymen to protect the Spanish. Napoleon took the blame; he wanted the Spanish to beg him to restore Joseph to his throne.

South of Burgos, the French army advanced in march order, except for cavalry flankers, as it approached the Guadarrama mountains. It was the world's most magnificent in uniforms and equipment, especially the cavalry – each regiment in its own uniform and on matching horses. The whole army swung along to the music of regimental bands or beat of drums. But suddenly, on 30 November, at the Pass of Somo Sierra, the column halted.

At the top of the pass were 9,000 men under Benito San Juan, who had sixteen cannon trained on the one road to his position. It was a narrow road, carved into cliffs above the Duraton River, widening only near the top of the pass. The Spanish guns had fired on the skirmishers leading the advance, who had fallen back, stalling the whole army.

Somo Sierra

Napoleon rode forward with his guard, Polish *chasseurs* of the Imperial Guard, eighty-seven officers and men on matching grey chargers, under Colonel Jan Koziutelski. The emperor peered through his field glass at the enemy, muttered curses, and then ordered Koziutelski to charge the Spanish guns.

The colonel in the lead, the Poles charged, but San Juan's cannon downed a third of them, including the colonel. They took cover behind some boulders. General Frédéric-Henri Walther, commanding the Guard Cavalry, urged Napoleon to turn over the attack to the infantry, which, he said, could outflank the Spanish guns. The emperor stormed, "My Guard will not be stopped by peasants!" He sent young Count Philippe de Ségur, his aide, forward with the order for another charge.

The Poles with horses formed and charged; Ségur with them. This time they overran the guns. The Spanish fled; Benito San Juan tried to rally his men, but they killed him. The road to Madrid was clear.

The price had been high. Forty-four Poles lay dead, sixteen were wounded seriously (including Koziutelski and Ségur), others had lesser wounds. Napoleon decorated them all – living and dead – with the Legion of Honor. He honored the Poles in his Bulletin of 2 December. They are still legendary in Poland.[14]

Napoleon in Madrid

On 2 December, the anniversary of Napoleon's coronation and of Austerlitz, the Grande Armée was before Madrid. On 4 December he entered the city and proceeded to govern Spain. He relegated Joseph to the Pardo, a hunting lodge nearby.

The French emperor abolished the Inquisition and seized its treasury, confiscated the property of rebels and began selling it at auction, and ordered his army to seize things France needed, from quinquina (for quinine) to Merino sheep for breeding. He put rebels and *mauvais sujets* before firing squads. He then announced that he would restore King Joseph to the throne, if *Madrileños* would sign oaths of allegiance to the king. They rushed to do so, but Napoleon kept wielding power, abolishing monastic orders,[15] confiscating the royal bank of Saint Charles, and more.

Les Anglais

Then, just before Christmas, Napoleon restored Joseph to his throne, and marched north with the Guard to fight *Les Anglais*. He had word that Sir John Moore, with a British army of 30,000, was near Salamanca. Moore had marched from Portugal to reinforce the Spanish rebels, who were too proud to admit their flight from the French. The British were in jeopardy from French corps nearby.

Napoleon had fought the British only at Toulon, and longed to test himself against them; his odds were ten to one. However, Moore, meanwhile, realized his situation and marched northwest, via Astorga, for Coruña, where the Royal Navy could meet him. Napoleon ordered Soult to pursue Moore, and Ney to block the route to Coruña (their corps were closest). Meanwhile, the emperor crossed the Guadarrama mountains in a snowstorm, with winds that blew men and horses off cliffs; he and his officers walked, leading their horses. On 24 December he was at Villacastin, north of the mountains, where shortly he began a forced march to join Soult.

On the march, however, Napoleon heard from Paris that Austria was mobilizing for war. More insulting, a plot was afoot to make Murat his successor if he were killed; the leaders were his sister (and Murat's wife) Caroline, Talleyrand, and Fouché. From Astorga, he ordered Soult to continue the pursuit and sent Ney a reprimand; in the murderous cold of the Galician mountains, he had failed to block Moore's path.

Napoleon went back to Valladolid. On 16 January 1809 he departed for Paris. He left orders giving Joseph command of the Armée d'Espagne (including all of the Grande Armée present). In a letter to the king, he promised to return in February. In fact, Napoleon never returned, which surely contributed to making the "Spanish Affair" so disastrous.

On the same day, Soult fought Moore at Coruña. Moore had lost 5,000 men during the retreat – fewer to the French than to the cold and abundant wine that induced men to sleep in the snow, never to wake. On 15 January, 10,000 men had gone aboard British vessels, but high seas kept the rest on shore. Moore fought Soult with 15,000 men, almost no cavalry, and nine guns; Soult had 16,000 men, more cavalry and forty guns. Despite French superiority, the British stood their ground, but Moore died in battle, his shoulder ripped away by a cannonball.

On 17 January 1809 the Royal Navy evacuated the rest of Moore's army. Soult thought he had cleared the Peninsula of the British – as did Napoleon.

After the Battle of Coruña, Soult moved into Portugal, held by 12,000 British troops. However, by April 1809 there were 25,000, plus 16,000 Portuguese, and Wellesley (Wellington), had arrived to take command. (He had been in London, answering charges from a parliamentary committee of being too soft on Junot after Vimeiro.) He marched north, crossed the Duero in the early hours of 12 May 1809, surprised Soult at Oporto (the marshal fled in his dressing gown), and drove him into Spain. (The troops nicknamed Wellington "Old Douro," Portuguese name of the river.)

Talavera

Wellington then marched to the Tagus valley, combined his force with a Spanish army under Cuesta, and they marched for Madrid (July 1809). Joseph devised a workable plan, by which the Allied army might have been destroyed, but he lacked the force to make his marshals execute it. Three corps under Soult (his own, Ney's and Mortier's) – 60,000 men – were to march south from Salamanca, block Wellington's avenue of retreat, and attack his rear. Meanwhile, Joseph with 45,000 men (corps of Victor, General Horace Sébastiani, and his Guard) would march from Madrid to meet the Allied army head on. However, the corps from Salamanca did not arrive in time.

Joseph met Wellington at Talavera (27–29 July 1809) with only the 45,000 from Madrid. The battle was indecisive, but bloody. On 27 and 28 July, Marshal Victor browbeat Joseph into making successive day and night attacks on Wellington's forces, on high ground, the strongest part of the Allied line. It was not the sector to attack; the Spanish, in the valley near the river, were more vulnerable. Each time the French reached the British line, but decimated and exhausted. As usual, the British delivered volley after volley of accurate musket fire, and, when the French were close, a volley followed by a bayonet charge; each time the French retreated.

On the 29th, Joseph got word that a small Spanish army was threatening Madrid. He left half his force to watch Wellington, and marched to meet it (remembering Napoleon's reaction to his losing the capital in 1808). Joseph and Sébastiani broke the Spanish army long before it reached Madrid.

Meanwhile, however, Wellington, was warned by Spanish guerrillas that French corps were approaching from the north, and beat a retreat to Lisbon. Around the vulnerable north flank of Lisbon, he built the Lines of Torres Vedras – two lines of forts and positions stretching from Torres Vedras, on the Atlantic, to the Tagus estuary, with a belt of obstacles in front of the lines. It was his base until he was able to go on the offensive.

Joseph had not done badly, considering the poor response of the marshals, but Napoleon did not agree. His opinion of Joseph's military performance never improved, although in 1810 the king, with Marshal Soult, conquered Andalusia, except for Cadiz, where the Spanish rebel government was defended by the British navy. During Joseph's triumph, Napoleon divided Spain into six military governments under officers responsible directly to him. Joseph was left "king of Madrid" and vicinity.

Meanwhile, Marshal Suchet had conquered Aragon and Valencia. Thus, at the beginning of 1812, the French held all of Spain except Cadiz. Guerrilla bands, based in remote mountain areas, took a steady toll of Frenchmen in any vulnerable post or convoy. Without the support of conventional armies, however, they were no threat to French control. Total victory for the French seemed imminent, and might have come but for the czar's challenge to Napoleon on 31 December 1810.

Masséna and Marmont vs Wellington

Meanwhile, Napoleon had defeated Austria again in 1809 (the Wagram Campaign; see next chapter), divorced Josephine, and in 1810 married the Archduchess Marie-Louise of Austria. The emperor had also decided that to subdue Iberia he must destroy "thirty thousand miserable *Anglais*" (Wellington's army) in Portugal; but he sent veteran marshals to do it.

In 1810 Napoleon gave Masséna command of a 60,000-strong Army of Portugal, with orders to destroy Wellington. However, *l'Enfant Cheri* of 1796–97 was old, battered, and war-weary. He had not wanted to go, but was persuaded by Napoleon. When he got there, though, he was less interested in fighting than finding palaces for himself and his 20-year-old mistress (prettily "disguised" as a cavalry officer). The marshal lucked into a victory over Wellington at Bussaco (September 1810) and pursued him to the Lines of Torres Vedras. But he could not break the Lines, which were manned by Portuguese militia, leaving Wellington's army (57,000 British and Portuguese) free to attack. In March 1811, with troops worn from failure, hunger, cold, and guerrilla attacks, Masséna limped back into Spain.[16]

In May 1811, Napoleon replaced Masséna with Marmont, who also invaded Portugal, but could make no headway. Wellington drove him back, and in January 1812 took Ciudad Rodrigo and in April Badajoz – the two key fortresses on the Spanish border.

In March 1812, as he left for Russia, Napoleon gave Joseph command of the armies in the Peninsula. He thought the Russian Campaign would be short, and he trusted Joseph more than any marshal. However, the appointment was a cardinal error. Joseph, after three years as a do-nothing king, was less the commander than he had been in 1809.

In June 1812, when Napoleon was invading Russia, Wellington, with 30,000 British and 20,000 Portuguese troops, invaded Spain and seized the forts at Salamanca, driving Marmont northward. The marshal, with 48,000 troops, fought his way back to Salamanca. Marmont called on Joseph for help (he had 18,000 troops at Madrid). The king responded, moving north with 14,000 men. However, the marshal was impatient. On 22 July 1812, he tried to outflank Wellington by moving south of Salamanca toward the Ciudad Rodrigo road, and let his army get grossly extended. Wellington, on the Arapiles (heights), had full view of the French, and ordered an attack (rare for him). He shattered Marmont's army, and the marshal fell with a severely mangled arm, which surgeons amputated. He was carried from the field unconscious.

Joseph arrived after Marmont's defeat; if it hadn't been for a warning from a friendly peasant (Joseph in person was charming) he might have been killed or captured by the British, but he was able to scurry back to Madrid.

Wellington was hard on his heels, and took Madrid. Joseph withdrew to Valencia with his army and court – a comic opera march during which Joseph's troops had to protect spoiled, carping civilians – men, women, and children –

while mounted Spanish guerrillas hurled insults from beyond musket range, occasionally charging, then fleeing and laughing.

With the loss of Madrid, Soult was forced to evacuate Andalusia, and reinforced Joseph at Valencia. At year's end Joseph and Soult recovered Madrid, but without engaging Wellington, a professional who preferred to avoid battle unless he had a clear advantage over his enemy, and retreated to the border fortresses, forecasting a better year in 1813.

Wellington takes charge

The tall, handsome, unflappable, and arrogant Earl of Wellington (Duke in 1813) had become a legend in Iberia. He was a commanding figure, though habitually in civilian clothes and without insignia. He purported to despise his men, whom he called "scum of the earth who have enlisted for drink," and could be a brutal disciplinarian. Yet his men respected and trusted him and would follow "Old Douro" anywhere. Astride his tall thoroughbred, he was everywhere during battles. He hated the Spanish and liked the Portuguese only a little better. To him the guerrillas were "scum and robbers," but he accepted their aid.

In late 1812, Wellington was made Allied commander in the Peninsula, an honor earlier blocked by Spanish pride. In the spring of 1813, he invaded Spain with an army of 100,000 British, Portuguese, Spanish regulars, and guerrillas.

Napoleon ordered Joseph to abandon Madrid and mass his forces to guard the border of France. The king moved very slowly, reluctant to abandon his Spanish followers to the guerrillas. He was outflanked at Valladolid and forced to shift northward until he was behind the Ebro.

Vitoria

On 21 June 1813, Joseph finally stood to fight at Vitoria. He had 70,000 men against Wellington's 100,000, but his forces were mostly French; Wellington fully trusted only his British and Portuguese troops. But Joseph and Marshal Jean-Baptiste Jourdan, his chief-of-staff, let corps commanders choose positions. The Allies charged in over an unguarded bridge, and then exploited gaps between French units.

Joseph was disastrously defeated; his troops fled into the Pyrenees by all roads. The king abandoned the army treasure, his carriages and crown, and yet barely escaped capture. (His mistress, the Marquesa de Montehermoso, was captured; the British "forwarded" her to Joseph.) Casualties were light for a decisive battle – some 8,000 French and 5,200 Allies.

Wellington has been adversely criticized for not pursuing the French. Nonetheless, his victory marked the end of the Bonaparte Kingdom of Spain and shortly enabled him to invade southern France. It influenced Austria to join the Allies in northern Europe. In 1814, after Napoleon retreated into France from Germany, he had to worry not only about his pursuers but also about Wellington in his rear.

11

THE WAGRAM CAMPAIGN, 1809
THE EMPIRE REACHES ITS HEIGHT, 1810

Austria prepares for war

On 24 January 1809, Napoleon, angry and impatient, was back in Paris. To his mind, *la guerre d'Espagne* was finished and he was ready to bleed Austria for her impertinence.[1] He deflated the "succession plot" by blaming Talleyrand, to whom he bawled "You are just ── in a silk stocking," and dismissed him from the post of grand chamberlain, but did not deprive him of his title (prince) or properties. Talleyrand betrayed Napoleon almost immediately by selling information to Austria.

In October 1808, the Austrian emperor, after Napoleon's departure for Spain with much of the Grande Armée, allied with Britain and got a loan to finance a war with France.[2] A war party formed that included the beautiful young empress, Maria Ludovica (Francis's third wife), Chancellor Philip von Stadion, the archdukes John and Ferdinand, and a loud bevy of foreign exiles with grudges against Napoleon – the Baron vom Stein, Friedrich von Gentz, Madame de Staël, and others. The German exiles touted pan-German nationalism, claiming that if Austria challenged Napoleonic France, the Germans would rise to support her and "win their freedom."

The Archduke Charles was not a "war hawk," primarily because he doubted that the Austrian army was ready to fight. Thus he saw danger in the Austrian nationalism generated by the war party, and did not believe that pan-Germanism existed, except in the minds of *idéologues*. As head of the *Hofkriegsrat* (War Council) he had begun army reforms with the introduction of a corps organization, but was unsure his officers could (or would) use it to best advantage. He had managed to retire many older officers or move them to semi-civilian posts (provincial governor and the like). But there were still too many traditionalists among veteran officers, and too many dashing but untrained younger ones. In the end, however, Charles joined the war party because he knew Austria was bent on war, and did not want to be left out, as in 1805.

Charles had built up the regular army to 300,000 men, and the *Landwehr* (National Guard) to some 150,000. He had numbers, but the troops were poorly trained.

Preliminaries to war

In March 1809, Charles proclaimed a "War of German Liberation" – to Napoleon a declaration of war.[3] Charles commanded the major army (209,000) in Germany. The Archduke John was to march on Italy with 72,000 men.

On 9 April, Charles marched into Bavaria, invading Napoleon's *Rheinbund*. As he had feared, the Germans showed scant interest in "liberation." However, there were obsessed enemies of Napoleon – Major Ferdinand von Schill, a Prussian, and the Duke of Brunswick (whose father had died at Auerstädt). Schill marched his battalion into Westphalia, and was disowned by the Prussian king, who was still in shock from Jena–Auerstädt and Tilsit.

Schill expected Jerome's officers to mutiny and join him with their troops, but virtually all kept their oaths to the king. Schill marched to Stralsund, where he and many of his men were killed. Brunswick organized a "Black Legion of Vengeance" in Bohemia which also marched into the *Rheinbund*, but was forced to flee to Hamburg where the Duke and most of his men were rescued by the Royal Navy. That was all. Napoleon's German allies fought the Austrians beside the French.

The armies – war begins (see Map 16)

In January 1809, from Spain, Napoleon called up the conscripts of the classes of 1809 and 1810. At the same time he ordered Berthier to Germany to reorganize the 90,000 French (two corps under Davout) already there, and troops from the *Rheinbund*. The chief-of-staff gave corps to Davout, Masséna and Oudinot, and shortly, when they arrived from Spain, Lannes and Lefebvre. Most of the Guard was called from Spain, as was Bessières, who took command of the cavalry reserve (*vice* Murat, king of Naples).

On 17 April 1809, at Donauworth, Napoleon took control of L'Armée d'Allemagne (Army of Germany) – referred to below as the French army or Grande Armée. He had 200,000 men, including 50,000 Germans, but half the French were green conscripts. Thanks to Berthier's preparations (adjusted, en route, by Napoleon), he was on the march the next day. The Archduke Charles's field army was larger, but was divided north and south of the Danube.

Napoleon struck south of the Danube, moving east. After a minor victory at Abensberg (20 April 1809), he directed the bulk of his army on Landshut, convinced that the Archduke's main force was there. But when he arrived (21 April) he found one Austrian division, which Bessière's cavalry stampeded. Napoleon had made a mistake; and proceded to compound it.

In driving south, Napoleon had left Davout's corps exposed near Eggmühl. Charles had taken Regensburg (Ratisbon), occupied by a single French regiment, as an avenue of escape across the Danube, and attacked Davout. Beginning at 2.30 p.m. on 21 April, Davout sent repeated reports to Napoleon, still at Landshut, that he was under attack by the main Austrian army at Eggmühl.

The French emperor did not move, however, because he believed that Charles was in retreat through Eggmühl to Vienna, via the south bank of the Danube. Thus, he would soon arrive at Landshut – where he would intercept and destroy him. Napoleon judged that if Charles did not appear at Landshut, he would move through Straubing. He ordered Masséna and Lannes to prepare their corps to march for Straubing (southeast of Regensburg).

As the day (21 April) waned, however, Davout's messages got more urgent. At 5 p.m. he wrote the emperor: "I will hold my positions, I hope . . . the troops are too overcome with exhaustion to dream of attacking positions with three times the artillery and troops that I have."[4] At 7 p.m. he sent General Henri Piré to persuade Napoleon that he was under heavy attack. Davout was saved from destruction by Lefebvre, whose corps was closest to him, moving without orders from the emperor.

Meanwhile, Napoleon had sent four divisions toward Eggmühl, with orders to arrive by 9 a.m. on 22 April. At 3 a.m. on 22 April, however, Napoleon was finally convinced that Charles was at Eggmühl. He ordered Lannes, just in from Spain, to assume command of the divisions marching on Eggmühl. At 4 a.m. he wrote Davout that he was coming to his support with 40,000 men.

On 22 April, Napoleon arrived in mid-afternoon at Eggmühl. The divisions under Lannes had seen action, but Davout had been saved by Lefebvre. Masséna, recalled from the vicinity of Straubing, arrived late. Napoleon ordered him back to Straubing, since he still thought Charles likely to go in that direction.

On 23 April, however, the Archduke withdrew through Regensburg to the north bank of the Danube, and was joined at Cham by his northern corps, bringing his field strength to 90,000. He withdrew east, picking up more troops, so that he had 100,000 men by the time he reached the vicinity of Vienna.

On 23 April, at midday, Napoleon arrived at Regensburg to find his army blocked by 6,000 men behind the crumbling walls of the fortress. Too impatient to undertake a siege, he ordered Lannes to storm the walls. Lannes' first attempt, at about 1 p.m., failed, but at 5 p.m. he took the fortress. Meanwhile, Napoleon had gone too far forward and been hit in the right ankle by a spent musket ball (one of two wounds in his whole career). It barely drew blood, but rumors spread that he was dead. He spent the day riding about, sometimes recklessly, to show the troops he was alive and with them.

Napoleon loses Charles again

Instead of following the Archduke Charles, Napoleon chose to march on Vienna. After his victories of 1805 he had not taken the Austrians seriously, and he fancied a few days in Schönbrunn Palace – and could use the fact as propaganda. He also held out hope that the Austrians so treasured Vienna that they would make peace. *Nevertheless, he had violated his long-standing rule – to pursue and destroy the enemy army, no matter where it went, not to waste time taking places.*

Napoleon took Vienna on 13 May, but found no Austrian emissaries waiting. He had no idea where the Archduke was, but thought perhaps he was in Moravia, where he had found the enemy in 1805. This was a dangerous pre-conception. The Danube bridges north of Vienna had been destroyed. Thus he began scouting the Danube for another place to cross, aware that he might be opposed, since some Austrian troops, mostly cavalry, were in evidence across the river.

He decided to cross the Danube at Lobau Island, in the river, 5 miles downstream. It had a narrow channel opposite the north bank, and one about 700 yards wide on the south. On 18 May he occupied Lobau, and his engineers erected bridges between the south bank and Lobau – three spans – the first 400 yards long, to a small island, the second, 300 yards long, from the island to Lobau Island. Several pontoon bridges – the longest 125 yards – were thrown from the north end of Lobau to the north bank.

Building the bridges was a smaller task than keeping them up. The Danube was swelling from spring rains, rising several feet a day. Also, at intervals, the Austrians sent barges and fireships down the river in attempts to destroy the bridges. Keeping them up was essential, because Napoleon did not plan to mass his army on Lobau before crossing to the north bank. If any of the southern spans went down, troops waiting to cross would be isolated on the south bank. The emperor might not have made such a plan if he had known how close he was to the enemy army.

Napoleon had only three corps (Masséna, Lannes, and Davout), the reserve cavalry (Bessières), and 8,000 of his Guard in the Vienna area – a total of 82,000 men. The Archduke had 100,000 just north of Lobau Island, and 16,000 more opposite Vienna.

Aspern–Essling (see Map 16)

Charles's cavalry had kept a close watch on the French. On 20 May, he had five corps of infantry and one of cavalry in the hills 6 miles north of Lobau, behind the Russbach River. He meant to organize them *after* the French appeared in force, either crossing the Danube or on the north bank. He chose not to try to outguess Napoleon as to where, exactly, he would cross, and knew that his Austrians were slow to respond to orders.

On 20 May Napoleon sent troops onto Lobau – first the cavalry of Lasalle (*"A cavalryman who is not dead by twenty-five is a jean-foutre!"*),[5] with a division of Masséna's infantry close behind. By midnight, Masséna's whole corps and Bessières Guard cavalry were across.

At 51, Masséna was an old man, arthritic and weathered from the rigors of campaigns and a dozen wounds.[6] Not without pain, he climbed the steps of the church steeple in Aspern, judged the number and position of the enemy by his campfires, and then aligned his corps between Aspern and Essling, anchored by positions in the stone buildings of the villages.

On 21 May Charles sent his cavalry, then his infantry, against the French bridgehead. However, the Austrians came on slowly, and their weight was not felt until 5 p.m., when the Archduke had almost 100,000 men and 260 guns opposite the French. Masséna and Bessières had fewer than 30,000 with some eighty guns, but held their own. In mid-afternoon, Lannes reinforced them with one division, then, about midnight, his whole corps, bringing French numbers to 45,000, with Davout's corps to come.

At dawn on 22 May, Napoleon arrived, bringing 8,000 Guard infantry and more reserve cavalry. Masséna opined that the major Austrian army was before them. Napoleon did not think so. Without waiting for Davout's corps, which had not crossed the Danube, he ordered Lannes to lead an offensive. Bonaparte was attacking 100,000 Austrians with 55,000 French.

Lannes led the charge, and caught the Austrians by surprise. By 7 a.m. he had pushed their center back over a mile, and an hour later by 2 miles. However, the French cavalry outran the infantry and all too soon were low on ammunition. Seeing them falter, the Archduke Charles seized the standard of the Zach regiment of his grenadiers and led them forward. Lannes' attack stalled.

At about the same time, Napoleon was informed that one span of the long, south bridge over of the Danube had been wrecked. Before dawn, the Austrians had cut loose a massive floating flour mill anchored some 8 miles upstream. It careered down the river, and smashed the bridge to splinters. Davout's corps, on the south bank, could not get onto Lobau. Napoleon's 55,000 were left alone on the north bank. They would get no more artillery and only supplies that small boats could carry. The emperor had taken his bridges for granted, although they had been broken and repaired four times before the fatal breach: on 20 May, twice on the 21st, and at about 4 a.m. on the 22nd.

At mid-morning, Lannes, on Napoleon's order, fell back to the Aspern–Essling line. The Austrians attacked in full force and fury. Masséna, commanding at Aspern, lost the village twice, but recovered and held it. In the center, Lannes' infantry stopped Austrian attacks, aided by sweeps of Bessières cavalry. On the French right, Essling fell at about 2 p.m., but Napoleon sent in four battalions of the Young Guard, who retook it.

Charles pulled back his infantry in favor of murderous artillery fire on French positions. Napoleon could not reply in kind or volume since he had fewer guns (less than eighty to 260) and was short of ammunition.

At about 3 p.m., Napoleon turned command over to Lannes and retired to Lobau Island. Hardly had he left when a cannonball smashed Marshal Lannes' legs. He was rushed to the rear, where Napoleon's surgeon, Baron Jean Larrey, had to amputate one leg. It did not occur to Napoleon that Lannes would die (nine days later). His first question to Masséna was "You don't think [the loss of Lannes] has demoralized the troops, do you?" The Marshal said no, but they could not hold against such odds.[7]

At about 5 p.m. Napoleon reluctantly ordered the evacuation of the beachhead. From fatigue and/or disorganization, the Austrians made no move to interfere, not even using their artillery. By about 3 a.m. on 23 May, the French withdrawal was complete. Masséna was the last man over the pontoon bridge before it was pulled back onto Lobau; the rearguard followed in rowboats. French casualties had been at least 15,000; Lannes lay dying; his corps had been shot to pieces; General Louis-Vincent St-Hilaire had been killed, as had General Jean-Louis Espagne, incomparable leader of heavy cavalry. Austrian casualties were higher, perhaps twice as many, but the French had left the field. Napoleon's first attempt to cross the Danube had failed.

The loss of Lannes was a extra blow to Napoleon. He was the first of the "unkillable" marshals to die (in battle, of wounds, or otherwise), and the last anyone expected to die. Lannes had survived more wounds than any soldier or officer in the French army. Perhaps the most handsome of the marshals, slender, broad-shouldered and blond, he was quarrelsome and violent, but of unexampled bravery in battle. Wrote Napoleon to his widow: "I [have lost] the most distinguished general in my army . . . and . . . my best friend."[8] The emperor wept openly.

Napoleon pronounced that his army had been defeated by the Danube, not the Austrians. He would not even give the enemy credit for destroying the bridges. "It was not Prince Charles who cut the bridges, it was the Danube, which rose fourteen feet in three days."[9]

The Austrians saw it differently. They celebrated a victory, and ignored that Charles had failed (not been able?) to punish the French as they withdrew, and had not even bombarded Lobau.

One thing is certain, Napoleon had not been able to scramble to victory on the Aspern–Essling line.

Digging in on Lobau

Fearful of tarnishing his myth of invincibility, Napoleon refused to order the evacuation of Lobau Island and any suggestion that he withdraw to or west of Vienna or seek another crossing site. "I would as soon return to Strasbourg right now as to recross the Danube!"[10] He dictated a bulletin depreciating the importance of the Battle of Aspern–Essling, exaggerating enemy strength and casualties, and giving low estimates of his own.[11] He then turned to preparing for another crossing from Lobau.

Napoleon gave first priority to ensuring that the Danube would not ruin his next attempt. He set engineers, aided by sailors called from the French fleet, to building a barrier of piles over 1,300 yards long across the main channel of the Danube to stop fireboats, mines, and of course floating mills. This was to protect the bridges downstream; this time there would be two (not one) to Lobau from the south bank. On the north bank of Lobau he ordered no fewer than twenty pontoon bridges readied to be extended over the Danube. To protect all of this, he formed a fleet of six gunboats and a floating, armored battery of 18-pound guns.

He was determined also to have superior numbers during the second crossing, evidence that he had developed greater respect for the Archduke Charles. While the bridges were built (which took three weeks), he was assembling his army, drawing in the maximum number of corps. He also called on Eugene's Army of Italy, which had been fighting a war of its own.

The war in Italy and Hungary

In March, the Archduke John, with some 50,000 men, had marched on the Kingdom of Italy. (Of his 72,000-man army, he had sent 10,000 into the Tyrol and 12,000 into Dalmatia.) On 16 April 1809 he defeated Viceroy Eugene, with some 35,000 Italians and French, at Sacile, in Venetia. (Eugene's army comprised 37,000 Italians and 15,000 French, not counting detachments.) The viceroy was forced to retreat behind the Piave, then the Adige.

At news of Napoleon's victories in Germany, however, John began withdrawing over the Alps to reinforce the Archduke Charles. Eugene pursued, wreaked huge casualties at the Piave and Tagliamento rivers, and dogged John until he reached Hungary.

Eugene then went to consult Napoleon, leaving General Jacques Macdonald, with 15,000 men, to continue the pursuit. On 27 May he was with Napoleon. The emperor issued a bulletin praising Eugene and the Italian Army. "The Viceroy displayed . . . the *sang froid* and perception that marks a great captain."[12] He sent Eugene back to his army, however, with reinforcements (bringing it to 45,000), and the mission of preventing the Archduke John from reinforcing with the Archduke Charles.

John had marched down the Raab River, to the town of Raab, near the confluence of the Raab and Danube – 60 miles east of Vienna. There, he expected to be heavily reinforced by Hungarians from the "Insurrection" (rally of nobles), but was disappointed. On 14 June, Eugene (45,000) attacked John (35,000) at Raab, where the Archduke had to fight with a force of exhausted veterans and raw recruits. The viceroy first led his infantry in person, supported by the artillery of Sorbier (later commander of the artillery of the Guard). He then scattered the Austrians at the head of cavalry. The Archduke John crossed the Danube with 12,000 men, but was forced to retreat downstream – away from Vienna. He was unable to join the Archduke Charles before Napoleon forced him to fight. However, Eugene reinforced Napoleon with 30,000 men.

Armies and preparations (see Map 16)

On 30 June, Napoleon's army on and near Lobau numbered 190,000 men and 480 guns (including the Army of Italy). The Archduke Charles had 140,000 men and 450 guns. Rain continued to fall almost daily, and the Danube rose steadily, but Napoleon's new bridges held up. In the first days of July, Napoleon put his army on Lobau and the south bank of the Danube in attack positions.

Charles withdrew 115,000 men behind the Russbach River, 6 miles north of the river, and left 25,000 on the Aspern–Essling–Enzersdorf line. The latter were to delay the French, after they crossed to the north bank, while the Archduke organized his army. He was certain that Napoleon would cross from Lobau, but it could be anywhere on 5 miles of north shoreline.[13]

Battle of Wagram (see Map 16)

Napoleon's army crossed the Danube on the night of 4–5 July in torrential rain and hail, with thunder and lightning. Macdonald wrote that it was ideal for the crossing.[14] (Surely the enemies' heads were down.) The first units crossed on the east side of Lobau, outflanked the Aspern–Essling–Enzersdorf line, and drove the 25,000 defenders into retreat; this freed the numerous other bridges for use, and the French crossed *en masse*.

On 5 July the armies tested each other. At day's end, Charles's troops were behind the Russbach, and the French opposite them. At dusk, Napoleon ordered three corps to cross the river, led by the Army of Italy, which had crossed the Danube late and was fresh. Macdonald suggested to Eugene that they question Napoleon about it. Eugene snapped, "My God *no*. He gave the order to attack, we attack!"[15] Macdonald forced the Russbach, but was counter-attacked, and his tired troops fled. Grenadiers of the Guard, bayonets fixed, forced them back into line, but they could not resume the attack.

On the morning of 6 July the Archduke launched an enveloping attack on the French left (the weak side). Klaus von Klenau's corps, marching stolidly, broke through the French cavalry screen, just north of the Danube. Klenau was then to break through the French line – destroy the bridges south of Aspern–Essling, and – with John-Charles Kolowrat's corps – sweep into the French rear. Meanwhile, Charles bombarded the French center for two hours with heavy artillery, then launched a massive infantry attack. The blow struck Bernadotte's Saxon corps of 18,000 men, which broke and retreated in disorder. Before the infantry attack, the marshal had left his advance division, in column, under artillery fire for an hour. Napoleon sent Bernadotte from the field in disgrace. Masséna, on the Saxon corps' left, shifted his corps into the gap left by Bernadotte until Macdonald and Eugene relieved him.

Napoleon then sent Masséna to stop the enveloping attack, and he moved out briskly. During Charles's attack on the French center, Klenau had broken the one French infantry division near Aspern, and seemed about to drive into the French rear. However, he halted when he saw Masséna's divisions in motion and that Kolowrat's corps, to his left rear, was not advancing.

While French cavalry kept the Austrians back, Masséna – in full view of the enemy – made a sweep across the field. When he came opposite the Austrians, he sent his infantry forward, firing and closing with the bayonet. Masséna stopped Klenau, and by mid-afternoon had driven him out of Aspern and slowly

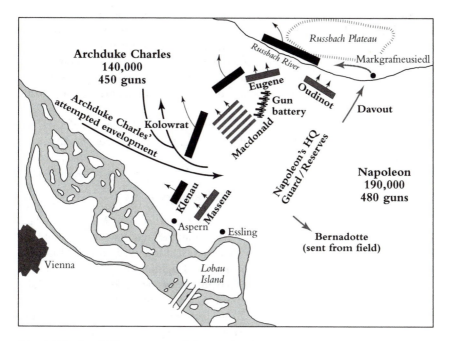

Map 16 Battle of Wagram, second day, 6 July 1809

westward. Masséna's losses were small, but the cavalry had suffered. The bold Antoine Lasalle was killed, and Marshal Bessières wounded.

At about 3 p.m., Napoleon rearranged the army to strike back, using formations at his headquarters, a mile behind the left center of the line. He had the Guard (20,000 men and 60–70 guns), the reserve cavalry (8,000), Wrede's Bavarian division (7,000), and Marmont's corps of Dalmatians (12,500). He sent Marmont to reinforce Masséna.

Meanwhile, he detached Macdonald's corps from Eugene's army to mount an attack on the Austrian center, supported by a battery of 112 guns. After a heavy barrage, Macdonald went forward with eight battalions in line, two abreast, flanked by nine battalions in column on either side. The Austrians gradually gave ground, but their artillery wreaked havoc among the attackers, taking no fewer than 5,000 casualties. The enemy then rallied, with Austrian cavalry driving its infantry forward with the flat of the sword.

Macdonald's offensive stalled, but Napoleon reinforced him with Wrede's Bavarian division and a brigade of Guard cavalry. The tide began to turn, and Napoleon gave Macdonald impetus by sending up all the battalions of the Young Guard.

Macdonald succeeded, and Eugene, on his right, took Wagram. This set the stage for the key action of the battle (though Napoleon never acknowledged it), which was the attack on the Austrian left by Davout's corps, which had been at work all day. During the early morning hours, Davout had cleared the south bank of the Russbach of Austrian forces, and by about 10 a.m. had positioned his artillery to blast Markgrafneusiedl from two sides. About noon, his infantry crossed the river and captured the town. Davout then turned the enemy flank, widening his front until he was driving west along the river, rolling up Charles's line. By 3 p.m. fatigue had all but stopped the movement of corps, but the battle was really over anyway.

By 4 p.m., the French were advancing in all sectors. Charles saw that he had lost, and executed a phased withdrawal; after nightfall, he retreated north toward Moravia.

Outcome and analysis

Napoleon's victory was not so final as that at Austerlitz. The Archduke's attack *sur les derrières* of the French had failed, but was an inspired move, and might have beaten him if the Austrian corps commanders had followed orders. Moreover, Charles still had at least 80,000 men capable of fighting. Napoleon, of course, insisted to everyone that he had scored a triumph. In a letter to Josephine (7 July) he called the battle "decisive and complete."[16] Davout's III Corps had sealed Napoleon's victory, and Masséna's actions had prepared the way. The emperor, however, gave Macdonald major credit for victory and made him a marshal, along with Marmont. In 1810, Bonaparte made Davout Prince of Eckmühl (Eggmühl) and Masséna Prince of Essling.

Of course, victory was also the result of Napoleon's preparations and mustering of maximum numbers of men and guns. Of his first Italian campaign, he said: "We were always outnumbered three to one, but . . . *la force morale* more than numbers was decisive to victory."[17] In 1809 he was enamoured of numbers, but he was still the improviser. His direct role in the victory was the *ad hoc* organizing of Macdonald's column and gun battery.

Surprisingly, massing the great battery of cannon, generally seen as totally Napoleonic, he had learned from the Austrians. At Aspern–Essling, Austrian artillery had forced his withdrawal to Eylau. After that battle, he began assigning sixty or more guns to the Imperial Guard artillery, solely as a base for forming batteries. He also decided that massed artillery was a good substitute for skirmishers (*voltigeurs* or *tirailleurs*) who tried to disorganize the enemy before major attacks.

The peace

After Wagram, the Archduke Charles had to fight bloody rearguard actions during his retreat. He was tired and ill (an epileptic), and was not sure that his army, though strong in numbers, could fight another major battle. He expected that his retreat would influence the czar (who wanted Austrian Galicia) to send more troops against the Austrians in Poland.

On 12 July Charles asked for a truce, which Napoleon granted; he then retired – permanently – from the army. The Austrian emperor delayed making peace until October 1809, when the British expedition to Belgium (Walcheren Island) was recalled.[18] Meanwhile, Napoleon lived in the Schönbrunn Palace.

Napoleon was happy to have peace, though loath to admit it. His bulletins claimed total destruction of the Austrian forces, and he "robbed" Francis I as if that were true. He took the remaining Austrian lands in the Balkans, gave the czar part of Austrian Galicia, and annexed the rest to the Duchy of Warsaw; he returned the Tyrol to Bavaria, and gave her Salzburg, Berchtesgaden, and other small territories. Other Austrian lands were given to German allies.

The new marriage

While Napoleon occupied the Schönbrunn Palace, he worried over the future of his dynasty. He had no legitimate heir. The constitution allowed him to adopt one; but that had been a Roman practice, seldom seen since. He doubted that his successor would be accepted by the hereditary monarchs of Europe. Ergo, he must produce a male heir (in France, a girl would not do) by a new wife from an old dynasty.

After exploring possibilities, he contracted a marriage with the Archduchess Marie-Louise, daughter of Francis I of Austria – a Habsburg, of the oldest reigning family in Europe. In November 1809 he divorced Josephine (who got Château Malmaison and an empress's income), and in March 1810 remarried. He was certain he could father a boy.[19] In February 1810 (before he was married), Napoleon gave his prospective son the title "King of Rome," and named Rome the second capital of the Empire.

What he had won by talent and by the sword, he proposed to preserve by compromising with the *ancien régime*.

Marriage and the warrior

We need not retell the story of Napoleon's meeting in March 1810 with Marie-Louise at Compiègne (he, 40; she, 18), and his hurried possession of his bride. (Actually, they were already married, if by proxy, in Vienna, which spoils the tale.) Napoleon apparently succeeded in overcoming her inbred fear of the French and the "ogre" she had married, and also negated the influence of his sister Caroline (queen of Naples), who had travelled with the bride, and pictured him as ill-tempered and intolerant of pets. (Caroline wanted her children to be in the imperial succession.) She had induced the bride to get rid of her lap dog, but otherwise just made her nervous. With her beauty, that did not matter. Marie-Louise was at ease with Napoleon long before their spectacular marriage (2 April 1810) in Notre Dame cathedral.

The marriage was extraordinarily happy. Napoleon could not stop talking about the charms of German girls. He lost interest in travelling unless

Marie-Louise went with him. When she became pregnant (June, 1810), he was ecstatic, and even more a homebody. However, the emperor of the French could not afford this sort of happiness. He neglected duties requiring travel or physical exertion, and became fat and sedentary.

Nonetheless, in 1809–10, the Empire reached its height. At the end of 1810, France had 130 departments (up from eighty-three in 1789.) Holland, as well as Illyria, Tuscany, and the Duchy of Warsaw were technically part of France. The satellite kingdoms of Italy, Naples, Spain, and Westphalia still existed. Napoleon ruled the Confederation of the Rhine and Swiss Confederation. There were many lesser Napoleonic states – for example, the Grand Duchy of Berg and the Duchy of Frankfurt (in Germany), and the Principality of Piombino (in Italy). Every state in Europe and Russia were allied with France.

Much had been added to the Empire in 1809 and 1810. Napoleon drove his brother Louis from the throne of Holland and annexed it to France in 1810. He annexed the Hanse cities and much of north Germany to France (to enforce the Continental System). The states taken included Oldenburg, a possession of the czar's brother-in-law. In 1809, the emperor had named Elisa Bonaparte Bacciochi, his sister, Grand Duchess of Tuscany; she also ruled adjacent Parma and Piacenza. He organized former Austrian Balkan territories as the Illyrian Provinces (after the Roman name for the area). It comprised Villach, Austrian Istria, Hungarian Dalmatia, and Trieste (ceded by Austria in 1809), Venetian Istria and Dalmatia (given to Italy in 1805), Ragusa (seized 1808), and the Ionian Islands (captured by Russia, 1799, returned to France 1807). He divided the Papal States between the Kingdom of Italy and France, which took Rome. (In May 1809, Pius VII had excommunicated Napoleon, who heard just after Aspern–Essling; the Pope was precipitously imprisoned at Savona.)

Moreover, the emperor seemed to be working to dismantle his system of satellite kingdoms. Holland disappeared. In Spain, he put most provinces under military governors and behaved as if he wanted Joseph to abdicate. In Westphalia, he allowed Davout to levy taxes, and King Jerome asked if he should abdicate. In Naples, he threatened Murat by concentrating French troops at Gaeta. Italy, he told Eugene, was to go to Napoleon's son after twenty years. It appeared that Napoleon's son would inherit all the kingdoms' lands – in addition to France.

Despite the formidable extent of the Empire and the irresistible appearance of its armies, it had weaknesses. The "Spanish war" went on. In 1809 Wellington had threatened Madrid and marched to safety in Portugal. There were rumblings of discontent in France. Draft evasion and desertion were high (12,000 deserters in 1808, 10,500 in 1809, with 7,000 more "missing"). Prussia was allied to France against her interest and will, as was Austria, despite the imperial marriage. Anti-French sentiment had increased Europe-wide by heavy conscription quotas, war taxes, levies of food and equipment.

Yet, Napoleon seemed to see no limit to his power. He had become short-tempered, impatient of disagreement, foul-mouthed, and tyrannical. This was disturbing even to his friends.

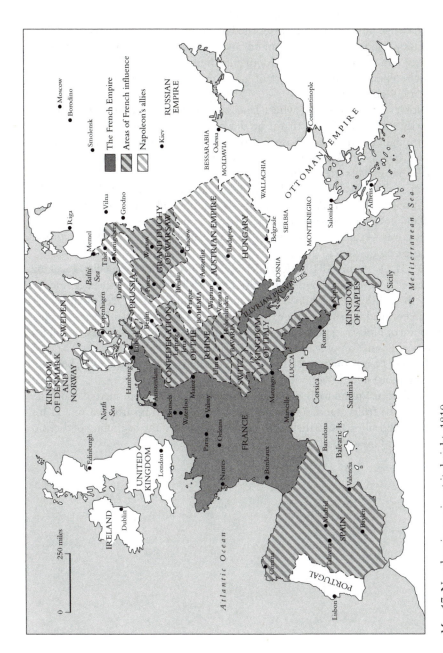

Map 17 Napoleonic empire at its height, 1810

The czar throws down the gauntlet

The czar was uncertain that Napoleon could be stopped, but he decided he had to challenge him. Napoleon had violated his promises of sharing power with him in Europe and the Ottoman Empire, and instead had sent military advisers to Turkey and Persia (Iran). The Continental System was ruining his economy – which depended on the export of grain, timber, and other raw materials to Britain or elsewhere.

Nobles owned the vast wheat-lands and forests, and were losing income directly. Alexander feared that if he did not renounce the French alliance his court might resort to the "Russian national sport," the assassination of czars. His father had been killed by disgruntled nobles. His courtiers' pride and pocketbooks had suffered since 1807.

Russia had no allies, though Britain would surely be one if Russia left the Continental System. Russia's industry was almost nil. Her population, at 31 million was about the same as that of France proper (without annexations), but spread over 24 million square miles. To defy Napoleonic Europe was irrational, but the czar decided to do it.

On 31 December 1810, Alexander issued a ukase (that is, an edict) breaking with the Continental System and the French alliance. He then began negotiations with Sweden for an alliance, and with Turkey for peace (to end a war Napoleon had fomented). By early 1812, he had both. Sweden's price was the promise of Norway, a possession of Napoleon's ally, Denmark; Turkey settled for Russian evacuation of Moldavia and Wallachia.

In 1811 Napoleon devoted himself to preparing for war with Russia, but kept talking peace until the eve of the campaign.

He declined to go to Spain, as we know, and the war continued. Napoleon's empire was truly grand, and he would be able to call up troops from all his puppets and allies. Nevertheless, the year 1812 marked the beginning of the end for him and his empire.

12

THE RUSSIAN CAMPAIGN, 1812

Napoleon in 1812

In 1812, at Borodino, deep in Russia, an angry Marshal Ney bellowed: "Why is the Emperor in the rear of the army? If . . . he is no longer a general . . . then he should go back to the Tuileries [Paris] and let us be generals for him."[1] Napoleon's behavior was atypical and even strange on the Russian Campaign. Philippe de Ségur attributes his lack of attention to duty to colds and other minor illnesses. There are more dire theories.[2]

At any rate, Napoleon kept to his command tent, called councils of war (which he had always despised), seldom checked the condition of troops in the field, and persisted in an unrealistic view of his enemy. He also wasted time discussing new political arrangements with the Lithuanians and others – while the army moved ahead without him.

Probably, the explanation of Napoleon's behavior is dirt simple. He was middle-aged, overweight, and out of condition from his soft life since 1809. Fatigue discouraged him from scouting in person, or keeping close contact with his troops, or even keeping well informed. That also explains his short attention span and lapses of memory.

Of course there are other factors. Napoleon was a master of maneuver with small armies; even at Austerlitz he had whittled his army down to a comfortable size, and then improvised his tactics. The campaigns of 1806–07 and 1809 had shown that he had trouble with larger ones. Further, his marshals were aging, Masséna had retired, and he had lost confidence in others. Then, no doubt, he had become megalomanic from many years of success, which made disappointments in Russia loom much larger, and his confidence was shaken in the solidity of the Austrian alliance. Finally, he had gradually become aware that his taxation and conscription had made him unpopular, to a degree, everywhere.

In terms of peace of mind, war is simple: there is the enemy and he needs to be beaten. An emperor's life is complex and demanding, and enemies are never clearly identifiable; the pressures had chastened Napoleon. He was old before his time. Perhaps the admission he made to Caulaincourt in November 1812 – after the retreat from Moscow began – he should have made to himself before he took command: "*Late hours, hardship, war are not for me at my age. I love my bed, my repose, more than anything; but I must finish my work.*"[3]

As recently as late 1809, Napoleon had been a battle-hardened general who prided himself sharing the hardships of his troops, who roamed about at night, visiting the troops and harassing the generals, and took catnaps on the ground during the day.

In Russia the emperor lived in luxury. His staff (once skeletal) was 7,000 strong. His household (without Berthier's) had 150 saddlehorses, 500 other horses and mules, 50 carriages, and a mobile hospital. Liveried servants served him on sets of silver and plate, bearing the imperial arms. He had chefs, valets, and secretaries. The ministers who accompanied him were equally well served. His headquarters had provisions for all these people for sixty days (while the troops lived off the land). The tents for his headquarters and staff covered acres. The emperor's tent had two drawing rooms, a study, and a bedroom. He was guarded on the march by a cavalry squadron (about a hundred strong), given the honor for a day or so; plus two infantry battalions, and *Gendarmes d'Elite* (military police). At Borodino, 30,000 Imperial Guards formed a square around his tents.

The armies

For the Russian Campaign, Napoleon mustered overwhelming numbers of troops; he thought it probable that he could cow the czar into surrender without a fight. In June 1812, his field army numbered 611,000 men with 2,000 guns and 250,000 horses. The "first wave" was to be 490,000 strong; 121,000 would follow. In Germany and the Rhineland were over 130,000 more, making his total force around 750,000.

The Grande Armée of 1812 was a European army, and reflected Napoleon's domination of Europe. Of the 611,000 who invaded Russia, 200,000 were French (born within the boundaries of 1789), and 100,000 were from new departments – thus actually Dutch, Belgian, German, Swiss, or Italian. The remaining 311,000 comprised 130,000 Germans from the *Rheinbund*, 90,000 Poles and Lithuanians, 27,000 Italians and Illyrians, 5,000 Neapolitans (the Royal Guard), 9,000 Swiss, and finally 30,000 Austrians and 20,000 Prussians. Also, French corps had many Spanish, Portuguese, and others; the Imperial Guard was international. The Guard (47,000) and reserve cavalry (60,000) are included in the totals above.[4]

Czar Alexander had about 450,000, including 30,000 from Finland and 60,000 men from the Ottoman frontier secured by pre-war diplomacy. No more than 130,000 were ever massed for battle.

Preliminaries

In May 1812, Napoleon travelled across Germany, escorted by the cavalry of the Guard, drawing crowds in every village and town, even at night. They usually saw him in his carriage, but in larger cities he rode his grey Arabian horse, dressed in his faded green "good luck" coat, making stark contrast to his flamboyant Guardsmen, with colorful uniforms and larger horses.

On 16–17 May, in Dresden, the Austrian emperor and all the kings and princes of Germany arrived to greet him. Days of talks and festivities followed. He meant to show the Russians that his allies supported him, and he did, but in vain.

The invasion (see Map 18)

On 30 May, at Posen, Napoleon took command of the Grande Armée, initially, divided into three armies. He commanded the northern army (250,000) in East Prussia. King Jerome Bonaparte headed the southern army (80,000) in Poland. Between them Viceroy Eugene de Beauharnais had a third army (80,000). Macdonald's corps (30,000) and the Prussians (20,000), under Johann Yorck von Wartenburg guarded the north flank of the Grande Armée. The Austrians (30,000), under Prince Karl von Schwarzenberg, were on the south flank.

Jerome Bonaparte (28) was a handsome, rakish, younger version of Napoleon. As a teenage naval officer he had been an insubordinate hellraiser and womanizer, and continued his habits in Westphalia.[5] Westphalian officers rated him a good commander, but Napoleon distrusted him, despite his service in the campaigns of 1806–07 and 1809. Eugene (31), was balding and wore a heavy moustache – the cavalryman personified – if a bit too tall. He had won respect of the military in 1809.

Directly opposing Napoleon was the Russian general, later field marshal, Prince Mikhail Barclay de Tolly (a Livonian of Scottish ancestry) with an army of 130,000. Barclay had risen from the ranks and was praised by the czar after Eylau. To the south, opposite Jerome, was Prince Piotr Bagration, with 50,000 troops. This Georgian was the senior commander; he had commanded advance guards, then rearguards at Austerlitz, Eylau, and Friedland. South of the Pripet Marshes, out of play, were 40,000 men under Tomassov. Other Russian forces were far to the rear. Barclay alone had to meet Napoleon's initial assault.

On 24–25 June 1812, Napoleon's main force crossed the Niemen into Russia at Kovno. The Russians retreated, and for days the French saw only Cossacks of the rearguard, who hit Murat's advance screen of cavalry then galloped out of range.

On 26 June the army marched, unresisted, into Vilna, the capital of Lithuania. Napoleon ordered that work begin on a major base at Vilna, which could be supplied from Königsberg and Danzig via the Baltic Sea and the Niemen River. He had brought enough of the French fleet to the Baltic to secure these supply

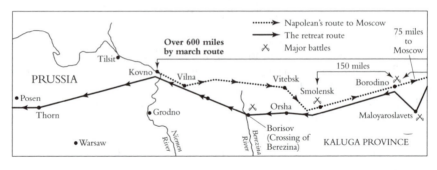

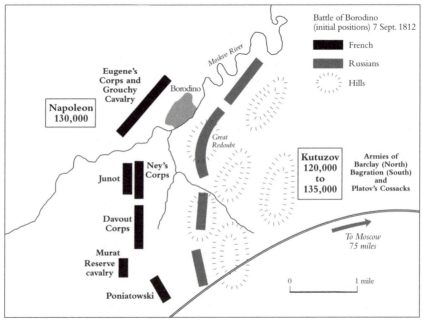

Map 18 The Russian Campaign, 1812, and the Battle of Borodino, 7 September 1812

lines.[6] He tarried in Vilna, principally deciding whether to restore the Kingdom of Poland, including Lithuania. The locals celebrated with a *Te Deum*, balls and dinners. However, the Polish Diet, assembled in Warsaw, was divided. The emperor gave Lithuania its own government, and finally departed to join his army.

Meanwhile, Murat and the cavalry were leading the army toward Vitebsk, following Barclay. The men trudged in heat and dust, then pouring rain, then unusual cold, which made men ill.[7] After their five-day ration of hard tack and dried beef gave out, men began to starve, and horses too. The pace set by Murat's cavalry was too fast for foraging, and fodder wagons for the horses could not keep up. There was food on farms not far from the march route, but the men had no time to find it. Russian peasants did not cooperate in the official "scorched earth" policy; burning crops meant starvation. Cossacks or, rarely, other army units set villages afire – line soldiers were also peasants. By early July, the French were falling out from hunger and fatigue, or deserting, and horses were dying.[8] Napoleon surely knew that, but his priority was catching and destroying the Russian army. In mid-July, Napoleon reached the army with his Guard and headquarters.

Meanwhile, Jerome had departed for Westphalia – principally as a result of miscommunication – and Davout had taken over his army. Napoleon had ordered the king to prevent Bagration from reinforcing Barclay, and thought he was not moving fast enough. On 1 July, from Vilna, the emperor sent Marshal Davout, with 35,000 men, to head off Bagration – assumed to be moving east – and trap the Russian between his and Jerome's forces. Davout took Minsk, but wrote Napoleon that there was no sign of Jerome. Napoleon lost his temper and on 6 July ordered Davout to take command of Jerome's army when they made contact.

Jerome had started late, after attending the meeting of the Polish Diet (by Napoleon's order). He had been delayed by heavy rains and swollen rivers, but was following Bagration, who had skirted Minsk and gone south, through Mir (10 July), and was marching to cross the Berezina at Bobruisk. On 14 July, Jerome heard that Davout was at Minsk, and sent a messenger asking him to join in the pursuit; the messenger returned with Napoleon's orders placing Davout in command. Jerome, furious, left the army and returned to Westphalia. (Napoleon covered his desertion with orders.) By the time Davout organized his forces, Bagration had escaped to the north and joined Barclay.

One can hardly fault Napoleon for preferring Davout to Jerome as an army commander. *What is odd is that the emperor did not send him home earlier.* Jerome had been brought to Warsaw to become king of Poland; the army command was a "cover." At Vilna, Napoleon decided to delay a solution on Poland; meanwhile Jerome had marched with the army. The only certainty is that dismissing him gained Napoleon nothing in the short term. A few days were lost, however, in changing the command; in that time it is possible that Jerome could have stopped Bagration, and put a new complexion on the campaign.[9]

Napoleon soon united his army with those of Davout and Eugene. He expected Barclay and Bagration to turn and fight at Vitebsk, about 300 miles into Russia, but they did not. So the army continued the pursuit toward Smolensk – on the road to Moscow – but without Napoleon. The emperor remained fifteen days (29 July to 12 August) in Vitebsk, where he organized a provincial government (in a Russian city – if once Lithuanian). Why is a good question. Militarily, he was wasting time.[10]

Napoleon's army was shrinking, although it had not fought a major battle. At Vitebsk one-third of the men were missing – victims of hunger, thirst, disease, fatigue, and the pounding of the elements. The weather had turned very hot again, and the army was marching in clouds of stifling dust, with Murat's cavalry setting the pace, and losing more men.

Smolensk

On 16 August, the French approached Smolensk, 400 miles into Russia by the march route, and received artillery fire from the city. Barclay and Bagration seemed ready to fight at last. Smolensk was protected by a wall on the west and the Dnieper River on the east; the wall was 3 miles long, 25 feet high, 10 feet thick, and protected by a moat. On 17 August the French attacked and breached the wall in a few places, but at great cost in lives.

On the morning of 18 August they found the wall deserted, and buildings in the city ablaze. Cautiously, they went through the city to the Dnieper River, where they received cannon fire from the opposite bank. For most of the day, the artillery of the two armies duelled across the river.

Unbeknown to the French (or Napoleon) Bagration (actually the senior general), disregarding Barclay de Tolly's orders, had begun withdrawing toward the Moscow road. Barclay was forced to follow during the night of 18–19 August, and the next morning was marching away briskly, covered by a large rearguard.

On the 19th the Russian armies were still separated, however, and vulnerable. The day before (18th), Junot, on Napoleon's order, had crossed the Dnieper southeast of Smolensk. When he moved up the Russians seemed to be on the river line, and his orders said to attack the flank. When Junot saw that they were marching, he pulled back into the woods, near Lubino, and awaited orders. Murat appeared and urged him to attack the Russians, but he refused to move. Murat, Davout, and Ney crossed the river and went into pursuit, but in uncoordinated movements. Again, the enemy got away.

Throughout the extended battle, Napoleon had remained in his headquarters, out of touch with his corps commanders or Murat. Had he not been, he might have won the war at Smolensk as late as 19 August, when the Russian armies were still separated. Neither the corps commanders nor Murat kept Napoleon informed, but in earlier years he would have been near the front. On the 19th he seems not to have known either the position of the enemy or of his own troops. Napoleon was culpable, but put the blame on Junot, an easy scapegoat since his failure in Portugal (1808). Late on the 19th, at Lubino, Ney defeated the Russian rearguard. The emperor arrived as the battle ended, praised the marshal and his corps, made promotions and passed out medals. The enemy was gone, however. The only result of the battle was to run up the French casualty figure from 4,500 to 9,000. Again, the Russians retreated toward Moscow, and the French followed.

Napoleon had begun the campaign with an outrageous numerical advantage over the Russians, but his edge was steadily dropping. He reached Smolensk with 156,000 men and left with about 148,000. He had under his direct command five corps – Eugene, Davout, Ney, Junot, and Poniatowski – plus Murat's reserve cavalry and the Guard under Bessières. The march had taken a heavy toll, and the emperor had left detachments in seven towns. In Smolensk, he ordered another major depot established, which reduced his numbers. He had sent the corps of Oudinot and Saint-Cyr (combined, 28,000) to help Macdonald and Yorck guard his ever-widening northern flank, and Reynier's corps to help Schwarzenberg keep Tomassov south of the Pripet Marshes. On his south flank (but under his direct command), Napoleon had a cavalry corps (4,000), under Latour-Maubourg and a Polish division (6,000) under Dombrowski. His main column had fewer than 148,000.

The emperor again put the army on the march while he remained behind for a week, with the Guard. Murat's cavalry led the way, with the usual disastrous effect on the infantry. When Napoleon caught up with the army, Murat and Davout appeared at headquarters, the one damning the infantry for slowing the advance, the other accusing the cavalry of killing the infantry. They were about to draw swords when Napoleon intervened and promised Davout that he would slow Murat's troopers. After Davout left, however, the emperor ordered Murat to go ahead at full speed.

The killing pace resumed, and the awesome spaces of Russia, terrifying to men accustomed to the ordered plots of western Europe, increased the malaise of an army getting weaker from hunger, thirst, and oppressive weather. It was hot, cold, and rainy by turns, and the nights were getting colder. French foragers, half mad with hunger, handled the peasants brutally.

Napoleon was short-tempered too. At Vyazma, 95 miles from Moscow, he found French soldiers looting a vodka and wine shop. He jumped from his carriage and ran at them, cursing in French and Italian and hitting them with his riding crop.[11]

Meanwhile, the czar had made Marshal Prince Mikhail Kutuzov commander of the Russian armies. Alexander thus entrusted the fate of his empire to the general whose advice he had scorned at Austerlitz (for which defeat Kutuzov accepted blame). Kutuzov had since fought largely against the Ottoman Turks, scored consistent victories, and had become the most respected of Russian generals. He was 67, ill, and so fat that he had to be hoisted onto a horse, but his commands were sure to be obeyed. The czar wanted Moscow defended. Kutuzov elected to stand near the village of Borodino, 75 miles west of the one-time capital.

Borodino (see Map 18)

On 1 September, at Gzhatsk, Napoleon's cavalry scouts brought word that the Russians were preparing battle positions 5 miles away – at Borodino, on the Kalatsha River. The emperor ordered a halt for three days, while his officers "counted heads." After the brutal 150-mile march he did not know how many men he had – or guns. The count was 130,000 men, 587 guns. They would face 120,000 Russians, with 640 guns. The enemy troops were ragged, but physically strong, and in prepared positions.

On 4 September Napoleon ordered the advance. On the 5th, the army swept away the Russians' delaying positions, and on the 6th the Grande Armée was before the enemy positions. Napoleon's headquarters were near Valuyeva, 2 miles from the enemy lines. The Guard infantry (30,000 present) was in a square around his tents, and bivouacked there.

On 6 September, the day before battle, Napoleon did not visit his troops. In 1809 he had advised Eugene: "When you are in the presence of the enemy, bivouac with your troops. I've done that for a long time . . . It sets the right example for everybody."[12] At Borodino, however, he was in his headquarters, except for three trips in daylight to view enemy positions through his telescope.

Napoleon's plan was for a dawn attack on 7 September. After artillery barrages, Poniatowski was to break through enemy positions on the old Smolensk road and turn the Russian left (south) flank. Eugene was to take Borodino and then attack the Great Redoubt (the Russians' central fortification). Davout, Ney, and Murat were placed to attack *fleches* (small fortifications) on the Russian left (south center); Junot's corps and the Guard were in reserve. The written order read: "Once the combat is joined, orders will be given according to the dispositions of the enemy." That was vintage Napoleon, but he did not behave accordingly.[13] On 7 September at 2 a.m. the French army mustered for battle. Regimental commanders read Napoleon's proclamation to the troops, which finished with: "The victory depends on you . . . It will give you abundance, good winter quarters, and an early return home".[14] The marshals and key generals were briefed by Napoleon at Valuyeva, and were confident but edgy.[15] The emperor moved his headquarters to a rise about a mile behind the front. From there he could not see much of his line, but that was indicative of his attitude. He was not very active during the Battle of Borodino. Philippe de Ségur wrote that Napoleon stayed in or near his headquarters all day, quite ill with a cold and fever, caught the day before.[16]

The day began with blunders – Napoleon's fault in that he had not scouted the terrain. At 5 a.m. Poniatowski went forward, but was trapped by the dense undergrowth in the forest along the old Smolensk road. He could not turn the Russian flank, and it was 8 a.m. before he reached the line of battle.

The artillery had been late (6 a.m.) and ineffective. The balls fell short of the enemy because of the abnormal cold. It took an hour to reposition the guns; at 7 a.m. some 100 guns finally began to fire with effect. This enabled Davout and Ney to advance on the *fleches*, and Eugene on Borodino.

About 7.30 a.m., Davout led his corps forward against the Russian left. It captured the south *fleche*, but the Russians counter-attacked, backed by their Guard cavalry and many guns. Davout's horse was blown from under him by an artillery ball, and he fell to the ground, dazed and bruised. True to form, after a few minutes, he found another horse and resumed command.

At about 8 a.m., Ney came up on Davout's left, with Murat close behind, and they attacked the Russian center and left. Ney assailed the *fleches*, and took and lost them several times, finally holding them with help from Murat's cavalry. At about 9 a.m. Junot's corps moved up between Davout and Ney, and by 10 a.m. the French had all the *fleches* and Ney's infantry was on the

Semyonovskaya Ridge beyond them. About 11 a.m., however, Bagration counter-attacked and retook the *fleches*, but was mortally wounded.

Poniatowski, meanwhile, had finally come up on Davout's right, and joined the attack. At about noon, the French had all the *fleches* again. The Russian center and left fell back. Murat charged repeatedly with one of his cavalry corps, and pushed the enemy eastward, but he could not break the Russians.

At about 1 p.m., Ney and Murat rode to Napoleon's camp and demanded that he commit the Guard. Murat was in a frenzy, as he often was in battle, and colored his pleas with obscenities in the Gascon patois of his youth. They told Napoleon that the battle could be won with a final assault, if they had the Guard.

Napoleon displayed "a hesitation never known before."[17] He ordered Marshal Bessières (commanding the Guard) to make a reconnaissance, which took half an hour, and then refused to send the Guard forward. Instead he reinforced his right with one division of the Young Guard – to be used in case of a Russian counter-attack. "If I have a battle tomorrow [and have no Guard]," Napoleon asked,"how will I win?"

The marshals were angry. They would always believe that the battle could have been won at midday by committing the Guard.[18] Maybe they were right. What is certain is that Napoleon's hesitation gave the Russians some time to reorganize and dig in on a line of hills to the east. On the French right (the Russian left and center), fighting gave way to artillery fire for the rest of the day.

Meanwhile, on the French left, Eugene had taken Borodino by 9 a.m., crossed the Kalatsha River, and attacked the Great Redoubt. He captured the Redoubt and then lost it. At about 11 a.m., Murat reinforced him with General Montbrun's cavalry corps, and Eugene retook the Redoubt – but Montbrun was killed. Eugene's north flank was then hit by Platov's Cossacks and Uvarov's cavalry corps. He gave up the Redoubt to reinforce Grouchy's cavalry, on his north flank – and the Russian horse was repulsed.

About 2 p.m. Eugene was able to hit the Redoubt again, reinforced by the same cavalry corps, but led by Auguste de Caulaincourt. He took the Redoubt, but Caulaincourt was killed. The Russians gave ground; Grouchy's cavalry pursued them, but was stopped by Russian Imperial Guard cavalry. Napoleon was shocked at the death of Montbrun, an old comrade, and Caulaincourt, whose brother, Armand, was with him (as grand equerry; later foreign minister).

About 4 p.m., Napoleon finally mounted his horse "with effort,"[19] rode to the heights of Semyonovskaya, and looked over the Russian positions – his only reconnaissance of the day. Back at his headquarters a group of marshals and generals, including Ney and Murat, pleaded with him to commit the Guard. He consulted Berthier, who said if they made an attack it should be with the whole army, not just the Guard. Bessières said gravely: "Europe lies between [Your Majesty] and France. You are 800 leagues (1,900+ miles) from Paris."[20]

Napoleon refused to commit the Guard, instead ordering artillery preparation for the next day; but there would be no next day. Carl von Clausewitz, who was on the Russian side, wrote:

> The masses of infantry had melted away . . . less than one-third [were]
> still in action: the rest . . . were dead, wounded, engaged in carrying
> away the casualties or rallying in the rear . . . The mighty artillery . . .
> now spoke only by sporadic shots, and . . . did not seem to ring out in
> . . . thunderous style, but sounded languid and muffled.[21]

At dawn on 8 September the Russians were gone, leaving their sick and
wounded behind – unusual for the Russians. Murat pursued. The Grande Armée
– or the 95,000 left of it – rested for several days, then marched on to Moscow.

Russian casualties were about 45,000; French casualties 28,000 to 31,000,
including forty-seven generals (sixteen of whom were killed). Napoleon was
visibly affected. He moved his headquarters to Mojaisk, a few miles east, but for
several days returned to the battlefield to walk through the carnage of battle,
still and frozen contorted bodies and wrecked equipment and arms, mutter-
ing to himself. Wrote Ségur: "The losses were immense and out of proportion
to result . . . What mourning in Paris; what a triumph for the enemy; what a
dangerous subject . . . in Germany."[22]

Regiments of 3,000 to 4,000 been reduced to 1,000 or fewer. The men sensed
they had won an empty victory; they did not sing or laugh at the campfires.
Officers were morose and fearful.[23]

Whose victory?

Napoleon, of course, proclaimed victory. Privately, he was depressed and
frustrated. He felt he had won every battle with the Russians, but it seemed
to mean nothing – and he said so, over and over, to Caulaincourt and others
in the weeks to come. Kutuzov also claimed victory. He had made a strategic
withdrawal. The French were no closer to winning the war, and their forces
were reduced by one-third.

Napoleon would have to draw reinforcements from units detached during his
march – or from Germany or France, 700 to 1,600 miles away. Supplies could be
had from Smolensk or Vitebsk or Vilna, but that would deplete the depots.
Convoys had to be heavily guarded; east of Smolensk, they required an escort of
1,500 infantry, cavalry, and artillery.

Moscow

On 14 September 1812, Napoleon entered Moscow with 95,000 men. There
had been no resistance on the 75-mile route from Borodino. He found Moscow
undefended and almost deserted. Kutuzov had gone south to the provision-
rich Kaluga province. The emperor took over the Kremlin for himself, the
Guard, his staff and retinue. In the streets hardly anyone was visible except
madmen and prisoners released by the mayor, Count Fedor Rostopchin, on his
departure. Soon there emerged a considerable French community (merchants,

businessmen, others), and some Russians. The French were happy to see them, but they later had to be evacuated, which burdened the army.

On the night the French entered, the city was set afire by Rostopchin's prisoners; the fires spread quickly in a city of wooden buildings. For five days the Grande Armée fought fires. On 20 September, Napoleon wrote Czar Alexander that: "The beautiful . . . superb city of Moscow no longer exists. Rostopchin had it burned." He went on to say that the czar could have prevented the battle at Borodino, or his entry into Moscow, by simple request. He obliquely proposed that they make peace, and avoid further destruction and death.[24] Alexander did not answer. In mid-October, Napoleon had still not heard from him. The emperor had no option but to hold Moscow as long as possible and keep pressure on the czar for peace. Winter would come soon; it was too late in the year to march on St Petersburg.[25] To pursue Kutuzov seemed fruitless. He had beaten him at Borodino; another victory would be meaningless.

Moreover, if he withdrew, his European allies might defect – especially Austria and Prussia. His enemies had been encouraged too much already by the news from Spain, where Wellington had taken Madrid (temporarily). His whole alliance system might collapse. In France, especially in Paris, Napoleon feared a setback might fire up his opposition. There was always the danger of a coup when he was away. Merchants were already nervous.

Finally, supplying his army through the winter would be difficult, perhaps less so if he fell back to his depot at Smolensk, or Vilna. However, any withdrawal would signal weakness, and invite heavier attacks on his supply lines. Napoleon had predicted a short campaign; that had not come about. To finish the war with Russia in 1812 he had to bring the czar to terms.

The French were soon suffering from malnutrition, boredom combined with anxiety – and even exposure, since they tended to congregate around fires for company, although one-quarter of the city had survived the fire. There were furs and diamonds to be had in Moscow, but no shoes. There was vodka, liqueur, wine, jams, jellies, and sugar, but no bread and meat.[26] Initially, there had been stores of grain and flour in the city, and cabbages and meat could be bought at the markets. However, the French did not collect and store the food, and, under threat from Kutuzov's soldiers, peasants stopped bringing any to the markets, and sometimes killed foraging parties. Supply trains from the west brought little food. Meanwhile, the weather got colder, with rain and fog. Men lost hope, and sat staring vacantly at their fires. Occasionally one would collapse, dead. Replacements barely took the places of men who had died. Hospitals were inadequate. Horses were dying daily, as well, for lack of fodder – some 20,000 during the month in Moscow – and only the infantry could move without them. The cavalry began slaughtering horses to eat.[27]

Kutuzov and his army were in the Kaluga province, south of Moscow, where there was plenty of food and fodder. He drew in reinforcements, organized and armed bands of peasants, sent his Cossacks to interdict French supply routes, but put little direct pressure on Moscow. It was unnecessary.

Kutuzov threatened Moscow only on the south. Cossacks were bivouacked on the south bank of the Nara River, opposite Murat's cavalry on the north bank. There was an informal truce; French and Russians met, talked, and traded. Murat was delighted to find that the Cossacks considered him "one of them." Platov had given orders that "the King of Naples, with the high plume," was not to be killed. The Gascon, susceptible to flattery, talked of winning the Cossacks to the French side.

Napoleon, within the Kremlin walls, analyzed possible plans, reviewed the Guard, and sometimes other units, presenting medals and making promotions. He gave irrational orders, for example to Maret, the foreign minister, in Vilna, to procure 14,000 horses in Germany and Poland, although they could not possibly arrive before winter struck.[28] He decreed that the markets be opened, and guaranteed protection for peasants who brought food.[29] He did dispatch cadres back to France to train new regiments, and the like, and had the Comédie-Française reorganized.

In the evenings, he played cards or read books from his travelling library. He reprimanded his bookseller in Paris, M. Barbier, for not sending him the latest works.[30]

Finally, however, Napoleon had to evacuate Moscow. On 17 October he ordered preparations for departure. On 18 October the Russians (who had a ready-made spy system) attacked Murat across the Nara River. He was surrounded and almost captured, but cut his way out with most of the cavalry, and joined Napoleon.

The emperor decided to withdraw to Smolensk, where he had a depot, but not via Borodino. Instead he opted to travel south, via Kaluga and Elnya, then east, through country with food and forage. Even by the southern route, Smolensk was only 14 days' march away. Napoleon hoped to evacuate every man in his army, including wounded and sick, and the French community of Moscow. He ordered transportation to every soldier who could not walk, using every available vehicle – carriages, wagons, caissons, and carts.

On 19 October the Grande Armée marched southward, and for five days met little opposition. On 24 October, however, at Maloyaroslavets, the Russians stood in force behind the Luzha River. Eugene's corps took the brunt of the fighting, taking and losing the village ten times before nightfall. The viceroy sealed a victory by committing an Italian division (Domenico Pino) and his Italian Royal Guard (5,000). They were heroes, but were almost wiped out.

After dark, Napoleon held a council of war, something he steadily advised against. Continue on the Kaluga route? Return to the Borodino road? Murat wanted to fight on: Davout proposed a route (via Medyn) to Smolensk which avoided Borodino. Murat shouted that Davout's plan was stupid, and they went for their swords, but Napoleon silenced them. The council, assuming that Kutuzov meant to contest every foot of the Kaluga route, decided to return to the Borodino–Smolensk route.[31]

To Borodino and westward

On 25 October the army marched northward. Cossacks would have captured Napoleon – but did not recognize him. Berthier and Armand de Caulaincourt jumped from the emperor's carriage and drew their swords, but Guard cavalry came up and the Cossacks rode away laughing. The army moved on, and on 27 October passed the battleground of Borodino, still littered with frozen corpses and the debris of the armies. All went well, despite harrassing attacks by Cossacks, Russian cavalry, and occasionally peasant militia bands. Some men had to discard their loot to keep up, and much of the French community turned back to Moscow. Kutuzov was content to march parallel at a distance.

The weather did the Russian army's work for it. On 4 November there was heavy snow. After 6 November there was always ice and snow on the ground. The withdrawal lost cohesion. Temperatures dropped to 50 degrees below freezing (–17 Fahrenheit; –21 Réaumur; –26 centigrade).[32] Men died by thousands from hunger and exposure; warming sips of wine and vodka meant a permanent nap in the snow. Some 15,000 horses also died. When the army reached Smolensk (9–13 November), half of the cavalry was afoot, and much artillery and most vehicles had been abandoned. The Guard cavalry and artillery had seized the remaining horses. The men had long since eaten the food they carried (in theory, four days' rations). Those able to march were sustained by horse flesh. Starving men sometimes carved up cold-stunned horses before they were dead.

Smolensk

On 13 November, when last of the column straggled into Smolensk, the army numbered 50,000 of almost 100,000 who had left Moscow – of the 50,000, maybe 30,000 were battleworthy. Napoleon said in the 29th Bulletin (3 December 1812): "Until 6 November the weather was perfect, and the army executed its movement very well."[33] True. But then the snow wrecked the army, which became a mob, except for rare units. The soldiers looted the depots of Smolensk, making it impossible to winter there.

On 12 November, Napoleon ordered the march to continue to Vilna; on the 13th, he and the lead elements departed. Such was the disorder in Smolensk, however, that it was 18 November before the rearguard – Ney's III Corps – marched. It comprised 6,000 men – 3,000 (of 37,000) of his original corps and 3,000 replacements. At Krasnii, a few miles from Smolensk, their way was blocked by 30,000 Russians under General Miloradovich, who demanded that Ney surrender. Ney shouted NEVER, with obscenities, and shortly attacked, holding the Russians at bay until dark.[34]

Leaving campfires to deceive the enemy, Ney got his corps across the Dnieper on the ice, eluding the mass of Russian troops. The next morning Ney, on foot among his men, was fighting in deep woods against Cossacks and irregulars.

Eugene returned to reinforce him, and the two marched to join the main column. He had "saved" his corps, but only 900 of the 6,000 remained.

On 19 November, Napoleon wrote Maret that he had lost 30,000 horses in the past week. His greatest need, he said, was for horses.[35] Their loss increased human casualties. Napoleon's effectives dropped by the day. The organized units were followed by perhaps an equal number of stragglers.[36]

The Berezina

The army soon was threatened from the north by the Russian corps of Wittgenstein (30,000), opposed by the reduced corps of Victor (12,500) and and Oudinot (11,000). Kutuzov, with 80,000 men, was behind the French; Tshetshakov, with 35,000, was in a blocking position behind the Berezina at Borisov. Napoleon's army was in danger of being boxed in. A way of avoiding destruction was for the army to fight its way across the Berezina and march to Vilna, where there were masses of supplies. Napoleon decided to take that chance. At Orsha, he directed the army on Borisov.

When Napoleon made his decision, the Berezina was frozen over, but rising temperatures melted the ice and made the river a formidable obstacle. On 24 November, as the remnants of the army approached Borisov, Napoleon had perhaps 25,000 men who could fight and a dozen guns. For cavalry, he had a squadron of four companies of 150 men each, commanded by General Grouchy; generals served as captains, colonels as lieutenants. However, the emperor was reinforced at Borisov by Oudinot and then Victor, whose corps were half-sized but in fair condition and well equipped. They brought his forces to about 48,000. However, the forces of Wittgenstein and Tshetshakov, combined, outnumbered them, were in better condition, and had much more artillery.

Before it reached the Berezina, Napoleon's reputation probably saved the remnants of the Grande Armée from destruction. The Russian generals were loath to attack him. Moreover, with their view obscured by snow and fog, they could not tell how many men he had; the column was several miles long. Kutuzov slowed his march, either from prudence or in the belief that Wittgenstein and Tshetshakov could dispatch Napoleon.

A last victory for Napoleon
(see Map 18)

Napoleon had sat in his coach for days in an almost catatonic state, but on 25 November, when the army neared Borisov, he came alive and took charge. The river was deep and wide and full of ice floes; Tshetshakov (35,000) was on the opposite bank. Wittgenstein was closing in from the north.

However, cavalry colonel Jubenal Courbineau rode in to tell the emperor of a ford 8 miles north, at Studenka. Napoleon also learned that General J.-B. Eblé, his chief engineer, had disobeyed his order to destroy his bridge train, and still had his forges and tools. Timber for bridges was available in the buildings of Studenka, which he could dismantle.

On 26 November the French noisily feinted at Tshetshakov. Upstream, Polish cavalrymen rode across the river, carrying infantrymen behind them who established a bridgehead on the opposite bank. That done, General Eblé began construction of two bridges, one for foot traffic and one for vehicles, each 100 yards long, across the Berezina. They were finished by 2 p.m., and Oudinot's corps went across at dark. On 27 November what remained of the corps of Ney, Davout, Junot, and Eugene, the reserve and Guard filed across slowly, well into the night.

On the 27th, however, Tshetshakov finally attacked the bridgehead. Oudinot blocked him. In the afternoon, the larger bridge broke, dropping wagons, horses and men into the icy waters. While it was repaired, men ran for the other bridge, creating a crush that pushed many into the water. Then Oudinot was wounded and his men fell back. But Marshal Ney seized command; the men rallied, and the French line held.[37]

On the 28th, with Wittgenstein moving in, Victor guarded the bridges while thousands of stragglers went across. During the night he withdrew his corps to the west bank, leaving the bridges to Eblé and a rearguard. On the morning of the 29th, Wittgenstein's artillery was firing on the bridges. Eblé held until 9 a.m., but Wittgenstein's infantry was closing in. He withdrew his last men and burned the bridges. Some stragglers perished on the burning bridges; perhaps 10,000 were left behind. Napoleon had a victory. He escaped the Russians with 100,000 men (though only about 50,000 fighters, the rest stragglers). Due credit should go to Courbineau, Eblé, Victor, Oudinot, and Ney. However, Napoleon had "awakened," and it made a difference. The road to Vilna was open to the remnants of the Grande Armée.

On 5 December, at Smorgoni, Napoleon turned the Grande Armée over to Murat and departed for Paris. He had to raise another army, and the French were jittery over his long absence. In October, there had been an attempted coup against his government, the "Malet Conspiracy."[38] With his army free to march to Vilna, he decided he was needed more in Paris.

Napoleon travelled incognito, with Caulaincourt, by sledge and then carriage. Before dawn on 19 December he was in the Tuileries. Three days before, the *Moniteur* had printed the 29th Bulletin of the Grande Armée (3 December 1812). The emperor admitted that the army had suffered a "calamity," but blamed it on the weather. There were no casualty figures, and no mention of the ghastly condition of the men. Rather, he praised the "*bonne humeur*" and "*gaieté*" of the soldiers. Most space was given to the crossing of the Berezina, emphasizing the heroism and downplaying the suffering and death. He exaggerated the number of Russian prisoners taken in that action. Overall, he gave the impression that the army had suffered, but could recover. The Bulletin ended: "The health of the emperor has never been better."[39] That seems arrogant, but was meant to reassure the French.

Murat commands the army

Napoleon had given Murat the army because he was the ranking officer (king and marshal), and because he felt Murat's "follow me" style of leadership would get the army to Vilna. It did, but Murat had developed an obsession with returning to Naples. He was afraid that his spider queen, Caroline Bonaparte, would seize control and ally with the British. Murat had exuberantly led the way to Moscow, but during the retreat he had become morose, and even voiced doubts about Napoleon's future.

On 8 December, Murat led the army (minus 20,000) into Vilna, where some 4 million rations of biscuit and meat were stored – enough for the rest of the winter. But the troops looted the depot and Murat became anxious about Russian pursuers. "I will not be trapped in this chamber pot!" On 9 December he ordered the army to march on to Kovno, abandoning men in hospital and those still stumbling into town.[40] On 19 December the army was in Königsberg, which Murat might have held, but he led on to Posen, in East Prussia – 400 miles west of Kovno.

In mid-January 1813, at Posen, Eugene, Berthier, Ney, and Davout began reorganizing what troops remained. Fewer than 40,000 men were left of the main army, not counting 20,000 stragglers, some wounded or incapacitated by frostbite, some raving mad from the horrors they had seen. Other survivors were Macdonald's corps (12,000); Poniatowski's corps (8,000, half of them reinforcements from Poland), and the corps of Reynier, Augereau, and Grenier (total, 30,000), which were barely engaged in the campaign. Yorck, with his Prussians, had gone over to the enemy on 30 December. Schwarzenberg and his Austrians assumed a neutral posture behind the Vistula.

On 17 January, Murat deserted the army, leaving the command to Eugene, and galloped away for Naples. Napoleon confirmed the viceroy's authority: "My son, take command . . . It pains me that I did not give it to you before I departed." Eugene held Posen for twelve days, then conducted a masterful retreat across Germany. He stopped the Allies on the Elbe and held positions hinged on Magdeburg until Napoleon came with a new army in April.

Casualties and Napoleon's image

It is difficult to calculate the precise extent of Napoleon's losses in Russia. French records show that 210,000 Frenchmen alone were killed, captured, or disappeared in 1812, but they were not all in Russia. Records for other nationalities in the Grande Armée are spotty. Russian records show that over 170,000 men were captured between Moscow and the Vistula.[41] However, Napoleon's total losses must have been above 500,000 men – roughly the difference between the number who entered Russia and those who returned (counting Prussians and Austrians). Those killed in action or who died of disease or exposure must have been at least 330,000.[42]

Napoleon's performance in Russia disillusioned his marshals and generals in varying degrees, and the officers and NCOs at large became more skeptical. However, the French people remained generally loyal to the government. Evasion and desertion increased, but there were a fair number of enthusiastic recruits and draftees for the next campaigns.

Nevertheless, the myth of Napoleon's invincibility, which he had carefully cultivated since 1796, was forever damaged.

13

CAMPAIGNS OF GERMANY AND FRANCE, 1813–14

France's enemies

Because of his enemies' failure to unite, or other factors, Napoleon had fought one great power at a time in his earlier campaigns.[1] In 1813, early on, Bonaparte had against him only Russia and Prussia (plus Britain, at sea). He had greater numbers than his enemies, and was in Germany before he was expected (see below). Eventually, however, he had to face the combined armies of the major (and minor) European powers, who had twice his forces, and no allies but Eugene, in Italy. It was the same in 1814. That would make a great difference in the campaigns of 1813–14.

Yorck's Prussians had deserted the French and joined the Russians on 30 December 1812. Frederick William III of Prussia silently approved of Yorck's action, but watched and waited. On 28 February 1813, after Russian troops crossed the Oder River, he allied with the czar. On 17 March, after French troops left Berlin, he appealed to "my people" and the army to expel the French, and declared war on France. Meanwhile Bernadotte, acting for the king of Sweden, signed a treaty with Britain (3 March) that gave him a healthy subsidy to remain among the Allies. On 27 March the Russians occupied Dresden, and the king of Saxony fled to Bavaria. He swore continuing loyalty to France, but he was wavering, as was the king of Bavaria.

Finally, Austria, after enlarging her army, refused Napoleon's request (20 April 1813) to put it at his disposal. Clement von Metternich, the new chancellor, informed him that Austria would act as "armed mediator" for the time being. Ultimately, Austria's stand would depend on French military fortunes in 1813. The same applied to *Rheinbund* states.

The Grande Armée of 1813

On 30 April 1813, Napoleon took command at Naumburg of a new Grande Armée of 300,000, with 40,000 cavalry and 1,250 guns. Eugene's Army of the Elbe (90,000) was the nucleus. Napoleon had transferred 180,000 French National Guardsmen to the army, and called up 487,000 conscripts of the classes of 1814, 1813, and 1809–12 (but not all were sent to Germany).[2] His German allies furnished 40,000 troops, despite losses of 90–95 percent sustained in Russia.[3] Poniatowski and 10,000 Poles were present for duty.

At peak strength, in August 1813, Napoleon's Grande Armée numbered 430,000, including 88,000 in foreign contingents. The cavalry, however, was not of the quality of that lost in Russia; too many were green riders on second-rate mounts. The infantrymen were mostly conscripts (fewer than called because of desertion or evasion). There were volunteers, however, some under age, who were excited over serving the emperor, reflecting a male urge – in a society with a military tradition – to follow the glory road their brothers or fathers had told them about. The French army, however, was neither tough nor well trained. In all arms there were jaded veterans of the Russian disaster. Finally, Napoleon commanded through uninspired marshals and generals (with some exceptions). The army was big, but weaker than any Napoleon had commanded before. Both size and weakness created problems.

Lützen and Bautzen

Napoleon had decided to divide his forces into several armies, but pending that he marched with 120,000 men. He was faced by about 110,000 Russians and Prussians, under Wittgenstein and Blücher, but neither commanded the whole force.[4]

The French emperor was not aware, however, of his advantage in numbers or his enemies' lack of central command. Neither did he know the precise location of the enemy, but that never bothered him. On 1 May, the day after his arrival, he ordered his army across the Saale River and marched on Leipzig. The Allies fell back, opposing his advance only sporadically.

In one of these skirmishes, however, near Weissenfels, Marshal Bessières was killed by a cannonball. Napoleon was stunned. The marshal had served him on every major campaign since 1796, and had now been killed by the first shots of the enemy – a bad omen. He was only the second marshal to be killed (or die of any cause). Napoleon gave him an epitaph worthy of a Gascon: "Bessières lived like Bayard; he died like Turenne."[5]

On 2 May, at Lützen, with some difficulty, Napoleon won a victory over the Allies. Wittgenstein and Blücher had 73,000 of their troops massed, whereas Napoleon's corps were widely separated. (He was not blessed with the Grande Armée of 1805.) The Allies advanced, and Napoleon fought back with 45,000, but by dusk had 110,000. He attacked, and after hours of bloody combat, committed the Guard (under Soult, vice Bessières), and drove the Allies into retreat. His cavalry was too weak to pursue.

Nevertheless the emperor was jubilant. His proclamation to the troops compared Lützen to Austerlitz, Jena, Friedland, and Borodino. His bulletin said the French had annihilated the Prussian Royal Guard, and decimated the czar's guard.[6] "I am again the master of Europe," he exulted.[7] As usual, he exaggerated the enemy's casualties and understated his own.

He appealed to French pride (and repaired his image) by describing wounded soldiers passing him in ambulances: "The young soldiers . . . hid their suffering and cried '*Vive l'Empereur!*' For twenty years . . . I have commanded the armies of France, and I have never seen such bravery and devotion."[8]

He wrote to his German allies of certain victory in the war.

As to Napoleon's performance, Marmont wrote, "It was probably the day when, in his whole career, he most courted danger."[9]

At this juncture Napoleon sent Eugene back to Italy, and in June, the viceroy sent 38,000 Italians to the Grande Armée in exchange for 50,000 French for his army.

The emperor brought up replacements, building his numbers to 250,000. Responding to an obsession on punishing the Prussian traitors, he gave Ney command of a separate army of four corps (plus cavalry), with orders to march on Berlin. Napoleon then followed the retreat of the Allies.

On 16 May, the cavalry found the enemy near Bautzen, 100 miles to the east in Saxony; spies estimated the enemy strength at 150,000. (It was actually 96,000.) Napoleon sent most of his army west of Bautzen. He ordered Ney (marching for Berlin) to bring two corps (his own and that of Lauriston) and attack the Allies from the north. Reynier and Victor (with Sebastiani's cavalry) were to continue the march on Berlin. Ney misunderstood and came south with his whole army, which was to the good.

On 19 May at 10 a.m., Napoleon reached Bautzen; he spent the day putting 115,000 men in position west of the Spree River. When Ney (85,000) arrived, he would have 200,000. Wittgenstein, with Prussians and Russians (96,000), was east of the Spree River (which runs roughly north and south) with the south-center of his position in the fortified town of Bautzen, a second line on hills a mile to the rear, and the reserve a mile behind it. However, there was no fighting on the 19th, only scouting and probing.

Napoleon's plan for the 20th was to hold the enemy in position with the corps of Oudinot, Macdonald, Bertrand, and Marmont, plus the Guard if needed, while Ney hit the enemy's north flank and rear. But only Ney's advance guard reached the battle site early enough to see action.

On 20 May, about noon, the French bombarded the enemy center. Then the infantry attacked across the Spree, with the engineers throwing up bridges under fire. At day's end, the French had captured Bautzen and pushed back the first Allied line. Ney's, Lauriston's and Reynier's corps were approaching.

On the 21st, Oudinot was to attack the enemy in the south, and Macdonald and Marmont the enemy left and center, while Ney drove south into the enemy rear. Soult, with Bertrand's corps (he was ailing), the cavalry of Latour-Maubourg and the Guard (if needed) on Napoleon's order, would hit the enemy right and seal the victory.

On the morning of the 21st the Allies hit Oudinot on the south flank, before he could attack them. In mid-morning he asked Napoleon for reinforcements. The emperor refused help and told him to hold. By 11.30 a.m. Marmont and

Macdonald had made forward progress, and Ney was attacking from the north. At 12 noon, Napoleon sent Soult forward, and by 2 p.m. he had pushed Blücher's corps back a mile. But then the attack stalled. Ney was assaulting Preititz (which he should have bypassed). Lauriston was moving too slowly, and Reynier had not arrived. The battle turned into a slugging match, with the French sustaining heavy losses but making progress.

At dusk, Napoleon committed the Guard in Bertrand's sector, and it drove Blücher's corps steadily back. But Ney and Lauriston had not cut the Weissenberg and Görlitz roads, which allowed the enemy to make a fighting withdrawal. At 10 p.m. a violent rainstorm ended the battle. In the morning the Allied army was gone. The French, exhausted and short of cavalry, did not pursue. Each side had suffered about 20,000 casualties.

Napoleon had won another victory, but by fielding twice the numbers of his enemy and committing the Guard. Hardly a triumph. The czar had interfered with Wittgenstein's operations, which helped Napoleon. Principally, however, the French emperor had failed to win handily because he had inferior troops, especially cavalry, and was short of effective commanders. He had sent Davout to take Hamburg, which was not yet of importance in the war. Lannes was dead; Masséna was in *de facto* retirement; as was Augereau; Murat was in Naples (and up to no good); so it went.

Truce

The French took Dresden, which, in theory, put Saxony back in Napoleon's camp. Davout took Hamburg, securing the lower Elbe. The French emperor thus recovered some of power in Germany.

Napoleon's army, however, had problems. His cavalry was not combat ready. Cossacks roamed about the French rear. Two battles had taken 40,000 casualties. There were some 90,000 sick and stragglers. Green French troops, having seen the horrors of battle, were fearful and unhappy. Some had cut off their trigger fingers or shot themselves in the hand or foot, hoping to be sent home. Napoleon had ordered that two offenders from each corps be shot by firing squad before the whole corps.[10]

On 2 June the Allies asked for a cessation of hostilities; Napoleon agreed. On 4 June an armistice was signed, extending the truce until 20 July, then 16 August. Napoleon agreed to the truce in order to rest, reorganize, discipline, reinforce, and resupply his army. The Allies had similar reasons, and also hoped to bring Austria into the war on their side.

Austria swings the balance

On 14 June, the czar, inspired by Metternich, proposed a congress at Prague to discuss general peace. On 26 June, Metternich went to Dresden to interview Napoleon. The French emperor offered to pay Austria a subsidy for her neutrality; Metternich, rather than respond, urged him to participate in the Prague congress. Napoleon finally agreed to send Armand de Caulaincourt, but believed that Austria intended to join the Allies. "I will beat you," he shot at Metternich, who replied, "But I have seen your troops, they are boys and old men."

The same evening, 26 June, news arrived of Wellington's victory over Joseph Bonaparte at Vitoria (21 June 1813), marking the end of the Bonaparte kingdom of Spain and making it possible for Wellington to invade southern France. Vitoria, in effect, brought Austria into the war on the Allied side.

On 19 July Austria agreed (the Reichenbach Convention) to join the Allies if Napoleon declined the terms offered by the Prague Conference. For peace, he was to cede the Duchy of Warsaw to Russia and Illyria to Austria, restore Prussia to her boundaries of 1805, and dissolve the *Rheinbund*. Otherwise his empire would stand. Napoleon refused, scorning Allied strength. Austria had raised 300,000 troops, and was calling up more; Russia and Prussia had strengthened their armies, and Bernadotte had agreed to command troops, encouraged by British subsidies and the promise of Norway (from Denmark) at the peace. In Naples, Murat and Caroline were negotiating with the Austrians. It was probable that Napoleon's German allies would defect if he lost a major battle. On 12 August, Austria joined the Allies. Blücher, a violent Francophobe, resumed fighting on 13 August, four days early.

The armies

Napoleon found himself at war with all the major European powers; their armies were partially financed by the British and they had the British navy at their service.[11]

Soon arrayed against him were four armies, the strength of which would grow as the campaign progressed. They were: the Army of Bohemia (Austrian Prince von Schwarzenberg, 240,000), the Army of the North (Swedish Crown Prince Bernadotte, 120,000), the Army of Silesia (Prussian Field Marshal Blücher, 95,000), and the Army of Poland (Russian Marshal Bennigsen, 60,000), making a total of 515,000, which would soon exceed 600,000.

Napoleon's forces had expanded also – but by more green French troops and foreign contingents that might defect. He formed three armies: Marshal Oudinot (120,000; including 35,000 under Davout at Hamburg), Marshal Ney (85,000), Napoleon (165,000), plus detachments and fortress garrisons (60,000), making a total of 430,000 with a field army of 370,000 at the maximum.

Despite these dispositions, Napoleon was in command of the whole army. He ordered Ney about, and drew troops from Oudinot. Nevertheless, the army under his personal command numbered 250,000 at best, and shrank with every battle he fought.

Meanwhile, Napoleon had sent Soult to command the Army of Spain, soon fighting in southern France against Wellington. But Murat was back, by his order. Napoleon needed Murat. Murat came because Napoleon was winning when he left Naples. Napoleon knew about his contacts with the enemy, but felt that if Murat were with him he would be loyal; the Gascon's heart was with him, if Caroline's was not.

Campaign plans (see Map 17)

Napoleon first considered placing the corps close together for quick concentration – and awaiting the next Allied move. That might have saved his men's strength, and allowed him to strike if the enemy made mistakes – carrying his battlefield tactics to the strategic level. However, he settled on a plan under which his three armies would operate separately, and Oudinot's beyond the range of support of the others. Oudinot was to take Berlin and destroy Bernadotte's army. Again, Napoleon was driven by the obsession with punishing King Frederick William and Bernadotte ("traitors" both), and dispersed and wasted his strength. Ney was to advance into Silesia against Blücher; Napoleon into Bohemia against Schwarzenberg.

Napoleon consulted his marshals on these plans, something he had always decried. "In military operations, I consulted no one but myself."[12] Marmont said the three-army plan would deprive two armies of the presence of His Majesty on the battlefield – a flattering objection.[13] The others said little and the plan prevailed.[14] However, the French army was not very optimistic. Wrote Jean de Marbot: "The least clairvoyant of officers sensed that we were on the eve of great catastrophes."[15]

The Allies agreed to the "Trachenburg Plan," which was to fight Napoleon's subordinates but avoid battle with Napoleon. An army commander was to retreat if attacked in force by Napoleon, while the others closed in on his flanks. This plan worked very well until Allied numbers made it unnecessary. Obviously, if Napoleon had kept the Grande Armée massed, the Trachenburg Plan would not have been effective.

Dresden

On 23 August, near Berlin (Grossbeeren), Oudinot was defeated by Fredrick-William Bülow's Prussians (of Bernadotte's army), and driven southward. Meanwhile (contrary to plan), Napoleon (with Ney) marched to engage Blücher in Silesia, leaving Saint-Cyr's corps to guard Dresden, but Saint-Cyr, soon under attack by Schwarzenberg's Army of Bohemia, sent a rider to ask Napoleon for help. Since Blücher was in retreat, Napoleon marched for Dresden with the Guard, leaving Macdonald to face Blücher with the "Army of the Bober" (two infantry and two cavalry corps). However, Blücher attacked suddenly (26 August) on the Katzbach River, and wrecked Macdonald's force, capturing 15,000 men and 100 guns.

On 26 August, Napoleon was at Dresden, preparing to meet Schwarzenberg. Saint-Cyr had fortified the city, which allowed Bonaparte to defend while building up his forces. Schwarzenberg was hampered by the presence of the emperor of Austria and the king of Prussia (and shortly the czar), who "advised" him. Contrary to the Trachenburg Plan, he opted to fight, since he had 170,000 men and 400 guns.

On 27th Napoleon attacked with 120,000 men and 250 guns. Murat, with the corps of Victor and the cavalry of Latour-Maubourg hit the Austrian left flank; Ney, with Mortier's corps and Nansouty's cavalry, attacked the Austrian right. Saint-Cyr and Marmont, backed by the Guard, held fast in the French center. This scheme was supposed to produce a double envelopment of the enemy, but did not. However, the Allies had 38,000 casualties (four times the French); they had fought in heavy rain in a sea of mud, caused by the overflow of a tributary of the Elbe that divided their army. Their artillery was bogged down, depriving them of a firepower edge.

On the night of 27–28 August, Schwarzenberg retreated. On the 28th, Napoleon ordered pursuit, but his inept cavalry could not execute the command.

Napoleon had another victory, but it was offset by the defeats of his subordinates. It was his last victory in Germany.

Leipzig

Enraged by Oudinot's defeat by Bernadotte (Bülow) Napoleon sent Ney to command his army. The emperor went after Blücher.

Meanwhile, the Allies got lucky. Napoleon sent Vandamme to cut across the Austrian route of retreat and destroy their trains. On 29 August, an Austrian corps, under Ostermann, blocked him at Kulm, but Vandamme had the larger force and prepared to attack. But on 30 August, Kleist's Austrian corps, retreating from Dresden, blundered into Vandamme's rear, and he was suddenly outnumbered 54,000 to 30,000. The French corps fought well, but had 50 percent casualties and Vandamme was captured.

Ney was marching against Bernadotte. On 6 September he was badly defeated at Dennewitz, only 70 miles north of Dresden. Bernadotte again had led with his Prussian corps under Bülow and Tauenzien, a hero to his countrymen at Jena (1806).

Meanwhile, Napoleon had advanced against Blücher, picking up Macdonald's corps as he went, but the Prussian retreated before him and notified Schwarzenberg, who marched on Dresden. Napoleon returned to Dresden, but Schwarzenberg withdrew, by which time Blücher again was edging toward Macdonald. On 22 September, Napoleon told Macdonald to attack Blücher, but the marshal was already in retreat, and Dresden was menaced by Bernadotte, Blücher and Scharzenberg.

The French emperor was unaware of the Trachenburg game, but saw that Allied armies were closing in on him from the north, east, and south, and soon might cut his communications with France. Cossacks were already wreaking havoc to the west. The weather was getting worse, with rain and the hint of ice and snow to come, and the roads were rutted in deep mud. And Marshal Berthier, Napoleon's perennial chief-of-staff was ill. "It is a horrible time," the emperor wrote Marie-Louise.[16]

On 24 September he ordered a withdrawal behind the Elbe River, moving on Wittenberg and Magdeburg – both in French hands. In early October, Napoleon marched west, and sent Marmont to help Ney against Bernadotte. But Blücher combined with Bernadotte, and they drove Ney southward. Blücher, then Bernadotte, crossed the Elbe, threatened Napoleon's rear, and blocked his retreat on Wittenberg and Magdeburg. Saint-Cyr, meanwhile, was left to defend Dresden. Murat, with three corps plus cavalry south of Dresden, was driven toward Leipzig by Schwarzenberg. Bennigsen's Army of Poland blockaded Dresden (surrendered by Saint-Cyr on 11 November).

By 15 October most of Napoleon's army was in Leipzig.

Battle of the Nations

At Leipzig, on 16–19 October 1813, Napoleon met the Allied armies in a four-day battle – his last in Germany.

On 16 October Napoleon had 177,000 men and 700 guns; the Allies had over 200,000 under Schwarzenberg in the south and 54,000 under Blücher in the northwest. Napoleon attacked Schwarzenberg with six corps, cavalry and the Guard, supported by a 100-gun battery under Drouot. French infantry made some advances, but was weakly supported by artillery and cavalry. Every advance ended in a withdrawal behind Drouot's guns. On the same day, Marmont was attacked by Blücher at Möckern, and retreated toward Leipzig.

On the 17th Napoleon attempted to negotiate with the Allies, but in vain. Reynier's corps (18,000+) reinforced the French, bringing their total to 195,000. However, Bennigsen (70,000) and the next morning, Bernadotte (85,000), joined the Allies, bringing their total to 410,000 men and 1,500 guns. Action was light, but Napoleon decided to withdraw west.

Early on 18 October Napoleon drew his army into a tight circle around Leipzig and secured his line of retreat over the Elster and Luppe rivers, and through Lindenau. The Allies attacked the French on all quarters, however, and the battle raged all day. The French held, despite the defection of their Saxon allies; after dark, the withdrawal began in earnest.

On 19 October the Allies stormed Leipzig as the defenders departed, but the French rearguards held, while the various corps, in disorder and confused by fire from former German allies, crossed the Elster River bridge and filed along the Leipzig–Lindenau causeway. Then, at about 1 p.m., a panicky corporal put a match to explosives prematurely and blew up the Elster River bridge.

The corps of Macdonald, Poniatowski, Lauriston, and Reynier were trapped. They fought, but were driven to the river bank. Macdonald swam to safety. Poniatowski – made a marshal three days before – already twice wounded, tried to swim the river on his horse and drowned. Lauriston, Reynier, and 30,000 French were captured, and some 38,000 had been killed or wounded (total casualties, 68,000). Allied losses were 54,000.

During the battle, Napoleon sent Murat off for Naples with a public embrace, fearing that Caroline might take Naples into the Allied camp (she already had, tentatively, on 17 October). He counted on Murat's guilt and loyalty to delay overt treason.

Over the Rhine

Napoleon made for the Rhine, and behind him his German empire collapsed.[17] He left the army for Paris on 7 November, and by the end of November what remained of the Grande Armée of 1813 was across the Rhine, except for troops left in strongholds in Germany – Hamburg, Magdeburg, Erfurt, Würzburg, Wesel, Mainz, Wittenberg, and lesser places. Davout held Hamburg until after Napoleon abdicated in April 1814.

Meanwhile, on 8 November, the Allies offered Napoleon rule of France within her "natural boundaries" – the Alps and the Rhine – in return for peace. Austria and most of the German states simply wanted the French out of Germany and Italy. They were not for destroying Napoleonic France, since that might allow Russia to dominate central Europe, an unwelcome prospect. Already, the czar had founded a Russian-controlled kingdom of Poland. He was also the champion of Prussia, whose king he had promised Saxony, and he had made clear that he wanted a say in the disposition of all the German states. Moreover, he had a candidate for king of France – Bernadotte – whom he hoped to control.

Napoleon refused the offer, however. The Allies then mutually pledged to invade France (1 December 1813).

Campaign of France (see Map 19)

Napoleon began the defense of France against Allied invaders with a field army of about 120,000, comprising veterans of the German campaign, conscripts, and National Guardsmen. He also had Soult, with the 100,000-man Army of Spain, battling against Wellington in the south of France. Eugene had 50,000 Frenchmen in the Army of Italy, but he fought his own war for his kingdom.

Beginning on 29 December, Blücher (110,000) crossed the Rhine. Schwarzenberg (210,000) was moving through Switzerland. Bernadotte (100,000) was approaching through the Netherlands, but had little part in this war. Blücher and Schwarzenberg planned to unite on the Langres Plateau, between the Marne and Seine, and march on Paris.

Napoleon's plan was to get between Blücher and Schwarzenberg, drive their armies apart, and destroy them separately. Of course, in getting between the enemy armies Napoleon risked being crushed between them – a grave risk, considering the poor quality of his troops.

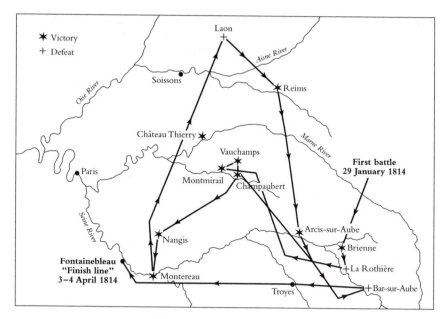

Map 19 The Campaign of France, Napoleon's battles

Return of the scrambler

In January 1814, Blücher (72), Napoleon's most inveterate enemy, marched into Champagne, en route to Paris, without waiting for Schwarzenberg. He personally commanded only 53,000 men, and had no plan to consolidate his widespread corps. On 29 January, Napoleon, with 30,000 troops, surprised him at Brienne, and drove his troops to the winds.

However, Blücher reorganized 5 miles to the southeast, at La Rothière, and Schwarzenberg sent him reinforcements, bringing his numbers to 110,000. On 1 February, Napoleon (40,000) attacked him anyway, but could not match Blücher's numbers. He was beaten, but retreated in good order.

The Allied generals agreed that Blücher would march on Paris via the Marne valley, while Schwarzenberg went down the Seine to the south. However, Blücher moved with his corps dispersed.

Napoleon took advantage, and with only 31,000 troops beat Blücher's corps in four successive battles. On 10 February he destroyed Olssufief's corps at Champaubert. On 11 February he bloodied and dispersed Sacken's corps at Montmirail, 12 miles to the west; and the same day he hit Yorck, disrupting his attempt to reinforce Sacken. On the 12th, his forces sent Sacken and Yorck across the Marne at Château Thierry and into retreat.

Napoleon, meanwhile, was stalking Blücher (32,000) with two corps and some cavalry. Marmont found Blücher near Champeaubert, and led him westward while Napoleon drew in available forces (31,000, including Marmont). On 14 February, Napoleon annihilated Blücher's advance guard at Vauchamps. The Prussian retreated, but Grouchy's cavalry galloped around him and attacked. He lost 7,000 men, but got away.

French villagers turned out to cheer the emperor. Any illusions of better times without Napoleon had been ruined by Allied soldiers' looting and pillaging. Cossacks, lent to the armies by the czar and often drunk on stolen wine, had viciously burned, killed, robbed, and raped as they went. Peasants were even forming partisan bands to kill the enemy. They also produced food for Napoleon's men – stocks normally hidden from friend and foe.

Napoleon left Mortier and Marmont to guard the approaches to Paris with their corps (reduced to about 6,000 each), while he moved south with 70,000 men. Schwarzenberg had his army concentrated, but was vulnerable to attack in detail. On 17 February, at Nangis, Napoleon surprised Wittgenstein's corps, and drove it into Wrede's Bavarians (formerly of the Grande Armée) who were saved by nightfall. On the 18th he hit the corps of the Prince of Württemberg at Montereau and drove him into the Seine. Schwarzenberg withdrew southward.

Congress of Châtillon

The Allies called a congress at Châtillon that offered Napoleon France with the boundaries of 1792 in return for peace. He refused, ignoring the advice of Caulaincourt, now foreign minister. He was giddy from victory, distrustful of the Allies, and thought he could win the war.

Napoleon's inability to even think of defeat apparently made him oblivious to the fact that his forces were shrinking from casualties and desertions. He had been forced to commit the Guard, repeatedly, to win and sometimes just to escape. Further, the Guard was a pitiful shadow of its former self. Old Guard regiments numbered a few hundred. The Young Guard was somewhat stronger, but composed of veterans of the campaign of 1813 and draftees. There were dead and wounded – and also desertions, unheard of in the Guard.

After Napoleon's victory at Montereau, Blücher marched for Paris. Napoleon ordered Macdonald, with 40,000 men, to follow Schwarzenberg, and went after Blücher with 30,000. On 27 February, at Bar-sur-Aube, Schwarzenberg turned on Macdonald and won a smashing victory.

Meanwhile, Blücher was reinforced to 85,000 from Bernadotte's army (corps of Winzengerode and Bülow). Napoleon's strength when they met was 37,000, including local forces. He hit Blücher at Laon on 9 March, but the battle extended into the 10th, and the French were beaten. Marmont left the Paris area to reinforce the emperor, and approached Laon with 9,000 men; he was driven away. Napoleon retreated to Soissons.

Napoleon still hoped to defeat the Allied hordes. He heard of an isolated Prussian corps at Reims, marched across Blücher's front, destroyed it, and then raced south to strike at Schwarzenberg. On 20 March, at Arcis-sur-Aube, he met the Austrian on almost even terms, 21,000 to 20,000, and won. But Schwarzenberg had more troops than were engaged. He heard of Napoleon's descent on Reims, and ordered his forces to concentrate between Troyes and Arcis-sur-Aube.

On 21 March, Napoleon marched his army south, but was blocked by 90,000 Austrian troops. Macdonald (30,000) was 40 miles away, near Paris. Napoleon withdrew eastward.

The race for Paris

The Allies, after palavering for days and reorganizing, marched on Paris again. Meanwhile, Napoleon had conceived a new plan, which was to march across the Allied rear, destroying their supply and communications lines. He and Macdonald marched for a the upper Marne, south of Vitry, and ordered Marmont and Mortier to join him. They obeyed, but found Schwarzenberg's army before them. On 25 March, at La Fere Champenoise, they were bloodied and driven back to Paris.

On 27 March, Napoleon got news of their defeat and marched for Paris via Bar-sur-Aube, Troyes, and Fontainebleau. However, on the 30th, at Troyes, the army was flagging. He left it with Berthier, rode with a small escort to Fontainebleau, and then, with five companions, to within 11 miles of Paris. Early on 31 March, at Essonnes, he found that Paris had been surrendered.

Abdication

Napoleon returned to Fontainebleau, assembled 60,000 troops and proposed to march on Paris. His troops cheered, but while he prepared, on 3 April 1814, Talleyrand persuaded the French senate to depose the emperor and formed a provisional government. On 4 April, Napoleon's marshals refused to march. He confronted them shouting "The army will obey me!" Ney replied, "The army will obey its chiefs."[18] The marshals present – Oudinot, Macdonald, Moncey, and Lefebvre – nodded agreement.

The same day (4 April 1814) Napoleon abdicated in favor of his son (the king of Rome; prospective Napoleon II). But the French senate and the Allies refused to recognize him. On 6 April, the emperor abdicated unconditionally.

On 29 March, Joseph Bonaparte, head of the French government in Napoleon's absence, had fled Paris with the Empress Marie-Louise and Napoleon's son, Napoleon-François-Charles-Joseph, king of Rome. Their journey ended at Blois, where Marie-Louise awaited Napoleon's invitation to join him. He neither invited nor ordered her to come, waiting to see if she could love a fallen emperor. Probably she would have come if asked. But on 10 April Allied troops found her and the king of Rome, and took them to her father, Francis I of Austria. Napoleon never saw them again.

Murat and Eugene

Murat, after leaving the Grande Armée, was back in Naples on 5 November 1813. On 8 November he told the Austrian ambassador that he was ready to ally with Austria in return for a guarantee of Naples, with the addition of the Papal States, Tuscany, and Sicily. In December, however, influenced by Caroline Bonaparte, Murat decided to settle for Naples. On 11 January 1814 he allied with Austria.

Murat was soon facing Eugene and his Italian–French army. He commanded 30,000 Neapolitans and an Austrian corps under General Count Laval von Nugent, in Field Marshal Bellegarde's army, which was trying to conquer the kingdom of Italy.

In the fall of 1813, Eugene had been begged by his father-in-law, the king of Bavaria, to defect to the Allies. He had a tentative promise from the powers to make Eugene king of Italy (rather than viceroy). His wife, Augusta, wanted him to take the offer for the sake of their children. Eugene, however, felt honor-bound to fight for Napoleon.

Murat, conscience stricken, tried to avoid fighting Eugene. Nugent tried to trick him into the war by involving some of his troops, but failed. On 14 April – after Napoleon's abdication, though this was unknown to him – Murat ordered his Neapolitans into battle, but only after repeated demands from Bellegarde and threats from Lord Bentinck, representing Britain.

In February, Eugene had withdrawn his forces into a more defensible area behind the Mincio and Po rivers, including the fortresses of Piacenza, Mantua, and Peschiera. On 16 April, when he was informed of Napoleon's abdication, he still held this area, and was making attacks on the Allies. With Napoleon de-throned, Eugene made a truce with Bellegarde, and appealed to the Congress of Vienna, hoping to keep his kingdom. But the Austrians saw to it that Eugene's appeal was not heard, bribed corrupt officials to oppose him, and paid agitators to foment riots in Milan and elsewhere. He had to choose between causing a civil war and abdicating. He chose to step down, and went into exile in Bavaria. King Max Joseph of Bavaria provided him with an estate and titles.[19]

Murat was in despair after Napoleon's abdication. "Never doubt my heart," he wrote the emperor, "it is worth more than my head!" His agitation was increased by the scorn of the Allies. The Austrians felt he had not lived up to his promises. Lord Wellington, representing Britain (temporarily) in Vienna, hated a traitor, even an enemy one. Murat felt that his kingdom was in jeopardy, and he was right.

Elba

Napoleon was sent into exile on the island of Elba, between Corsica and the Italian mainland, over which he was to rule.[20] To him, however, life was hardly worth living. On the night of 12–13 April he tried to commit suicide, using poison he had carried in Russia, but it only made him sick. He accepted his fate and recovered quickly. On 20 April he said farewell to the Old Guard, drawn up in the White Horse Court of the château of Fontainebleau:

> *Adieu, mes enfants*! Would that I could press you all to my heart; at least I can embrace your banner! . . . General Petit, seizing the Eagle, came forward. Napoleon . . . kissed the flag. The silence . . . was broken only by the sobs of soldiers.[21]

Napoleon, repressing tears of his own, was helped into his carriage and driven away. On 4 May he was in Elba. Louis XVIII had been returned "in the baggage of the Allies." Wellington thought him hardly a regal figure: "A perfect walking sore, not a part of his body sound; even his head let out a sort of humour."[22] The contrast with Napoleon was a factor in causing his unpopularity with the French.

14

THE HUNDRED DAYS AND WATERLOO, 1815

Napoleon on Elba

Reaching Elba (3 May 1814), Napoleon assumed rule of an "empire" of 86 square miles. The population of 12,000 Italian-speaking inhabitants was initially hostile, since he had kept Elba under military government since 1802.

The emperor gradually won over the people by creating jobs and by personal attention. He set up a government and court, remodelled the palace in Portoferraio and four other residences, and financed the improvement of mining, agriculture, and fishing. Rich visitors, mostly British, came (and he received some of them). He paraded his little army of 1,600, including 600 of his Old Guard.

However, by the end of 1814 Napoleon had spent 1 million francs and netted only 200,000 from taxes. Louis XVIII had not sent the 2 million francs (per year) specified in the Treaty of Fontainebleau. The Allies refused to allow Marie-Louise and his son to join him. There were rumors that Marie-Louise had been seduced by her "guardian," Count von Neipperg.[1] His son, soon the Duke von Reichstadt, was being brought up at the Austrian court. Napoleon's mother came to live with him, and his sister Pauline came from Italy to arrange entertainments. Madame Walewska visited. But Napoleon was bored, going bankrupt, and haunted by the suspicion that the royalists (or Talleyrand) were plotting to have him murdered by Barbary pirates.[2]

He was cheered only by the disputes among the former allies at Vienna, and problems of Louis XVIII in France.

Vienna/France

In September 1814 the Congress of Vienna, hosted by the Austrian emperor, opened with lavish celebrations. The czar and a galaxy of kings and princes were there, with their foreign ministers and advisers. Only opposition to Napoleon had united them, however. Now, the czar and king of Prussia plumped for a kingdom of Poland (including Galicia and Lithuania) under Russian control, and the annexation of Saxony by Prussia. Austria and Britain (Metternich and Castlereagh) opposed, fearing Russian domination of central Europe.

Talleyrand, representing Louis XVIII, took advantage of the dissension. He insisted that France have great-power status, since her king, as he reminded Metternich, had been enthroned by the Allies. "Allies against whom?" he asked. "Surely not against the king of France: He is the guarantee . . . of the peace." He got his wish, and put France on the side of Austria and Britain.[3]

Murat's tenure in Naples was in question as well. Metternich supported "legitimacy" (the restoration of old dynasties), and thus preferred the Bourbon king, Ferdinand, but kept his options open; Murat's treaty with Austria was unratified, so he could turn against Murat at will. Castlereagh supported Metternich, in return for a free hand in colonial matters. Actually, the British opposed Murat, who had been a weak ally and was a *turncoat* (Wellington had pronounced thunderously) – against Napoleon; but it did not matter. The czar preferred Murat to Ferdinand, but would not sacrifice his interests in northern Europe for him. Murat's crown was in jeopardy; he knew it and prepared for the worst.

In France, Louis XVIII, to Napoleon's delight, was supported largely by the former *émigrés* and other royalists, such as the Vendéans, among the people, and Lafayette among the nobility. Many *émigrés* were disgruntled, however, because the king had not restored their influence or property, except for unsold "national properties" (other purchasers were alarmed all the same). Louis had found that his *émigré* followers lacked experience and/or talent to run his government or command his army. He was forced to employ ex-revolutionaries and Bonapartists in government and retain Napoleon's marshals to control the army. The king had promulgated a "Constitutional Charter," which established a parliamentary monarchy, with guaranteed rights and freedoms. However, freedom of the press and speech gave way to censorship, when Republicans and Bonapartists began taking advantage of it. To the people, Louis personified the *ancien régime*. Some clergy confirmed it by denying sacraments to Republicans and Bonapartists. Of course, the "lily banner" was back and the tricolor was banned. Further, Louis found the economy in chaos, and raised taxes.

The army was a shambles. Although some marshals and generals had sworn loyalty to Louis (only to be snubbed at court), serving officers and NCOs were split, with the majority loyal to Napoleon.[4] The army was much reduced in size; thousands of "regular" officers and NCOs had been discharged on half pay. Talk of the glories of battle under imperial France and toasts to *l'Empereur* resounded in every tavern and bistro.

Napoleon judged that France wanted him back, and that surely the divided Allies could not oppose him if he came in peace.

Flight of the eagle

On 1 March 1815, the "*thunderer of the scene*" (Lord Byron's words) landed on the Gulf Juan, between Cannes and Antibes, and marched for Paris. He and his staff had blithely sailed from Elba on the night of 26 February 1815 aboard the brig

Inconstant with 1,000 officers and men, including his Guard, in smaller ships. They took roads flanking the Alps to avoid the royalist Rhône valley. People turned out to cheer him. On 7 March, however, near Grenoble, his Guard confronted troops of the 5th Regiment of the Line; he recognized their standard.

According to Napoleon's own account, dictated to General Henry Bertrand on St Helena, he was mounted, rode forward alone to within earshot, and shouted "Soldiers of the Fifth, kill your emperor, if you dare!" The men ran toward him, shouting *Vive l'Empereur*, all trying to touch him.[5]

The usual account is more theatrical. Napoleon pushed past his Guard, and opened his coat and walked forward. "Soldiers of the 5th," he shouted, "I am your Emperor . . . If there is a man among you who would kill his Emperor, here I am!" There was silence, then *Vive l'Empereur!* as the troops joined him.

In any case, he then made a triumphal procession to Paris, gaining more troops as he went. At Auxerre, Marshal Ney, who had promised King Louis to bring him to Paris in an iron cage, fell into his arms. On 20 March 1815 the emperor entered Paris, from which the rotund and puffing Louis XVIII had fled, and was carried by a cheering crowd into the Tuileries. He was emperor of the French again – for a "hundred days" (20 March to 22 June 1815).

The Hundred Days

Napoleon represented French glory, and the years of his reign had been mostly prosperous. The common man's emotional attachment to him was great. He could have ignored politicians and appealed to the people, but did not want to "become king of a *Jacquerie*." He believed that "There can be no social revolution without terror."[6] He meant that the people would require new leadership, and only a new Terror could eliminate the old. He chose to rule with the existing "establishment," the *notables*.

Napoleon had "made" – or improved the status of – most of the *notables*. Nevertheless, some were quietly hostile, and many supporters were fearful and tentative. To please them, Napoleon amended the imperial constitution, with an "Additional Act" providing for an appointed Chamber of Peers and an elected Chamber of Representatives. It pleased no one altogether, and put secret enemies in the chambers, but got his government going. He assembled a ministry of all talents, including Joseph Fouché, Armand de Caulaincourt, and Lazare Carnot. His brothers Joseph, Jerome, and Lucien rallied to him.[7] He began rebuilding the army.

Napoleon pledged to the European monarchs that he would keep the peace and rule France within her existing borders. But the Allies had already (13 March 1815) declared him an outlaw and "Enemy and Disturber of the Tranquillity of the World." On 25 March, Austria, Prussia, Russia, and Britain each promised to provide 150,000 troops until Napoleon was defeated, a total of 600,000. German states promised another 100,000. Napoleon's foreign minister, Caulaincourt, repeatedly affirmed Napoleon's pacific intentions, while the emperor tried to divide the Allies, for example by sending Czar Alexander a copy of Talleyrand's secret military alliance among France, Austria, and Britain.

All efforts were fruitless. War became Napoleon's only hope of survival as emperor.

Murat starts the war

To Murat, in Naples, Napoleon's return provided a chance to salve his conscience, and not only to save his kingdom, but to make himself king of *all* Italy. Queen Caroline Bonaparte demurred, but Murat, for once, went ahead with his plan. His ministers, notably Antonio Maghella and Francesco Ricciardi (freemasons and/or Carbonari) had convinced him that all Italy would rise to fight for unification and independence, and add 150,000 men to his army.

On 19 March, Murat marched northward, with his 100,000-man Neapolitan army, to attack the Austrians in Eugene's former kingdom. On 30 March, at Rimini, he proclaimed Italian independence to the cheers of a paid claque. He expected a flood of volunteers, but there was none. The average Italian, at this time, was loyal to his city or province, and against Italian unification. Even if he understood it, he was unwilling to risk his life for it.

Murat marched forward anyway, serene in the knowledge that he had the Austrians outnumbered two to one. The enemy retreated, but then, in chance encounters, found that Murat's army was a "paper tiger." The Austrians went on the offensive, and the Neapolitan army was soon in flight to the south. On 3 May, Murat managed to pull a sizeable force together at Tolentino and personally led infantry and cavalry attacks. Nonetheless, his army was demolished.

The king fled to Naples, where he growled angrily to Queen Caroline: "You seem surprised to see me Madame; I assure you I have done my best to die." Caroline cared little; she had surrendered Naples to Admiral Lord Robert Campbell, commanding a British fleet in the harbor. Murat fled to Marseilles, and wrote Napoleon, offering his sword. Napoleon did not answer, probably a mistake. He could have used Murat at Waterloo.

After Waterloo, Murat went to Corsica, recruited 300 men, and returned to Naples, landing near Pizzo in October 1815. He purported to believe that the Neapolitans would restore him to the throne, but may have been bent on suicide. At any rate, he was captured by Bourbon troops, tried by court-martial, and executed by firing squad. Brave and vain to the end, he ordered the soldiers: "Spare the face; aim for the heart." Then he gave the order to fire himself. It was a sad end, but the "First Horseman of Europe" surely would have been unhappy in the nineteenth century, when there was much talk and little action.

Napoleon's war plans

Napoleon put together a field army of 125,000 (out of 300,000 regulars and 170,000 National Guardsmen available). Troops had to be sent to defend the frontiers and stand watch in the royalist Vendée and Rhône areas, and a reserve of 20,000 was assembled near Paris. The Allies had 400,000 men under arms and a potential of 700,000. His only hope was to defeat the enemy armies one at a time, and quickly.

The emperor had decided to attack the two nearest armies, both in Belgium: Wellington, at Brussels, with an Anglo-Dutch-German army of 110,000,[8] and Blücher, at Liège, with 120,000 Prussians. He planned to hit Wellington first, under the belief that a hard blow to "*Les Anglais*" would send them running for the British fleet at Ostend. He remembered – perhaps too well – Sir John Moore's retreat to Coruña in 1809. With Wellington out of play, he would go after Blücher. However, Napoleon expected that if he defeated Wellington, Lord Liverpool's Tory government in Britain would fall, and a Whig ministry replace it. Any Whig government (in the tradition of Charles James Fox) would be more likely to seek an accord, and if the British left the coalition he thought it would collapse.[9]

Napoleon's Army of the North

Many of Napoleon's marshals were not available. Masséna and Lefebvre had retired. Alexandre Berthier, his faithful chief-of-staff, was ill and in Bavaria with his German wife. (He died on 1 June.)[10] Most of the marshals fit to command had gone into exile with the king, or had not rallied to Napoleon (Marmont, Victor, Macdonald, Gouvion Saint-Cyr). Napoleon had refused to employ Murat, Augereau, and Oudinot. He was left with marshals Davout, Soult, Ney, and Mortier.

Napoleon made Davout (the best independent commander of them all) minister of war and commander of the reserve army. He appointed Soult chief-of-staff – although the marshal was unpopular and had little staff experience. The emperor made Marshal Ney (in effect) his "deputy commander," although he was a firebrand and some thought deranged by the pressure and horror of the latter campaigns. Jerome Bonaparte was given only a division, but commanded it with great bravery at Waterloo.

Napoleon created one new marshal – Emmanuel Grouchy, a marquis of the *ancien régime* and a renowned cavalryman. He was assigned suitably to lead the cavalry reserve, but in the field was given command of one-third of Napoleon's army, and did not perform well.

Napoleon's infantry corps commanders were second line. Honoré Reille had served largely in Iberia. Of Georges Mouton, Comte de Lobau, Napoleon had said: "Mon Mouton est un lion" (My sheep is a lion); but more than courage was needed to lead a corps. He had been captured in 1813, and would be again at Waterloo. Dominique Vandamme was brave, but had been several times "destituted" and recalled. J.-B. Drouet, Comte d'Erlon, had commanded a corps in the Army of Spain, but was not well respected; his peers addressed him as "count," never "general." Maurice Gérard had been a corps commander briefly in 1813 and 1814.

Good cavalry commanders were available, however. Kellermann had been many times a hero since his crucial role at Marengo; Exelmans, Milhaud, and Pajol had excellent records. All had the cavalryman's impetuousness, however, which, mated with Ney's impulsiveness, made for spectacular blunders at Waterloo.

The army was not as strong as it looked. Of five infantry corps, four had 18,000 to 25,000 men, but Lobau's reserve corps had only 10,000. All were heavy on green troops. The Imperial Guard infantry numbered 13,000 in twenty-three battalions (eight Old Guard and fifteen Young Guard) – an average of 565 men per battalion (normal strength 840). The Old Guard had absorbed the Middle Guard and had many officers and men from line regiments; the Young Guard had been reinforced with men from line regiments and even conscripts, chosen for spirit and appearance (notably height, 5'9" or above). The cavalry had 4,100 men in five regiments and one squadron (normally, about 6,500). The cavalry corps were also small; Kellermann had the largest, 3,400, little more than a brigade. Napoleon named his army the Armée du Nord, reverting to the nomenclature of a Revolutionary army on the Belgian border. If weak, it was spirited and splendidly uniformed.

The campaign begins (see Map 20)

On 15 June 1815, Napoleon crossed the Sambre River at Charleroi and advanced into Belgium. He sent Ney toward Brussels with 45,000 men and kept 80,000 under his command. On 16 June Napoleon fought Blücher, with 85,000 Prussians, at Ligny. Ney, meanwhile, found the enemy at Quatre-Bras – 8,000 men under the Prince of Orange. But thinking he faced Wellington, whose habit of keeping troops in defilade he well knew, he was cautious.

Blücher had marched precipitously, leaving a detached corps (Bülow) behind. Wellington had taken a casual stance toward "Boney." On the 15th, the Duke had learned from Blücher, among others, that Napoleon had crossed into Belgium but had done little. He thought the French might strike to the west, where most of his troops were stationed – between the Charleroi–Brussels road and the sea – but gave them no orders to move.

On the evening of the 15th, Wellington was in Brussels at a ball given by the Duchess of Richmond (as was the Prince of Orange). Just after midnight, he got news that the French had driven the Prussian advance guard from Charleroi.[11] Wellington sent the Prince of Orange south to defend Quatre-Bras, gave orders for his army to concentrate there, and continued to dance until 2 a.m. (16th).

Wellington rose early, however, and reached Quatre-Bras about 11 a.m. on 16 June. The Prince of Orange (8,000 men) was holding out against Ney's 45,000. Wellington brought in troops as fast as possible, and at dusk had 36,000. Meanwhile he rode over to confer with Blücher and Gneisenau, his chief-of-staff, at Brey, near Ligny, only 5 miles away. Wellington promised to reinforce

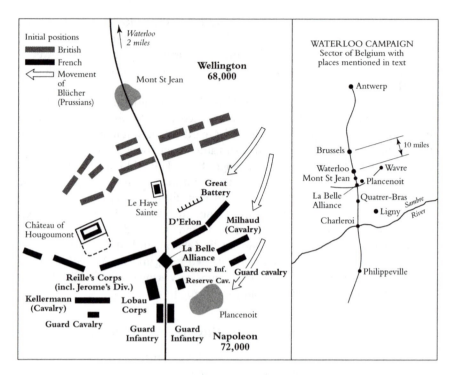

Map 20 The Waterloo Campaign and the Battle of Waterloo, 18 June 1815

Blücher if he could, but did not because he feared Ney might break through at Quatre-Bras.

Ligny

Blücher (73), had rushed his army to Ligny, spoiling to be first to fight Bonaparte. The old Prussian rode with several aides, with one assigned to keep his pipe filled and another to keep his brandy bottle ready. Blücher, a legend in the army, was called "*Alte Vorwärts*" (Old Forward) by the troops. He was always urging his "*kinder*" (children) along, shouting, cursing, and joking with them, and sometimes whacking them with the flat of his sword. He wanted to capture Napoleon and have him shot. The men he commanded at Ligny were not well organized or in peak condition. Regiments were full of green recruits and volunteers, many from recently annexed territories, and some were almost spent from forced marches.[12] Still, they fought like tigers.

At about 2 p.m., Napoleon hit the Prussian left with two corps and the cavalry. The Prussians recoiled. Sensing victory, the emperor sent an aide to d'Erlon (of Ney's army) ordering him to attack Blücher's right flank. Comte d'Erlon obeyed, but Ney heard that he was leaving, and angrily ordered him back. Almost to Ligny, d'Erlon turned back to Quatre-Bras, and thus fought in neither battle. His failure to arrive probably cost Napoleon a decisive victory, but he beat the Prussians.

With bayonets, the French pushed the Prussians through Ligny and Sombreffe. At about 8 p.m., Napoleon committed the Old Guard and Milhaud's cavalry; they shattered the Prussian center. Blücher hit back by leading a cavalry charge in person, but his horse was shot from under him, and he was lost from sight. Fearing his chief was dead, Gneisenau ordered a retreat on Wavre, marching about 10 miles east of Wellington. Meanwhile, Blücher's aides found him, pinned under his dead horse, pulled him out, fortified him with brandy, and found another horse. He galloped after the army and was in his headquarters just after midnight.

Quatre-Bras

Meanwhile, at Quatre-Bras, Ney was advancing almost timidly. Early in the day, he surely could have broken the 8,000 men under the Prince of Orange and defeated Wellington's units coming from Brussels. Since the rest of the Anglo-Dutch–German army was to the west, he might have taken Brussels. However, Ney was familiar with Wellington's tactics in the Peninsula, and feared that redcoats in legion might be on the reverse slopes of hills in front of him. Thus he had sent Reille's corps (20,000) marching slowly, through forest and farms, to press the Allies back on Quatre-Bras. By about 4 p.m., however, Wellington had brought up 20,000 men, and stopped Reille. Ney called for d'Erlon (20,000), but learned he was marching toward Ligny. Ney called him back, but attacked without him.

At that point, Ney fell into a fury that often overtook him in battle. He ordered Kellermann's cavalry to charge into Quatre-Bras, and goaded Reille's troops ahead. Kellermann took the crossroads, but British artillery drove him out. At about 6.30 p.m. Wellington, now with 36,000 men and 100 guns, counterattacked. Ney fell back, awaiting d'Erlon; night fell and the battle ended.

On 16 June, Napoleon had won an indecisive victory at Ligny; Ney had a draw. However, Napoleon now planned to keep Blücher at bay while he defeated Wellington.

Rain began late on the 16th, and poured down all night and the next day.

The march north (see Map 20)

At dawn on the 17th, the Prussians were retreating on Wavre, Wellington marched to Mont Saint-Jean, 10 miles to the north and 8 miles west of Wavre. He told Blücher by messenger that if the Prussian could reinforce him with "even one corps," he would fight Napoleon at Mont Saint-Jean. (That is, Waterloo, where he put his rear-echelon HQ.) Blücher promised two corps or more.

The Allied army trudged northward in driving rain, with deep mud underfoot. Their wagons, caissons, and gun carriages often had to be pushed through the sticky mire when their teams of horses could not make progress. They left rutted roads for the French, who followed.

On the 17th, Napoleon ordered Grouchy to pursue Blücher with 33,000 men – two corps (Vandamme and Gérard) and two cavalry corps (Exelmans and Pajol). He assumed (as did Grouchy) that Blücher was retreating eastward, toward Liège or Namur. The upshot was that Grouchy went in the wrong direction. He spent the night of the 17th at Gembloux and only on the 18th moved toward Wavre after his cavalry picked up the Prussians' trail.

Meanwhile, early on the 17th, Ney asked Soult for orders, but the chief-of-staff gave him none. At about 11 a.m., Napoleon ordered Ney to attack Quatre-Bras, while he marched from Ligny to hit Wellington's flank. However, Ney found that Wellington had marched away, and the emperor simply joined Ney at about 2 p.m.; they then followed Wellington north.

The rain continued, so the French marched in mud, sometimes knee-deep, with men helping to push and drag the artillery along. The troops were delayed also by the horse artillery of the British rearguard, under Henry Paget, Lord Uxbridge (a hero of Sir John Moore's retreat to Coruña in 1809). When the French least expected it, he would bombard them from the hills and ride away, leaving dead and wounded and ruined vehicles behind. It took the French 10 hours to march the 10 miles between Quatre-Bras and the battlefield Wellington had chosen south of Mont Saint-Jean. They halted in the black of night under fire from Wellington's army , already generally positioned to fight.

Positions at Waterloo (see Map 20)

Wellington's army was on a ridge at the north end of a plateau that ran south from Mont Saint-Jean to Maison-du-Roi. Napoleon placed his army on a similar ridge about a mile to the south, centered on La Belle Alliance.

Wellington intended to fight a defensive battle, at least in the beginning. The forward slope of his ridge (facing the French) was steeper than the reverse slope, which lent itself to putting troops in defilade, shielded from fire, and concealing their positions and numbers. On its west side, the ridge curved south, making the Allied front concave.

Wellington

Wellington's force at Waterloo was 68,000, with 157 guns. By evening, however, Blücher would be there, and the numbers near to 140,000. The core of the Allied army was a small seasoned British force of 20,000 infantry and 8,000 cavalry, including 5,000 infantry and 2,000 cavalry of the King's German Legion (KGL); the remainder of the 68,000 consisted of Dutch (16,000) and German troops from Hanover (13,000), Brunswick (5,000), and Nassau (6,000).

A majority of the senior British officers and half the men had served under Wellington in the Peninsula; so had most of the KGL. Many British units had traditions far older than any of the French, of which they were fiercely proud. On the Allied left were the Royal Scots, Black Watch (Royal Highland regiment), the Gordon Highlanders; Kempt's Brigade of Peninsular veterans; and Picton's division, with the Cameron Highlanders and eight Peninsular battalions. Behind Picton was Ponsonby's cavalry brigade, with the Scots Greys (Royal North British Dragoons). On the right was the Ompteda's KGL brigade and brigades of Coldstream Guards, 73rd and 71st Highlanders, and the Royal Inniskilling (Irish) Fusiliers. On the extreme right was Maitland's brigade of Guard Infantry. The Peninsular veterans imbued the whole army with confidence in Wellington.

The Duke had fortified two advance posts. In front of the Allied right was the Château of Hougoumont commanded by the giant Lieutenant-Colonel James Macdonnell, a Peninsular veteran, and defended by companies of the Coldstream and 3rd Guards and Hanoverian and Nassau light infantry. Before the Allied left was the farmhouse of La Haye Sainte, manned by KGL infantry and three companies of the 95th Rifles.[13]

Napoleon

Napoleon's army numbered 72,000, with about 250 guns. Reille's corps, including Jerome Bonaparte's division was on the French left; behind it was Kellermann's cavalry corps and a division of Guard cavalry. On the right was the corps of d'Erlon, backed by Milhaud's cavalry corps and a division of Guard cavalry. Lobau's corps was in reserve, with the Guard infantry and two divisions of cavalry. A battery of 80 guns was placed 500 yards in front of d'Erlon's corps. If Grouchy had arrived, Napoleon would have had over 100,000 troops. Instead, Blücher reinforced Wellington to almost 140,000 at day's end.

Both commanders, perforce, showed confidence before the battle. Wellington, riding his lines on his chestnut thoroughbred, Copenhagen, said to Colonel Friedrich von Müffling, Blücher's representative: "Now Bonaparte will see how a general of Sepoys can defend a position."[14] (He had heard that Napoleon called him a "Sepoy general" because of his service in India.) On the morning of Waterloo he stormed at Soult, who had recommended he call for reinforcements: "Because he beat you in Spain you think he is a great general . . . this is going to be a picnic."[15]

Waterloo (see Map 20)

The day of 18 June 1815 was sunny and clear, but the ground was muddy. The guns of the "great battery" were dragged forward, however, and shortly after 11 a.m., began firing.

At about 11.30, Reille attacked toward Hougoumont. Jerome's division drove in the German infantry outside the walls of the château. However, the château held. The French battered the walls and main gate, held shut briefly by the huge Scottish commander, Lieutenant-Colonel Macdonnell, with his back against the inside. At 1.30 p.m., the French broke through, but Wellington reinforced the outpost with four companies of Coldstream Guards, and the attackers were driven out. The château stood all day. Jerome Bonaparte fought there throughout the battle, and left the field a hero.

At about 1.30 the 80-gun battery fired again in preparation for the attack by d'Erlon's corps that went at the Allied center at about 2 p.m. The vanguard was stopped by Picton's veterans, lying behind a hedge (though Picton was killed), and Uxbridge launched his cavalry into their flank. The Scots Greys and Household Cavalry cut through the French, joined by infantry of the 92nd Highland Regiment, while their pipe major played "Hey, Johnny Cope, Are Ye Waulkin' Yet." The Greys attacked the Great Battery, cutting down the gun crews, but had gone too far. They were hit on the flank and badly bloodied by French lancers (*chevaux légers lanciers*). Nevertheless, d'Erlon's attack failed. At about 4 p.m., Ney led d'Erlon's corps forward again, once more attacking the Allied center, but was thrown back. Each time the French had been forced by heavy fire to bypass La Haye Sainte, held by the King's German Legion and 95th Rifles.

Meanwhile, just after 1 p.m., the French sighted a mass of troops approaching from the northeast. Napoleon hoped it was Grouchy, and sent an aide to find out, who returned quickly. "What news?" asked the emperor. "Bad, Sire." "They are Prussians, *non*?" "Yes, Sire." It was Bülow's corps.[16]

Grouchy

At about 10 a.m., Napoleon received a message from Grouchy that he was pursuing the Prussians toward Wavre. At 1 p.m. the emperor sent an order to Grouchy: "March on Wavre and drive out the Prussians." But after Napoleon confirmed the approach of the Prussians, he added a postscript that informed Grouchy of the fact, and said: "Thus you should maneuver to join with our right."[17] Grouchy received Napoleon's order, probably around 4 p.m., when he was attacking the Prussian rearguard at Wavre. He could hear the cannon at Waterloo, but continued the attack on Wavre. Napoleon's orders were contradictory, but one may question Grouchy's judgment, if not his courage. He never marched for Waterloo; Napoleon was deprived of almost one-third of his army.

Ney and the cavalry

Around 4 p.m. Bülow's Prussians threatened Plancenoit, to the right rear of Napoleon's headquarters. He ordered Lobau to defend the village, which left him with no reserve, save the Guard. He focused his attention on stopping the Prussians.

Ergo, Ney took command against Wellington. The enemy center began to fall back (in fact, moving on order behind the crest for better protection from cannon fire). Ney thought Wellington was retreating, and went in for the kill. Waving his sword, he ordered Milhaud to follow him; by accident or Milhaud's request, the Guard cavalry of Lefebvre-Desnouëttes followed also. Thus 2,800 *cuirassiers* went forward, heavy horses making the ground tremble, followed by 2,000 lancers and *chasseurs* – almost 5,000 men and horses. Trotting, trotting, plumes flying, sabers drawn, they awaited the order to charge. Finally, Ney raised his sword high and went into a gallop; the mass followed in splendid array.

Over the crest of Wellington's ridge they went – and were met by British artillery fire at point-blank range, and then the fire of the infantry, in squares, the men formed three deep, firing and changing places. The British infantry, unlike the French, were trained shooters, if not marksmen, and each rank, on order, delivered punishing fire. The cavalry charged and veered around the squares; hardly penetrating Wellington's formations. If the men were brave, the horses sensed danger, and balked in front of the British squares, forcing the riders to go to the sides, where they took more fire. The French cavalry, badly bloodied, withdrew pell-mell.

Ney, furious that he had not broken the Allied line, reorganized the survivors, ordered in Kellermann's cavalry corps of 3,400 heavy and light cavalry, plus the Guard cavalry of Guyot, also mixed, and led another attack, this time of some 8,000 horse. Again the French were greeted with artillery fire and then braved the squares, but again the attack failed. Ney, still in a battle frenzy, reorganized the mass again and led it forward; he had lost his shako, but the men were guided on by his flying red hair. The sad story of attack and repulse was replayed. At about 6 p.m., Ney finally let the cavalry rest.

Ney remained determined to shatter the Allied line. He did not know it, but his cavalry had broken one British regiment, and badly shaken others. However, he had the impression that his attacks had hurt the enemy; he decided to attack again with infantry and cavalry. Ney called additional infantry from Reille's corps, alerted d'Erlon's survivors, and brought back much of the cavalry for another charge.

One more solid blow! Ney led, hatless and wielding a broken sword; the men followed. This time he took La Haye Sainte, where the KGL infantry and 95th Rifles had run out of ammunition, but no more. If the Guard infantry was to be committed, this could have been the perfect time. Ney could not throw in the emperor's last reserve, however, and Napoleon was still near Plancenoit, reinforcing the defense.[18]

Plancenoit

Since about 4 p.m., when Napoleon had committed Lobau's corps on his right flank, he had lacked any reserve but the Guard. After Ney's cavalry attacks, he had no whole units apart from twenty-three battalions of Guard infantry – fifteen of Old Guard and eight of Young Guard.

Lobau's corps had met Bülow's Prussians east of Plancenoit. He had been steadily pushed back, however, as more Prussian troops came up, led on by "*Alte Vänwarts,*" Blücher himself. By 5 p.m. the Prussians held Plancenoit. Napoleon sent in four battalions of the Young Guard, then four more (Young Guard) who retook the village, but were driven out. The emperor committed two battalions of his precious Old Guard, which took and held Plancenoit. He had thirteen Guard battalions left.

Napoleon judged that he must break Wellington's center, or the Prussians would smash through his rear.

The Guard

At about 6.30 p.m. Napoleon led twelve battalions of the Old Guard down the slope into attack position. The band played "La Marche des Bonnets à Poil" (March of the Bearskins) which refers to the shakos of the Grenadiers.[19] On the appearance of the emperor with the tall *Grenadiers* and *Chasseurs à Pied* of the Guard, the men of the front divisions raised the cry of "*Vive l'Empereur!*" The wounded rose to cheer, or tried.

Napoleon, never ready to admit that he could lose, nevertheless had left a battalion at Maison du Roi, in his rear, in case of retreat. He detached another at the front and stationed it near La Haye Sainte. He then turned eleven battalions over to Ney and went off to check on the action at Plancenoit. At this juncture, Ney was not a man to be handed troops without orders. Four horses had been killed under him that day, and he was on a fifth. Still without a hat and clutching a broken sword, the madness of battle possessed him.

Marshal Ney had the Guard infantry, and was disposed to use it. Just after 7 p.m. the drums of the Guard sounded the *pas acceléré* (double time), and Ney led six battalions forward, followed at an interval by five more, all in battalion column, sixty men abreast. Between the battalions were pairs of horse artillery. The column was not a good attack formation against seasoned troops, such as Wellington's Scottish regiments and Guards.

The Imperial Guardsmen were an awesome sight, all the same, tall shakos bobbing, bayonets gleaming. The tired and battered troops of d'Erlon and Reille were urged forward in support of the Guard by officers shouting that Grouchy had arrived to save the day – a deliberate falsehood spread by Napoleon.

At around 8 p.m. the drummers beat the charge as the Guard neared the crest, but their pace remained deliberate, almost sinister, and they did not maneuver into line, for greater firepower, as they approached the Allied position. They came on as if they were the agents of death, as so often they had been. On the march, they had somehow veered to the left, and came up against Wellington's freshest infantry (protected all day by Hougoumont), but lying down in tall grain, invisible to the Guard.

Suddenly, some 30 yards from the Guard's front ranks redcoats without number appeared, as if by magic. It was Maitland's Brigade of (Royal) Guards. Wellington had ridden up behind them and shouted, "Now, Maitland, now's your time!" The general had ordered "Stand up!" and "Fire!" The first volley took down the officers and 400 men of the leading battalion of French Guards. They moved forward again, but were hit by volley after volley until 1,200 Guards and 60 officers lay dead. The Guardsmen halted and milled about, and, despite appeals to their honor from officers and NCOs, went into retreat.

Waterloo: the end

"*La Garde recule!*" was shouted all across the French line, and "*Sauve qui peut!*" (Every man for himself!). The French army broke up and ran, swirling about the square of Guards near La Haye Sainte, which stood heroically, and past the few other units still fighting. Ney tried to rally the center, shouting "Come see how a Marshal of France dies!" but he ended up inside the square of Guards in the valley along with Soult, hundreds of Guards and officers – and Napoleon. At about 9 p.m. Wellington galloped forward, waving his hat, and his army advanced almost unopposed.

Meanwhile, Napoleon, on his little Arabian mare, Marengo, rode rapidly out of the beleaguered square of Guards at La Haye Sainte, escorted by cavalry and grenadiers, and reached his square of Guards at Maison du Roi. Thence he went by carriage to Genappe, where he mounted a horse, and, accompanied by Ney, Soult, and others, rode for Paris.

At La Belle Alliance, Wellington and Blücher met (on horseback); Blücher embraced the astonished Duke, roaring "*Kamerad!*" and "*Quelle affaire!*"

Two "defenders"

At Waterloo two "defenders" had faced each other. Napoleon had often begun battles, but always held back a heavy reserve and pounced when the enemy made a mistake, as at Austerlitz.[20] Wellington almost always defended selected positions, but would attack (as at Salamanca, 1812) when the odds were heavily in his favor. Wellington behaved typically at Waterloo. Napoleon began typically, but ended with all-out frontal attacks because he had no other choice.[21] He had to win – and on 18 June. If Blücher joined Wellington, he would be outnumbered – even if Grouchy reinforced him. Wellington was not under such pressure.

Since Blücher did join Wellington, and Grouchy failed to show, Napoleon was outnumbered two to one at the end of the battle. He was beaten for the last time. His military career was over; his political career would end in four days.[22]

The significance of Waterloo

The campaign of Waterloo was dramatic and left both sides bathed in glory. Napoleon left the world stage to the thunder of cannon and Wellington became a British legend. Since 1803, if not before, the British had felt that only the Royal Navy stood between them and subjugation to a tyrant (whom they pictured, justly or not, as bent on setting up the guillotine in London). To most others, the relief that he had been beaten for good and all was more qualified. The French were of course divided.

Epilogue

In Paris, Napoleon found Joseph Fouché heading the government, supported by the Marquis de Lafayette, leader of the Chamber of Representatives. At the Tuileries, crowds of Parisians urged him to fight on. Paris had been prosperous and proud under the Empire (at least compared to the successive fragile governments of the Revolution). To Parisians, he was the alternative to the restoration of the *ancien régime*.

Napoleon could not but marvel at the people's loyalty, when so many *notables* had turned against him. He said to Benjamin Constant, who was with him: "Do you see them . . .! They are not the ones I loaded with honors and gorged with money. What do they owe me?" With their support, he went on, he could destroy the government in an hour. Then, sadly: "I did not return from Elba to see Paris washed in blood."[23]

Napoleon could have fought on. Davout's reserve army, near Paris, had swollen to almost 120,000 (mostly conscripts, but amazingly eager to serve the emperor). Grouchy was withdrawing from Belgium, and could reinforce him; so could the survivors of Waterloo, the National Guard, and frontier forces. However, Napoleon saw that continuing the war would only mean more bloodshed. There was not time to make conscripts into soldiers. At Waterloo, he had seen the Guard destroyed; France could not quickly replace it. He decided to try to leave France to his son, who would be Napoleon II.

On 22 June 1815 he abdicated in favor of his son, avowing dramatically that he offered himself as a sacrifice to the hate of the enemies of France. Through his brother, Lucien, he tried to get the senate to accept his son as Napoleon II, and initially seemed to have succeeded. But then the senate and the Chambers approved the restoration of Louis XVIII; both ex-*émigrés* and other nobles, such as the Marquis de Lafayette, had remained loyal to the Bourbon dynasty, but for most legislators it was simply the safest thing to do. Meanwhile, the armies of Wellington and Blücher entered France, Blücher still determined to have Napoleon shot; Wellington opposed (he won out).

Napoleon went to Malmaison, where most of his family gathered to say their farewells. Surely he also said a silent farewell to Josephine, whose château it had been from 1798 until her death in 1814. The gardens and grounds showed her loving touch. Napoleon then went to Rochefort, where Joseph had chartered a ship for New York. He offered it to Napoleon, whom he planned to impersonate while he escaped. (He might have succeeded; he resembled Napoleon, and the British had not seen the emperor since 1803.) But Napoleon declined his offer.

Instead, he took a boat to HMS *Bellerophon*, lying in the harbor, and surrendered himself to her captain, Frederick Maitland. He hoped to find sanctuary in England, and had written the Prince Regent of England (George III was in a spell of mental incapacity): "I come, like Themistocles, to settle by the hearth of the British people . . . which I beseech of Your Royal Highness, as the most powerful, the most constant and most generous of my enemies."[24] He charmed the *Bellerophon*'s officers and crew, who were at his beck and call by the time they reached England.

The British ministry refused to let him land, fearful that he would win over the Prince Regent, and declared him a prisoner. The Allies requested that the British exile him to a place remote from Europe, from which he could not escape. They sent him to St Helena, in the South Atlantic, 1,300 miles from the nearest point in Africa, and 2,400 from Brazil. There he lived out his life as "General Buonaparte" to his "jailer," Sir Hudson Lowe, and as "His Majesty the Emperor" to his retainers. He died of stomach cancer on 5 May 1821, a day officially commemorated in France every year, even in the twenty-first century.

In December 1840, at the request of King Louis-Philippe, Napoleon's remains were returned to Paris (as he had asked in his will) and interred in Les Invalides, where they still rest. Lord Rosebery described the arrival of his casket in the chapel, where King Louis-Philippe, princes, and ministers awaited it:

> Suddenly a Chamberlain appearing at the door announced in a clear and resonant voice, "*L'Empereur*," as if it were a living sovereign: and the vast and illustrious assembly rose with a common emotion as the body was borne slowly in. The spectators could not restrain their tears.[25]

Dictating "memoirs"

Napoleon spent much time on St Helena "writing" (dictating) the history of his reign and military campaigns, but also on a startling variety of other subjects, from the campaigns of Caesar to those of Condé and Turenne and Frederick the Great. He dictated to Emmanuel de Las Cases for the famous *Mémorial de Sainte-Hélène*. He talked to members of his suite, such as generals Gourgaud, Montholon, and Bertrand, whose writings comprise the so-called *Mémoires* of Napoleon, and to the Irish surgeon Barry O'Mearas whose *Napoleon in Exile* was an instant bestseller in Great Britain, and dozens more.

The fallen emperor also described his own campaigns, but said that Waterloo would erase the memory of his victories.[26] He was guilty of some petty, sometimes reprehensible, alterations of facts, however. For example, he said that at Marengo he, Napoleon, had drawn out the Austrian army so that Desaix, with the "reserve", could finish it off.[27]

The myth [cleverly built on truth] he created was mostly political. As emperor, he said, he governed for the people in France. His desire for Europe was to give the nationalities the benefits of the French Revolution in a "Federation of Free Peoples." He insisted that he would be remembered for the Code Napoléon, not his conquests. (In fact, he is remembered for both, but especially his campaigns.)

The "Art of War"

Napoleon, on St Helena, said many things about the *Art de Guerre*, sometimes contradicting himself. He said: "The art of war is a simple art . . . everything is common sense", but also, "The art of war has invariable principles".[28] More true to his own thinking were: "[The first quality of a great general] is the courage of the *improviste* . . . War is composed altogether of accidents . . . A [great] commander never loses sight of what he can do to profit by these accidents."[29] "In military operations, I consulted no one but myself".[30] "The most essential quality of a general-in-chief is the strength of character and resolution to win at all costs."[31] "In war . . . it is one man [the commander] who is everything."[32] "Generals are beaten who . . . follow the principles which they have been taught [principes qu'on leur a inculqués]. There are too many diverse elements in war."[33]

"In war, three-quarters are factors of morale; the balance of real forces make up the other quarter."[34] His maxims are studied in military academies today, and might serve executives in any organization.

Napoleon was probably the greatest commander of all time, but he never had a tactical plan, and only vague strategic ones. His success resulted as much from "scrambling" as from genius.

15

CONCLUSIONS

The French military of the *ancien régime* laid the foundations for armies (and navies) of both the French Revolution and Napoleon. Little changed during the Revolution as to the armies' organization, weapons, tactics, and strategy. It was the same with Napoleon, except for the introduction of the corps. His forte was using everything better than anyone ever had, and taking great liberties with tactics (as great commanders always have).[1] Of course, armies grew in size after the introduction of national conscription (the *levée en masse*, 1793).

A root cause of the Revolution was the population explosion of the eighteenth century.[2] It pushed peasants off the land and into cities, especially Paris, which became crowded with hungry, angry workers, easily led by demagogues or idealists promising a better life. However, the "surplus" population later benefited the army by making possible a successful *levée en masse*.

In 1789, the first step of the revolution – limitation of royal power by a National Assembly – rattled the thrones of Europe, and challenged the established rights of the aristocracy. The rulers of Austria and Prussia called on Europe's monarchs to oppose the Revolution, but in vain. Nevertheless, the French Assembly managed to feel threatened and, announcing a mission of bringing *"liberty and equality"* to all peoples, pushed Louis XVI into declaring war on Austria; Prussia joined her.

As early as July 1789 the National Guard (commanded in Paris by Lafayette) was created to guarantee internal peace, but was soon used to augment the army. In 1791 and 1792 there were calls for volunteers, followed by levies, raised very like the king's militia. These measures brought enough men to reinforce the regular (royal) army. But they were untrained when Louis XVI declared war.

The French Revolutionary armies initially lost, and badly, which Rochambeau and Lafayette had predicted, outraged that the Assembly was pressing Louis XVI to declare war when the armies were not prepared.[3] Moreover, the army had a plethora of problems: the first army commanders were aristocrats and not fully trusted – Rochambeau, Arthur Dillon, Lafayette, Dumouriez, *et al.* Commanders depended too much on *zeal*. There was a shortage of officers, formerly almost all aristocrats, some 55 percent of whom had fled the country; they were replaced by middle-class volunteers and former NCOs who (at first) were obeyed selectively, if at all. The troops were infected with vague democratic ideas, which emboldened them to question their generals' orders and demand votes, with catastrophic results.

The king was the victim of defeats in the Austrian Netherlands (Belgium) and the invasion of France by Prussians under the Duke of Brunswick. Louis XVI was overthrown on 10 August 1792 and executed on 21 January 1793. The monarchial powers united in hostility, but not as allies. United action had to wait – which undoubtedly saved the Revolution – until other issues were settled.

However, *the French Republic had the WAR it needed to sustain revolutionary spirit and perpetuate itself.* No war could have suited their purposes better than war against the *ancien régime* – monarchs, aristocrats, and their minions. The government made them loathsome by propaganda, including the "Marseillaise," which urged the French to fill the furrows of their fields with the blood of tyrants' "ferocious soldiers."

The rule of the new Republic became *Victory or the Guillotine* for aristocrats and potential traitors. Custine, Houchard, and Arthur Dillon were victims of the policy. Lafayette fled (and was locked up by the Austrians as a "dangerous revolutionary"). Dumouriez, expecting to be accused, went over to the enemy. Under the Terror, loyal officers died at the guillotine simply because they were aristocrats – for example the Vicomte de Beauharnais (first husband of Josephine, Napoleon's empress). Minor aristocrats who were promoted to high command, such as Napoleon Buonaparte and Nicolas Davout, fared best.

Oddly enough, the workers of Paris (led by more materially successful *sans-culottes*) forced enactment of the *levée en masse*, the major military innovation of the era. Demanding the right of "the people" to man and control the armies, they threatened mass action. In August 1793, to placate them, the Terror government instituted the *levée*, making all able-bodied males between 18 and 25 liable for military service. Lazare Carnot was responsible for implementing the *levée en masse*, which raised a million troops on paper; 850,000 in fact – too many to use on battlefields as war was fought at the time – but a reserve and a continual threat to France's enemies. The *levée* became raw conscription under the Jourdan–Delbrel Law of 1798, and was continued by Napoleon.

The armies of the Revolution became truly victorious (ignoring earlier flukes, such as the Battle of Valmy) when the officers gained experience, discipline was restored, and particularly after the reforms of Carnot under the Terror (1793–94). In addition to the *levée en masse*, the government made participation (in some capacity) in the war effort a duty of every citizen – man, woman, and child. It took control of all material resources. Carnot was responsible for reforming the officer corps, under a policy of "careers open to talent" (often attributed to Napoleon). It vaulted Captain Napoleon Buonaparte to brigadier-general, and eight of his future marshals to brigadier-general or higher.

Overall, a pattern was set for national wars, with citizen-soldiers, total involvement of the population, and propaganda, which whipped up nationalist feelings. *Ultimately the French were emulated by all major nations. However, during the Revolutionary/Napoleonic era, France's enemies followed her example only tentatively and for short periods.* The old monarchs were too fearful of the masses to arm them, appeal to popular passion, or institute conscription. Spanish nationalism, *or the perception of it in the rest of Europe, along with the myth of constant grass roots fervor, played a part in bringing Napoleon down.* However, the kings of England and Prussia and the emperors of Austria and Russia continued to depend largely on professional armies. In the final struggle against Napoleon, however, they did benefit from anti-French sentiment, heightened by Napoleon's conscription and taxes in conquered areas. From 1813 to 1815, pan-German and Italian nationalism existed largely in the minds of intellectuals, and became a vital force only in the nineteenth century.

Napoleon (like the French revolutionaries) provoked all his wars, and blamed his enemies for them. He won steadily until 1812 (ignoring the Egyptian fiasco) because he was a master of improvisation and a "scrambler," capable of turning failure into victory. Moreover, for most of his career he had an army of regulars. He built a standing army from men from the old royal army, volunteers, and conscripts who chose to remain in service. He retained conscription for filling the ranks, but allowed the purchase of substitutes, and drafted an average of only 73,000 men a year (for an army of 600,000), until 1812–14.

Napoleon's strategy involved moving his corps parallel, ideally a day's march apart, in the general direction of the enemy, so they could concentrate quickly. He devised his tactics on the battlefield. The only constants were that he held back a large reserve and usually let the enemy attack first, then exploited his mistakes. No two battles were the same.

Neither Napoleon nor the generals of the Revolution before him could maneuver great masses of troops, given the primitive state of communications; nor could their economies support them. Napoleon assembled 750,000 troops for the Russian campaign, but two-thirds of them were non-French. He fought his greatest battle in Russia, at Borodino, with 140,000 men.

Napoleon's only organizational innovation was the corps as the standard unit-of-all-arms, a force of 20,000 to 30,000 troops capable of fighting alone. In major national armies, the corps is still the basic unit of all arms. He waged economic war via the Continental System, and set tariffs in Europe to benefit France.

Napoleon ultimately failed because he: (a) overreached his military capa-bilities, (b) developed a touch of megalomania, (c) made too many compromises in efforts to gain acceptance by monarchs of established European ruling houses, (d) granted constitutions and bills-of-rights to conquered nations that the people did not understand, and (e) at the same time, burdened the people with higher taxes and conscription.

In the stunned hush after Waterloo, Frenchmen and other Europeans must have thought that nothing had been accomplished by the Revolution or Napoleon. The old monarchs were back; to peasants, surely, it seemed that the established Church had also returned. The people were ignorant of Napoleon's ultimate plan to build either a European state or (as he said in exile) a "federation of free peoples."

Napoleon's legacy to France and Europe embodied much that is beyond the scope of this book – best represented by the liberal (for the time) Code Napoléon. However, it seems clear that he was one of a kind. None of the other ambitious generals had his combination of talents. Napoleon utilized the nationalism of the Revolution to the maximum. "The Imperial Guard always marched to the "Marseillaise,'" he said at St Helena.[4] His propaganda, which dramatized his triumphs and celebrated the victories and heroes of the Grande Armée, raised national pride to such heights that his name is still synonymous with French glory. Further, his wars had essentially no effect on population growth in France and Europe. Europeans, at the time, were skeptical about the constitutions and bills-of-rights that he had offered. In the nineteenth century, however, the centers of revolution were in areas that Napoleon had controlled.

Military men have generally studied Napoleon's campaigns and neglected those of the Revolution. An unusual example is General Vo Nguyen Giap, the architect of the North Vietnamese army. He did once compare his soldiers to the volunteers of Valmy, but he named as his "tutors" Napoleon and Lawrence of Arabia, along with Sun Tzu, Mao Zedong, and Ho Chi Minh. He described Napoleon's battles in detail, with diagrams, for one reporter.[5] As for Sun Tzu's *The Art of War*, Giap said, "Sun Tzu has interesting ideas. [But] he said that . . . if enemy forces are ten times larger, then we should not fight. If I had followed him we would still be in the jungle."[6]

There was perpetual war throughout the French Revolutionary and Napoleonic periods, ending only when all Europe (and Great Britain) combined their armies to crush Napoleon's.

The Revolutionary/Napoleonic era was not a turning point in the history of warfare. However, the innovations in mobilizing manpower (via conscription), national support (via propaganda) and resources (through government law and force), set the stage for mass warfare that would reach its zenith in the World War of 1914–18, the most savage and wasteful of life ever fought.

NOTES

INTRODUCTION

1 Napoléon I, *Correspondance de Napoléon Ier, publiée par ordre de l'Empereur Napoléon III*, 32 vols (Paris, 1858–70), XXXI, 51–52.

1 THE EIGHTEENTH CENTURY: THE FRENCH MILITARY AND ITS ENEMIES – THE REVOLUTION BEGINS

1 *La France et ses Armées* (édn 1971), 79–80, in *Les Écrits militaires de Charles de Gaulle: Essai d'Analyse thématique*, ed. by Pierre Messmer and Alain Larcan (Paris, 1985), 228–229.

2 Alan Forrest reminds us that in the eighteenth century, Diderot's *Encyclopédie* described infantrymen as the lowest forms of humanity and that society was contemptuous of soldiers. See Alan I. Forrest, *Soldiers of the French Revolution* (Durham, N.C., 1990), 30.

3 Peter Paret, *Understanding War: Essays on Clausewitz and the History of Military Power* (Princeton, N.J., 1992), 58.

4 De Gaulle, *Écrits*, 226: "Au XVIII . . . Frédéric II de Prusse, porte à sa perfection l'art guerrier d'Ancien Régime."

5 Brent Nosworthy, *With Musket, Cannon and Sword: Battle Tactics of Napoleon and His Enemies* (New York, 1996), 104–105.

6 Geoffrey Parker, *Military Revolution: Military Innovation and the Rise of the West* (Cambridge, Mass., 1988), 149–150.

7 Ken Alder, *Engineering the Revolution: Arms and Enlightenment in France, 1763–1815* (Princeton, N.J., 1997), 40–43; Parker, *Military Revolution*, 148.

8 Under Napoleon, snipers used powerful *silent* air rifles.

9 Lee Kennett, *The French Armies in the Seven Years War* (Durham, N.C., 1987), 81.

10 Marie-Joseph-Paul-Yves-Roch-Gilbert du Motier, Marquis de La Fayette (1757–1834).

11 Kennett, *The French Armies in the Seven Years War*, 72.

12 The *règlement Ségur* was in force until 29 July 1790 – a year into the French Revolution. George A. Kelly, *Victims, Authority, and Terror: The Parallel Deaths of d'Orléans, Custine, Bailly, and Malesherbes* (Chapel Hill, N.C., 1982), 96.

13 Alder, *Engineering the Revolution*, 56–57, 76, 83.

14 "Si la France, en 1790, a mis si promptement sur pied de bonnes armées, c'est qu'elle avait un bon fond, que l'émigration l'améliora plutôt qu'elle ne le détériora."

Napoléon I, *Correspondance de Napoléon Ier, publiée par ordre de l'Empereur Napoléon III*, 32 vols (Paris, 1858–70), XXIX, 342.

15 The inspector-general of infantry was Jean Martinet, whose name became a generic word for disciplinarian. Kennett, *The French Armies in the Seven Years War*, 77.

16 His musketeers boasted the swordsman-poet Cyrano de Bergerac.

17 Charles II of Spain, who died in 1700, willed the throne of Spain to Louis XIV's grandson. Louis ignored a treaty ceding Spain to Charles von Habsburg, brother of the Emperor Joseph I, and sent his grandson to Spain as Philip V. War ensued, with France losing to the armies of the Duke of Marlborough (John Churchill) and Prince Eugene of Savoy. However, in 1711 Joseph I died; Charles stood to gain all Habsburg lands, including Spain. The "Grand Alliance" collapsed, and the Treaties of Augsburg left Philip V on the Spanish throne.

18 Martin van Creveld, *The Training of Officers* (New York and London, 1990), 19ff.

19 See Kennett, *The French Armies in the Seven Years War*; Christopher Duffy, *Military Life of Frederick the Great* (New York, 1986); Dennis E. Showalter, *The Wars of Frederick the Great* (London and New York, 1996).

20 Voltaire (François Arouet), *Le Siècle de Louis XIV* (1751).

21 The *livre* was worth about $0.20 US or one English shilling. It became the *franc*, in effect, during the Revolution.

22 It can be argued that Louis XIV's legacy belongs in the causal pattern of the French Revolution of 1789. Since his successors, Louis XV and XVI, did not have the force, industry and talent to occupy the "genius seat" he left them, the French government deteriorated in the eighteenth century – to a point where only a revolution could repair it.

23 See John M. Sherwig, *Guineas and Gunpowder: British Foreign Aid in the Wars with France, 1793–1815* (New York, 1969).

24 Parker, *Military Revolution*, 148.

25 For example, the British East India Company operated in India, Burma, Malaya, China, and the East Indies; its worth grew by 1,000 percent between 1789 and 1815. The French equivalent, despite government subsidies, went bankrupt in 1769 and was abolished. In 1785, a combined East and West India Company was founded, but it, too, failed and was dissolved during the Revolution.

26 The value rose from 120 million *livres* in 1716 to over 500 million in 1789 – over 400 percent (*livre* = $0.20 US).

27 In 1789, a *livre* equaled about one British shilling (one-twentieth of a pound) or $0.20 in United States currency. The purchasing power of money, however, was about forty times what it is in 2005.

28 Except the insane and those convicted of a felony.

2 THE REVOLUTION AND WAR: FIRST CAMPAIGNS, 1789–93

1 Workers; *sans-culottes* means "without knee-britches," these being worn by the upper classes. Ideally, workers wore long trousers; in fact contemporary drawings show that many wore cast-off culottes.

2 The ancient fortress, built in the 1300s, since 1660 a prison, rumored to hold many political prisoners, had none. The inmates were five forgers and two insane men (there by request of relatives). One madman, who thought he was a medieval bishop, busily blessed people all day.

3 They sold locks, chains, keys, and even stones from the Bastille. (Lafayette got a gift key, and sent it to George Washington; it is displayed at Mount Vernon in Virginia.)

4 François-Claude-Amour, General Marquis de Bouillé.

5 Charles-François du Périer, called Dumouriez.

6 The Duc d'Orléans was the king's cousin, but joined the successively more radical leaders as the Revolution became more violent. He was a Jacobin and supported the Terror under the name Philippe Égalité; he went to the guillotine all the same.

7 *Histoire militaire de la France*, 4 vols, Sous la direction de André Corvisier (Paris, 1992), II, 262.

8 Poland would disappear from the map after the Third Partition (1795) and reappear in 1919 as an independent nation.

9 Luckner commanded the Rhin (December 1791); the Nord (May 1792); the Centre (July 1792) and was Generalissimo (August–September 1792). He was executed on 4 January 1794.

10 Ramsay Weston Phipps, *The Armies of the First French Republic and the Rise of the Marshals of Napoleon I*, reprint, 5 vols (Westport, Conn., 1980), II, 66–67.

11 "Courtisan de Versailles, favori de Marie-Antoinette, rival des Besenval et des Lauzun, Dillon . . . surnommé, Dillon le Beau, n'était qu'un général de cour . . ." See Arthur Chuquet, *Les guerres de la révolution*, 11 vols, 6th edn (Paris, 1914), II, 251.

12 Ibid., I, 46–47.

13 General Armand-Louis de Gontaut, Duc de Biron.

14 One of his generals was the Duc de Chartres, later King Louis-Philippe.

15 Steven T. Ross, *Quest for Victory: French Military Strategy, 1792–1799* (South Brunswick, New York and London, 1978), 39.

16 Son of a cartwright, he had assumed the "*de* Beurnonville" in the chaotic time before the Revolution, when many men stole the noble "de" (including Maximilien de Robespierre). Beurnonville exaggerated his feats and bolstered the myth of the invincible citizen-soldier. Napoleon made him a count; later, Louis XVIII made him a marquis. See Chuquet, *Les guerres*, II, 151–152.

17 The "Phrygian bonnet" or *bonnet rouge* – a red stocking cap – was one of many revolutionary symbols drawn from the ancient Roman Republic. By legend, it was brought to Rome by slaves from Phrygia (in modern-day Turkey), and represented freedom and resistance to tyranny. There is a Roman coin with the head of Brutus, and on the reverse the bonnet, suspended over a dagger. See C. H. V. Sutherland, *Roman Coins* (London, 1974), pp. 102, 326.

18 Actually, as detailed on p. 27, it also had Austrian troops, and several thousand French *émigrés*.

19 Written in 1792 by Rouget de Lisle for the Army of the Rhine, it was not popular. However, it scored with the National Guard of Marseilles. It was a call to arms, exhorting the people to slaughter the minions of tyrants until their blood filled the furrows of their fields.

20 Always a supporter of the Bourbons (he had wanted them to rule with a parliament), he helped Napoleon deal with the Americans, briefly, but from 1814 to 1815 helped to bring him down.

21 With Lafayette gone, Dumouriez, as ranking officer in the Nord, assumed the title "Lieutenant-General commanding the Nord," and on 19 August was officially made commander.

22 Chuquet's count was 40,000 Prussians, 29,000 Austrians, 5,532 Hessians and 4,500 *émigrés*. Chuquet, *Les guerres*, I, 145.

23 Like many officers of the old army, he had accepted the Constitution of 1791, and hoped the Revolution was over. Chuquet, *Les guerres*, I, 229–249.

24 François-Étienne-Christophe Kellermann (1735–1820).

25 After commissioners sent to arrest him for treason certified to his *civisme* (patriotism). He went to the guillotine, however, under the next government.

26 Chuquet, *Les guerres*, I, 203.

27 Luckner suggested that troops in Alsace attack the German rear at Koblenz, but was ignored.

28 Phipps, *Armies*, I, 118.

29 Some reached Châlons, where Luckner rounded them up.

30 At this juncture Luckner was recalled to Paris. Officially retired in January 1793, Luckner went to his home in the Vosges. However, he made the mistake of asking for his pension during the Terror. Branded "le vil courtisan et l'esclave titré d'un tyran conspirateur," he was guillotined on the 4 January 1794. It is ironic and sad that "La Marseillaise" was originally the "Chant de guerre pour l'Armée du Rhin, *dédié au Maréchal Luckner*." Beurnonville took command at Châlons. Phipps, *Armies*, I, 117.

31 Ibid., II, 179.

32 Ibid., 20–21.

33 The artillery, overall, still had 42 percent of its officers. Ken Alder, *Engineering the Revolution: Arms and Enlightenment in France, 1763–1815* (Princeton, N.J., 1997), 83.

34 Chuquet, *Les guerres*, II, 207.

35 Brent Nosworthy *With Musket, Cannon, and Sword: Battle Tactics of Napoleon and His Enemies* (New York, 1996), 107.

36 Phipps, *Armies*, II, 27–28.

37 Ross, *Quest for Victory*, 41.

38 Chuquet, *Les guerres*, III, 251–255

39 Ibid., II, 220–221; Baron Antoine-Henri Jomini, *Histoire critique et militaire des guerres de la révolution*, 16 vols, new edn (Paris, 1820–22), II, 121; Alan I. Forrest, *Soldiers of the French Revolution*, (Durham, N.C., 1990), 116; Ross, *Quest for Victory*, 33. T. C. W. Blanning credits both artillery volunteers in *The French Revolutionary Wars, 1787–1802* (London and New York, 1996), 77.

40 "[L]e corps militaire est l'expression la plus complète de l'esprit d'une société. . . . *Qui pense à la Révolution sans évoquer les Volontaires?*" Charles de Gaulle, *Les Écrits militaires de Charles de Gaulle: Essai d'Analyse thématique*, ed. Pierre Messmer and Alain Larcan (Paris, 1985), 238. In that – and perhaps that alone – de Gaulle agreed with the generations of left-leaning historians, such as Mathiez, Lefebvre and Soboul, who held that French "minute man" won the Battle of Valmy. See also John A. Lynn, *The Bayonets of the Republic: Motivation and Tactics of the Army of Revolutionary France, 1791–94* (Chicago, 1984).

41 Luckner commanda l'armée [du Rhin] 14 déc. 1791 au 6 mai 1792 ; La Morlière, du 7 mai au 20 juillet [1792]; Biron, du 21 juillet au 16 décembre [1792]; Deprez-Crassier, du 16 décembre au 14 mars 1793 (intérimaire et subordonné à Custine); Custine, du 15 mars au 17 mai [1793]; Diettmann, du 18 au 29 mai (subordonné 'à Houchard); Beauharnais, du 30 mai au 17 août; Landremont du 18 août au 20 septembre; Munnier, du 30 septembre au 1 octobre; Carlenc, du 2 au 26 octobre ; Pichegru, à dater du 27 octobre 1793. Chuquet, *Les guerres*, VI, footnotes 5–6.

42 Ibid., 47.

43 Ibid., 57.

44 In 1795, a partition removed Poland from the map.

45 Nosworthy. *With Musket, Cannon, and Sword*, 103.

46 Phipps, *Armies*, I, 142. Ross accepts the "mighty volunteer" myth. "Finally, the weight of numbers . . . forced the Hapsburg generals to withdraw to avoid annihilation." Ross, *Quest for Victory*, 39.

47 The Revolutionary calendar had not been devised, however, and was not put into effect until September 1793.

48 The radicals took the high seats on the speaker's left, and called themselves Montagnards (Mountaineers), or as a body La Montagne (The Mountain). The

Girondins, now conservatives, sat on the right; the uncommitted majority in the center. This is the origin of Left, Right, and Center, referring to political conviction. Earlier, assemblies had seats surrounding the speaker.

49 On 14 December 1792 the Convention decreed regulations for generals in conquered areas, asserting authority over them. Generals were to abolish tithes, feudal dues, and aristocratic privilege; convoke assemblies to organize Republican governments; confiscate the property of aristocrats and the Church. They were to buy supplies with paper money backed by confiscated property of nobles and the Church. Thereby the nation's enemies would finance the war.

50 The Jacobin Club was organized in 1789 at Versailles, as the Breton Club, and in Paris became the Jacobin Club when it moved into a confiscated Dominican "Jacobin" monastery. It had been dominated, in turn, by Lafayette's constitutional monarchists, the Girondins, and finally by the radicals. In 1793 the radicals organized the Terror, giving "Jacobin" its still-current meaning.

51 There was no great difference in wealth or social origins of the Girondins and Montagnards. The Girondins were simply less favorable to centralization and bureaucratization and more jealous of property rights than the Montagnards.

52 The king defended himself, *extempore*. He was formally defended by an appointed ex-judge and a *philosophe* and once royal minister, Malesherbes (72), who paid with his life in 1793.

53 From 8 p.m. on 16 January, all night, and into the afternoon of the 17th, deputies filed to the rostrum and voted aloud. Surprisingly, 288 voted for imprisonment or exile, while 46 favored reprieve (delay of sentence). However, 361 flatly voted for death, and 26 more for death with reprieve.

54 Most Girondins had voted him "guilty," but on the death sentence with qualifications – delays, approval by the people, etc. Those for exile included the American Tom Paine.

55 The King of Spain had offered to receive Louis as an exile and guarantee his non-interference in French affairs. His ambassador had also paid millions in bribes, obviously in vain.

56 Phipps, *Armies*, I, 151.

57 Ibid., 152, gives grand total of 122,293.

58 Ross, *Quest for Victory*, 44.

59 Phipps, *Armies*, I, 154.

60 Ibid., 155.

61 For a terse account of these battles, see Ross, *Quest for Victory*, 46.

62 Once the property of the Knights Templars of the Crusades.

63 Veteran of the American Revolution and crusader in Venezuela.

64 Phipps, *Armies*, I, 160–161. The Austrians held them until December 1795, then exchanged them for Princess Marie-Thérèse, daughter of Louis XVI.

65 He devoted himself to supporting counter-revolutionaries in France, making daring trips to Paris in disguise, and courted the exiled Comte de Provence (future Louis XVIII). On Louis' restoration (1814–15), Dumouriez expected to be made a marshal, but was not. He retired to England and died there in 1823.

66 He of the Jennings family of Kilmaine, County Mayo, who had been brought to France when he was eleven by his father, a physician in Tonnay-Charente. He had begun his career in the cavalry, had served under Rochambeau in America, had then risen rapidly under the Revolution, and would survive to fight in Napoleon's famous first Italian campaign.

67 Phipps, *Armies*, I, 187.

68 Ross, *Quest for Victory*, 49.

69 Jomini says that the "military Vendée" was bordered in the north by the Loire, in the south by the Sèvre niortaise, on the east by the highroad from Saumur to Niort,

and the west by the ocean. It comprised parts of the departments of the Loire-inférieure, of Maine-et-Loire, Deux-Sèvres and most of Vendée. Jomini, *Guerres de la révolution*, III, 382. This does not take into account the areas of Brittany and Normandy in rebellion.

70 In 1791 the nobles in the Loire valley had formed a counter-revolutionary organization, and it survived, but was useful only to supply leaders and communicate with *émigrés*.

71 Jomini, *Guerres de la révolution*, III, 385.

72 The Girondins' founder, Brissot, was executed. The "last *philosophe*," Condorcet, was captured later, but finished his *Progress of the Human Mind* before he died in prison (probably a suicide). An astonished prisoner was Tom Paine, of American Revolutionary fame. After a year the US minister, James Monroe, got him freed.

73 Federal because the Girondins were "federalists," favoring strong local government. Girondins also raised revolts in sixty departments, which collapsed for lack of coordinated leadership.

74 The "right to subsistence" was in the Constitution of 1793, never promulgated. And see Richard Cobb, *The People's Armies*, trans. from the French by Marianne Elliott (New Haven, Conn., 1987).

3 THE TERROR: POLITICS AND ARMY REFORM, 1793–94

1 His better portraits show a weary and impatient man, with an expression startlingly like that of W. T. Sherman in photos made during the American Civil War. Wrote Palmer: "Carnot is the one man of the Twelve who today is a French national hero." R. R. Palmer, *Twelve Who Ruled: The Year of the Terror in the French Revolution* (Princeton, N.J., 1969), 81. Arthur Chuquet, *Les guerres de la révolution*, 11 vols, 6th edn (Paris, 1914), IX, 35.

2 Charles de Gaulle, *Les Écrits militaires de Charles de Gaulle: Essai d'Analyse thématique*, ed. Pierre Messmer and Alain Larcan (Paris, 1985), 235. There was a minister of war, however, Jean Bouchotte, who had great influence. His ministry quietly built a huge bureaucracy to administer Carnot's large army, and became politically powerful. Howard G. Brown, *War, Revolution, and the Bureaucratic State: Politics and Army Administration in France, 1791–1799* (Oxford, 1995), 74–75ff. Palmer, *Twelve Who Ruled*, 83–84.

3 She had visited politely and stabbed him as he sat writing in his medicinal bath (he had skin ailments).

4 "*Homère de l'ordure.*"

5 Via Hérault de Séchelles. Another *représentant*, Marc-Antoine Jullien (18) wrote (Feb. 1794): "At Nantes I saw Carrier acting like a satrap . . . an assassin of . . . liberty." R. R. Palmer, *From Jacobin to Liberal: Marc-Antoine Jullien* (Princeton, 1993), 42. Carrier was executed after Robespierre fell.

6 The French foot (*pied*) = 33 cm. The British, 31.7 cm. This has led to disputes over, for example, the height of Napoleon.

7 This was the first national draft, so the government was roundly hated. Evasion and desertion were easy; rural villages protected offenders, birth and death records were unreliable, communications were poor, and police methods primitive. Further, the law was enforced only in 1793/94, and was renewed only in 1798. Alan I. Forrest, *Conscripts and Deserters: The Army and French Society During the Revolution and Empire* (New York, 1989), 44–45ff.

8 According to Brown: "The republican army reached its zenith in September 1794: an astounding 750,000 effectives. However, this is [an] estimate; the government

[could not] provide an accurate figure at the time. In the summer of 1794 the [government] was unable to identify each army unit, let alone its location or strength." Brown. *War, Revolution and the Bureaucratic State*, 131–132.

9 The demi-brigade was essentially the "regiment" of the old army. Napoleon restored the regiment, but by his time battalions had grown from 1,000+ to 3,500; companies from 60–120 men.

10 Brown writes: "Carnot . . . had opposed this law partly because it entailed a huge amount of administrative work difficult to accomplish during wartime." In fact, it produced a bureaucracy which gave greater power to the War Ministry. Brown, *War, Revolution, and the Bureaucratic State*, 130.

11 The Republic had only two grades of general – of brigade and of division. Army commanders were sometimes given the grade of lieutenant-general, but were usually called "General of the Army" (of the North, or Rhine, or whatever). Marshals had been branded creatures of the *ancien régime* until Napoleon reintroduced them.

12 Palmer, *Twelve Who Ruled*, 86.

4 THE TERROR AND WAR, JULY 1793–JULY 1794

1 Early leaders were Jacques Cathèlineau, a teamster, and Gaston Bourdic, a wigmaker; both were dead by June 1793. Gaston became a legend, nevertheless, celebrated in the courts of Europe. *Représentants* reported him everywhere in the military Vendée – as the Marquis de Gaston, Colonel Gaston, and by other titles – always as a dashing figure. The Comte de Fersen, Marie-Antoinette's chevalier, hoped to send him arms, money, and even troops. Arthur Chuquet, *Les guerres de la révolution*, 11 vols, 6th edn (Paris, 1914), XI, 120–121.

2 Marquise de la Rochejacquelein, *Memoirs*, trans. Cecil Biggane (London, 1933), 37–38, *passim*. Antoine-Henri Jomini, *Histoire critique et militaire des guerres de la révolution*, 16 vols, new edn (Paris, 1820–22), III, 384–385.

3 First husband of the Marquise de La Rochejacquelein.

4 Jomini says the men fought well because their former lords marched with them. *Guerres de la révolution*, III, 388.

5 They were the Armée d'Anjou, La Grand Armée, and the Armée du Marais.

6 See Reynald Secher, *Le génocide Franco-Français: La Vendée-Vengé* (Paris, 1986), 253–264.

7 Armand-Louis de Gontaut, Duc de Biron, whom we met on the Rhine; he came from the Armée du Var (on the south coast).

8 Kléber, an Alsacian, had been an officer in the Austrian army, but returned to France to serve in the army of the Revolution. In the Vendée, he was initially under Jean-Baptiste-Annibal Aubert du Bayet (Dubayet), but Dubayet was recalled.

9 La Rochejacquelein's troops; the cavalier lay wounded.

10 Kléber's men were angry because he had not got the command; some began negotiations to join the Vendéans, but the rebels broke off the talks. Jomini thought the Vendéans thereby lost a chance for victory. Given the amateur character of both sides, it is possible. Jomini, *Guerres de la révolution*, IV, 310–311.

11 "La fureur guidait les Vendéens." Jomini, *Guerres de la révolution*, IV, 315.

12 Under Michel-Armand de Beaupuy and Nicolas Haxo, the first an officer of the royal army (captain after twenty years' service, 1791), the second an ex-sergeant. Haxo was killed in the Vendée in 1794; Beaupuy in Germany in 1796.

13 He was called to Paris after the Vendéans were finally defeated in December, and tried and executed in March – not for brutality but as a Dantonist (and for scorn of *représentants*).

14 General Eisenhower's first European HQ after D-Day, 1944.

15 Jomini, *Guerres de la révolution*, IV, 329.

16 His cousin was with the rebels.

17 Secher, *Le génocide*, 243.

18 Jomini, *Guerres de la révolution*, IV, 348.

19 Jean-Baptiste Kléber, *Mémoires politiques et militaires: La Vendée, 1793–1794*, ed. Roger Nougaret (Paris, 1989), 229.

20 Secher, *Le génocide*, 243–244.

21 He fought in 1795 and was captured and shot in 1796.

22 See Jomini, *Guerres de la révolution*, V, 257–277, for detail on the post-Savenay operations; also Ramsey W. Phipps, *The Armies of the First French Republic and the Rise of the Marshals of Napoleon I*, 5 vols (London, 1926–29; reprint, Westport, Conn., 1980), III, 31–35; R. R. Palmer, *From Jacobin to Liberal: Marc-Antoine Jullien* (Princeton, N.J., 1993), 43.

23 Reynald Secher counts 117,257 "disappeared" (killed) of 815,029 (14.38 percent) in the Vendée *militaire* in uprisings from 1792 to 1802. He is conservative; probably nearer 300,000 died. Remaudière (pop. 744), lost 102, of whom 23 were under age 10. Secher, *La génocide*, 253, 260–261.

24 The *représentant* Marc-Antoine Jullien wrote Robespierre (February 1794) from Nantes: "A crew of generals . . . rich with what they have stolen, run . . . their carriages [over] *sansculottes* on foot; they are always with women . . . or at sumptuous meals that insult the public misery." Palmer, *From Jacobin to Liberal*, 43.

25 R. R. Palmer *Twelve Who Ruled: The Year of the Terror in the French Revolution* (Princeton, N.J., 1969), 216.

26 However, he later proved an effective general. Napoleon made him a marshal (1804), but he was overtly Republican and was forced to retire in 1807; however, he served Napoleon in 1815.

27 Late of the *Moniteur*, the official newspaper.

28 This is the English spelling; the French is *Marseille*, without the "s" at the end. Similarly Lyons, below, is *Lyon*.

29 Samuel F. Scott, *From Yorktown to Valmy: The Transformation of the French Army in an Age of Revolution*, (Niwat, Colo., 1998), 174.

30 The "fameuses fusillades sur la place des Broteaux" were executed by a Belgian revolutionary-cum-French general, Nicolas Declaye. He considered the Lyonnaise to be royalists, and took revenge for the death of his three children during the revolution in Belgium. Chuquet, *Les guerres*, XI, 288–289.

31 Ship decks were unsteady, and rocked by cannons' recoil; no gyroscopic equipment had been invented to keep the guns level.

32 Carteaux's wife ran the headquarters, signed orders, and was with her husband when he received officers, and not silent.

33 Carteaux later commanded L'Armée d'Italie and L'Armée des Alpes, was imprisoned as "unpatriotic," but survived. He served the Directory and (in civil posts) Napoleon. Phipps, *Armies*, III, 217–219.

34 Napoleon willed 1,000,000 francs to Dugommier's son or grandson as a "token of remembrance": ibid., 117.

35 Steven T. Ross, *Quest for Victory: French Military Strategy, 1792–1799* (South Brunswick, New York and London, 1978), 75.

36 The *Représentants* nominated Buonaparte to be general-of-brigade on 22 December; the promotion was confirmed by the government in February 1794. Two future marshals were also promoted, Masséna to major-general, and Victor to brigadier.

37 Jean-Paul Bertaud, *La Révolution Armée: Les soldats-citoyens et la Révolution française* (Paris, 1979), trans. R. R. Palmer as *The Army of the French Revolution: From Citizen Soldiers to Instrument of Power* (Princeton, N.J., 1988), 144.

38 His courageous and beautiful daughter-in-law, Delphine de Custine, had sat near him at the trial. Judges were threatened with accusations if her presence swayed them. Phipps, *Armies*, I, 189–190.

39 Palmer, *Twelve Who Ruled*, 85.

40 With his troops in columns, then moving into line, supported by skirmishers. Brent Nosworthy, *With Musket, Cannon, and Sword: Battle Tactics of Napoleon and His Enemies* (New York, 1996), 105.

41 Palmer, *Twelve Who Ruled*, 96.

42 After few weeks under General Charles-Édouard-Jennings de Kilmaine (1751–99), Irish-born but reared in France, already commanding the Armée des Ardennes.

43 Palmer, *Twelve Who Ruled*, 102–103.

44 He denied paternity of Hortense, their second child, born 1783.

45 Beauharnais, Houchard, staffs, and four *représentants*.

46 Chuquet, *Les guerres*, VIII, 107.

47 *Représentants* Borie, Milhaud, and Ruamps. In Paris, Fouquier-Tinville, prosecutor of the Revolutionary Tribunal, accused him of complicity in the treason of Custine, and of facilitating the enemies' capture of Mainz. However, the *représentants* managed to send him into retirement.

48 Phipps, *Armies*, II, 58.

49 Chuquet, *Les guerres*, IX, 30.

50 Phipps, *Armies*, II, 80; Chuquet, *Les guerres*, IX, 67.

51 Phipps, *Armies*, II, 86; Chuquet, *Les guerres*, IX, 71.

52 "Hoche is the Republican hero to many writers, a distinction one suspects to be much due to his early death, which prevented his ambition from being shown . . ." Phipps, *Armies*, II, 84.

53 Chuquet, *Les guerres*, IX, 452.

54 He died of fever a year later before Luxembourg.

55 Carnot mobilized resources and technicians to construct a balloon – "aerostatic globe" – which was used for artillery observation at Fleurus. It was a hundred feet in circumference, and floated 500 feet from the ground, held by a long rope. Captain Coutelle, in charge of the monster, remained aloft for nine hours during the battle. A number of generals went up for shorter periods. Soldiers maneuvered the balloon with the rope; bulletins were slid down the rope from observers. The value of the balloon is in doubt, but perhaps it encouraged French troops. Palmer, *Twelve Who Ruled*, 355–366.

5 THE GOVERNMENT OF THERMIDOR AND ESTABLISHMENT OF THE DIRECTORY, JULY 1794–OCTOBER 1795

1 General Hoche estimated the total number of French killed in the Vendée rebellions, on both sides, at 600,000 – including one-fifth of the population of the Vendée militaire.

2 Napoléon I, *Correspondance de Napoléon Ier, publiée par ordre de l'Empereur Napoléon III*, 32 vols (Paris, 1858–70), XXXI, 418.

3 After Thermidor, Buonaparte had been jailed briefly as a Jacobin, then sent to the staff of the Armée d'Italie, then called 'Nord', in a move to disperse Corsican officers.

4 The term of Thomas Carlyle in his *French Revolution* (1832). The French call this affair L'Émeute de Vendémiaire.

5 Napoléon I, *L'Oeuvre et l'histoire*, ed. Jean Massin, Jean Tulard, *et al.* (Paris, 1969), 1/1, 293–296. Murat was not mentioned, but later Napoleon made him a marshal.

He married Napoleon's sister Caroline, and became Grand Duke of Berg and King of Naples.

6 Ibid., 1/1, 296.

7 In March 1796 Pichegru was replaced by Moreau and called to Paris, but acquitted of royalism. He was elected to the lower house of the legislature in 1797, but ousted in 1798 and exiled to Guiana. However, he escaped to England, and returned to France with French royalists in 1803 (see p. 118). *Histoire militaire de la France*, 4 vols, Sous la direction de André Corvisier (Paris, 1992), II, 272.

6 WAR IN ITALY AND GERMANY, 1796–97

1 Louis Marchand, his valet, measured his body after his death, and recorded *"cinq pieds, deux pouces"* (five feet, two inches). If the figures are in French measure (the French foot = 33 cm; the British 30.47 cm), then he was 5'6" plus. But Napoleon had decreed the metric system official in France, so it is unlikely that Marchand had an *ancien régime* measuring tape. Thus his figures are almost surely in English feet and inches.

2 Except for the radiant Madame Juliette Récamier, whom artists vied to paint. She met his advances with witticisms.

3 Napoléon I, *Correspondance de Napoléon Ier, publiée par ordre de l'Empereur Napoléon III*, 32 vols (Paris, 1858–70), XXXI, 417.

4 Ibid., XXXII, 286.

5 Constant (Louis Constant Wairy), *Mémoires intime de Napoléon I*, One-vol. edn (Paris, 1967), 255, 268, *passim*.

6 Lieutenant-general was a temporary grade; that of marshal had been abolished, but would be restored by Napoleon as emperor.

7 André Masséna, *Mémoires*, 7 vols (Paris, 1849–50; new edn 1966), II, 131.

8 A. F. L. Viesse de Marmont, *Mémoires*, 9 vols (Paris, 1857), I, 148.

9 Masséna, *Mémoires*, II, 11; Joseph Bonaparte, *Mémoires et correspondance*, 10 vols, ed. A. du Casse (Paris, 1851–54), I, xi.

10 Napoléon I, *L'Oeuvre et l'histoire*, ed. Jean Massin, Jean Tulard, *et al.*, 12 vols, (Paris, 1969), 2/1, 218.

11 The term "corps" had no fixed meaning until Napoleon made it the standard unit-of-all-arms (1803).

12 Napoléon I, *L'Oeuvre et l'histoire*, I, 311–312.

13 Marmont, *Mémoires*, I, 178.

14 Jean Tulard, *Le Mythe de Napoléon* (Paris, 1971), 84.

15 Napoléon I, *Correspondance*, XXIX, 107.

16 Napoléon I, *L'Oeuvre et l'histoire*, 2/1, 283.

17 John W. Croker, *The Croker Papers: 1808–1857* (London, 1884), 94.

18 Saint-Cyr became a marshal. Desaix might have been one, but was killed at Marengo (1800), after saving Napoleon from defeat.

19 Marmont, *Mémoires*, I, 257–258.

20 Eysturlid feels that the Archduke was too bound by rigid rules, but covers his campaigns in a few paragraphs. Lee W. Eysturlid, *The Formative Influences, Theories, amd Campaigns of the Archduke Carl of Austria* (Westport, Conn., 2000), 125, *passim*.

21 Wurmser was forced to surrender Mantua after six months, and the loss of 8,000 troops and 6,000 civilians. Napoleon declined to take his sword. The old warrior died within months.

22 Short 2,500. Napoléon I, *Correspondance*, XXIX, 231.

23 Charles went to Vienna to get Francis II to make peace, but had to settle for a truce. Eysturlid, *Archduke Carl*, 11.

24 The *coup d'état* of 18 Fructidor, Year V. The elections of 1797 had returned a dangerous number of royalists to the legislature (councils of Elders and "500"). Augereau took command of troops in Paris, expelled the royalists, and sent prominent ones to prison or into exile, restoring a moderate government.

25 Austria confirmed French possession of Belgium and the west bank of the Rhine, and recognized the Batavian and Cisalpine republics. France was to participate in remapping Germany (to compensate princes for losses to the French). Austria got Venetia; France the Ionian Islands. Some historians see in this evidence of Napoleon's desire to be a "New Alexander the Great."

7 EGYPT AND THE *COUP D'ÉTAT DE BRUMAIRE*, 1798–99

1 Louis-Charles-Antoine des Aix, Chevalier de Veygoux.

2 The Knights had ruled the place since the Crusades, recently under British protection. Nelson expelled the French in 1799; Britain occupied Malta until 1815, when they annexed it.

3 Brueys had about as many ships as Nelson, and more firepower, but in any case would have lost the transports.

4 A.-F.-L. Viesse de Marmont, *Mémoires*, 9 vols (Paris, 1857), I, 367.

5 On St Helena, Napoleon described the division squares in detail. Napoléon I, *Correspondance de Napoléon Ier, publiée par ordre de l'Empereur Napoléon III*, 32 vols (Paris, 1858–70), XXIX, 432.

6 Les Mameluks avaient un magnifique corps de cavaliers, couverts d'or, d'argent, armés des meilleures carabines et pistolets de Londres, des meilleurs sabres de l'Orient, et montés peut-être sur les meilleurs chevaux du continent. Napoléon I, *L'Oeuvre et l'histoire*, ed. Jean Massin, Jean Tulard, *et al.*, 12 vols (Paris, 1969), I, 414.

7 They were motivated in part, surely, by the tenet of Islam that promised immediate entry into heaven for those killed "in defense of the faith." Their heaven had no clouds and harps, but beautiful women, attentive to the warrior's every wish.

8 To the Directory, 24 July 1798. Napoléon I, *L'Oeuvre et l'histoire*, 1/1, 418–419.

9 Before the message arrived, the future Duke of Wellington had defeated Tippu and restored British control.

10 What happened to Napoleon's army? Kléber took over, as ordered, but was assassinated in 1800. General Jacques Menou (who had become a Moslem, Abd Allah Menou) then took over. He was defeated by the British expedition of Sir Ralph Abercromby (March 1801), and captured with his army. The survivors were repatriated during negotiations for peace with Britain (Treaty of Amiens, 1802).

11 Paris, 18 brumaire an VIII (9 novembre 1799). "Citoyens Représentants . . . Nous voulons une république fondée sur la vraie liberté . . . sur la représentation nationale; nous l'aurons! . . . je le jure! Je le jure en mon nom et en celui de mes compagnons d'armes!" Napoléon I, *L'Oeuvre et l'histoire*, 1, 463.

12 Charles de Gaulle, *Les Écrits militaires de Charles de Gaulle: Essai d'Analyse thématique*, ed. Pierre Messmer and Alain Larcan (Paris, 1985), 231. "Pour toutes sortes de raisons, et d'abord à cause de la puissance de l'armée qui a gagné «force, ordre, honneur» et qui est indignée par la faiblesse, la licence, les vices, l'avènement de Bonaparte est acclamé par l'opinion unanime."

8 MARENGO AND THE GRAND ARMÉE, 1800–05

1 Later Prince Italijsky (Italy).
2 Quoted by Steven T. Ross, *Quest for Victory: French Military Strategy, 1792–1799* (South Brunswick, New York and London, 1978) 240.
3 Napoléon I, *L'Oeuvre et l'histoire*, ed. Jean Massin, Jean Tulard, *et al.*, 12 vols (Paris, 1969), 2/2, 121.
4 Ibid., 208.
5 "[In late afternoon] the enemy advanced along his whole line following the fire . . . of more than a hundred cannons. The roads were jammed with fugitives, wounded, debris; the battle seemed lost . . . [But at] San Giuliano the division of Desaix was arrayed for battle . . . All the fugitives formed behind it . . . To cries of *Vive la République! vive le premier consul!* Desaix charged the enemy . . . Kellermann . . . with his brigade of heavy cavalry . . . charged with full force . . . All the army followed . . ." Napoléon I, *Correspondance de Napoléon Ier, publiée par ordre de l'Empereur Napoléon III*, 4910, 15 June 1800.
6 In 1803 Napoleon ordered the Dépôt de la Guerre to produce a new account. The result expanded Bonaparte's role in the victory, but not enough. In 1805, as emperor, he had the history revised again. In this account the Austrian force suddenly jumped to 45,000, with 200 cannon. Desaix was sent toward Novi, but ordered to return if a battle developed near Marengo. Castel Ceriolo was held all day by Brigadier-General Carra Saint-Cyr (whereas it was well documented that it had been lost early on, and recaptured only after the French counterattack began). Moreover, Castel Ceriolo was presented as a pivot on which the French line had shifted, changing the front against the Austrians from one running roughly north–south to an east–west line (Napoléon I, *L'Oeuvre et l'histoire*, 2/2, 167). Carra Saint-Cyr became a hero of the battle. Desaix's status was reduced from that of *the* hero to that of a valiant general following Napoleon's orders. Bonaparte controlled the retreat in order to give Desaix time to reach San Giuliano.
   Napoleon stuck to this account, and at Saint Helena even composed a maxim to explain his victory:
   "*Le grand art des batailles* is to change, during the action, your line of operations . . . That is how I won a victory at Marengo: The enemy threw himself on my line of operations to cut it; I had changed it, and he found himself cut up instead." Ernest Picard, *PrécepTes et jugements de Napoléon* (Paris, 1913), 23; Baron Gaspard Gourgaud, *Sainte-Hélène: journal unédit*, ed. E. H. de Grouchy and A. Guillois, 2 vols (Paris, 1899), II, 425.
   See David Chandler, "Tuning the Record," *Proceedings of the Consortium on Revolutionary Europe, 1981* (Athens, Ga., 1982).
7 The Archduke Charles had temporarily retired.
8 Nosworthy quotes a British officer (1802) who praised Moreau's scientific approach to battle, but noted that he had lacked "*boldness and fire.*" It was the latter that Napoleon wanted. Brent Nosworthy, *With Musket, Cannon, and Sword: Battle Tactics of Napoleon and His Enemies* (New York, 1996), 111.
9 Bonaparte offered Moreau the hand of Hortense de Beauharnais; he refused it, and post-haste married another.
10 Moreau was implicated in a royalist plot and imprisoned. His co-conspirators were condemned to death. He was exiled, probably because Joseph Bonaparte intervened on his behalf.
11 It reconfirmed the provisions of the Treaty of Campo Formio (1797), recognized the new Helvetic and Ligurian (Genoa) "sister Republics." (Napoleon chose not to revive the Roman or Parthenopean Republics; Rome and Naples reverted to their old rulers. Tuscany went to France.)

12 Britain was to return all her conquests except Ceylon and Trinidad, and evacuate Elba and Malta. France was to respect the independence of Naples, Portugal, and the Batavian Republic, and further promised to trade with Britain on favorable terms. On trade, Lord Cornwallis, representing Britain, took the word of Joseph Bonaparte, representing France, who had become his friend. He did not consider that Napoleon, not Joseph, would decide whether France would honor the treaty – and the First Consul did not intend to. The treaty lasted only a year.

13 The Pope quietly received back the Papal States, minus Bologna and Romagna (to the Italian Republic). Roman Catholicism was pronounced the "religion of the great majority of Frenchmen," but not the established Church (Napoleon granted freedom of religion in his civil code). The French head of state was to nominate bishops; the Pope to consecrate them (or refuse). France was to pay the clergy; the Pope agreed not to challenge revolutionary confiscations of Church property. The Concordat reunited the Catholic clergy in France (in schism since 1790, over the oath of loyalty to the revolutionary government).

14 The top grade in revolutionary armies was major-general (general of division). Under Napoleon, grades were brigadier, major-general, and lieutenant-general (temporary) and marshal.

15 John R. Elting, *Swords Around a Throne: The Grande Armée of Napoleon* (New York, 1987), 183. Quoting from Elzéar Blaze, *La Vie militaire sons l'Empire, on moeurs de la garrison, du bivonac et de la caserne,* (Paris, 1890), 59.

16 Charles de Gaulle, *Les Écrits militaires de Charles de Gaulle: Essai d'Analyse thématique,* ed. Pierre Messmer and Alain Larcan (Paris, 1985), 243.

17 "Lorsque Napoléon vient au pouvoir, il trouve 'une armée incomparable, forgée par huit années de campagne, sûre d'elle-même, avide d'honneur, ambitieuse de grandes entreprises Le Directoire a légué au premier consul un système nouveau de recrutement proposé par Jourdan, la conscription . . ." De Gaulle, *Écrits,* 233.

18 De Gaulle (*Écrits,* 243) confirms this: "La Grand Armée qui depuis Ulm jusqu'à Friedland fit voler en éclats tous ses adversaires se composait essentiellement de briscards."

9 SUBDUING THE EUROPEAN POWERS: AUSTERLITZ–JENA–AUERSTÄDT–FRIEDLAND, 1805–07

1 His first choice was Admiral Louis-René-Le Vossor La Touche Tréville, an aggressive seaman, but he died in 1804.

2 *Reichdeputationshauptschluss.*

3 He spent eight years in the United States. But in 1813 he took service with the czar against Napoleon, and was killed, some say by a cannonball from the artillery of the Imperial Guard.

4 Napoleon wrote detailed instructions to Berthier for the operation, naming the commander, troops, mode of crossing the Rhine, and much else. *L'Oeuvre et l'histoire,* ed. Jean Massin, Jean Tulard, *et al.,* 12 vols (Paris, 1969), 1/2, 67–68.

5 The crown from Aachen (Aix-la-Chapelle); it rests near the remains of Charlemagne in the cathedral (*chapelle Palatine,* built 805).

6 Pope Pius VII, whose distant predecessor had crowned Charlemagne Roman Emperor in AD 800, watched passively.

7 Brought from Monza, it was called the "Iron Crown" because embedded in it were nails "from the cross of Christ."

8 In 1797 France had taken the Ionian Islands (Treaty of Campo Formio). In 1799 they were made a Russian protectorate by Czar Paul I, who also became Grand

Master of the Knights of Malta. Alexander wanted to keep the title and the islands, to improve Russian naval presence in the Mediterranean. His interests in the Balkans were threatened by the Napoleonic kingdom of Italy.

9 Napoléon I, *L'Oeuvre et l'histoire*, 2/2, 248, citing *Correspondance*, 7859 and 8243. He ordered Marshal Murat to leave Boulogne on 26 August, posing as a Colonel Beaumont, to go via Ulm to the border of Bohemia, and return up the Danube, again checking Ulm, and be in Strasbourg on 24 September. To Marshal Berthier, 25 August 1805. *L'Oeuvre et l'histoire*, 2/2, 266–267.

10 And he kept reminding Eugene to see that they were supplied. See, for example, Napoléon I, *Correspondance de Napoléon Ier, publiée par ordre de l'Empereur Napoléon III*, 32 vols (Paris, 1858–70), 8983, 14 July 1805.

11 John Keegan, *The Price of Admiralty: The Evolution of Naval Warfare* (New York and London, 1988), 28–29.

12 Napoléon I, *Correspondance*, XI, 176–177, 204.

13 Specifying routes of march for each. Napoléon I, *L'Oeuvre et l'histoire*, V, 205–206.

14 Napoleon's letters described his corps as 50,000 each, making the army 350,000+, to alarm the enemy if his letters were captured. See *Correspondance*, XI, 268.

15 Pan-German nationalism was yet to come.

16 The Austrians possibly ignored that the Russians were on the Julian calendar, with dates twelve days behind the Gregorian, in use in Europe – or vice versa.

17 He wrote Murat on 11 October to move quickly on Mack's army; "if he escapes, he will stop at the Lech." *L'Oeuvre et l'histoire*, 2/2, 252.

18 Ibid., 292.

19 Mack was sentenced to twenty years in prison by a military court. Francis II paroled him, but his military career was over.

20 *L'Oeuvre et l'histoire*, 2/2, 294.

21 Ibid.

22 Napoléon I, *Correspondance*, XI, 204.

23 He damned Murat and his messenger: "such a brute (*bête*) that he can explain nothing." *L'Oeuvre et l'histoire*, 2/2, 297.

24 A.-F.-L. Viesse de Marmont, *Mémoires*, 9 vols (Paris, 1857), I, 357.

25 In the 30th Bulletin of the Grande Armée, Napoleon mentions the gullibility of Alexander's advisers. He had received several in his headquarters; they went away certain that the French army was very weak. *L'Oeuvre et l'histoire*, 2/2, 322–324.

26 Napoleon, however, wanted the public and posterity to believe he could read the enemy's mind. There is an order in the *Dépôt de la Guerre*, dated 1 December 1805 (the day before the Austerlitz), which reads: "When they march to turn my right [south] flank, they will expose their flank to me [and I will attack and destroy them]." That is what happened. Henry Lachouque discovered, however, that this order was written on 2 December, after the battle began. Lachouque was an authority on Napoleon (best known for his *L'Histoire de la Garde Impériale* (1962). The improvisor's actions did not surprise him, but he was saddened by the deception involved. Napoléon I, *Correspondance*, 9533; *L'Oeuvre et l'histoire*, 2/2, 308–310.

27 Annexed to the Kingdom of Italy, but in 1809 Istria and Dalmatia became part of the new Illyrian Provinces.

28 The continental part of Naples–Sicily; Sicily was protected by the British navy.

29 He wanted direct control of the Netherlands, particularly because he thought the Dutch had "all the money in the world" and wanted Louis to get him more of it. This did not work out.

30 Napoléon I, *Correspondance*, 10629.

31 Napoléon I, *L'Oeuvre et l'histoire*, 2/2 396–397.

32 Ibid., 399.

33 He wrote Soult that he planned thus to win without risking anything. *L'Oeuvre et l'histoire*, 2/2, 403.

34 See Napoléon I, *Correspondance*, XXXII, 238–242.

35 In 1807, when Scharnhorst began reforming the army, he was forced into retirement.

36 Made Prince von Wahlstatt after Waterloo.

37 Meanwhile, Bernadotte came close to committing treason. He had refused to march with Davout. On 14 October he could hear the guns of both Jena and Auerstädt, but stayed at Dornburg, and fought in neither battle. His only excuse was misleading orders. However, he was not punished, but merely reprimanded, undoubtedly because he was a member of the Imperial family (married to Desirée Clary, sister of Joseph Bonaparte's wife, Julie).

38 Napoléon I, *L'Oeuvre et l'histoire*, 2/2, 423–424.

39 Louis-Nicolas Davout, *Correspondance*, 4 vols (Paris, 1885), I, 276–79.

40 Ibid., 179–180.

41 Napoléon I, *L'Oeuvre et l'histoire*, 2/2, 426–428.

42 He was a Prussian of a family originally French.

43 Josephine came as far as Mainz, but was told Poland was dangerous, and went back to Paris. Walewska became like a second wife to Napoleon, who gave her a house near the Tuileries. He made their son, Alexandre Walewski, born 1810, one of his heirs.

44 On the march, his Cossack cavalry captured French orders, giving Bennigsen the locations of the French corps.

45 Napoléon I, *L'Oeuvre et l'histoire*, 2/2, 480.

46 Napoléon I, *Correspondance*, 14276.

47 Napoléon I, *L'Oeuvre et l'histoire*, 2/2, 485.

48 The school still exists, and obeys Napoleon's rule on soldiers' daughters.

49 The attack was planned for 4 June, but Bennigsen postponed it until the 5th. Lestocq did not get the order, attacked Bernadotte on the 4th, and was thrown back. On the 5th, he and Bennigsen attacked again, but by then Napoleon was moving forces to support Bernadotte.

50 Napoléon I, *Correspondance*, 12755.

51 Savary, in Napoléon I, *L'Oeuvre et l'histoire*, 2/2, 554.

52 Often called Grand Duchy because of its size.

10 "THAT MISERABLE SPANISH AFFAIR": THE PENINSULAR WAR, 1808–13

1 The British name for Napoleon's Iberian war. The French say *la guerre d'Espagne* (the war in Spain), which it was, mostly.

2 The French said *les Anglais*. Napoléon I, *Correspondance de Napoléon Ier, publiée par ordre de l'Empereur Napoléon III*, 32 vols (Paris, 1858–70), XXXII, 265.

3 See Charles Esdaile, *The Peninsular War: A New History* (Houndmills, UK, and New York, 2003), 501–05. Alan I. Forrest, *Napoleon's Men: The Soldiers of the Revolution and Empire* (London & New York, 2002), 13, 130.

4 André Palluel, *Dictionnaire de l'Empereur* (Paris, 1969), 532. To Montholon on St Helena, November 1820.

5 For those interested, there are numerous books on this war, the latest being *The Peninsular War: A New History* (2003) by Charles Esdaile. The bibliography in Esdaile's book has biographies of participants, and relevant memoirs, letters, and the like.

6 Since 1795, when defeated by French revolutionary armies.

7 On evasion and desertion, see Esdaile, *The Peninsular War*, 111–112, and *passim*.

8 Ibid., 265. He also writes: "the people's real loyalty was rather to a Spain in which they would no longer be subject to the demands of Church, State and señor." Ibid., 112.

9 On this see Gabriel Lovett, *Napoleon and the Birth of Modern Spain* (New York, 1965), who names and describes heads of bands.

10 Esdaile, *The Peninsular War*, 124–126, 264–265, *passim*.

11 Others: Garcia de La Cuesta, Don Joaquin Blake (of Irish ancestry), Francisco Castaños, Theador Reding (Swiss), Felix Jones (Irish), and the Marquis de Coupigny (French *émigré*).

12 Esdaile, *The Peninsular War*, 64.

13 Ibid., 100, quoting J. Leach, *Rough Sketches in the Life of an Old Soldier* (London, 1830), 50–51.

14 Napoléon I, *Correspondance*, 14524.

15 But Joseph was to execute the order, and never did.

16 Esdaile concludes that despite Wellington's stand in Portugal, guerrilla actions, and the use of seapower, Masséna's invasion "eroded the foundations of Spanish resistance still further." French victories elsewhere "brought the day closer when the *partidas* could be exterminated." Esdaile, *The Peninsular War*, 338.

11 THE WAGRAM CAMPAIGN, 1809

1 Napoléon I, *Correspondance de Napoléon Ier, publiée par ordre de l'Empereur Napoléon III*, 32 vols (Paris, 1858–70), 14571.

2 He allied with Prussia, but not actively. Napoléon I, *L'Oeuvre et l'histoire*, ed. Jean Massin, Jean Tulard, *et al.*, 12 vols (Paris, 1969), 2/2, 566.

3 Ibid., 575. Napoleon to A. de Caulaincourt, 21 March 1809.

4 Ibid., 617–618.

5 Thiébault called him an amiable lunatic, but fearless leader. Paul Thiébault, *Mémoires du Général Baron Thiébault* (Paris, 1962), 58ff.

6 After this campaign he wanted to retire, but Napoleon sent him to Spain, as we know.

7 André Masséna, *Mémoires*, 7 vols (Paris, 1849–50), VI, 256.

8 Napoléon I, *L'Oeuvre et l'histoire*, 2/2, 654.

9 Ibid., II, 643. Napoleon: St Helena, replying to criticisms of General Rogniat, commanding IV Corps Engineers, Aspern–Essling.

10 Masséna, *Mémoires*, VI, 256.

11 Napoléon I, *Correspondance*, 15246.

12 Ibid., 15272.

13 Charles, of course, was not reinforced by the Archduke John (12,000). The Archduke Ferdinand had an army of 20,000, but it was threatened from Saxony by Jerome Bonaparte (12,000 Westphalians) and from Poland by Prince Poniatowski (30,000 Poles).

14 Napoléon I, *L'Oeuvre et l'histoire*, 2/2, 677.

15 Ibid., 678.

16 Ibid., 686.

17 Ernest Picard, *Préceptes et jugements de Napoléon* (Paris, 1913), 62; Emmanuel Las Cases, *Mémorial de Sainte-Hélène*, 8 vols (Paris, 1823–24), III, 303–304.

18 Launched to take pressure off Austria, it came too late. The army, prostrated by unidentified fevers, was evacuated.

19 He had a son by a former mistress (and three girls by others). Moreover, a child was due in 1810 by Countess Walewska, his Polish mistress; he expected a boy, and he was right.

12 THE RUSSIAN CAMPAIGN, 1812

1 Philippe-Paul de Ségur, *Histoire de Napoléon et la Grande Armée en 1812* (Paris, 1824), 184.
2 Some writers have contended that he already had cancer, which would kill him in 1821. That seems unlikely, however, since he fought campaigns in 1813, 1814, and 1815 – and was on St Helena for six years before he died.
3 Adrien Dansette (ed.), *Napoléon: Pensées . . .*, (Paris, 1969), 412.
4 Napoléon I, *L'Oeuvre et l'histoire*, ed. Jean Massin, Jean Tulard, *et al.*, 12 vols (Paris, 1969), 2/3, 111–114.
5 Where he had a wife, Catherine von Württemberg, and three mistresses, all at once.
6 Napoléon I, *L'Oeuvre et l'histoire*, 2/3, 130–131.
7 Raimond-A.-P.-J de Fezensac, *The Russian Campaign, 1812*, trans. Lee Kennett (Athens, Ga., 1970), 8.
8 Horses can keep up with men over long distances, but must be taken along slowly – at the walk and trot – and fed well. A slow gallop for three miles, without rest, can kill a horse; at top speed, two miles.
9 See Abel Mansuy, *Jérôme Bonaparte et la Pologne en 1812* (Paris, 1931).
10 He reviewed the Guard, ordering his medical personnel, publicly, to improve food supply and hospital care. "But," wrote Fezensac, "it is not enough to give orders: the orders must be capable of execution." The country was ravaged, of food and everything else of use. Fezensac, *Russian Campaign*, 21.
11 Fezensac, *Russian Campaign*, 28.
12 André Palluel, *Dictionnaire de l'Empereur* (Paris, 1969), 533 (10 May 1809).
13 Napoléon I, *Correspondance de Napoléon Ier, publiée par ordre de l'Empereur Napoléon III*, 32 vols (Paris, 1858–70), 19181.
14 Ibid.
15 As dawn broke, Napoleon declaimed: "Behold, the Sun of Austerlitz!" The response was muted. Fezensac, *Russian Campaign*, 31.
16 Ségur, *Histoire de Napoléon . . . en 1812*, 181.
17 Ibid., 180.
18 Ibid., 184.
19 Ibid., 187.
20 Ibid., 188.
21 Quoted by Rory Muir, *Tactics and the Experience of Battle in the Age of Napoleon* (New Haven, Conn., 1998), 236.
22 Ségur, *Histoire de Napoléon . . . en 1812*, 189.
23 Fezensac, *Russian Campaign*, 39.
24 Napoléon I, *Correspondance*, 19213.
25 He had considered it. Ibid., 19237, n.d.
26 Fezensac, *Russian Campaign*, 45.
27 Ibid., 46.
28 Napoléon I, *Correspondance*, 19234.
29 Fezensac, *Russian Campaign*, 46.
30 Napoléon I, *Correspondance*, 19236.
31 The famed British observer with the Russians, General Sir Robert Wilson, wrote that Kutuzov was about to run.
32 According to the famous *Carte Figurative* of the Russian Campaign by M. Minard, Inspecteur Général des Ponts et Chausées (ret.), the first of its kind, dated 20 November 1869.
33 Napoléon I, *Correspondance*, 19365.
34 An officer asked Ney, "What are we going to do?" "Cross the Dnieper," said Ney. "Where is the road?" "We will find it." "And if it isn't passable?" "It will be." Fezensac, *Russian Campaign*, 79.

35 Napoléon I, *L'Oeuvre et l'histoire*, 2/3, 191 (11 November), to Maret, captured by Cossacks.

36 The luckiest were taken in by Russian peasants. Some returned to their homes decades later, to the consternation of wives who had remarried.

37 Fezensac wrote: "That famous warrior, who had saved the Third Corps [at Smolensk], now saved the entire army and the emperor himself". Fezensac, *Russian Campaign*, 96.

38 For a few hours, ex-General Claude François de Malet had seized ministerial offices with some regiments of the Paris garrison, having convinced them that Napoleon had died in Russia.

39 Napoléon I, *Correspondance*, 19365.

40 He could have taken his time. Kutuzov reached Kovno long after Murat had passed on into East Prussia, and the Russian had only 35,000 men. His army had dwindled also.

41 Napoléon I, *L'Oeuvre et la histoire*, 2/3, 199.

42 David G. Chandler gives casualties of 570,000, including 200,000 captured, in his *The Campaigns of Napoleon* (New York, 1966), 853. John Elting says 400,000 – see John R. Elting and Vincent Esposito, *Military History and Atlas of the Napoleonic Wars* (New York, 1964), opp. map 126.

13 CAMPAIGNS OF GERMANY AND FRANCE, 1813–14

1 In 1796 and 1797, Austria (with other French armies). In 1798 and 1799, Egypt. In 1800, Austria. In 1805, Austria at Ulm; largely Russia at Austerlitz. In 1806 and 1807, Prussia at Jena–Auerstädt; largely Russia at Eylau and Friedland. In 1808 and 1809, personally, Spain. In 1809, Austria. In 1812, Russia.

2 During the next year, 635,000 more were called, but the draft of March 1814, for 160,000, was negated by Napoleon's abdication.

3 Westphalia, for example, sent 22,000 to Russia; 760 stood muster at Küstrin in January 1813; perhaps 700 others returned.

4 Kutuzov had been commander of Russian and Prussian forces, but died in April; the czar had not named a successor.

5 Napoléon I, *L'Oeuvre et l'histoire*, ed. Jean Massin, Jean Tulard, *et al.*, 12 vols (Paris, 1969), 5, 416.

6 Napoléon I, *Correspondance de Napoléon Ier, publiée par ordre de l'Empereur Napoléon III*, 32 vols (Paris, 1858–70), 19951, 19952.

7 A.-F.-L. Viesse de Marmont, *Mémoires*, 9 vols (Paris, 1857), V, 25.

8 *Correspondance*, 19952.

9 Marmont, *Mémoires*, V, 26.

10 Ibid., 177.

11 In Germany, pan-nationalism was a generation or more away. Though historians of the Prussian School – H. von Sybel, H. Treitschke, *et al.* – would say that Napoleon had been expelled by patriot armies in 1813, he was actually beaten by regular armies augmented (in Prussia) by a few volunteers.

12 Ernest Picard, *Préceptes et jugements de Napoléon* (Paris, 1913), 114; Napoléon I, *Correspondance*, 15332 (to Clarke, 11 juin 1809).

13 Marmont, *Mémoires*, V, 204–208.

14 It seems inexplicable that Oudinot rather than Davout was given the second largest army. Davout had triumphed, alone, at Auerstädt (1806); his corps had decided battle after battle.

15 Jean Mistler, *Napoléon et l'Empire*, 2 vols (Paris, 1969), II, 219.

16 Napoléon I, *L'Oeuvre et l'histoire*, 2/3, 203.

17 King Max (Maximilian Josef) of Bavaria had deserted to the Allies on 8 October, before Leipzig. Saxony had been occupied by the Russians since March; her troops went over to the Allies during the Battle of Leipzig, as noted on p. 193. Württemberg joined the Allies after Napoleon passed through in late October. Jerome Bonaparte fled Westphalia on 26 October, and the dukes of Brunswick, Hesse-Kassel, Hanover (the English king), and other minor rulers recovered their lands. In November, Prussia took over her former lands in Westphalia, the Rhineland, Switzerland, plus the Grand Duchy of Berg, composed of former territories of Prussia, Bavaria, Nassau, and Münster. The Grand Duchy of Frankfurt reverted to its parts – the Imperial cities of Frankfurt and Wetzlar and the principalities of Hanau and Fulda. This, and the claims of some 300 princelings whose lands had been ceded to larger states (in the end thirty-nine), had to await disposition by the Congress of Vienna (1814–15).

18 Felix Markham, *Napoleon* (New York, 1963), 216.

19 Eugene was Duke von Leuchtenberg and Prince von Eichstädt.

20 Marie-Louise became Duchess of Parma. The Bonapartes all retained their property and wealth. Josephine was left with Malmaison, where she died suddenly in May 1814.

21 Napoléon I, *Correspondance*, 21561.

22 John R. Elting, *Swords Around a Throne: The Grand Armée of Napoleon*, (New York, 1987), 623–624.

14 THE HUNDRED DAYS AND WATERLOO, 1815

1 She married him after Napoleon's death.

2 John R. Elting, *Swords Around a Throne: The Grand Armée of Napoleon* (New York, 1987), 637.

3 In January 1815 the three signed a secret military alliance.

4 Marshals in Louis' service were Berthier, Ney, Marmont, Jourdan, Brune, Augereau, Mortier, Victor, Macdonald, Oudinot, Suchet, and Gouvion Saint-Cyr.

5 "Aussitôt que l'Empereur . . . s'avança à seul au galop, et, quand il fut à portée de la voix, il leur dit: '*Soldats du 5e, 'tuez votre Empereur, si vous l'osez!*'" To General Henry Bertrand: Napoléon I, *Correspondance de Napoléon Ier, publiée par ordre de l'Empereur Napoléon III*, 32 vols (Paris, 1858–70), XXXI, 51–52.

6 "Je vous a refusé . . . d'être le roi d'une jacquerie . . . Règle generale: pas de révolution sociale sans terreur. A revolution is . . . one of the greatest evils that the anger of God can inflict on a nation." Ibid., XXXII, 344.

7 But not Louis, who resented losing the throne of Holland.

8 Peter Hofschröer, summarizing his revisionist findings for the BBC in May 2004, said: "The . . . army was a mixture of Germans (the largest contingent), Netherlanders (. . . 'Dutch-Belgians') and British (many . . . from Ireland). The [veteran] . . . British and King's German Legion units [held] together this . . . mixture of men, some . . . had fought for Napoleon only the previous year."

9 David Chandler, *Waterloo: The Hundred Days* (London, 1980), 25.

10 Berthier fell from a window in Bamberg; suicide or foul play were rumored, but the cause was probably illness.

11 Probably Wellington *should* have known much earlier, and been more active on the 15th or before. He can be seen as leaving Blücher to take the brunt of the French attack. Peter Hofschröer, *1815: The Waterloo Campaign: Wellington, His German*

Allies, and the Battles of Ligny and Quatre-Bras (London and Mechanicsbury, Pa., 1998), 210–215.

12 Hofschröer, *Waterloo*, 67–69.

13 Ten miles to the west, at Hal and Tubize, Wellington stationed 17,000 troops – Belgians, with a British brigade and Hanoverian cavalry. They took no part in the Battle of Waterloo. Wellington may have put them there to cover a possible retreat (Chandler, *Waterloo*, 120). More likely, he did not trust the Belgians; they had been quiet under Napoleon's rule, but resented the Dutch king the Allies gave them in 1814.

14 Elizabeth Longford, *Wellington: The Years of the Sword* (London, 1969), 448; Christopher Hibbert, *Wellington: A Personal History* (London, 1997), 177.

15 Hibbert, *Wellington*, 177.

16 Henry Lachouque, *Waterloo: Fin d'un monde* (Paris, 1958), 134.

17 Ibid., 140.

18 It was an hour before the Guard attacked. "By then, Wellington had reconstructed his line . . . and brought into the centre two brigades of light cavalry from the extreme left [now held by the Prussians]." Rory Muir, *Tactics and the Experience of Battle in the Age of Napoleon* (New Haven, Conn., 1998), 236–237.

19 *Bonnets à Poil* translates, literally, "fur hats," called "bearskins" by the British.

20 "The whole art of war consists of a well reasoned defense . . . and a bold and rapid offense". Napoléon I, *Correspondance*, 10558 (1806).

21 "Napoleon did not manoeuver at all. He just moved forward in the old style, and was driven off in the old style." Wellington to Beresford, quoted by M. Glover in U. Pericoli, *1815: The Armies at Waterloo*, (New York, 1973), 70.

22 Ney was executed for treason. A court-martial declared itself incompetent, but Louis XVIII convened the Chamber of Peers as a high court, which passed sentence. It included marshals Kellermann (the elder), Pérignon, Sérurier, Victor, and Marmont.

23 Quoted by Chandler, *Waterloo*, 178, and others.

24 Napoléon I, *Correspondance*, 22066.

25 Lord Rosebery, *Napoleon: The Last Phase* (London, 1900), 220.

26 Napoléon I, *Correspondance*, XXXII, 275.

27 Ibid., XXX, 388.

28 Ibid., 171, 263.

29 André Palleul, *Dictionnaire de l'Empereur* (Paris, 1969), 530 (*Mémorial*, 15 Dec. 1815); Ernest Picard, *Préceptes et jugements de Napoléon* (Paris, 1913), 41 (*Correspondance*, XXXII, 99); Picard, *Préceptes*, 42 (*Mémorial*, II, 39).

30 Napoléon I, *Correspondance*, 15332 (to Clarke, 11 juin 1809); Picard, *Préceptes*, 114.

31 Picard, *Préceptes*, 120.

32 Napoléon I, *Correspondance*, 14283; Picard, *Préceptes*, 114.

33 Emmanuel Las Cases, *Mémorial de Sainte-Hélène* (Paris, 1823–24), 5 décembre 1815; Palluel, *Dictionnaire*, 529–530.

34 Napoléon I, *Correspondance*, 14276.

15 CONCLUSIONS

1 De Gaulle confirms the contributions of the *ancien régime*, the Revolution, and Napoleon in *La France et ses Armées*, where he treats the army as an institution apart, one that developed, irrespective of governments, from the eighteenth century onward – an attitude much like Napoleon's. See Charles de Gaulle, *Les Écrits militaires de Charles de Gaulle: Essai d'Analyse thématique*, ed. Pierre Messmer and Alain Larcan (Paris, 1985), 228–229.

2 See Chapter 1, pp. 16–17.

3 Arthur Chuquet, *Les guerres de la révolution*, 11 vols (Paris, 1914), I, 24. "Je ne puis concevoir comment on a pu déclarer la guerre, en n'étant prêt sur rien." (Lafayette to the Minister of War, 6 May 1792.)

4 La Garde impériale a toujours marché à la Marseillaise. Napoléon I, *Correspondance de Napoléon Ier, publiée par ordre de l'Empereur Napoléon III*, 32 vols (Paris, 1858–70), XXXI, 224.

5 Peter MacDonald, *Giap: The Victor in Vietnam* (New York and London, 1993), 23. Among other disciples of Napoleon were the generals on both sides in the American Civil War, Lawrence of Arabia (World War I), George Patton and Erwin Rommel (World War II), and Charles de Gaulle, cited several times in the text. More contemporary generals, like Norman Schwarzkopf, tend to quote an interpreter of Napoleon, usually Clausewitz, rather the man himself. Nonetheless, he still has influence in military circles.

6 Cecil B. Currey, *Victory at Any Cost: The Genius of Viet Nam's General Vo Nguyen Giap* (Herndon, Va., 1996), 517.

BIBLIOGRAPHY

Bibliographies and references

Alison, Sir Archibald, *Alison's Atlas of the Wars in Europe, 1792–1815*, reprint, Tyne and Wear, 1994. (Original editions Edinburgh and London, 1848 and 1850.)

Bertaud, Jean-Paul (ed.), *Dictionnaire historique de la Révolution française*, Publie sous la direction scientifique de Jean-René Suratteau et François Gendron; comité de redaction, Jean-Paul Bertaud *et al.*, 1st edn, Paris, 1989.

Bourguet, Marie-Noëlle, *Déchiffrer la France: La statistique départmentale à l'époch napoléonienne*, Paris, 1988.

Caldwell, Ronald J., *The Era of the French Revolution: A Bibliography*, 2 vols, New York, 1985.

—— *The Era of Napoleon: A Bibliography of the History of Western Civilization, 1799–1815*, 2 vols, New York, 1990.

Chandler, David G., *Dictionary of the Napoleonic Wars*, New York, 1979.

Chronique de la Révolution, 1788–1799, Paris, 1989 (Larousse).

Clausewitz, Carl von, *On War*, trans. Peter Paret and M. Howard, Princeton, N.J., 1986.

—— *Historical and Politcal Writings*, ed. and trans. Peter Paret and Daniel Moran, Princeton, N.J., 1992.

Connelly, Owen (ed.), *Historical Dictionary of Napoleonic France*, Westport, Conn., 1985.

Dupaquier, Jacques, *Histoire de la population française*, 3 vols, Paris, 1988.

Gendron, François, *Dictionnaire historique de la Révolution française*, Paris, 1989.

Godechot, Jacques, *Les institutions de la France sous la Révolution et l'Empire*, 2nd edn, Paris, 1968.

Histoire militaire de la France, 4 vols, Sous la direction de André Corvisier, Paris, 1992.

Israel, Jonathan I., *The Radical Enlightenment: Philosophy and the Making of Modernity 1650–1750*, New York, 2001.

Paret, Peter, *Understanding War: Essays on Clausewitz and the History of Military Power*, Princeton, N.J., 1992.

Parker, Geoffrey, *Military Revolution: Military Innovation and the Rise of the West*, Cambridge, Mass., 1988.

Pope, Stephen, *Dictionary of the Napoleonic Wars*, New York, 1999.

Reinhard, Marcel, *Étude de la population pendant la Révolution et l'Empire*, Paris, 1963.

Ross, Steven, *Historical Dictionary of the Wars of the French Revolution*, Reprint, Lanham, Md., 1998.

Scott, Samuel L. and Rothaus, Barry, *Historical Dictionary of the French Revolution*, New York, 1985.

Showalter, Dennis E., *German Military History, 1648–1982: A Critical Bibliography*, New York, 1984.

Tulard, Jean, *Bibliographie critique des mémoires sur le Consulat et l'Empire*, Geneva, 1971; and *Nouvelle bibliographie critique des mémoires sur l'époque napoléonienne écrits ou traduits en français* (Jean Tulard; avec le concours de Jacques Garnier, Alfred Fierro et Charles d'Huart), Nouv. edn, Genève, 1991.

Tulard, Jean, *Dictionnaire Napoléon*, Paris, 1987.

Van Creveld, Martin, *The Training of Officers*, New York and London, 1990.

Primary sources: Revolution

Archives de la Bastille d'après des documents inédits, 10 vols, Reprint, Geneva, 1975.

Barras, Paul-Jean-François-Nicolas, Vicomte de, *Mémoires de Barras, membre du Directoire . . .*, 4 vols, Paris, 1895–96. New edn, condensed, Geneva, 1968.

Carnot, Lazare, *Mémoires historiques et militaires*, Paris, 1824.

Charette de La Contrie, François Athanase, *Mémoires sur la Vendée*, Paris, 1823.

Chateaubriand, René, Vicomte de, *Mélanges historiques: contenant les mémoires sur M. le duc de Berry, de la Vendée etc. suivis mélanges politiques contenant Napoléon et les Bourbons, Compiègne, reflexions politiques, etc.*, Paris, c. 1850.

Kléber, Jean-Baptiste, *Mémoires politiques et militaires: La Vendée, 1793–1794*, ed. Roger Nougaret, Paris, 1989.

La Bouère, Antoinette Charlotte Le Duc Gazeau, Comtesse de (1770–1867), *Souvenirs. La guerre de La Vendée, 1793–1796*, Mémoires inédits publies par Madame la ctesse. de La Bouère, belle-fille de l'auteur, Paris, 1890.

La Rochejaquelein, Marie-Louise-Victoire, Marquise de (1772–1857), *Mémoires de Mme. la marquise de La Rochejaquelein*, Paris, 1822. English trans. Cecil Biggane, London, 1933.

Les Armées françaises à l'époque révolutionnaire: 1789–1804, Paris, 1989.

Marat, Jean Paul (1743–1793), *Oeuvres politiques, 1789–1793*, 10 vols, Brussels, 1989–95.

Palmer, R. R., *From Jacobin to Liberal: Marc-Antoine Jullien*, Princeton, N.J., 1993.

Poirier de Beauvais, Bertrand, *Mémoires . . . sur la guerre de la Vendée*, Niort, 1886.

Recueil des actes du Comité de Salut Public, 27 vols, Paris, 1889–1956.

Robespierre, Maximilien, *Oeuvres complète de Maximilien Robespierre*, 10 vols, Pub. of Société des études Robespierristes, ed. Albert Soboul *et al.*, Paris, 1955–69.

Société des Jacobins: Recueil de documents pour l'histoire du Club des Jacobins de Paris, 6 vols, ed. F.-V.-Alphonse Aulard, Paris, 1889–1897. Reprint, AMS, New York, 1973.

Thiébault, D.-A.-Paul-F.-C.-Henri, *Mémoires du Général Baron Thiébault*, Paris, 1962. (Orig. 5 vols, 1892–95.)

Tulard, Jean, *et al.*, *le livre de la mémoire, 1793–1993*, Préface de Philippe de Villiers [Clichy], Valmonde, 1993.

Turreau de Garambouville, General Baron Louis-M., *Mémoires pour servir à l'histoire de la guerre de la Vendée*, Paris, 1824, New edn, Cholet, 1992.

Turreau de Linières, Louis Marie, Baron (1756–1816), *Mémoires pour servirà l'histoire de la guerre de la Vendée*, Paris, 1824.

Primary sources: Napoleon

Napoléon I, *Correspondance de Napoléon Ier, publiée par ordre de l'Empereur Napoléon III*, 32 vols, Paris, 1858–70. *Supplement*, ed. A. du Casse, Paris, 1887.

—— *Correspondance inédite de Napoléon Ier, conservée aux Archives de la Guerre*, 5 vols, ed. E. Picard and L. Tuetey, Paris, 1912–25.

—— *Dernières lettres de Napoléon*, 2 vols, ed. Léonce de Brotonne, Paris, 1903.

—— *Inédites Napoléoniens*, ed. A. Chuquet, Paris, 1913.

—— *Lettres de Napoléon à Joséphine*, 2 vols, ed. Mme de Faverolles, Paris, 1933.

—— *Lettres de Napoléon à Josephine et . . . de Joséphine à Napoléon*, Paris, 1959.

—— *Lettres de Napoléon à Marie-Louise écrits de 1810 à 1814*, Paris, 1960.

—— *Lettres, décisions et actes de Napoléon à Pont-de-Briques et au camp de Boulogne, An VI (1798)–An XII (1804)*, ed. Fernand Beaucour, Levallois, 1979.

—— *Lettres inédites de Napoléon*, 2 vols, ed. L. Lecestre, Paris, 1897.

—— *Lettres inédites de Napoléon*, ed. L. de Brotonne, Paris, 1898.

—— *L'Oeuvre et l'histoire*, ed. Jean Massin, Jean Tulard, *et al.*, 12 vols, Paris, 1969.

—— *Mémoires pour servir à l'histoire de France sous Napoléon écrits à Sainte-Helénè, sous la dictée de l'Empereur, par les géneraux qui sont partagé sa captivité . . .* 9 vols, Paris, 1823–25. English trans.: *Memoirs*, Reprint, 4 vols, New York, 1985.

—— *My Dearest Louise: Marie Louise and Napoleon 1813–1814: Unpublished letters from the Empress with previously published replies from Napoleon*, ed. C. F. Palmstierna, trans. E. M. Wilkinson, London, 1958.

—— *Ordres et Apostiles*, 4 vols, ed. A. Chuquet, Paris, 1911–12.

—— *Oeuvres litteraires et ecrits militaires*, 3 vols, ed. Jean Tulard, Paris, 1969.

—— *Proclamations, ordres du jour et bulletins de la Grande Armée*, ed. Jean Tulard, Paris, 1964.

★ ★ ★

Beauharnais, Eugene de, *Mémoires et correspondance*, 10 vols, ed. A. du Casse. Paris, 1858–60.

Bigarrré, Auguste J., Gen. Baron, *Mémoires*, Paris, 1899.

Blücher von Wahlstatt, Prince G. L., *Blüchers Briefe*, ed. W. von Unger, Stuttgart and Berlin, 1913.

Bonaparte, Jérôme, *Mémoires et correspondance du roi Jérôme et de la reine Catherine*, 7 vols, Paris, 1861–66.

Bonaparte, Joseph, *Mémoires et correspondance*, 10 vols, ed. A. du Casse, Paris, 1851–54.

Bourrienne, Louis-Antoine Fauvelet de, *Mémoires*, 10 vols, Paris 1829.

Carnot, Lazare, *Mémoires . . . rédigés d'après ses manuscrits . . .*, par P.-F. Tissot (ed.), Paris, 1824.

Caulaincourt, Armand A.-L., Marquis de, *Mémoires*, 3 vols, ed. Jean Hanoteau, Paris, 1933.

—— *With Napoleon in Russia*, trans. G. Libaire, New York, 1935.

Chlapowski, Dezydery, *Memoirs of a Polish Lancer*, Chicago, 1992.

Constant, Louis (Wairy), *Mémoires intimes de Napoléon I*, Paris, 1967. (Original in 6 vols, Paris, 1830–31.)

Croker, John Wilson, *The Croker Papers, 1808–1857*, London, 1884.

Dansette, Adrien, *Napoléon: Pensées . . .*, Paris, 1969.

Davout, Louis-Nicolas, Marshal, *Correspondance*, 4 vols, Paris, 1885.

Driault, Édouard, *Napoléon: Pensées pour l'action*, Paris, 1943.

Dumas, Mathieu, Général Comte, *Souvenirs*, 3 vols, Paris, 1839.

Fezensac, R.-A.-P.-J. Gen. Duc de, *Souvenirs Militaires*, Paris, 1863.

—— *The Russian Campaign, 1812*, trans. Lee Kennett, Athens, Ga., 1970.

Foy, Maximilien S., Gen. Comte, *Histoire de la guerre de la Peninsule sous Napoléon*, 4 vols, Paris, 1827.

Gourgaud, Gaspard, Baron (1783–1852), *Journal de Sainte-Hélène, 1815–1818*, edn augm. d'après le texte original, Intro. and notes par Octave Aubry, Paris, 1944.

Grouchy, Emmanuel de, Marshal, *Mémoires*, 5 vols, Paris, 1873–74.

Macdonald, Jacques-E.-J.-Alexandre, Marshal, *Souvenirs*, Paris, 1892.

Marchand, Louis, *Mémoires*, 2 vols, ed. J. Bourguignon and H. Lachouque, Paris, 1952–55.

Marmont, A.-F.-L. Viesse de, Marshal, *Mémoires*, 9 vols, Paris, 1857.

Masséna, André, Marshal, *Mémoires*, 7 vols, Paris, 1849–50. New edn, 1966.

Murat, Joachim, Maréchal, *Lettres et documents, 1787–1815*, 8 vols, ed. Paul Le Brethon, Paris, 1908–14.

Ney, Michel, Marshal, *Mémoires*, 2 vols, Paris, 1833 (fragmentary).

Palluel, André, *Dictionnaire de l'Empereur*, Paris, 1969.

Picard, Ernest, *Préceptes et jugements de Napoléon*, Paris, 1913.

Rapp, Jean, Général, *Mémoires*, Paris, 1824.

Roederer, Pierre-Louis, *Autour de Bonaparte: Journal*, Paris, 1909.

Savary, A.-J.-M.-René, Duc de Rovigo, *Mémoires*, 8 vols, Paris, 1828.

Ségur, Philippe-Paul, Comte de, *Histoire et Mémoires*, 7 vols, Paris, 1873.

—— *Histoire de Napoléon et la Grand Armée en 1812*, Paris, 1824. (Many later editions in French and major foreign languages.)

Soult, Jean de Dieu, Marshal, *Mémoires*, 3 vols, Paris, 1854.

—— *Mémoires . . . Espagne et Portugal*, Paris, 1955.

Staël, Anne-Louise-Germaine Necker, Baronne de, *Mémoires: Dix ans d'exil*, ed M. le Duc de Broglie and le Baron de Staël, Paris, 1821.

Talleyrand de Périgord, Prince, *Lettres de Talleyrand à Napoléon*, ed. Jean de Bonnot, Paris, 1967.

Walter, Jakob, *Diary of a Napoleonic Foot Soldier*, New York, 1991.

Wellington, Arthur Wellesley, Duke of, *Dispatches*, 12 vols, ed. Lt.-Col. Gurwood, London, 1834–38.

★ ★ ★

Gourgaud, Gaspard, Baron, *Sainte-Hélène: journal inédit*, 2 vols, ed. E. H. de Grouchy and A. Guillois, Paris, 1899.

Las Cases, Emmanuel, *Mémorial de Sainte-Hélène*, 8 vols, Paris, 1823–24.

Montholon, C.-J.-T. de, *Récits de la captivité de l'Empereur Napoléon*, 2 vols, Paris, 1847. First pub. in London as *History of the Captivity of Napoleon at Saint Helena* (1846).

O'Meara, B. E., *Napoleon in Exile*, 2 vols, London, 1822.

Secondary works

Armies and navies: France and opponents, and related

Androlenko, General D., *Histoire de l'armée russe*, Paris, 1967.

Angeli, M. von, *Erherzog Karl als Feldherr und Heeresorganisator*, 6 vols, Wien, 1895–97.

Bescrovny, L. G., *Russkaia armiia i flot v XIX veke*, Moscow, 1973.

Blaze, Elzéar, *La Vie militaire sous l'Empire, ou moeurs de la garrison, du bivouac et de la caserne*, Paris, 1890.

Blond, Georges, *La Grande Armée, 1804–1815*, Paris, 1979. English edn, *La Grand Armée*, trans. Marshall May, London, 1995.

Bucquoy, Eugène L., *La garde impériale*, 2 vols, Paris, 1977.

Bukhari, Emir, *Napoleon's Cavalry*, San Francisco, 1979.

Choury, Maurice, *Les Grognards de Napoléon*, Paris, 1968.

Corvisier, André, *Armies and Societies in Europe, 1494–1789*, trans. Abigail Siddall, Bloomington, Ind., 1979.

Davies, David Tudor, *Nelson's Navy: English Fighting Ships, 1793–1815*, 1st US edn, Mechanicsburg, Pa., 1997.

Davies, G., *Wellington and His Army*, London, 1954.

Duffy, Christopher, *Military Life of Frederick the Great*, New York, 1986.

Elting, John R., *Swords Around a Throne: The Grande Armée of Napoleon*, New York, 1987.

Fletcher, Ian, *Wellington's Regiments: The Men and their Battles from Rolica to Waterloo, 1808–1815*, Staplehurst, Kent, 1994.

Gallaher, John G., *Napoleon's Irish Legion*, Carbondale, Ill., 1993.

Glover, Richard, *Peninsular Preparation: The Reform of the British Army, 1795–1809*, Cambridge, 1963.

Guy, Alan J. (ed.), *Road to Waterloo: The British Army and the Struggle Against Revolutionary and Napoleonic France, 1793–1815*, Stroud, Gloucestershire; Wolfboro Falls, N.H.; London, 1990.

Jany, C., *Geschichte der königlich-preussischen Armee*, 4 vols, Berlin, 1933.

Johnson, David, *Napoleon's Cavalry and Its Leaders*, New York, 1978.

Kennett, Lee, *The French Armies in the Seven Years War*, Durham, N.C., 1987.

Lachouque, Henry, *Napoléon et la garde impériale*, Paris, 1957. Adapted from the French as *The Anatomy of Glory: Napoleon and His Guard* by Anne S. K. Brown, London and New York, 1961. Fourth edn intro. by Col. John R. Elting, London and Mechanicsburg Pa., 1997.

Maffeo, Steven E., *Most Secret and Confidential: Intelligence in the Age of Nelson*, Annapolis, Md., 2000.

Muir, Rory, *Tactics and the Experience of Battle in the Age of Napoleon*, New Haven, Conn., 1998.

Rothenberg, Gunther E., *Napoleon's Great Adversaries: The Archduke Charles and the Austrian Army, 1792–1814*, Bloomington, Ind., 1982.

Schneid, Frederick C., *Soldiers of Napoleon's Kingdom of Italy: Army, State, and Society, 1800–1815*, Boulder, Colo., 1995.

Shanahan, William O., *Prussian Military Reforms, 1786–1813*, New York, 1945.

Showalter, Dennis E., *The Wars of Frederick the Great*, London and New York, 1996.

Sparrow, Elizabeth (Elizabeth Mary), *Secret Service: British Agents in France, 1792–1815*, Rochester, N.Y., 1999.

Tranie, J., *Les Polonaise de Napoléon*, Paris, 1982.

Ward, S. G. P., *Wellington's Headquarters, 1809–1814*, London, 1957.

Wars of the Revolution

Alder, Ken, *Engineering the Revolution: Arms and Enlightenment in France, 1763–1815*, Princeton, N.J., 1997.

Andress, David, *Massacre at the Champ de Mars: Popular Dissent and Political Culture in the French Revolution*, (Rochester, N.Y., 2001.

Bertaud, Jean-Paul, *La Révolution Armée: Les soldats-citoyens et la Révolution française*, Paris, 1979, trans. by R. R. Palmer as *The Army of the French Revolution: From Citizen Soldiers to Instrument of Power*, Princeton, N.J., 1988.

—— *La vie quotidienne des soldats de la révolution 1789–1799*, Paris, 1985.

Bittard des Portes, René, *Histoire de l'armée de Condé pendant la Révolution française (1791–1801)*, Reprint, Genève, 1975.

Blanning, T. C. W., *Origins of the French Revolutionary Wars*, London, 1986.

—— *The French Revolutionary Wars, 1787–1802*, London and New York, 1996.

Bordonave, Georges, *La Guerre de Vendée*, Paris, 1964.

Brown, Howard G., *War, Revolution and the Bureaucratic State: Politics and Army Administration in France, 1791–1799*, Oxford, 1995.

Chuquet, Arthur, *Les guerres de la révolution*, 11 vols, 6th edn, Paris, 1914.

Cobb, Richard, *The People's Armies*, trans. from the French by Marianne Elliott, New Haven, Conn., 1987.

Deschard, Bernard, *L'armée et la Révolution: du service du roi au service de la nation*, Paris, 1989.

Forrest, Alan I., *Soldiers of the French Revolution*, Durham, N.C., 1990.

Fremont-Barnes, Gregory, *The French Revolutionary Wars*, London, 2001.

Griffith, Paddy, *The Art of War of Revolutionary France*, London and Mechanicsville, Pa., 1998.

Hampson, Norman, *Saint-Just*, Oxford (UK) and Cambridge, Mass., 1991.

Hopkin, David, *Soldier and Peasant in French Popular Culture, 1766–1870*, Woodbridge, Suffolk and Rochester, N.Y., 2003.

Jomini, Antoine-Henri, *Histoire critique et militaire des guerres de la révolution*, 16 vols, new edn, Paris, 1820–22.

Kelly, George A.. *Victims, Authority, and Terror: The Parallel Deaths of d'Orléans, Custine, Bailly, and Malesherbes*, Chapel Hill, N.C., 1982.

Kramer, Lloyd S., *Lafayette in Two Worlds: Public Cultures and Personal Identities in an Age of Revolutions*, Chapel Hill, N.C., 1996.

Lynn, John A., *The Bayonets of the Republic: Motivation and Tactics of the Army of Revolutionary France, 1791–94*, Chicago, Ill., 1984. Paperback edn, Boulder, Colo., 1996.

Martin, Jean-Clément, *La Vendée et la France*, Paris, 1987.

Palmer, R. R., *Twelve Who Ruled: The Year of the Terror in the French Revolution*, Princeton, N.J., 1969.

Phipps, Ramsey W., *The Armies of the First French Republic and the Rise of the Marshals of Napoleon I*, 5 vols, London, 1926–29. Reprint, Westport Conn., 1980.

Pivka, Otto von, *Napoleon's German Allies*, London, 1978.

Quimby, Robert S., *The Background of Napoleonic Warfare*, New York, 1957.

Ross, Michael, *Banners of the King: The War of the Vendée, 1793–4*, London, 1975.

Ross, Steven T., *European Diplomatic History, 1789–1815: France Against Europe*, Garden City, N.Y., 1969; Malabar, Fla., 1981.

—— *Quest for Victory: French Military Strategy, 1792–1799*, South Brunswick, New Jersey and London, 1978.

—— *From Flintlock to Rifle Infantry: Tactics, 1740–1866*, Rutherford, N.J. and London, 1979.

Scott, Samuel F., *The Response of the Royal Army to the French Revolution*, New York, 1978.

—— *From Yorktown to Valmy: The Transformation of the French Army in an Age of Revolution*, Niwat, Colo., 1998.

Secher, Reynald, *Le Génocide Franco-Français: La Vendée-Vengé*, Paris, 1986.

Soboul, Albert, *Les soldats de l'an II*, Paris, 1959.

Tackett, Timothy, *When the King Took Flight*, Cambridge, Mass., 2003.

Wetzler, Peter, *War and Subsistence: The Sambre and Meuse Army in 1794*, New York, 1985.

Whitridge, Arnold, *Rochambeau*, New York, 1965.

Wilkinson-Latham, Robert, *British Artillery on Land and Sea, 1790–1820*, Bristol, 1973.

Woloch, Isser, *The French Veteran from the Revolution to the Restoration*, Chapel Hill, N.C., 1979.

Wars of Napoleon: General

Bertaud, Jean Paul, *Histoire du Consulat et de l'Empire: chronologie commentée, 1799–1815*, Paris, 1992.

Camon, Hubert, *La guerre napoléonienne: Les systèms d'operations*, Paris, 1907.

—— *Génie et métier chez Napoléon*, Paris, 1929.

—— *La guerre napoléonienne: précis des campagnes*, 2 vols, Paris, 1925.

—— *Quand et comment Napoléon a conçu son système de manoeuvre et . . . a conçu son système de bataille*, Paris, 1931–33.

Chandler, David G., *The Campaigns of Napoleon*, New York, 1966.

Connelly, Owen, *Blundering to Glory: Napoleon's Military Campaigns*, Wilmington, Del., 1987 (revised edn 1999).

Dodge, T. A. *Napoleon: A History of the Art of War*, 4 vols, New York, 1904–07.

Dumas, Mathieu, Gen. Count, *Précis des événéments militaires ou essais historiques sur les campagnes de 1799 à 1815*, 27 vols, Paris, 1817.

Durova, N. A. (Nadezhda Andreevna, 1783–1866), *Zapiski kavalerist-devitsy*. English: *The Cavalry Maiden: Journals of a Russian Officer in the Napoleonic Wars*, trans, intro., and notes by Mary Fleming Zirin, Bloomington, Ind., 1989.

Elting, John R., *The Superstrategists*, New York, 1982.

Elting, John R. and Esposito, Vincent, *Military History and Atlas of the Napoleonic Wars*, New York, 1964.

—— *Atlas for the Wars of Napoleon*, West Point Military History Series, Gen. ed. Thomas E. Griess, Wayne, N.J., 1987.

Esdaile, Charles, *Wars of Napoleon*, London and New York, 1995.

Forrest, Alan I., *Conscripts and Deserters: The Army and French Society During the Revolution and Empire*, New York, 1989.

—— *Napoleon's Men: The Soldiers of the Revolution and Empire*, London and New York, 2002.

Gaulle, Charles de, *La France et ses Armées*, Paris, 1971.

—— *Les Écrits militaires de Charles de Gaulle: Essai d'Analyse thématique*, ed. Pierre Messmer and Alain Larcan, Paris, 1985.

Gregory, Desmond, *Malta, Britain, and the European Powers, 1793–1815*, Madison, Wis.; London; Cranbury, N.J., 1996.

Hall, Christopher D., *British Strategy in the Napoleonic War, 1803–15*, Manchester UK and New York, 1992.

Halweg, Werner (ed.), *Klassiker der Kriegskunst*, Darmstadt, 1960.

Haythornthwaite, Philip J., *British Infantry in the Napoleonic Wars*, London, 1987.

—— *Napoleon's Military Machine*, New York, 1988.

—— *The Napoleonic Source Book*, London, 1990.

—— *The Armies of Wellington*, London and New York, 1994.

—— *Weapons and Equipment of the Napoleonic Wars*, London and New York, 1996.

—— *Die Hard!: Dramatic Actions from the Napoleonic Wars*, London, 1996.

Haythornthwaite, Philip J., *et al.*, *Napoleon: The Final Verdict*, Foreword by David G. Chandler, London and New York, 1996.

Horne, Alistair, *How Far from Austerlitz?: Napoleon, 1805–1815*, New York, 1996.

Jurgenson, Luba, *La Dourova: une amazone russe*, Paris, 1995.

Lachouque, Henry, *Napoléon: 20 Ans de campagnes*, Paris, 1964. Trans. Roy Monckorn as *Napoleon's Battles: A History of His Campaigns*, New York, 1967.

Liddell-Hart, B. H., *The Ghost of Napoleon*, London, 1933.

Longridge, C. N., *The Anatomy of Nelson's Ships*, Drawings and plans by E. Bowness and G. F. Campbell; revised by E. Bowness, Annapolis, Md. and London, 1981.

Loy, Capitaine, *Deux femmes soldats picardes du temps de l'epopée Révolution-Empire: le grenadier Françoise Pellehette, Veronique Vivien: d'apres des documents inédits*, Paris, 1912.

Lyons, Martyn, *Napoleon Bonaparte and the Legacy of the French Revolution*, Basingstoke and New York, 1994.

Marshall-Cornwall, J., *Napoleon as Military Commander*, London, 1968.

Muir, Rory, *Britain and the Defeat of Napoleon, 1807–1915*, New Haven, Conn., 1996.

Neillands, Robin, *Wellington and Napoleon: Clash of Arms, 1807–1815*, London, 1994.

Nosworthy, Brent, *With Musket, Cannon, and Sword: Battle Tactics of Napoleon and His Enemies*, London, 1995; New York, 1996.

Oman, C. W. C., *Studies in the Napoleonic Wars*, London, 1930.

Page, F. C. G., *Following the Drum: Women in Wellington's Wars*, London, 1986.

Paret, Peter, *Yorck and the Era of Prussian Reform, 1807–1814*, Princeton, N.J., 1966.

—— *Understanding War: Essays on Clausewitz and the History of Military Power*, Princeton, N.J., 1992.

Paret, Peter and Moran, Daniel (eds and trans.), *Carl von Clausewitz: Historical and Political Writings*, Princeton, N.J., 1992.

Petre, F. Loraine, *Napoleon and the Archduke Charles*, Reprint, San Francisco, Calif., 1991.

Rogers, Hugh C. B., *Napoleon's Army*, London, 1974.

—— *Wellington's Army*, London, 1979.

Ross, Steven T., *From Flintlock to Rifle: Infantry Tactics, 1740–1866*, 2nd edn, Portland, Oreg., 1996; London, 1997.

—— *Napoleon and Maneuver Warfare*, US Air Force Academy, Colo., 1985.

Rothenberg, Gunther E., *The Art of Warfare in the Age of Napoleon*, Bloomington, Ind. and London, 1978.

Rowe, Michael (ed.), *Collaboration and Resistance in Napoleonic Europe: State Formation in an Age of Upheaval, c. 1800–1815*, Basingstoke, 2003.

Schneid, Frederick C., *Soldiers of Napoleon's Kingdom of Italy: Army, State, and Society, 1800–1815*, Boulder, Colo., 1995.

Sherwig, John M., *Guineas and Gunpowder: British Foreign Aid in the Wars with France, 1793–1815*, New York, 1969.

Strawson, John, *The Duke and the Emperor: Wellington and Napoleon*, London, 1994.

Tulard, Jean, *Napoléon: Le Pouvoir, la nation, la légende*, Paris, 1997.

Urban, Mark, *The Man Who Broke Napoleon's Codes*, New York and London, 2002.

Van Creveld, Martin, *Command in War*, Cambridge, Mass., 1985.

Woloch, Isser, *Napoleon and His Collaborators: The Making of a Dictatorship*, New York, 2001.

Yorck von Wartenburg, Count, *Napoleon as a General*, 2 vols, London, 1902. Trans. from *Napoleon als Feldherr*, 2 vols, Berlin, 1885–86.

Italian campaigns (1796–97 and 1800)

Burton, R. G., *Napoleon's Campaigns in Italy*, London and New York, 1912.

Clausewitz, Carl von, *La Campagne de 1796 en Italie*, Paris, 1899.

Cugnac, G.J.M.R., *La campagne de l'armée de réserve en 1800*, 2 vols, Paris, 1900–01.

Fabry, Gabriel, *Histoire de l'armée d'Italie 1796–1797*, 3 vols, Paris, 1901.

Ferrero, Guglielmo, *The Gamble: Bonaparte in Italy, 1796–1797*, London, 1961.

Jackson, William, *Attack in the West: Napoleon's First Campaign Re-read Today*, London, 1953.

Pescasio, Luigi, *Mantova assediata, 1796–1797*, Suzzara (Italy), 1989.

—— *Mantova 1799: un nuovo assedio*, Suzzara, 1990.

Rocca, Gianni, *Il piccolo caporale: Napoleone alla conquista dell'Italia, 1796–97 e 1800*, Milano, 1996.

Rodger, A. B., *The War of the Second Coalition 1798 to 1801*, New York, 1961.

Ross, Steven T., *Quest for Victory: French Military Strategy, 1792–1799*, South Brunswick, New York and London, 1978.

Thiry, Jean, *Bonaparte en Italie*, Paris, 1974.

Egyptian campaign, 1798–99

Barthorp, Michael, *Napoleon's Egyptian Campaigns, 1798–1799*, London, 1978.

Benoist-Mechin, J.G.P.M., *Bonaparte en Egypte*, Lausanne, 1966.

Deane, Anthony, *Nelson's Favourite: HMS Agamemnon at War, 1781–1809*, Annapolis, Md., 1996.

Derogy, Jacques, *Bonaparte en Terre sainte*, Paris, 1992.

Herold, J. Christopher, *Napoleon in Egypt*, London and New York, 1961.

Hibbert, Christopher, *Nelson: A Personal History*, Reading, Mass., 1994.

Jabarti, Abd al-Rahman (1754–1822). [Tarikh muddat al-Faransis bi Misr. English]. *Napoleon in Egypt: Al-Jabarti's Chronicle of the First Seven Months of the French Occupation, 1798*, trans. Samuel Moreh; intro. Robert L. Tignor, Princeton, N.J., 1993.

Laurens, Henry, *Les origines intellectuelles de l'expedition d'Egypte: l'orientalisme islamisant en France (1698–1798)*, Istanbul, 1987.

—— *L'Expedition d'Egypte: 1798–1801*, Avec le collaboration de Charles C. Gillispie, Jean-Claude Golvin, Claude Traunecker, Paris, 1989.

Lloyd, Christopher, *The Nile Campaign*, New York, 1973.

Mackesy, Piers, *British Victory in Egypt*, London and New York, 1996.

Marcus, G. J., *The Royal Navy in the Age of Nelson*, New York, 1971.

—— *A Thirst for Glory: The Life of Admiral Sir Sidney Smith*, London, 1996.

Pocock, Tom, *Horatio Nelson*, New York: Knopf, 1988.

Thiry, Jean, *Bonaparte en Egypte*, Paris, 1973.

—— *Victory: The Life of Lord Nelson*, Boston, Mass., 1958.

Warner, Oliver, *The Battle of the Nile*, London, 1960.

Campaigns of 1805–07

Bonnal, H., *La manoeuvre de Jena, 1806*, Paris, 1904.

Burton, R. G., *From Boulogne to Austerlitz: Napoleon's Campaign of 1805*, London, 1912.

Casaglia, Gherardo, *Una zattera per l'Europa: Alessandro e Napoleone a Tilsit: 25 giugno 1807*, Prefazione di Jean Tulard, Pisa, 1993.

Chandler, David G., *Austerlitz 1805: Battle of the Three Emperors*, London, 1990.

Duffy, C. J., *Austerlitz, 1805*, London, 1977.

Ellis, Geoffrey, *Napoleon's Continental Blockade*, London and New York, 1981.

Finley, Milton, *The Most Monstrous of Wars: The Napoleonic Guerrilla War in Southern Italy, 1806–1811*, Columbia, S.C., 1994.

Flayhart, William H. III, *Counterpoint to Trafalgar: The Anglo-Russian Invasion of Naples, 1805–1806*, Columbia, S.C., 1992.

Glover, Richard, *Britain at Bay: Defense Against Bonaparte, 1803–1814*, London, 1973.

Henderson, E. F. *Blücher and the Uprising of Prussia against Napoleon, 1806–1815*, London, 1911.

Howarth, David A., *Trafalgar: The Nelson Touch*, New edn, New York, 1969.

Lachouque, Henry, *Napoléon à Austerlitz*, Paris, 1960.

—— *Jena*, Paris, 1961.

Lettow-Vorbeck, C. von, *Der Krieg von 1806–1807*, Berlin, 1892.

Maine, René, *Trafalgar*, New York, 1960.

—— *The Ulm Campaign, 1805*, New York and London, 1912.

Maude, F. N., *The Jena Campaign, 1806*, London and New York, 1909.

Nowak, Holger and Brigitt Hellmann, *Die Schlacht bei Jena und Auerstedt am 14. Oktober 1806*, 1. Aufl., Jena, 1994.

Parker, H. T., *Three Napoleonic Battles*, New edn, Durham, N.C., 1983.

Petre, F.L., *Napoleon's Campaign in Poland, 1806–1807*, London and New York, 1901.

—— *Napoleon's Conquest of Prussia, 1806*, London, 1907; reprint, 1972.

Schuster, Wolf-Jorg, *Man ladt uns ein zum Stelldichein: Napoleon in Thuringen 1806*, Jena, 1993.

Thiry, Jean, *Ulm, Trafalgar, Austerlitz*, Paris, 1962.

Tranie, Jean and Carmigniani, J.-C. (eds), *Napoléon et l'Allemagne: La Prusse, 1806*, Paris, 1984.

—— *Napoléon et la Russie: Les années victorieuses, 1805–1807*, Paris, 1984.

Willbold, Franz, *Napoleons Feldzug um Ulm: die Schlacht von Elchingen 14. Oktober 1805 mit der Belagerung und Kapitulation von Ulm*, 1. Aufl., Ulm, 1987.

Peninsular War, 1807–14

Anton, James, *Retrospect of a Military Life: During the Most Eventful Periods of the Last War*, Cambridge, UK, 1991.

Alexander, Don, *Rod of Iron: French Counterinsurgency Policy in Aragon During the Peninsular War*, Wilmington, Del., 1985.

Arteche y Moro, José Gomez de, *Guerra de la independencia: Historia militar de España de 1808 a 1814*, 14 vols, Madrid, 1868–1903.

Artola Gallego, Miguel, *La España de Fernando VII*, Madrid, 1968.

Aymes, J. R., *La guerre d'independance espagnole*, Paris, 1973.

Chastenet, J., *Godoy: Master of Spain, 1792–1808*, London, 1953.

Connelly, Owen, *The Gentle Bonaparte: A Biography of Joseph*, New York, 1968.

Davies, D. W., *Sir John Moore's Peninsular Campaign*, The Hague, 1974.

Esdaile, Charles, *The Spanish Army in the War*, Manchester, UK, and New York, 1988.

—— *The Duke of Wellington and the Command of the Spanish Army, 1812–14*, New York, 1990.

—— *The Peninsular War: A New History*, New York and Houndmills, UK, 2003.

Fletcher, Ian and Poulter, Ron, *Gentlemen's Sons: The Guards in the Peninsula and at Waterloo, 1800–1815*, Turnbridge Wells, 1992.

Girod de l'Ain, Gabriel, *Joseph Bonaparte*, Paris, 1970.

Glover, M., *The Peninsular War, 1807–1814*, Hamden, Conn., 1974.

Grandmaison, G., *L'Espagne et Napoléon, 1804–1814*, 3 vols, Paris, 1908.

Hibbert, Christopher, *The Battle of Corunna*, New York, 1961.

Horward, Donald D., *Napoleon and Iberia: The Twin Sieges of Ciudad Rodrigo and Almeida, 1810*, Tallahassee, Fla., 1984.

Lachouque, H., Tranie, J., and Carmigniani, J. C., *Napoleon's War in Spain*, trans. Janet Mallender and J. R. Clements, London, 1982.

La Parra Lopez, Emilio, *La alianza de Godoy con los revolucionarios: España y Francia a fines del siglo XVIII*, 1992.

Lopez, J. P., *La guerra de la independencia, 1808–1814*, Madrid, 1947.

Lovett, Gabriel, *Napoleon and the Birth of Modern Spain*, New York, 1965.

Marti Gilabert, F., *Motin de Aranjuez*, Pamplona, 1972.

Mercader Riba, D. Juan, *José Bonaparte, rey de España*, Madrid, 1972.

Muir, Rory, *Salamanca, 1812*, New Haven, Conn., 2001.

Napier, Sir William F. P., *History of the War in the Peninsula and in the South of France, 1807 to 1814*, 6 vols, London, 1886.

Oman, Sir Charles, *History of the Peninsular War*, 7 vols, London, 1902–30.

Paget, Sir Julian, *Wellington's Peninsular War: Battles and Battlefields*, London, 1990.

Pelet, J. J., *The French Campaign in Portugal, 1810–1811*, trans. and ed. Donald D. Horward, Minneapolis, Minn., 1973.

Pouzerewsky, Col., *La charge de la cavalerie [Polonaise] de Somo Sierra (Espagne), le 30 novembre 1808*, Paris, 1900.

Ramisa i Verdaguer, Maties, *Els catalans i el domini napoleonic: Catalunya vista pels oficials de l'exercit de Napoleo*, Barcelona, 1995.

Read, Jan, *The War in the Peninsula, 1807–1814*, London, 1977.

Reynaud, Jean-Louis, *Contre-guérilla en Espagne (1808–1814): Suchet pacifie l'Aragon*, Paris, 1992.

Roux, Georges, *Napoléon et le guepier espagnol*, Paris, 1970.

Surtees, William (1781–1830), *Twenty-five Years in the Rifle Brigade*, New edn, London and Mechanicsburg, Pa., 1996.

Tone, John Lawrence, *The Fatal Knot: The Guerrilla War in Navarre and the Defeat of Napoleon in Spain*, Chapel Hill, N.C., 1994.

Toreño, José M., Conde de, *Histoire du soulèvement, de la guerre, et de la révolution d'Espagne*, 4 vols, Paris, 1838.

Webber, William (b. 1787), *With the Guns in the Peninsula: The Peninsular War Journal of 2nd Captain William Webber, Royal Artillery*, ed. Richard Henry Wollocombe, London and Novato, Calif., 1991.

Weller, Jac, *Wellington in the Peninsula, 1808–1814*, London, 1962.

Young, Peter and Lawford, J. P., *Wellington's Masterpiece: The Battle and Campaign of Salamanca*, London, 1973.

Campaign of 1809 (Wagram)

Arnold, James R., *Crisis on the Danube: Napoleon's Austrian Campaign of 1809*, London, 1990.

—— *Napoleon Conquers Austria: The 1809 Campaign for Vienna*, Westport, Conn., 1995.

Binder von Krieglstein, Karl, Freiherr, *Der Krieg Napoleons gegen Oesterreich 1809*, 2 vols, Berlin, 1906.

Bond, Gordon C., *The Grand Expedition: The British Invasion of Holland in 1809*, Athens, Ga., 1979.

Bonnal, Henri C., *Le manoeuvre de Landshut*, Paris, 1905.

Castle, Ian, *Aspern & Wagram 1809: Mighty Clash of Empires*, London, 1994.

Comeau, Baron S. J. de, *Souvenirs des guerres d'Allemagne*, Paris, 1900.

Epstein, Robert M., *Napoleon's Last Victory and the Emergence of Modern War*, Lawrence, Kans., 1994.

Fleishmann, Theo, *Expedition anglaise . . . en 1809: Conquete de l'Ile de Walcheren et menace sur Anvers*, Reprint, Brussels, 1973.

Gill, John H., *With Eagles to Glory: Napoleon and his German Allies in the 1809 Campaign*, London and Novato Calif., 1992.

Loy, L., *La Campagne de Styrie en 1809*, Paris, 1908.

Meinecke, Friedrich, *Age of German Liberation*, trans. Peter Paret and Helmut Fischer, Berkeley, Calif., 1977.

Menge, August, *Die Schlacht von Aspern am 21. und 22. Mai 1809; eine Erlauterung der Kriegführung Napoleons I und des Erzherzogs Carl von Oesterreich*, Berlin, 1900.

Pelet, Gen. J. J. G., *Mémoires sur la guerre de 1809*, Paris, 1825.

Petre, F. L., *Napoleon and the Archduke Charles: A History of the Franco-Austrian Campaign in the Valley of the Danube in 1809*, London, 1909; reprint London and Novato, Calif. 1991.

Rauchensteiner, Manfried, *Die Schlacht bei Deutsch Wagram am 5 und 6 Juli 1809*, Wien, 1977.

Saski, G. G. L., *La campagne de 1809*, 3 vols, Paris, 1899–1900.

Thiry, Jean, *Napoléon Bonaparte*, Paris, 1966.

Tranie, J. and Carmigniani, J. C., *Napoléon et Austriche: La campagne de 1809*, Paris, 1984.

Welden, Franz Ludwig, Freiherr von (1782–1853), *Der Krieg von 1809 zwischen Oesterreich und Frankreich: von Anfang Mai bis zum Friedensschlusse . . .*, Wien, 1872.

Wober, Ferdi Irmfried, *1809: Schlacht bei Aspern und Essling*, Perchtoldsdorf, 1992.

Russian campaign, 1812

Austin, Paul Britten, *1812*: I. *The March on Moscow*; II. *1812: Napoleon in Moscow*; III. *1812: The Great Retreat*, London and Mechanicsburg, Pa., 1990–95.

Belis, Roger, *La campagne de Russie, 1812*, Cannes, 1966.

Brett-James, Antony, *1812: Eyewitness Accounts of Napoleon's Defeat in Russia*, New York, 1966.

Burton, R. G., *Napoleon's Invasion of Russia, 1812*, London, 1914.

Cate, Curtis, *The War of the Two Emperors: The Duel between Napoleon and Alexander: Russia 1812*, New York, 1985.

Chuquet, Arthur (1853–1925), *Human Voices from the Russian Campaign of 1812*, Selections trans. from *Etudes d'Histoire* by M. Harriet M. Capes, Cambridge, UK, 1994.

Clausewitz, Carl von, *The Campaign of 1812 in Russia*, London, 1843. Trans. from *Feldzug 1812 in Russland*. New edn intro. by George F. Nafziger, London and Novato, Calif., 1992.

Duffy, Christopher, *Borodino*, London & New York, 1972.

Faber du Four, C. W. von, *La campagne de Russie*, Paris, 1895.

Fabre, M. A., *Jérôme Bonaparte, roi de Westphalie*, Paris, 1952.

Jackson, W. G. H., *Seven Roads to Moscow*, London, 1958.

Josselson, Michael and Josselson, Diana, *The Commander: Barclay de Tolly*, New York, 1980.

Mansuy, Abel, *Jérôme Bonaparte et la Pologne en 1812*, Paris, 1931.

—— *Jérôme Bonaparte*, Paris, 1979.

Melchior-Bonnet, B., *La conspiration de Général Malet*, Paris, 1963.

Nafziger, George F., *Napoleon's Invasion of Russia*, Chicago, Ill. 1988.

Nicolson, Nigel, *Napoleon, 1812*, New York, 1985.

Olivier, Daria, *The Burning of Moscow, 1812*, New York, 1966.

Palmer, Alan W., *Napoleon in Russia*, New York, 1967.

Parkinson, Roger, *Fox of the North: The Life of Kutuzov*, New York, 1976.

Riehn, Richard K., *1812: Napoleon's Russian Campaign*, New York, 1990.

Tarlé, E. V., *Napoleon's Invasion of Russia*, trans. from the Russian by N. Guterman and R. Manheim, New York, 1942.

Turner, A. E., *The Retreat from Moscow and the Crossing of the Beresina*, Woolwich, 1898.

Zamowski, Adam, *Moscow 1812: Napoleon's Fatal March*, New York, 2004.

Campaigns of 1813–14; first abdication

Brett-James, A., *Europe Against Napoleon: The Leipzig Campaign, 1813, from Eyewitness Accounts*, London, 1970.

Dupont, M., *Napoléon et la trahison des maréchaux, 1814*, Paris, 1970.

Foucart, Paul J., *Bautzen . . . 20–21 mai 1813*, Paris, 1897.

Friedrich, R., *Geschichte der Herbstfeldzuges 1813*, 3 vols, Berlin, 1903–06.

—— *Die Befreiungskreige 1813–1815*, 4 vols, Berlin, 1911–13.

Hofschröer, Peter, *Leipzig 1813: The Battle of the Nations*, London, 1993.

Houssaye, Henri, *1814*, Paris, 1888.

Janson, R. von, *Geschichte des Feldzuges 1814 in Frankreich*, Berlin, 1903.

Lachouque, H., *Napoléon en 1814*, Paris, 1959.

Lanrezac, C. L. M., *Mémoires: Lutzen*, Paris, 1904.

Lawford, J. P., *Napoleon: The Last Campaigns, 1813–1815*, London, 1977.

Leggiere, Michael, *Napoleon and Berlin*, Norman, Okla, 2002.

Maude, F. N., *The Leipzig Campaign, 1813*, London. 1908.

Mauduit, H. de, *Les derniers jours de la Grande Armée*, Paris, 1847.

Miguel, Pierre, *La campagne de France de Napoleon, ou, Les eclairs du genie*, Paris, 1991.

Mikhailovskii-Danilevskii, Aleksandr Ivanovich (*c.* 1789–1848), *History of the Campaign in France in the Year 1814*, trans. from the Russian, Cambridge, UK, 1992.

Nafziger, George F., *Napoleon at Dresden: The Battles of August 1813*, Chicago, Ill., 1995.

Petre, F. L., *Napoleon's Last Campaign in Germany, 1813*, London, 1912.

—— *Napoleon at Bay, 1814*, London, 1914.

Thiry, Jean, *Leipzig . . . 1813*, Paris, 1972.

Tournes, R., *La campagne de printemps en 1813: Lützen*, Paris, 1931.

Veltze, A., *Osterreich in den Befreiungskriegen*, 10 vols, Wien, 1911–14.

Wohlfeil, R., *Spanien und die deutsche Erhebung, 1808–1814*, Wiesbaden, 1965.

The Hundred Days / Waterloo / second abdication

Adkins, Mark, *The Waterloo Companion*, London, 2001.

Alexander, R. S., *Bonapartism and the Revolutionary Tradition in France: The Fédérés of 1815*, New York, 1991.

Beitzke, Heinrich, *Geschichte des Jahres 1815*, 2 vols, Berlin, 1865.

Blond, Georges, *Les Cent-Jours: Napoleon seul contre tous*, Paris, 1983.

Brett-James, Antony, *The Hundred Days*, New York, 1963.

Chalfont, Lord (ed.), *Waterloo: Battle of Three Armies*, London, 1980.

Chandler, David, *Waterloo: The Hundred Days*, London, 1980.

Cubberly, R. E., *The Role of Fouché during the Hundred Days*, Madison, Wis., 1969.

Dallas, Gregor, *The Final Act: The Roads to Waterloo*, 1st US edn, New York, 1997.

Duforcq, A., *Murat et . . . l'unité italienne en 1815*, Paris, 1898.

Fiore, Enzo, *Un re al bivio: Il tradimento di Murat*, Roma, 1972.

Godlewski, G., *Trois cents jours d'exil: Napoléon à l'ile d'Elbe*, Paris, 1961.

Griffith, Paddy (ed.), *Wellington, Commander: The Iron Duke's Generalship*, London, 1985.

Hamilton-Williams, David, *Waterloo: New Perspectives: The Great Battle Reappraised*, London, 1993.

—— *The Fall of Napoleon: The Final Betrayal*, New York, 1994.

Herold, J. C., *The Battle of Waterloo*, London, 1967.

Hibbert, Christopher, *Waterloo: Napoleon's Last Campaign*, New York, 1967.

Hofschröer, Peter, *1815: the Waterloo Campaign: Wellington, His German Allies and the Battles of Ligny and Quatre-Bras*, London and Mechanicsburg, Pa., 1998.

Hofschröer, Peter <www.bbc.co.uk/history/war/waterloo/three_commanders> British Broadcasting Corporation, 2003.

Houssaye, Henri, *1815*, 3 vols, Paris, 1894–1914.

Howarth, David, *Waterloo: Day of Battle*, New York, 1968.

Keegan, John, "Waterloo," in *Face of Battle*, New York, 1976.

Kennedy, Gen. Sir John, *Notes on the Battle of Waterloo*, London, 1865.

Lachouque, H., *Waterloo: Fin d'un monde*, Paris, 1958.

—— *The Last Days of Napoleon's Empire: From Waterloo to St. Helena*, London, 1966.

—— *Waterloo, 1815*, Paris, 1972. English edn, *Waterloo*, intro. David Chandler, London, 1975.

Longford, Elizabeth, *Wellington: The Years of the Sword*, London, 1969.

MacKenzie, Norman, *The Escape from Elba: The Fall and Flight of Napoleon, 1814–1815*, New York, 1985.

Müffling, Friedrich Karl Ferdinand, Freiherr von, *Aus meinem Leben*. English edn: *The Memoirs of Baron von Müffling: A Prussian officer in the Napoleonic Wars*, New intro. by Peter Hofschröer, London and Mechanicsburg, Pa., 1997.

Naylor, John, *Waterloo*, London, 1960.

Neely, Sylvia, *Lafayette and the Liberal Ideal, 1814–1824*, Edwardsville, Ill., 1991.

Nofi, Albert A., *The Waterloo Campaign, June 1815*, London, 1993.

Paget, Sir Julian and Saunders, Derek, *Hougoumont: The Key to Victory at Waterloo*, London, 1992.

Pericoli, Ugo, *1815: The Armies at Waterloo*, New York, 1973.

Sauvain, Philip Arthur, *Waterloo*, New York and Toronto, 1993.

Sibirne, William, Capt., *History of the Waterloo Campaign*, Reprint, London, 1995.

Siborne, Herbert T., *Waterloo Letters*, Reprint, London, 1993.

Sutherland, John P., *Men of Waterloo*, London, 1965.

Thiry, Jean, *La Chute de Napoléon*, 7 vols, Paris, 1941–45.

Uffindell, Andrew, *The Eagle's Last Triumph: Napoleon's Victory at Ligny, June 1815*, London and Mechanicsburg, Pa., 1994.

Uffindell, Andrew and Corum, Michael, *On the Fields of Glory: The Battlefields of the 1815 Campaign*, London and Mechanicsburg, Pa, 1996.

Veve, Thomas Dwight, *The Duke of Wellington and the British Army of Occupation in France, 1815–1818*, New York, 1992.

Weller, Jac, *Wellington at Waterloo*, New York, 1964. New edn, London and Novato, Calif., 1992.

Wood, Evelyn, Sir (1838–1919), *Cavalry in the Waterloo Campaign*, Facsim. edn, Felling, Tyne and Wear, 1992.

Wootten, Geoffrey, *Waterloo 1815: Birth of Modern Europe*, London, 1992.

Naval warfare

Arthur, Charles B., *Remaking of the English Navy by Admiral St. Vincent: Key to the Victory over Napoleon: The Great Unclaimed Naval Revolution (1795–1805)*, London, 1986.

Cormack, William S., *Revolution and Political Conflict in the French Navy, 1789–1794*, Cambridge, UK, and New York, 1995.

Dull, Jonathan R., *The French Navy and American Independence*, Princeton, N.J., 1975.

Goodwin, Peter, *Nelson's Ships: A History of the Vessels in Which he Served, 1771–1805*, Mechanicsberg, Pa., 2002.

Hibbert, Christopher, *Nelson: A Personal History*, Reading, Mass., 1994.

Keegan John, *The Price of Admiralty: The Evolution of Naval Warfare*, New York and London, 1988.

Longridge, C. N., *The Anatomy of Nelson's Ships*, Drawings and plans by E. Bowness and G. F. Campbell; revised by E. Bowness, Annapolis, Md. and London, 1981.

Morriss, Roger, *Naval Power and British Culture, 1760–1850*, Burlington, Vt., 2004.

Palmer, Michael, *Stoddert's War: Naval Operations During the Quasi-War with France, 1798–1801*, Columbia, S.C., 1988.

Pocock, Tom, *Horatio Nelson*, New York, 1988.

Southey, Robert (1774–1843), *The Life of Horatio, Lord Nelson*, London and New York, 1906; reprint, New York, 1993.

Howarth, David A., *Trafalgar: The Nelson Touch*, New York, 1975.

Howarth, David A., *Lord Nelson: The Immortal Memory*, 1st US edn, New York, 1989.

Napoleon: biography and life and times

Bergeron, Louis, *L'Episode Napoleonien: Aspects interieurs*, Paris, 1972.

Lovie, Jacques and Palluel, André, *L'Episode Napoléonien: Aspects Extérieurs*, Paris, 1972.

Carrington, Dorothy, *Napoleon and his Parents: On the Threshold of History*, New York, 1990.

Chandler, David, *Napoleon*, New York, 1974.

Chuquet, A., *La jeunesse de Napoléon*, 3 vols, Paris, 1897–99.

Colin, Jean, *L'Education militaire de Napoléon*, Paris, 1900.

Ellis, Geoffrey, *Napoleon*, London and New York, 1997.

Herold, J. Christopher, *The Age of Napoleon*, Reprint, New York, 1984.

Jomini, Baron Antoine-Henri, *Vie politique et militaire de Napoléon*, 4 vols, Paris, 1827.

Manfred, Albert, *Napoléon Bonaparte*, French edn trans. from the Russian by Patricia Champe, Moscow, 1980.

Markham, Felix, *Napoleon*, New York, 1963.

Mistler, Jean, *Napoléon et l'Empire*, 2 vols, Paris, 1969.

Ravignant, Patrick, *Napoléon*, Paris, 1985.

Rosebery, Lord, *Napoleon: The Last Phase*, London, 1900.

Roux, Georges, *Monsieur de Buonaparte*, Paris, 1964.

Sorokine, Dimitri, *La jeunesse de Bonaparte*, Paris, 1967.

Tarlé, Eugen, *Napoleon*, Berlin, 1968.

Tulard, Jean, *Le Mythe de Napoléon*, Paris, 1971.

—— *Napoléon ou le mythe du sauveur*, Paris, 1977.

—— *Le Grand Empire, 1804–1815*, Paris, 1982.

Weidhorn, Michel, *Napoleon*, New York, 1986.

Zaghi, Carlo, *Napoleone e l'Europa*, Naples, 1969.

Other biographies

Adelbert, Prince von Bayern, *Eugen Beauharnais, der Stiefsohn Napoleons*, Munich, 1940.

Ainval, Christiane d', *Gouvion Saint-Cyr: Soldat de l'An II, maréchal de l'empire*, Paris, 1981.

Bernhardy, Françoise de, *Eugene de Beauharnais*, Paris, 1973.

Cardigny, Louis, *Les maréchaux de Napoléon*, Paris, 1977.

Christophe, R., *Le Maréchal Marmont*, Paris, 1968.

Delderfield, R. F., *The March of the Twenty-Six: Napoleon's Marshals*, London, 1962.

Dunn-Pattison, R. P., *Napoleon's Marshals*, London, 1912.

Dupont, Marcel, *Murat, Cavalier, Maréchal de France, prince et roi*, Paris, 1980.

Erickson, Carolly, *To The Scaffold: The Life of Marie-Antionette*, New York, 2003.

Eysturlid, Lee W., *The Formative Influences, Theories, and Campaigns of the Archduke Carl of Austria*, Westport, Conn., 2000.

Foster, John T., *Napoleon's Marshal: The Life of Michel Ney*, New York, 1968.

Gallaher, John G., *The Iron Marshal: Louis N. Davout*, Carbondale, Ill., 1976.

Garnier, J. P., *Murat, roi de Naples*, Paris, 1959.

Graziani, Antoine-Marie, *Pascal Paoli: Père de la patrie Corse*, Paris, 2003.

Hayman, Peter, Sir, *Soult: Napoleon's Maligned Marshal*, London, 1990.

Hibbert, Christopher, *Wellington: A Personal History*, London, 1997.

Hourtoulle, H. F. G. L., *Davout le terrible*, Paris, 1975.

Humble, Richard, *Napoleon's Peninsular Marshals*, London, 1973.

Lamar, Glenn J., *Jerome Bonaparte: The War Years, 1800–1815*, Westport, Conn., 2000.

Macdonell, A. G., *Napoleon and his Marshals*, London, 1934.

Marshall-Cornwall, J., *Marshal Massena [sic]*, London, 1965.

Morton, John B., *Marshal Ney*, New York, 1958.

Oman, Carola, *Napoleon's Viceroy* [Eugene de Beauharnais], London, 1966.

Tulard, Jean, *Napoléon et la noblesse d'Empire: avec la liste complète des membres de la noblesse impériale (1808–1815)*, Paris, 1979.

Tulard, Jean, *Murat*, Paris, 1985.

Watson, S. J., *By Command of the Emperor: A Life of Marshal Berthier*, London, 1957.

Willette, L., *Le Maréchal Lannes: un d'Artagnon sous l'empire*, Paris, 1979.

Wolff, Jacques, *Le financier Ouvrard: l'argent et la politique*, Paris, 1992.

Young, Peter, *Napoleon's Marshals*, London, 1974.

The Revolution, Napoleon, Europe and the world

Bertaud, Jean Paul, comp., *Le Premier Empire, legs de la Révolution*, Paris, 1973.

Broers, Michael, *Europe under Napoleon 1799–1815*, London and New York, 1996.

Dwyer, Philip G., *Napoleon and Europe*, New York, 2002.

Ellis, Geoffrey James, *The Napoleonic Empire*, Atlantic Highlands, N.J., 1991.

Fick, Carolyn E., *The Making of Haiti: The Saint Domingue Revolution from Below*, Knoxville, Tenn., 1990.

Garnier, Michaël, *Bonaparte et la Louisiane*, Paris, 1992.

Gerosa, Guido, *Napoleone: un rivoluzionario alla conquista di un impero*, Milano, 1995.

Grab, Alexander, *Napoleon and the Transformation of Europe*, New York and Houndmills, 2003.

Grochulska, Barbara, *Ksiestwo Warszawskie*, Wyd. 2, Warszawa, 1991.

Hofmeister-Hunger, Andrea, *Pressepolitik und Staatsreform: Die Instututionalisierung staatlicher Öffenlichkeitsarbeit bei Karl August von Hardenburg*, Göttingen, 1994.

Hoobler, Thomas and Hoobler, Dorothy, *Toussaint L'Ouverture*, New York, 1990.

Kroczynski, Hieronim, *Wojsko Polskie na Pomorzu Zachodnim i Krajnie w 1807*, Wyd. 1, Warszawa, 1990.

Pachonski, Jan and Wilson, Reul K., *Poland's Carribean Tragedy: A Study of the Polish Legions in the Haitian War of Independence, 1802–1803*, Boulder, Colo and New York, 1986.

Schama, Simon, *Patriots and Liberators: Revolution in the Netherlands, 1780–1813*, New York, 1977.

Schulz, Andreas, *Herrschaft durch Verwaltung: die Rheinbundreformen in Hessen-Darmstadt unter Napoleon (1803–1815)*, Stuttgart, 1991.

Smets, Josef, *Les pays rhenans (1794–1814): le comportement des Rhenans face à l'occupation française*, Bern and New York, 1997.

Simms, Brendan, *The Impact of Napoleon: Prussian High Politics, Foreign Policy, and the Crisis of the Execution, 1797–1806*, Cambridge, UK, New York, 1997.

Tulard, Jean, *Le premier empire*, 1re édn, Paris, 1992.

Venohr, Wolfgang, *Napoleon in Deutschland: Tyrann und Reformator*, Erlangen, 1991.

Woolf, S. J., *Napoleon's Integration of Europe*, London and New York, 1991.

INDEX